TRAIN YOUR BRAIN
ENGAGE YOUR HEART
TRANSFORM YOUR LIFE

A Two Step Program to Enhance Attention; Decrease Stress; Cultivate Peace, Joy and Resilience; and Practice Presence with Love

A Course in Attention & Interpretation Therapy (AIT)

D1114535

AMIT SOOD, MD MSc
Director of Research & Practice
Complementary and Integrative Medicine Program
Chair, Mayo Mind Body Initiative
Associate Professor of Medicine
Mayo Clinic Rochester, MN

© Amit Sood, MD, MSc 2009, 2010
Morning Dew Publications, LLC

ISBN: 1452898057
ISBN-13: 9781452898056

Nurture a healthier brain

Enhance present moment awareness

Embody greater wisdom and love

Be kind to the self

End suffering

By

Cultivating heartfulness

To

All the World's Children

May each child rise to meet life's fullest potential

To

Your Every Kind Thought & Action

All profits to the author from this book will be used to support underprivileged children in the world

TABLE OF CONTENTS

Acknowledgments   3
The Journey you are about to Take   5
Preface   7

Section I: Train Your Brain Engage Your Heart Transform Your Life:
A Brief Survey   11
1. Introduction   13
2. Do Not Postpone Joy   17
3. Brain and its Two Centers   19
4. Mind and Suffering   21
5. Backstage with the Mind   28
6. Backstage with Attention and Interpretation   31
7. The Two Steps to Transformation   42
8. The Heartful Brain   51
9. Summary   55

Section II: The Brain And The Mind
10. The Brain: Introduction   65
11. Mind's Imperfections   68
12. The 3Ps (Principles, Prejudices, Preferences)   76
13. The Brain's Two Centers: Limbic and Cortical Loops   84
14. Skills, Loops, and Outcomes   94
15. The Brain and the Mind: Summary   105

Section III: Mindfulness, Heartfulness and AIT
16. Mindfulness and Heartfulness   111
17. Attention and Interpretation Therapy (AIT)   117

Section IV: Attention Training
18. Attention Training: Introduction   123
19. The Three Ds: Direction, Duration and Depth of Attention   127
20. Attention Training   133
21. Integrating Attention Skills   158

Section V: Refining Interpretations: Introduction
22. Refining Interpretations: Introduction   167

SECTION VI: GRATITUDE
23. What is Gratitude?   181
24. Why Practice Gratitude?   183
25. How to Practice Gratitude   188

SECTION VII: COMPASSION
26. Compassion: Concepts and Ideas   193
27. Cultivating Compassion   201

SECTION VIII: ACCEPTANCE
28. What is Acceptance?   209
29. Why Acceptance?   213
30. How to Cultivate Acceptance   227

SECTION IX: THE MEANING & PURPOSE OF LIFE
31. What is the Meaning & Purpose of Life?   247
32. The Three Types of Meaning   252
33. Meaning: Additional Perspectives   262
34. Why Find Meaning & Purpose?   268
35. How to Find Meaning & Purpose   276
36. When the Meaning is Threatened   291
37. Meaning: Putting it all Together   294

SECTION X: FORGIVENESS
38. What is Forgiveness?   303
39. Why Forgive?   305
40. How to Forgive   313

SECTION XI: RELATIONSHIPS: YOUR TRIBE
41. What is Your Tribe?   333
42. Why Develop Your Tribe?   337
43. How to Create Your Tribe   345

SECTION XII: THE BEGINNING OF AWAKENING (TRANSFORMATION)
44. Meditation   355
45. Faith, Prayer, and the Divine   365

SECTION XIII: AWAKENING (TRANSFORMATION)
46. The Awakening (Transformation)   375

Appendix I – Train Your Brain Engage Your Heart Transform
                Your Life: Tools and Tips   387
Appendix II – Breath and the Body   394
Appendix III – Physical Exercise   398
Appendix IV – Diet   402

References   411

Acknowledgments

I am thankful to my family for all their understanding, support, and love. My wife Richa and daughter Gauri spent many months playing together as I worked in the quiet of our basement. The cushion of understanding and love they have provided has allowed me to bring this work to completion. My parents introduced me to meditation and have been wonderful role models.

I am grateful to my colleagues at Mayo Clinic Rochester for their support and inspiration. I am appreciative of Drs. Victor Montori and Brent Bauer, Doug McGill, Carla Paonessa, my sister Sandhya Chandna, my mother Shashi Sood, my father Sahib D. Sood, my mother-in-law Kusum Sood, and my wife Richa for their critical review of the manuscript.

In this effort, I stand on the shoulders of thousands of researchers and authors who have developed a large body of work that contributes toward this book. I hold them in the highest esteem and am indebted for their contributions.

Most of all, I am thankful to the true embodiments of divine I have been blessed to serve over the last two decades—my patients. I have truly gained more from them than I could ever share.

Peace be on earth and may it come through you.

Amit Sood, MD MSc

September 2010

The Journey you are about to Take

Train Your Brain Engage Your Heart Transform Your Life is a complete program to walk with you on a journey that will take you from the past and future to the present moment; from lesser to higher wisdom; from suffering to joy; from ego to the self. The journey *trains your brain's higher center* to help you decrease the negative ruminations of the mind and enhance its engagement with the present moment and its contents. The journey *engages your heart* to fill the present moment with greater love.

The four wheels of the journey are *neurosciences, psychology, philosophy, and spirituality.* The voyage entails the progressive unfolding of *wisdom and love.* In this journey you will pick six precious jewels: *enhanced present moment awareness, gratitude, compassion, acceptance, forgiveness, and higher meaning and purpose.* The path overcomes five impediments: *ignorance, cravings, aversions, excessive ego, and attention deficit.* In the process you will likely experience four key milestones: *peace, joy, resilience, and altruism.* Each of these milestone points toward one common destination—*transformation (awakening).* The entire journey can be summarized in three words—*cultivating greater heartfulness.*

Increasing *peace,* contentment and equanimity take away much of anxiety, allow a more secure anchor in the present moment, and provide a deep sense of fulfillment and comfort. *Joy* is a welcome accompaniment of peace. This joy originates in freedom and is not contingent on something extraordinary happening externally. A healthy meal, a casual hello, a kind email, watching children play, sun shining in the sky—any or all of these can be a source of intense joy. *Resilience* refers to your ability to not only withstand adversity but bounce ever so higher, sometimes even because of adversity. Resilience emerges when you are grateful for your blessings, when you accept the present moment and its contents, when your compassion effortlessly flows toward self and others, when you cultivate greater forgiveness, and when you are anchored in a higher meaning and purpose of your life.

Peace, joy and resilience although hardwired within us, still remain hiding and have to be purposefully discovered. Discover how? In search of an answer, I am reminded of Michelangelo when he said, *"Every block of stone has a statue inside it and it is the task of the sculptor to discover it."* This process of discovery entails removing the extra rock and sand that hides the statue. That extra stuff within us likely is the excessive thoughts and feelings, the negative ruminations that originate in cravings and aversions.

Imbalanced cravings and aversions in turn depend on egocentricity and ignorance that give rise to excessive self focus with resulting deficits in *altruism*.

It is the progressive cultivation of *altruism,* the fourth milestone on this journey that helps you discover peace, joy and resilience. Altruism recognizes the universality of suffering and finiteness, and is deeply anchored in interconnectedness. Altruism believes we all have an innate capacity to decrease our individual as well as collective suffering. Developing altruism and its practical application—daily kindness, is a choice waiting for you to exercise.

So to awaken the Michelangelo within, we need to cultivate a deeper and purer wisdom and love that leads us toward altruism, which in turn balances our cravings and aversions. Such wisdom and love flow from us when our brain is trained and heart engaged in enhanced present moment awareness embodying greater gratitude, compassion, acceptance, forgiveness, and higher meaning and purpose—*a state of heartfulness.* The extra stuff, those excessive thoughts and negative ruminations, automatically get shed in the process. Peace, joy, resilience and altruism emerge from their hiding, your brain rightwires and the heart engages, as you walk on a path toward transformation.

Salmon swim upstream to spawn and thus secure the continuation of her species. We have to swim upstream to discover and unfold the highest being within us.

Preface

"Fix your thoughts on what is true, and honorable, and right, and pure, and lovely, and admirable. Think about things that are excellent and worthy of praise." This is what Cathy said when I saw her for the first time in the clinic. Then she broke down into tears. She had a serious diagnosis; each jab of pain reminded her of the finiteness of her life. She was also going through a difficult divorce and had significant financial constraints. Wiping the mist in her eyes she said, "I have read and memorized the right verses and books, I have deep faith and a personal relationship with Christ. I have a desire to serve others. I know I should be in the 'now.' Yet I do not know how to live in the 'now.' I do not know how to keep the noble thoughts within me when the stresses of life challenge me. I know I should forgive, but I am not able to... Can you help me with this doctor?"

Never had I received a request so direct, so moving, so intelligently and precisely articulated, and coming from someone who clearly seemed such an evolved soul yet was struggling with the vicissitudes of life, many not of her own creation. This book is written for Cathy and for each of you who believe that the brilliant sun is somewhere in the sky but the clouds presently seem too dense and you are not sure how to look past them. You know where you wish to reach, but may be unsure of the path that will take you there. I see this everyday—the finest of persons, salt of the earth, experiencing stress for no fault of theirs. Amongst other things, they are a victim of the imperfections of the human mind and of the evolutionarily inefficient systems inherent in the human brain. It is extraordinarily difficult to pick up these inefficiencies on your own using the mind itself as a tool to diagnose its very own imperfections.

The imperfections of the mind are reflected in the resulting symptoms— stress, anxiety, an empty feeling, inability to focus, sleeping difficulty, fatigue, irritability, pain, and many others. Most medical conditions and their related symptoms are worsened by the workings of an untrained mind. An untrained mind engages and empowers brain's lower center, decreases your efficiency, productivity, and creativity, and makes you escape from the present moment. Such a mind predisposes you to anger, reactionary decisions, lack of resilience, and suffering. Suffering is experienced when the sound of the present is lost as noise within the cacophony of the lost present or the present that is still unsure of what song it will sing. If you have experienced any of the above in the recent past, you might find some value in what I have to share.

A large proportion of the unfortunate events and unkind actions you see in the world are also a product of the untrained mind and brain. Understanding and correcting mind's imperfections and training and empowering brain's higher center is thus not a luxury—it is an absolute necessity if we hope to survive and thrive as a species.

I will help you understand the reasons behind the imperfections of our mind and the brain because of which we do not easily engage brain's higher center or make the present moment more "heartful." Based on my experiences with practicing medicine for over two decades and across two continents, and observing the world, I am convinced that human suffering is often not a human fault. Many of the imperfections affecting us found their seeds in the traits that helped ensure our evolutionary success. Once you have understood the process, I will then offer you a path that can help you transcend these imperfections. This path will help you train your higher center in the brain (predominantly the pre-frontal cortex) and engage your heart and thereby cultivate peace, joy, and resilience. It will help you decrease stress, anxiety, and attention deficit, and stay in a state of relaxed alertness throughout the day. This journey will teach you that just as avoiding predators and securing food was crucial to our survival in previous times, our future depends on sharing greater love and compassion.

Some of my greatest teachers have been the patients I have served. This book represents what my patients have taught me over the years and continue to teach me. I am humbled by your resilience, kindness, and wisdom. Each day I am blessed to meet someone who makes me feel hopeful about life and enthusiastic about how far we (and I) have to go. In our journey toward the current state, we have collectively experienced much suffering. As we begin the ascent I wish we traverse a path that provides us joy. In that sense this book represents my feelings of compassion and caring, and not of judgment or bias. I know you are good, I wish to offer you help so you also feel good.

My goal is to help you learn why the untrained brain (and mind) with their instinctive focus on threat or imperfections are instrumental in generating negative thoughts and excessive stress. Importantly I will also help you learn the skills that will enable you to train your brain and the mind and engage your heart so you are able to overcome this limitation. My desire is to be able to offer simple solutions for complex problems and share principles based higher order skills that are applicable to most life situations. An optimal program in the 21st century should tap on the wisdom of the scriptures as well as advances in science, particularly neurosciences, and also adapt to the needs and limitations of the present times. It is my humble hope that this program will offer you this combination.

It is my innermost desire through this effort to touch people of all generations, particularly those actively engaged in their homes, community, or work place. How you feel and what you do in the "now" will determine our collective future. While sharing information in this book, I have frequently received comments such as, "Why don't we teach this to all our kids in the schools?" Or "I wish I knew this when I was going to college." I could not agree more.

I have a few requests / directions as you read this book.

1. Please be participatory – This book is not a one-way dialog; it is an invitation for you to participate with me in this journey. Fill out the exercises and underline the text as you feel appropriate. Sometimes it also helps to place post-it notes at home and in the workplace or Outlook messages to serve as gentle reminders to practice the skills that you learn.

2. Remain open minded – I invite your skepticism but pray you to be open minded. Feel free to test each fact or opinion I present with the parameters of your own wisdom. There are times my ideas may not directly apply or appeal to you. I offer generalizations while your circumstances understandably are unique. As the statistician George E.P. Box said, *"Essentially all models are wrong, but some are useful."* I hope you find the model I share with you useful.

3. Share the skills with others – Exchange the concepts and skills you learn with others. It will be ideal to first embody what you read before you begin sharing. Your words will then come from a greater depth. The same words that come from a greater depth often assume an entirely different (and more profound) meaning.

4. Consider your brain and mind as an integrated tool – Just like any other part of the body, you can learn how best to train and use the brain-mind instrument to experience joy, find peace, and develop creativity and resilience. When I talk about engaging the heart, I primarily mean enhancing positive emotionality (love) in the present moment by engaging the heartful part of the brain.

Lastly I share two additional tips for reading this book:

- Each exercise in the text is italicized and has an underlying message. If you wish to proceed without completing the exercise, I urge you to at least read through the question in the exercise and the text that follows. That will provide you the spirit in which the exercise is written.

- Some of the more technical text is shaded and placed in a text box. If you do not wish to read scientific findings in greater depth you can skim through it or even skip it altogether. It is unlikely you will miss on the core concepts with this approach.

SECTION I: TRAIN YOUR BRAIN ENGAGE YOUR HEART TRANSFORM YOUR LIFE: A BRIEF SURVEY

Précis

• Your brain has two important centers that affect your well-being:
    • Higher cortical center: Decreases stress, increases resilience
    • Lower limbic center: Increases stress, decreases resilience

• You have a choice to engage and empower one or the other center

• This book teaches you two essential steps to train your brain and engage your heart to selectively awaken and empower your brain's higher center

• The two steps are:
    • Step 1: Training your attention
    • Step 2: Refining your interpretations

---

1. Introduction

Where do you mostly look when you drive your car? (Figure 1.1)

1) The road behind (area A) in your rear view mirror ☐
2) The road upfront (area B) well lit by your headlights ☐
3) Somewhere far ahead in the dark (area C) ☐

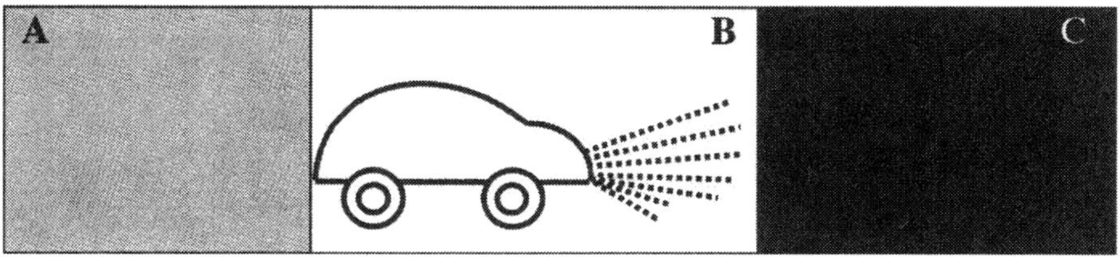

Figure 1.1 The three zones you can attend to as you drive

I am confident most of your attention remains upfront at the next few hundred feet—as far as the headlights show. You certainly have to periodically check the rearview mirror to keep a tab on the traffic behind. You also have to keep in mind what lies ahead and plan accordingly. Maybe there is a traffic jam you could avoid by taking a service road, or there is a state fair you want your kids to attend. However, obsessively looking too far ahead all the time would be counterproductive, just as looking in the rearview mirror for any longer than needed risks a major mishap. Both of these—constantly looking back in time or too far ahead—costs you dearly because in the process you miss out on one thing that will never come back—the present moment, the wonderful experience you could have in "the now" as you travel. In order to reach your destination safely and enjoy the ride, it will help if the majority of your time is spent looking at the next few hundred feet. *By paying attention, a few hundred feet at a time, you can travel hundreds of miles and arrive at your desired destination.*

Don't you think this is also the most efficient way to drive your life? To purposefully stay in the present and look at "what is" rather than spending too much time with "what was" or "what might be"? Most of our moments of peace and joy are experienced in the present moment. Many of our negative experiences including feelings of depression, anxiety, anger or stress, or habits such as smoking, recreational drug use, excess alcohol intake—are elaborate escapes from the present moment. Why do we harbor a propensity to escape from the present moment? One common theme is that the present moment becomes unacceptable if we have a large number of open files in our mind that we cannot close. These open files draw and sap your attention, and engulf your capacity to handle uncertainty. They originate in your propensity to incessantly plan and problem solve throughout the day. They are hosted by the lower stress producing center of the brain, activation of which produces overwhelming feelings of stress. Let us start our time together addressing the issue of stress.

Salt, spices, and stress

Stress is a bit like the salt or spices in your food. Food is bland if it misses salt; too much salt is not good either—for the taste of the food or for your health. What you seek is not a no-stress state—you seek a state wherein you have the optimal amount of stress. Individual taste for the salt and spices in the food varies. The ability to withstand stress also varies from one person to the next and even within a person from day to day, week to week, month to month, and year to year. In that case, how do you find out what is the optimal amount of stress for you?

You have optimal amount of stress if the challenges you face are evenly matched by your ability to respond while still maintaining well-being. This ability to maintain well-being while handling the stress and stressors is related to your resilience. Resilience is thus your ability to withstand adversity, to bounce back from reversals, and even rise as a result of adversity.

You have two options if at any instance the challenges you face overwhelm your capacity:

Option #1. Decrease the amount of stressors
Option #2. Increase your ability to handle stressors

It would be perfect if you could customize the amount and type of stressors that life throws at you. But unfortunately for most of us that is not always a realistic solution. So the logical next question is—is there a way you can increase your ability to handle stressors, and in turn enhance your peace, joy and resilience? The answer to this question, fortunately, is Yes!

What skills can help increase your peace, joy and resilience? In general, peace, joy and resilience correlate with increased activity in the higher cortical center of your brain, particularly the pre-frontal cortex. It would make sense then to practice approaches that can increase the activity of these centers in your brain. The cogent next question then is—are there skills that can help train your pre-frontal cortex?

A large body of scientific research conducted mostly in the last two decades hints at a number of approaches that are helpful to engage and empower your higher cortical center (the prefrontal cortex). As I looked at the sum total of data, a consistent theme took shape. Over a period of time I started incorporating elements from this theme into my "healing plan" with patients. The results were gratifying to miraculous. This journey not only helped, and sometimes transformed, the lives I was able to touch, but brought transformative changes to my own life too. It was when the majority of my patients and many of my colleagues nudged me to put the schematic I carried in my head on paper that I first thought of writing this book. In that sense this book is a work of compassion, hope, and optimism. There is no place for prejudice, judgment, or bias in it. I accept you as you are and wish to meet you where you are in your stage of life. Our goal isn't about becoming perfect; it is about reaching the highest level we can, whatever that may be for each of us.

The journey I embarked on has made me contemplate several aspects of the human condition—from the holiness of His Holiness the Dalai Lama to the greed of Bernard Madoff; from the evanescent nature of subatomic particles to the ultimate infiniteness of space and matter; from the grief that sometimes comes with partial cure to healing that may happen even without a cure. This book is an attempt to connect all those dots while offering tangible skills so you can benefit from the extensive research and clinical experience available. *It offers practical solutions and approaches that you can learn and imbibe in your own lives.* It is an invitation.

An Invitation

With this book I extend you an invitation to join me in a journey to together cultivate *higher order skills* based on the latest neurosciences research that will help us engage with "what is" and thus effortlessly arrive at "what might be." In the process I will help you learn in two simple steps how to transform your life by training your brain and engaging your heart.

This journey will take you away from excessively engaging the developmentally lower center of your brain toward awakening the higher cortical center. The higher center when engaged gives you such amazing attributes as peace, compassion, love, happiness, intellect, imagination, creativity, motivational drive, impulse control, strategic planning, organizational ability, long-term vision, efficiency, and effectiveness. The higher center is accessible to each of you yet awaits your purposeful attention and effort for it to be fully activated.

The two words I use to characterize the skills I will share are *higher order* and *practical*. *Higher order skills* are those that are based on eternal principles that transcend time. They are not individual value based judgments or captive of a particular paradigm. These skills permeate all aspects of your life and are applicable to most life situations. They existed five thousand years ago and will be taught five thousand years hence. From busy executives to patients with serious life threatening illnesses, I have taught and found useful the very same skills for a vast spectrum of people I have been blessed to serve. The skills that are helpful toward coping with an illness are also applicable to handling an economic downturn, planning the next steps to grow your business, for cultivating a deeper relationship with your child, and even for improving your golf swing. These skills have the potential to rewire (or, as I prefer to say, *"Rightwire")* your brain.

Another aspect of these skills is they are *practical*. I am convinced that behind all the complexity and chaos we see in the world, the basic uniting concepts are extraordinarily simple. You do not need esoteric or mystical ideas or a full understanding of quantum mechanics or evolution to find a path toward greater joy. In fact too much knowledge sometimes is an impediment since it loads us with excessive bias and sometimes tends to be divisive. If the notions are not simple, then we still have work to do to improve our understanding. In order to preserve this simplicity, I will stay clear of the maze of words or mystical concepts to the extent possible. I will convey the key concepts and ideas with a blend of explanations, examples, practice exercises, and measured repetition.

I will make every effort to stay within the paradigm of science. Science offers the two unique advantages of objective neutrality and ability to synthesize information from many observations to arrive at the probable likelihood of what will apply to you as an individual. Religion and spirituality on the other hand represent individual beliefs that are often not neutral. Science, religion, and spirituality thus wonderfully complement each other. Albert Einstein once said, *"Science without religion is lame. Religion without science is blind."* I will attempt to balance the two. Several thousand research studies support the individual components of the schema provided; information from about five hundred studies is included and referenced in this book.

In this section I provide a summary of the contents of the book that will then be expanded through the rest of the text. I begin the journey discussing what may seem obvious, gradually building into slightly more novel and contentious concepts. *Please be participatory as we walk together.*

2. Do Not Postpone Joy

Answer the following question by marking all that applies to your life.

Exercise 1. In which of the following aspects is your life presently challenged?

Relationships	☐
Children	☐
Health	☐
Finances	☐
Work	☐
Personal	☐
Others	☐

Based on your response, let us try to develop an insight into the nature of life with the following exercise.

Exercise 2. Do you think your challenges are likely to increase / decrease / go away / or remain the same over the ensuing years? (Table 2.1)

	Increase	Decrease	Go away	Unchanged
Relationships	☐	☐	☐	☐
Children	☐	☐	☐	☐
Health	☐	☐	☐	☐
Finances	☐	☐	☐	☐
Work	☐	☐	☐	☐
Personal	☐	☐	☐	☐
Others:	☐	☐	☐	☐
	☐	☐	☐	☐

Table 2.1 Direction of your life's potential future challenges

In most situations you may notice that the stressors change their form and intensity but do not completely go away. For example, as relationships change, sour relationships might get better while sweet ones become sour. Children go through different phases of life, each of which brings new challenges as well as rewards. For most of you, health-related issues will only increase with time. Your financial situation and work tend to be unpredictable. Personal issues such as self-esteem, growth, and the short term meaning of your life may also change with time, sometimes for good and others not so good. This leads to an important pearl I wish to share: **Do not postpone joy.**

Do not postpone joy waiting for a day when life will be perfect and all your stressors will be gone. Your opportunity to live the best you can is in this very moment. If you wait because you are too busy or stressed, it could be a wait of a lifetime. If you let go of this opportunity you might come back to it may be a decade later. You will always have some excuse to postpone your joy. I myself have never had a day when my boat was fully secure in the harbor, the water was a deep blue, the winds were quiet, and the sun was bright and shining in the sky. Waiting for such a day would be a very long wait. So I need to admit the reality and find fulfillment in the present moment accepting all its imperfections.

This is the day the LORD has made; let us rejoice and be glad in it (Psalm 118:24 NIV).

You might ask, if joy indeed is here and now then what is the reason that I am not able to find and sustain it for the long term? The answer is simple—your mind has a tendency to push the joy away and keep you logged off from life. Over a period of time this pushing away "wrongwires" your brain. Your brain wires itself to activate the lower stress producing center. In that state, you need not make any effort to invite stress—stress and suffering become a common event. Sounds very inefficient and maladaptive, doesn't it? This indeed is how your biology works—unless you choose to take action. It is only by purposeful action and training that you can "rightwire" your brain so that the higher cortical and not the lower limbic center predominates. Let us next look at these two centers.

3. Brain and its Two Centers

The brain is an unimaginably complex organ. A useful oversimplification for the present purpose will be to focus on the two centers of the brain that are of central importance to your well-being—the higher (cortical) and the lower (limbic) centers. ***Increased activity of the lower limbic center makes you anxious, unhappy, depressed, and stressed. Activation of the brain's higher cortical center helps you be calm, happy, joyous, and resilient.*** The relationship is almost mathematical. The main constituent of the lower limbic center is the amygdala, while the most significant component of the higher cortical center is the pre-frontal cortex. We will explore details about these components in the next section. *For the moment, know that the choice to activate one or the other brain center is squarely yours. Look at these centers as tools available to you to run your life.*

The higher cortical center helps us with many essential functions including, attention, judgment, decision making, memory, focus, postponing gratification, abstract thinking, compassion, forgiveness, handling complexity and novelty, and many more. With the present world being so fast paced and complex, this part of the brain, although much larger in us than any other species, still has to grow significantly to fully support our pattern of living. While we lack the ability to make it grow quickly, it is in our hands to increase our ability to engage, activate and rightwire this part of the brain.

Instinctively, however, many of us have a low threshold to activate the lower limbic center, particularly if we have an overactive mind. It is almost as if the connection to the limbic center is by a short, fast, broad band while that to the cortical center is by a long, slow, narrow band (Figure 3.1). Evolutionarily this pattern of connection helped us survive as a species. If you are born with a propensity to feel depressed, anxious, or stressed, you likely have a particularly active limbic system.

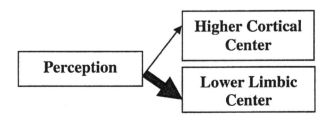

Figure 3.1 The "broad band" connection to the lower limbic center; "narrow band" connection to the higher cortical center

A good rule of thumb about the brain can be stated thus: if you engage a part of the brain, you awaken and empower it. Thus the limbic system (comprised mainly of the amygdala), once activated, makes its own connections stronger. *A key aspect of this whole process is that the chemicals (stress mediators) released in the stress response not only strengthen the limbic system but also disempower the higher cortical system. This keeps you within the trap of an activated limbic system for much longer than optimal (Figure 3.2).*

Here is a very important fact: Stress and depression do not just make you unhappy; they cause structural damage to your brain. So much so that scientists have begun to call the effect of stress on the brain as a reversible neurodegenerative disorder.[1]

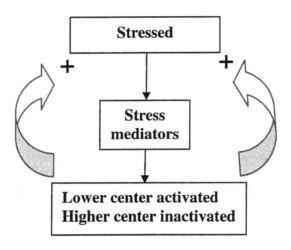

Figure 3.2 Feedback loops between stress, stress mediators, and the brain centers

Do you see the elaborate set up—how the inefficient systems in your brain can fence you into suffering and then enslave you into that state? This is like a boa constrictor—stress begets more stress because of this imperfection in our biology. This is more common than you may think. In fact, this faulty mechanism is ubiquitous and to my mind a very important contributor to the collective suffering on our planet.

The entity in charge of this operation that works in collaboration with the brain and allows this process to continue or can reverse the course if it chooses to is your mind. It is thus important as a next step to understand the workings of your mind particularly in relation to suffering.

4. Mind and Suffering

Most adverse situations in life affect multiple aspects of your being. The two domains of your life commonly affected by a negative experience are the *physical* and *emotional* (for the moment I am not addressing the spiritual component). A combination of these two equals your "total suffering."

Total Suffering = Physical Suffering + Emotional Suffering

Consider two examples—an ankle sprain and a verbal insult at work. The color black represents the physical suffering and grey the emotional suffering. The distribution of your suffering could be something like shown in figure 4.1.

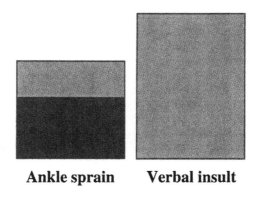

Ankle sprain   **Verbal insult**

Figure 4.1 Estimate of suffering associated with two common stressors. Physical suffering is shown in the color black while emotional suffering is shown in grey.

While the ankle sprain may cause you greater physical suffering, it is the verbal insult that often causes greater "total suffering." This is because of the greater emotional pain associated with a verbal insult. A verbal insult may be associated with several negative feelings, including sadness, anxiety, anger, diminished self-respect, sense of lack of control, feeling of futility, lack of faith in oneself, and loss of meaning in relationships. These elements in combination contribute to greater emotional pain.

Your quality of life and well-being depends on the "total suffering" and not just its individual elements. The two aspects of suffering are intimately related to and directly affect each other. An increase in emotional suffering over the long term may increase physical suffering and vice versa.

Disappointments

Emotional suffering commonly draws from everyday disappointments you face or anticipate. Disappointments can be represented in this simple equation –

Disappointments = Expectation – Reality (E-R)

Expectation is a mix of desires and beliefs related to how the future should transpire or past or present should have been. Excessive desire and self-focus both inflate expectations.

In an ideal world, success and happiness should be close relatives of each other. Often however, they do not live in the same dwelling. This is because of the E-R mismatch. *The mind's perception of discord between expectations and reality leads to disappointments.* Disappointments are particularly likely in the environs of excessive self-indulgence. In this state no amount of success can satisfy you because your thought process is dominated by unsatisfied needs. *The disappointments and related frustrations are the primary cause of unhappiness and suffering.* No wonder studies show that some of the happiest people on our planet (from Denmark) are so happy at least partly because they harbor the attitude of keeping low and reasonable expectations.

Generally it is not the major stressors that affect us the most. A major stressor is often accompanied by the societal response to enhance our coping. What bothers us most are the minor daily stressors that we allow to accumulate or the fear of a future major stressor.

A good understanding of this process provides the hint toward solutions—either change the expectations or change the reality. There is also a third solution unique to us humans—learn to accept the discord between expectation and reality. You can do this by accommodating in your world view the fact that such a discord exists and its acceptance provides a path toward greater joy, both in success as well as adversity.

Emotional suffering also occurs because of an *epidemic of low self-esteem in our society.*

Sadly, many of us have heard and absorbed repeated negative remarks emphasizing how imperfect, ineffective, and wrong we are. These remarks often come from the very individuals we depend on for our self-esteem—our life partner, loved ones, friends, and work colleagues. The resulting lowered self-esteem forces us to mistrust our wisdom. We begin treating ourselves poorly and start downplaying our strengths. Our confidence starts to shake; we feel inadequate and stop feeling loved. We may find it difficult to trust our friends or even may begin to feel that we are unworthy of friendship. I often tell my patients to look at themselves with their pet's eyes. *You are who your dog thinks you are—kind, caring, and compassionate.* Your pet does not care about your financial net worth, job, health, fame, etc. All it cares about is your love and your ability to express it. The loving you is the transcendental you that no one can rob. Peg your self-esteem on how loving you are, not on your material accomplishments.

How the mind multiplies suffering

We will take the next steps accepting the assumption that your mind is an active participant in every adverse and happy experience irrespective of its origin. Every experience of your life converges onto your mind. Your mind can keep you in bliss; alternatively, your mind can also craft and amplify your pain. Left to its own reserves, the human mind's natural tendency is to increase the pain.

The relationship between your stressors, reactions, and how you feel (your symptoms) are depicted in this triangle (Figure 4.2).

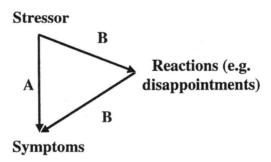

Figure 4.2 The two pathways connecting stressors to symptoms

There are two pathways that connect a stressor to symptoms:
- Pathway A: This is the direct pathway, e.g. an ankle sprain may cause you physical pain because of the sprain itself; and
- Pathway B: This is the indirect pathway, a result of your reaction to the stressor (related to E-R imbalance with resulting disappointments).

For each stressor or perceived stressor, your appraisal of that stressor has four components. These unfold in the following approximate sequence:
1) Assessment of the probability of the stressor materializing;
2) Assessment of the severity of the stressor;
3) Assessment of your ability to respond to the stressor; and
4) Assessment of the probability that your response will mitigate the stressor.

Most of this evaluation happens very quickly and often subconsciously. The sum total of this evaluation directs the extent of your reactions. The evaluator in this process is your own mind that is often not fully skilled to make accurate judgments about the threats or your ability to respond to them. The stress we see in our society is at least partly because of this limitation of our untrained mind. The conclusions made by such a mind are often flawed and lead to two fallacies that perpetuate your stress:

1) *The mind generally overestimates the severity of threat and the probability that it will materialize; and*
2) *The mind underestimates your ability to respond and the adequacy of that response.*

Most physical pains get a load of secondary emotional content added to it. The mind often catastrophizes the situation by imagining several worst case scenarios. In the example we just noted (ankle sprain), your mind might generate several thoughts such as:

1) What if I permanently damaged my ankle?
2) What if I remain in pain for several weeks?
3) What if because of the pain I am not able to work and end up losing my job?
4) What if my doctor misdiagnosed the problem?
5) What if the treatment does not work?
6) What if I react to the medication prescribed to me?
7) What if…..?

None of these concerns are independently wrong, but taken to an extreme these "what ifs" increase your emotional pain. They also do not serve your primary aim—to nurse and heal the sprained ankle. The mind generates these concerns to serve your instincts of self-preservation. **Mind, however, has a momentum problem.** It does not know very well when to stop and as a result overdoes it. At some point the mind might realize that its instinctive response may be maladaptive by the symptoms of stress that it generates. So it makes an effort to resolve the negative thoughts. The untrained mind's ruminations and efforts of thought suppression, however, are immature and take you deeper into the vortex. Research suggests that many negative emotions and predisposition to anger and aggression may originate in uncontrolled ruminations generated by an untrained mind.[2]

When faced with negative thoughts or feelings, your mind generates an *avoidance response*. The mind tries to suppress or delete these thoughts. *Your inside world, however, does not follow the same rules as the outside world.* You cannot throw away or recycle your thoughts the way you can with most of your possessions in the outside world. Thoughts do not come with the label "satisfaction guaranteed." Your thoughts are glued to each other—the more you try to suppress or remove them, the greater context you create for additional thoughts. Avoidance empowers your imperfections. While you may find occasional islands of peace in this process, this peace is unstable and does not last very long. Avoidance also keeps you away from the magnificence of life.

This is not all. The human mind has one final punch that multiplies your sufferings—your extraordinary ability to imagine. Your mind has the capacity to churn out your own version of a Harry Potter-like story every day. Spend some time with a four-year-old and you will be impressed with the imaginative capacity of the human mind! Further, your imagination has a unique quality to it. **Anything you imagine, your brain experiences as if it has already happened.** If you imagine your left leg is moving, the area of the brain involved in left leg movement becomes active. This quality of imagination supports your creativity and is the power that has allowed you to craft your beautiful world. Be it architects, lawyers, doctors, philosophers, poets, businessmen, plumbers, or entrepreneurs, most of us use our muscle of imagination to be creative and efficient.

Imagination, however, is a double-edged sword. On the one hand imagination helps creativity, yet on the other imagination about a threat makes the threat seem believably real. *When you imagine a threat, your brain goes through the same experience as if the threat has materialized.* So when you wake up in the middle of the night with a fear, your imagination forces you to go through all kinds of scenarios related to this fear. All this suffering is for nothing—just a thought that most likely will never materialize and does not represent reality. The vast majority of your fears will never come true. However, the stuff that never happens collectively hurts you more than what truly transpires. As Mark Twain very aptly said, *"I have been through some terrible things in my life, some of which actually happened."*

In many of life's situations, the triangle in figure 4.2 may actually be better depicted as shown below in figure 4.3.

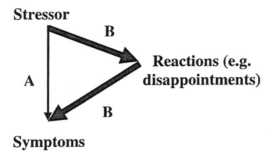

Figure 4.3 Symptoms associated with a stressor may sometimes be more related to reactions than the direct effect of the stressor itself

Do you see that the greater part of your suffering, particularly the emotional suffering, may sometimes result from the reactions of your untrained mind? The emotional needs of the mind may trump the biological needs, sometimes even the instinct of survival. The categorizations and judgments created by the mind are legion. Collectively they generate greater suffering than the primary stressor itself. Often times you may not have much control over the stressor. If you have already sprained your ankle, there is nothing you can do presently to go back in time and prevent it from happening. However, you always have control over how you respond to help it heal expeditiously.

In the instance of the ankle sprain, there are two things you can do to help decrease your suffering. First, go see your doctor and get appropriate medical help. Second and equally important, do not allow your mind to generate a maladaptive reaction. Seeing a doctor seems simple and straightforward; preventing a maladaptive reaction, however, needs a purposeful effort to train your mind.

Why is the training necessary? Will the mind not learn on its own? Training your mind and the brain is necessary because the innate wiring of your brain directs it to engage its lower center. Mind will also not learn on its own. Left to its own reserves, your brain and mind are designed to generate a strong stress response when they detect a stressor. This response is not all bad, it is actually sometimes beneficial—our ability to rapidly mount a stress response helps us survive major life threatening events.

The stress response, however, consumes considerable amounts of energy and becomes maladaptive in two situations:
1) If its intensity is disproportionate to the need; and/or
2) If it is activated for longer than desired.

In modern times, both of these errors are common. If I hold a glass of water above my head for a few minutes it won't bother me at all; if for half an hour it will start hurting me; but if I try for several hours, I might have to go to the emergency room. The same stressor when allowed to nag us for a long time can mutate into an illness. We thus overdo this response in terms of intensity as well as duration—and dearly pay for it. We often drive our life with the air bags already deployed! It might keep us safe but may not help our driving. The chronically activated stress response that was not designed for long-term stimulation creates inflammation in your body, decreases your immunity, interferes with sleep, delays healing, predisposes to many diseases, and worsens your quality of life. *Further, because of the peculiar mechanisms in your brain, the response once activated feeds on itself. Stress begets further stress.* This provides the basis for how our untrained brain and untutored mind increases our total suffering.

To reverse this process, when you begin training your mind, you start to train, engage and empower the brain's higher center. This process, once initiated, is self-propelling—train your mind, train, engage and empower your brain's higher center; train, engage and empower your brain's higher center, further train your mind. The mind thus changes the brain, which further changes the mind (Figure 4.4).

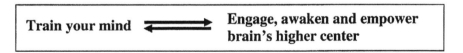

Figure 4.4 The interconnection between training the mind
and engagement of the brain's higher center

The foregoing description summarized the activity of the mind that is perceptible on the surface. In order to diagnose and fix the malfunction effectively, an engineer has to understand the underlying mechanics of the engine. So let us go backstage with our mind in an effort to develop a schematic to overcome its imperfections.

5. Backstage with the Mind

The mind is the sum total of all the processes that contribute toward your perceptions and actions. Consider the mind as the operating system of the brain. The brain and mind together constitute the primary tools that help you perceive the world, process the incoming information, and plan all your actions. Together they effect such important processes as attention, memory, monitoring, inhibitory control, judgment, decision making, intellect, and creativity.

The mind directs you to act based on what it perceives. Perception represents the sum total of your experience, external and internal. Perception involves obtaining sensory information and making a sense of this information integrating it with your memory and preferences. Awareness connotes ability to perceive. In this book we will use awareness and perception interchangeably, with awareness being used more in a contemplative sense. Perception depends on two integrated functions: attention and interpretation (Figure 5.1). *Attention works as the <u>gateway</u> into the mind; interpretation represents the <u>content</u> of the mind. Interpretation is thus related to the content of your thoughts and emotions.*

I have highlighted the boxes that offer the tools most amenable to change, i.e. attention and interpretation and the respective components of interpretation—*principles, prejudices, and preferences (**3Ps**)* (we will address all of these below).

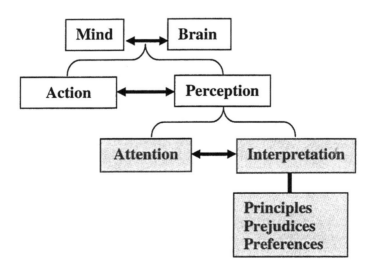

Figure 5.1 The components of the brain and mind and their relationships

Attention and interpretation are intimately related and together support all your actions (Figure 5.2).

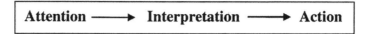

Attention ⟶ Interpretation ⟶ Action

Figure 5.2 The pathway from attention to interpretation and action

A sensory experience is first brought to you in its purity and originality by your power of attention. Attention, however, does not last very long. Within a fraction of a second your attention gets mixed with your memory, intellect, and a combination of principles, prejudices, and preferences (**3Ps**). Attention thereby progresses to interpretation. In general, once you have interpreted something, you do not stay with it but move on to the next thing. This "moving on" helps efficiency and allows you to keep learning new objects and ideas. This is adaptive to help us live a successful life in a complex, chaotic world. However, beyond a limit, this schematic enslaves us within the expectations and invariant beliefs that it creates. A premature deployment of interpretation disrupts the process of attention, makes your interpretation faulty because it is based on incomplete facts, and creates a state of attention deficit or mindlessness. This is further accentuated if you guide your interpretation based on prejudices rather than higher principles. You then become numb to new experiences; life goes past you very quickly without your stopping to smell the roses. You may see but not perceive, hear but not listen, touch but not feel. Days become dull, boring, and repetitive.

The quality of your perception (and in turn the quality of your entire life) thus depends on its two primary components: attention and interpretation. An optimal balance between attention and interpretation (*the AI balance*) is helpful toward continued growth, just like the yin and yang in traditional Chinese medicine (Figure 5.3).

Figure 5.3. Attention Interpretation (AI) Balance

The fast-paced modern world, however, forces many of us into attention-interpretation imbalance wherein we live a life with a combination of attention deficit and excess deployment of biased interpretations. The two important issues that may negatively affect the quality of your perceptions thus are:

1) *Attention deficit – generally accompanied by a state of attention inflexibility; and*
2) *Interpretation excess – premature, excessive, and biased interpretations*

Perceptions in our usual state thus have too little attention and excessive and biased interpretations. In this state you stop observing the world as it is. You look at the world as you would like it to be.

Attention and interpretation are the two wheels that carry the cart of perception. They are also the two entities most amenable to training and change. Hence it will help to peel another layer of the mind and go backstage with attention and interpretation to understand how they operate.

6. Backstage with Attention and Interpretation

Attention is the doorway into perception; interpretation represents the content of your perception. Together they create each of your experiences. ***Attention logs you on to your life; interpretation helps you discern and create the content.*** Both are needed and are mutually supportive. Understanding the integration of attention and interpretation in your brain might help you understand how you can strive to attain the optimal *AI balance.*

The cortex of your brain is organized in six vertically arranged layers that have extensive horizontal connections. Sensory input collected by the process of attention coming from below meets the narrative stored in our memory coming from the top. When they integrate they create an experience.

In general as shown in figure 6.1, untrained attention brings weak information. This is partly because like a leaking vessel with many holes, often our attention is simultaneously distributed in multiple directions. If you are talking on the cell phone, sipping a cup of coffee and driving at the same time, only a third of you really is paying attention to driving. Another reason for weaker attention is that most of our experiences from one day to the next are very similar, to the point of being boring. Such experiences thus do not engage our attention. Further, attention is met by a strong previously stored narrative which prematurely stops our attention. We stop seeing things as they are and mostly stick with our prejudices.

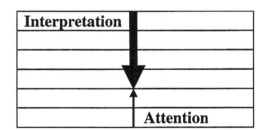

Figure 6.1 Attention and Interpretation within the brain with an untrained mind. Upward pointing slimmer arrow represents weaker attention; downward pointing thicker arrow represents dominating interpretation.

The trained attention, however, brings much richer information that is met by a less domineering labeling process (Figure 6.2). Such an attention allows you to experience the richness of life, to approach each moment and find novelty and newness in it. Changing the AI balance from the state depicted by figure 6.1 to one shown in figure 6.2 is at the core of training our attention and thus our brain, a process we will explore in greater details.

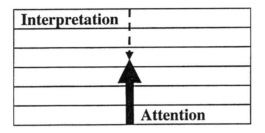

Figure 6.2 Pathways of Attention and Interpretation within the brain with a <u>trained mind</u>. Upward pointing thicker arrow represents strengthened attention; downward pointing slimmer arrow represents refined and optimized interpretation.

Attention

Attention is a skill involving a sustained and selective focus that allows you to register, imbibe, and transmit the sensory information. Attention is the common entry into all your mental processes that mediate thinking and emotions. The end product of successful attention is a transparent sensory experience that is perceived in its purity and originality. You register this experience, imbibe it, and then transfer it to your brain and mind to interpret. Attention thus depends on intact and engaged sensory apparatus and a mind-brain instrument that is ready to receive and process the sensory input. Three important aspects of attention are: its direction (toward the mind or the world), its depth, and its ability to sustain (duration). *The **3Ds** of attention thus are **D**irection, **D**epth, and **D**uration.* Let us next see what draws our attention.

Imagine you are driving on the streets of New York City and come across two sights—a dog on a leash and a stray elephant strolling on the sidewalk. There is a good chance you will not pay much attention to the dog. Watching the elephant, however, would be an exciting, or maybe even a scary event. It's very likely you will remember this experience all your life.

On the contrary, if elephants were a common part of our lives, just as dogs and cats are, you may not have paid attention.

Co-passengers in the train, colleagues at work, people in the mall—the list is long of persons, objects, and events we never pay much attention to. Sometimes this list might also include your close colleagues and even loved ones. Why is it that many of us remain in relative inattention? Simply because we are wired to pay attention only to the persons, objects, events, or experiences that have an extraordinary appeal or value—our attention depends on motivation. This value is called salience in neurosciences.

At any point in time your attention is drawn to entities that have one or more of the following three characteristics:
1) They are *potentially **T**hreatening;* or
2) They are *unusually **P**leasing;* or
3) They are ***N**ovel.*
These constitute the **TPN** of attention.

We pay attention to entities that have the promise of a high reward or knowing which might help our well-being or survival.[3] Most of this relates to what might constitute a threat. We thus have a little smoke detector in our head that preferentially attends to fear, anger and disgust.[4-6] Even infants as young as 7-months old pay greater attention to faces that express fear.[7, 8] This nature of our attention is thus instinctive and often useful because it helps us invest our energy wisely and facilitates task-focused learning. But taken to an extreme, it is this very habit that puts us into inattention. The reason for this is simple—*most of the time our world lacks material threats, unusual pleasure, or novelty.*

Most people I ask have fairly similar experiences from one day to the next. The vast majority of your thoughts are qualitatively similar from one day to the next. On most days the world provides only a limited dose of *innovation* or *unusual pleasure.* Similarly, the *threats* that the world provided a few thousand years ago when we foraged for food in the jungles side by side with wild animals are all but gone. Newer threats have emerged, but fortunately they do not grip us every day. As a result, unlike a young child who is constantly learning and engaged in the world, your senses may not find the world stimulating enough. Missing all the three elements (the TPN) that may excite you or draw your attention, the world is unable to hold your interest for very long.

This risks pushing you into a state of inattention with respect to the world— you just plough along disconnected. The common sequence followed by your mind with a unit of sensory experience is shown in figure 6.3.

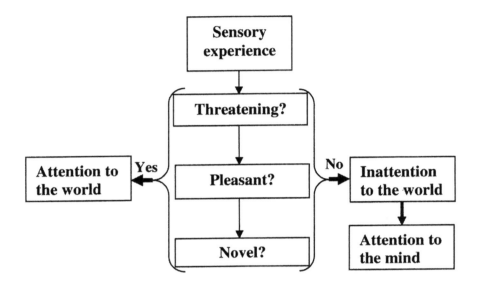

Figure 6.3 The effect of the interpretation of sensory experience on attention and inattention with respect to the world. Inattention to the world pushes your attention toward the mind.

The figure below represents the content of your perception in the default state of inattention—too little attention, too much interpretation (Figure 6.4).

Attention   **Interpretation**

Figure 6.4 Distribution of attention and interpretation within an untrained mind

The outcome of inattention: With the world seeming bland, your attention automatically turns to the other entity readily available—your mind.

Mind easily holds your attention because your mind is a storehouse of thoughts and ideas you could consider novel, pleasant, or threatening. These are in the form of fantasies, desires, and fears. Often these thoughts have I, me or mine as the focus. These thoughts of the past and future stored and imagined by your mind can keep you engaged for almost an indefinite period of time. In fact there is a network of neurons in the brain scientists call the "default network" that hosts these autobiographical thoughts. Research points to a certain "negativity bias" of our mind (propensity of our mind to pay greater attention to the negative), that particularly tends to affect us when we have wandering thoughts and are stuck within our default network.

No wonder, with the world failing to hold our consistent attention, many of us tend to spend an inordinate amount of time stuck in our mind. If you have this kind of attention, you are very likely to fail showing up in your life.

Figure 6.5 shows the two most common domains that keep your attention: the world and the mind. Notice that the past, present, and future within the mind are gelled into a continuum.

	Past	**Present**	**Future**
World ↑			
Mind ↓			

Figure 6.5 The two anchors of attention—world and the mind.
Notice the lack of distinction between the past, present,
and future within the mind.

Attention black holes: The propensity to direct your attention toward the mind is particularly strong if your mind harbors attention sumps that I prefer to call *attention black holes*. *Attention black holes*, like the black holes in outer space, have a very strong pull and incessantly and potently draw and bury your attention. These black holes represent one of two entities:

1) <u>Memories of past</u> negative experience/s (such as abuse, hurt, failure, regrets, rejection, accident, severe illness etc.) that collectively change your innocent view of the world; and/or

2) <u>Fear about future</u> significantly negative experience/s particularly related to the security (physical safety, health, finances) of self or loved ones. During times in your life when you feel vulnerable, potential for even a minor future imperfection could seem substantial and draw your attention.

(Mind also has Attention Oases that represent memories of positive experiences or optimistic future expectations. To keep the theme simpler, however, I will avoid adding attention oases to the model. In general, except for the most adept practitioners, it is the attention black holes not the oases that have a greater draw.)

These memories are stored in intricate neuronal connections within the brain. Such experiences generate prejudices and make you feel insecure about the future. Figure 6.6 shows an example of an attention black hole lodged in the recent past that pulls attention toward it away from the present.

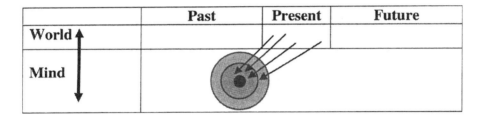

	Past	Present	Future
World			
Mind			

Figure 6.6 An attention black hole lodged in the recent past. Arrows represent the black hole drawing and burying attention within it. The resulting additional thoughts strengthen the attention black hole.

Attention black holes once created are difficult to dissolve. Carefully looking at the anatomy of an attention black hole thus might provide interesting perspective into learning how to prevent or treat them. At the core of such a black hole is the memory of the particular experience (Figure 6.7). This memory is then surrounded and protected by layers of additional context we create by ruminating about this experience, making its gravitational pull stronger. A strong effort to avoid thinking about the unhappy event also adds more contexts by creating a form of "negative attachment."

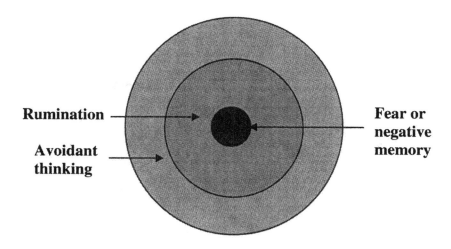

Figure 6.7 The anatomy of an attention black hole—kernel of fear or negative memory surrounded by layers of thoughts created by the mind

This black hole then becomes the common destination toward which your attention and thoughts converge. Greater the amount of attention and thoughts burying into this black hole, the stronger it gets. Such a black hole might become the defining aspect of your life. You might look at the world wearing lenses colored by this black hole. Every experience gets shaded and dulled by its presence.

Mind, thus, is very much like universe. It is as expansive and limitless as our universe is. Mind, in fact, is our universe. Just as there are numerous black holes in the universe, quite commonly the imperfections of your life create many such black holes in your mind in the domains of past as well as future (Figure 6.8). These black holes each may have a different context. They compete with each other and the sensory experiences of the world for your attention. Depending on the ongoing situation of life, you may spend time with one or the other black hole, or very commonly jump from one to the next. These black holes are the most common cause that prevents us from engaging with the splendor of the present moment within the world.

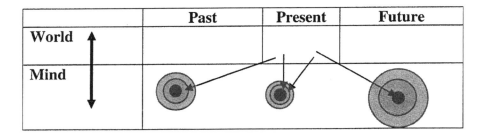

	Past	Present	Future
World ↕			
Mind			

Figure 6.8 The usual state of the mind with multiple attention black holes of different size and intensity

Attention black holes keep you locked in your mind. When your attention is captured by your mind, unless you are advanced in meditation, the multiple attention black holes do not allow you to stay in one time zone. You jump from one point to the other. Within your mind past, present, and future are enmeshed together in a continuum—you can free flow between multiple time points with ease. This free flow is accentuated because your instinctive approach toward imperfections within your mind is avoidance. You have learned that if you push away from negative thoughts, you can find peace for a short period of time. Thus, when within your mind, you do not stay at one place and are forced to time travel. This tendency to time travel is combined with another strong tendency of your mind—the habit of excessive thinking. Inside your head is a thought making machine that if not stopped can continuously churn out relevant and not so relevant thoughts. The common content of these thoughts is related to one of these five entities: desires, fears, hurts, regrets, and ordinary mundane thoughts.

Desires and fears keep you in the future; hurts and regrets lock you in the past. Based on where you are trapped (with desires, fears, hurts, or regrets), the bulk of your time with the mind may be spent in your past or future or (commonly) both (Figure 6.9).

	Past	Present	Future
World ↕			
Mind	Hurts, Regrets		Desires, Fears

Figure 6.9 The time spent in the past and future within the mind. When paying attention to the past or future, the present remains mostly inaccessible.

A large proportion of the time we spend within our mind may be unpleasant and unrewarding. Fears, hurts and regrets understandably are almost always unpleasant. Desires and their related fantasies on the other hand sometimes do bring pleasure, but more commonly degenerate into a sense of incompleteness. This incompleteness arrives because of the realization that many of our desires and fantasies will not be met or, even if they are met, we might not be able to retain and multiply all we acquire (the origin of E-R, or the expectation-reality gap). *In short, when your attention remains within your mind, you are likely to cycle between the past, present, and future, and the greater part of your time may be spent in the company of imperfections. In this state, the "present" mostly remains hidden and inaccessible and joy is postponed indefinitely.*

So simply because your attention instinctively seeks TPN (threat, pleasure, or novelty) and the world does not provide these on a consistent basis while the mind itself is a storehouse of desires, fears, hurts, and regrets— unless you make a purposeful effort, you are likely to spend a large part of your life drawn by the attention black holes within your mind. When you are "within your mind" you remain surrounded by imperfections of the past or presumed imperfections of the future. Since you are unwilling to accept most imperfections you repeatedly try to suppress or delete them, a process that does not work very well. Finally, because of your imaginative ability, you may repeatedly be hurting yourself by ruminating on and "experiencing" the disappointments of the past and presumed disappointments of the future. **Suffering is experienced when the sound of the present is lost as noise within the cacophony of the lost present or the present that is still unsure of what song it will sing.**

This pattern of thinking engages and empowers the lower limbic center of your brain and weakens (at least temporarily) the higher cortical center that in turn can create a chronic state of stress and anxiety. In order to run away from this anxiety, *your mind jumps from one point to the next—this may give rise to the state of attention deficit within the mind. When the mind does stop and tries to focus, it is often hypervigilant with an obsessive focus, characteristic of attention that is scouring for a potential threat. In a most inefficient way you slowly and surely invite stress and push joy away.*

Does this process sound familiar? Is this how you may have spent at least some part of your life? In my experience this state is extraordinarily common when someone is experiencing stress; in fact, to an extent, it is a rule rather than an exception. Studies show that people living their usual lives without significant stress may spend more than a third of their time during the day in the default mode disengaged from the world.[9, 10] Almost every individual I see with symptoms ascribable to stress acknowledges that this sort of thinking applies to them, partially or fully. ***No matter how materially accomplished your life, if you carry a load of attention black holes and spend an inordinate amount of time within your mind, you cannot be happy.***

There is another downside to being with your mind. While a constant engagement with the mind may keep you busy, the world keeps progressing at sixty seconds a minute. *You run the risk of missing out on life.* These black holes can sap your time, joy, peace and energy. Almost every day I am saddened to see people who have remained disengaged from their world—sometimes for decades, even an entire life time. What a loss, particularly because none of this happened out of their own volition. Their innate biological instincts imprinted into their brains coupled with an untrained attention pushed them into such a state.

The important question is, is there a path toward freedom from these imperfections? The answer is a resounding yes. We will soon begin exploring the steps of this path; first let us in brief look at the second aspect of perception, your interpretations.

Interpretations

Interpretations represent the content of your perception. The information you imbibe with paying attention is mixed with your stored database of memories, intellect, and the *3Ps (principles, prejudices, and preferences)*. This creates your overall "interpretations." Among these variables, memories and intellect are not easily modifiable. However, the 3Ps are amenable to learning and it is these three that will provide us the second step in our journey toward transformation. I will detail the 3Ps in the next section but will briefly mention them here.

- *Principles* represent higher order eternal laws that are based on the premise that every human being has a right to life, liberty, and the pursuit of happiness, just as you have. From these principles are derived individual skills and values including gratitude, compassion, acceptance, forgiveness, meaning and purpose, kindness, honesty, equanimity, humility, and love.

- *Prejudices* are a repository of interpretations and judgments that disregard the attention process and are based on pre-existing beliefs. Prejudices are shortcuts that are ready to be launched with each sensory experience and when in excess disengage you from the world.

- *Preferences* are your choices from among a number of possible alternatives. Preferences can either be *altruistic,* which incorporate the interests of others, or *egocentric,* which are primarily motivated to take care of the self. Predominantly egocentric preferences rely greatly on prejudices and when in excess increase your stress and suffering.

In general, principles and prejudices provide the basis for values, skills, and biases that generate your preferences (Figure 6.10).

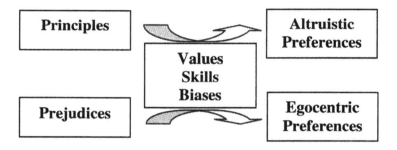

Figure 6.10 Principles and prejudices generate values, skills, and biases that may lead to altruistic or egocentric preferences

In a state of disconnectedness when you are mostly within your mind, your perception is suffused with prejudices and egocentric preferences that carry an ambience of invariance and certainty. This certainty prematurely interrupts attention. Your interpretations are thus inaccurate because they are based on an incomplete observation of the world. Such process engenders considerable stress and inefficiency. As a result we commit two errors in our interpretations:

1) *We interpret too soon and too much; and*
2) *Our untrained interpretations are predominantly based on prejudices*

Refining our interpretations entails correcting these two errors that constitutes the second of the two steps.

7. The Two Steps to Transformation

An ideal you has two wonderful aspects—one is a child and the other an adult. The child you is playful, gets excited, shares unconditional love, and is able to find joy in the mundane. The adult you has a mature perspective toward life, has learned the attributes of gratitude, compassion, acceptance, forgiveness, and is pursuing a higher meaning. Both the aspects are precious and together help you live a wholesome life.

In reality however, as you get older and the adult within you unfolds, the child within you gradually fades away. With this fading away you gradually gain maturity, however, you might lose the attributes of awe and wonder. This fading away is generally never complete—most of us maintain a vestige of the child we were within us, some more than others.

The process of the unfolding of the adult within you (correlating with the maturing higher cortical center) often does not carry to completion. Most of us do not achieve perfection in intellectual and spiritual maturity and may be found wanting in the practice of the higher principles.

Transformation entails addressing the child and the adult within you. In the time I have spent with His Holiness the Dalai Lama and other saints, I have uniformly found the transparency of a child within them and the maturity of an adult. The child within them is curious and ready to absorb with awe and wonder whatever is presented to their senses. The adult processes the information so received with principles-based skills of gratitude, compassion, acceptance, forgiveness, and higher meaning.

The first step toward transformation (training attention) reawakens the child within you who found joy in the mundane, extraordinary within ordinary, novelty within typical. In this state your higher cortical center exercises just the optimal amount of control—enough to suppress unacceptable or embarrassing behavior while at the same time allowing novelty to flourish. This ability to find novelty helps you cultivate a deep and purposeful attention with an ability to transparently absorb the sensory experience. It also helps nurture the creative artist within you. As Pablo Picasso once said, *"Every child is an artist. The problem is how to remain an artist once we grow up."* Awakening the child within you awakens that artist by training your brain.

The second step toward transformation (refining interpretations) appeals to the mature, loving and kind adult within you so s/he can attain greater intellectual and spiritual maturity. The fully mature adult within you guides the attention of the child by creating interpretations based on principles-based skills of gratitude, compassion, acceptance, forgiveness, higher meaning and purpose, kindness, honesty, equanimity, humility, and love. *Training the adult within you engages your heart.*

Attention training offers the optimal remedy for the first imperfection of the mind—its restlessness—while interpretation training heals the second imperfection of the mind—its ignorance. We will address these two imperfections later in this section.   With training attention and refining interpretations you offer your mind immediately accessible options to its negative ruminations. You rob suffering of its continuity.

The First Step: Train Your Attention

From the foregoing it may seem clear to you that the single most essential step of any program to enhance your well being will be to train your attention. The components of this training address the **3Ds** of attention—direction, depth, and duration.

When you are physically "here" but mentally "there," you have not showed up in your life. You are most likely still within your mind. When enslaved by your mind, you begin driving constantly looking into the rearview mirror or too far ahead—both ineffective and dangerous. The purpose of this training, however, is not to stop consulting the past or future. It is to go into the past and future in full control with an intention to serve the present. When you thus begin to serve the present, happiness and contentment manifest spontaneously.

Almost every deeply nourishing moment of your life has two common characteristics:
1) You are at one place mentally and physically; and
2) You are in one time zone mentally and physically.

Remember the moment you held your newborn baby for the first time. You were with the child physically as well as mentally, in total awe and admiration. Similarly in deep prayer you are one with your deity. When watching a beautiful sunset you admire and are one with the play of colors as they manifest. You don't tell Mr. Sun to add a shade of pink above or orange below. If you begin questioning your sensory experience, you are likely to stop enjoying it. When absorbed in a creative activity and in a state of "flow," hours may pass by in a blink. You do not feel tired, and actually may feel rejuvenated at the end of this rigorous work. This leads me to suggest the following hypotheses:

- *The joy you experience is <u>only partially</u> related to the specifics of the events itself.*
- *An event brings you joy by serving as a triggering factor to help you arrive at one place and one time.*

How much of the sunset would you enjoy if at the same time you were trying to absorb an undesirable business or personal news? The chances are that in this state you might not even notice the play of light on the firmament. With this understanding in mind, try to answer this question:

With a happy event, what do you think contributes toward your joy? Please pick one choice.

1. The specifics of the event   ☐
2. Your state of the mind   ☐
3. Specifics of the event + state of the mind   ☐

Both the event and the state of your mind, isn't it? Your physical and mental presence is essential for you to soak up your sensory experience. The happy event does bring you joy directly, but a larger part of your happiness comes about because such an event steers your attention into one place—the present moment. The sequence that progresses from a happy event to a state of joy is depicted in figure 7.1.

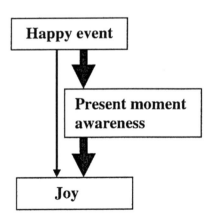

Figure 7.1 The two paths from happy event to the feeling of joy—Direct effect of the event and the effect of bringing the mind to present moment awareness

Armed with this hypothesis, I ask you a very important question:
Do you think it is possible for you to remain in the present moment and in the world without needing an outside event that is threatening / unusually pleasing / or novel?

    1. Yes   ☐
    2. No   ☐

I hope you answered yes, because that is the correct answer. It indeed is possible to train your brain, engage your heart and increase your presence in the here and now. My primary intention is to gently nudge you toward that state. Once you arrive in that state, happiness fills your experience of its own accord. You stop needing much from the world to feel happy. Your attention black holes gradually dry up and wither away.

The simple fact of life is that the world will not make every moment of yours materially fulfilling. You, however, have within your capacity to feel fulfilled despite the realities of the world by bringing about a shift in your attention. For such a shift to happen you do not have to join a laughter club or watch a hilarious movie. As a first step, you have to do one simple thing. Bring your attention to one place and one time, and mostly in the present.

You might ask, why just the present moment, why not past or future as long as you are in one time zone? The answer is simple. As we saw previously, past and future exist only in the mind not in the tangible world. Since past, present and future in the mind are in a continuum, it is extraordinarily difficult to remain in one time zone within the mind. The natural tendency is to shift from one time zone to the next. Further, mind in most instances harbors several attention black holes that are difficult to avoid particularly when you are under stress. Hence, at least initially in training, keeping attention focused is difficult when within your mind. It can more easily be achieved when you train your attention to be with the world.

Let us come back to the 3Ds of attention. First among the 3Ds of attention is the direction of attention that we have already agreed should optimally be the world and not so much the mind. For sustaining this direction it will help you to train the depth and duration of attention. As we will see subsequently (Section IV), to accomplish this you do not have to "invent" anything new or change your world. ***All you have to do is to "discover" the novelty that always existed in your world.*** The world remains the same; however, your trained attention floods the world with the light of *novelty*. You can imagine this as a *"circle of novelty"* that you implant in the world to keep your attention (Figure 7.2). This will train your ability to find the extraordinary within the ordinary.

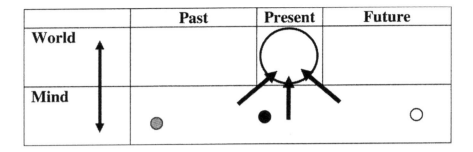

	Past	Present	Future
World			
Mind			

Figure 7.2 The effect of trained attention—Circle of novelty in the world draws your attention that gradually leads to disempowerment and transformation of the attention black holes

A peculiar aspect of the brain's structure and function is that if you do not use certain circuits, they gradually fade away. *Hence if you create an aptitude to bring your attention into the world in the present moment, then the attention black holes in your mind may gradually weaken.* By bringing your attention into the world you stop ruminations about negative experiences. This peels away the extra layers deposited around these experiences, leaving the kernel of experience that is much less potent in drawing your attention. Further, as you mature, you also re-interpret this experience and find meaning in it. Often with this meaning the negative experience may look less negative or even may start changing color to shades of grey or even white. Figure 7.3 shows the effect of this training with the transformation of the attention black holes. This may allow you to experience what is often called the phenomenon of post-traumatic growth.[11]

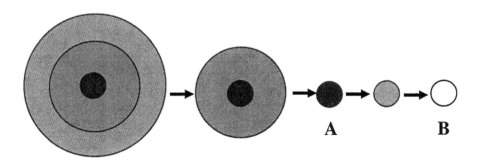

Figure 7.3 Evolution of an attention black hole. With training and practice, the attention black hole loses its extra outer layers until only the kernel of original experience or fear is left (A). With time you might reappraise the past (and future) and find meaning in every experience, good or bad. This eventually may transform the negative experience into a positive one (B).

An important caveat to keep in mind is that your attention black holes will not transform and the circle of novelty will not be created without your active participation. If you do not purposefully exercise your heart, lungs, or muscles, do they get stronger? Unlikely, isn't it? Similarly your attention has to be actively and purposefully cultivated. The initial few steps are the most difficult. Considerable energy is needed to pull your attention out of your mind into the world. This is akin to launching an object into space. To launch the space shuttle, the greatest energy needed is in the first few minutes for overcoming the gravitational pull of the earth. The attention black holes within the mind also have such a gravitational pull. They will draw your attention away from the world back into the folds of past and future. *Even without these black holes, your attention is strongly pulled inward by your mind because of the activity of a network of neurons in the brain called the default network.* [12, 13] That is just the nature of the brain and the mind. You will need a strong-willed, purposeful effort to break free of this pull. New thought patterns need to carve out newer connections in the brain and so are resisted and need considerable effort to implement. What kind of effort and how to go about it mechanistically? Several questions related to the process are pertinent at this point.

- What is the simplest technique to bring attention into the world?
- What will help you sustain this kind of attention, given that the mind has such a strong pull?
- If you bring your attention into the world, is the attention not likely to be drawn toward imperfections, thereby compounding the unhappy and stressed state?

I will spend a fair bit of time answering these very questions and sharing with you specific skills in Section IV. My intent is to help you recognize and remove the most likely impediments that prevent a deep and alert attention. The aim is to help your focus and concentration that keeps you mostly in the here and now both when life is going smoothly and also when challenges arrive, as they invariably will.

At this point I will turn to the second step, refining your interpretations. A deepened and balanced attention could easily get misdirected unless it is supported by refined interpretations.

The Second Step: Refine Your Interpretations

Refining interpretations means preferentially using the right blend of the 3Ps to interpret your sensory experience and decide on a particular action. The right blend comprises mostly of *higher principles* and *altruistic preferences* rather than *prejudices* and *egocentric preferences*. These principles are deeply imprinted in your heart.

The five core teachable skills based on higher principles that I have found most useful to refine interpretations are gratitude, compassion, acceptance, forgiveness, and meaning and purpose. *These are the outermost clothing we must wear all day long.* They can provide an immediately available alternative to negative ruminations.

Lack of gratitude, compassion, acceptance, forgiveness, and meaning and purpose to life when associated with pain equals suffering. The equation is:

Suffering = Pain + Lack of gratitude + Lack of compassion + Non-acceptance + Unforgiveness + Lack of higher meaning

Two of the most severe physical pains we know of are that of childbirth and passing a kidney stone. Millions of women the world over experience, and even welcome, the pain of childbirth, severe as it may be. Looking back, this pain is often not felt as suffering because of two reasons:
1) Women anticipate and accept this pain; and
2) There is enormous meaning associated with this pain—the gift of a child.

The same does not hold true for pain related to a kidney stone or most other pains, whether they be related to physical injury, emotional hurt, financial loss, or insecurity about the future. Such pains that often lack a positive meaning are associated with suffering.

Keeping gratitude, compassion, acceptance and forgiveness does not mean you passively resign to the fate of having the pain. These values allow your mind to better flow with adversity in order to conserve your resources and change the outward. With this attitude you are willing to approach rather than avoid. Gratitude, compassion, acceptance and forgiveness help stop the inner fight with yourself, which frees up your energy to fully engage with the external challenge. Many of our fights are fight with the self. Who will win if you fight yourself? Not you certainly. Cultivating these skills helps you step out of this fight—you become kinder to yourself.

The fifth component i.e. meaning behind the experience also greatly affects your well-being. A headache might bring considerable anxiety and thus feel more intense if you are concerned about a brain tumor; likewise, symptoms of chest pain may feel ominous if you are fearful of a heart attack. I have seen many patients with headaches objectively improve once their CT scan or MRI showed a normal brain with no evidence of tumor. Back pains sometimes get cured on finding a normal MRI; chest pains disappear with normal stress test results.

It is not that any of these pains are not real. They are. The underlying pain, however, is worsened by a fear that it might mean something ominous. Emotional suffering increases the physical suffering. Patients with fibromyalgia who suffer from chronic, sometimes severe, diffuse body pains often feel better once they know that this pain does not mean that their nerves, muscles, or some other body organs are getting permanently damaged. The meaning of a symptom or event is thus important and intimately related to how it is perceived. A credible and positive meaning or at least the lack of a threatening meaning decreases the emotional response. This is applicable not only to your physical symptoms but to most of your experiences in life.

When you thus refine your interpretations, you not only begin guiding your interpretations based on principles-based skills, but also correcting the first error of interpretation—of interpreting too soon and excessively. With the higher principles as your guiding force, the need and proclivity to interpret too soon goes away. This process brings you back to an optimal attention-interpretation (AI) balance as shown in figure 7.4. The refined interpretation here is shown as white instead of the grey of figure 6.4.

Attention   **Interpretation**

Figure 7.4 Optimal balance between attention and interpretation

Even a little refinement of interpretation when combined with a small increase in the depth and duration of attention will make you much better aware of your world and more joyous. The vast majority of the intensely pleasing moments of your life have a quality in which your perception is filled with pure attention, little interpretation, and a fully refined interpretation that allows you to be instinctively grateful, forgiving, accepting, compassionate, and anchored in your higher meaning (Figure 7.5).

Attention   **Interpretation**

Figure 7.5 Attention-Interpretation (AI) balance in a blissful state

Just as your attention won't deepen if you do not actively train it, the process of refining your interpretations also needs your purposeful effort. If you do not make a purposeful effort, there is a very good chance you may miss out on life weighed down by a potpourri of prejudices. The higher principles offer you an essential set of skills that will provide you the poise you need so you do not drown in your mind with prejudiced interpretations.

In the process you "practice presence with love" as your children (or grandchildren) attain important and not so important milestones. You begin creating islands of memorable experiences as you walk along your life. Your attention black holes transform into restful oases of attention that serve as rest areas in the long journey of life. Both you and I need rest areas in our long drives. Don't we?

8. The Heartful Brain

How to go about training your brain and engaging your heart? The primary tool to accomplish this is your mind. The brain, mind and heart are so intimately related that the separation between them may be artificial. Nevertheless this separation enhances our understanding so we will preserve it for this part of our journey. The two key operations of your mind as we saw are attention and interpretation. Training attention and interpretation has the potential to train and awaken brain's higher center and thus literally rewire (or rightwire) your brain. The two steps independently and together engage and empower the pre-frontal cortex. Your understanding of attention and interpretation thus provides tangible tools you can use to change your brain.

Such a brain is a resonating organ that has beautifully coordinated systems with optimal executive control of your attention and interpretation. The brain in this state has a fully engaged and empowered pre-frontal cortex and related areas and has a quiet limbic system that supports your well-being and happiness rather than intoxicating you with negative emotions. *Such a brain is a heartful brain.*

A heartful brain has optimal balance between the right and left cerebral hemispheres and generates coordinated brain wave patterns. A heartful brain spends more time in task related activities rather than ruminating in the default network. The process of training and rightwiring your brain by awakening the higher cortical center, once initiated, perpetuates itself by a lovely feedback loop that operates in your brain. To put it simply: the trained mind activates the brain's higher cortical center and quiets the lower limbic center; activation of the higher cortical center in turn helps train your mind (Figure 8.1). By training attention and refining interpretations, you stop feeding energy to the limbic center. This quiets the limbic center and empowers the cortical center.

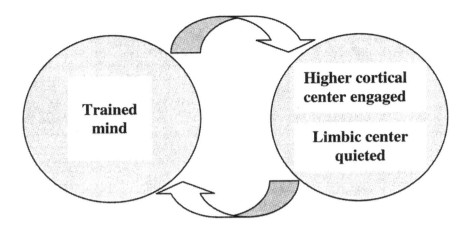

Figure 8.1 The feedback loop between training the mind and engagement of the higher cortical center and quieting of the lower limbic center

Your ability to deepen and prolong your attention and refine your interpretations provides the doorway to train your brain, engage your heart and transform your life. It is easy, doable, and worth the effort.

When your prejudices and egocentric preferences dominate your perception, they excessively engage and wrongly direct the content of interpretations. In this state, conscience-guided principles become subdued and the overload of negative interpretations keeps you surrounded by imperfections. You spend an inordinate amount of time in your mind away from the beautiful world.

At the level of the brain, the stress and attention deficit engendered in this process engages parts of the limbic system, particularly the amygdala, and suppresses the more evolved components, particularly the pre-frontal cortex. The innate systems and processes of your brain further increase your suffering because once your limbic system gets fully engaged it provides a positive feedback to itself. Almost every day I see people stuck in this state, sometimes for decades or even longer, because of this limitation in the functioning of our brains.

There is no doubt in my mind that you have a way out.

The first step to come out of this process is to understand how it operates. I have provided some of that understanding in the previous few pages. Once you know its underpinnings, the knowledge will likely make you enthusiastic about learning ways to deeply and securely engage your attention in the world. You accomplish this by taking your attention out of your mind into the world and deepening and sustaining your attention by delaying judgment and finding novelty. This is how you invite joy within the mundane. You practiced this as a child, and as a result were able to live every day of your life to the fullest. *You have to awaken that child within again if you wish to transform your life.*

Simultaneously with attention training, you refine your interpretations by bringing to them the attributes of gratitude, compassion, acceptance, forgiveness, and higher meaning and purpose to your life. Deeper more nourishing relationships by inviting a tribe around you, meditation, and devotional prayer provide additional tools to refine your perceptions. You started developing these attributes, but the advancement may have stalled at some point, likely because of the vicissitudes of the modern world combined with the imperfections of human mind and brain. *You have to discover and nurture that adult again.*

With these two steps your engagement with life will be sound and secure. You will be unstuck from the limbic mode and will have engaged and empowered brain's higher center, the pre-frontal cortex.

With this shift begins the process of transformation and awakening. You start noticing all the beauty around you that lies within the "normal and ordinary." The freedom allows you to attend to the splendor that was hitherto oblivious. You find an ordinary clock a miraculous object, so is a dishwasher, a vacuum, your pen, your pager, your car, your spouse, your child, and *you*. You increasingly notice that things are novel and perfect just as they are and you refrain from assigning too many judgments, neither good nor bad. You fill the present moment with love. Peace, joy, and resilience become effortless. They no longer remain a means to an end, they are the end. You become instinctively peaceful, joyous, and resilient. With this quality to your perception, you remain meditative throughout the day. Work becomes prayer, relationships become spiritual, your sense of self expands to include others, and forgiveness and compassion spontaneously flow as you progress toward the unfolding of transformation and awakening.

This is the journey I invite you to take—to bring the joy and wonder of a child along with the forgiveness and compassion of a realized adult. This journey helps you become fully what you are capable of. It is a tall order, will need purposeful effort, but truly is worth every moment of your time. It will be participatory, at times fun and at others serious, but all along purposeful. I am so glad you have joined me on this journey, in this book, and in life as a co-citizen of our precious planet. Rest assured that you have all the tools to complete this voyage. In our stroll together, consider me not as your therapist or instructor—accept me as your friend. All you need is a friend to hold your hands and walk with you with a promise to not part until the final lap is complete. Count me through this book as one such friend.

9. Summary

I wish to summarize all the concepts discussed in the previous chapters before we move on to the next section. In this chapter I will also introduce you to a signature image that we will use through the rest of this book.

The two essential skills that will help your journey away from stress toward resilience are:

Skill #1: <u>Training Attention</u> – Able to choose the direction, depth, and duration (3Ds) of attention giving you attention flexibility and helping you engage with the world as a learner who exudes "presence with love." Such a learner does not depend on explicit threat, pleasure, or novelty (TPN) in the world; s/he is guided by his/her purposeful effort and can find novelty within the ordinary. As you progress you will develop a broader awareness (meta-awareness) where you attend to attention; are aware of awareness; and think about your thoughts. *Attention training provides a cure for the restlessness of the mind.*

Skill #2: <u>Refining Interpretations</u> – Able to interpret based on principles-based skills and altruistic preferences rather than prejudices and ego-centric preferences. This will help you act with awareness, regulate your reactions, and become nonjudgmental and accepting. This will ingrain gratitude, compassion, acceptance and forgiveness within your instincts. *Refining interpretations provides a cure for the ignorance within the mind.*

The key concepts covered in this book are summarized in figure 9.1. Please spend a few moments with this figure since we will follow this schematic through the rest of the book.

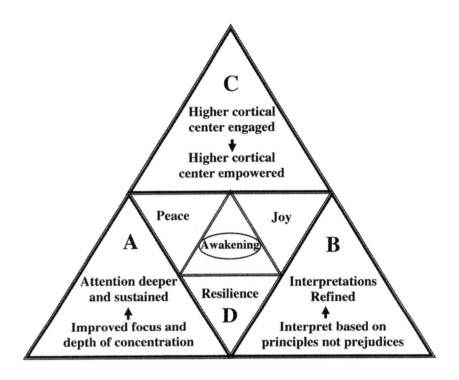

Figure 9.1 The two steps (attention and interpretation training,
A and B) help you cultivate a trained and right wired brain (C),
and all three together lead you toward peace, joy, and resilience (D),
and ultimately awakening (transformation)

Notice that the figure has four triangles. The bottom two supporting triangles consist of training attention (A) and refining interpretations (B). These two help you cultivate a brain that is trained and right wired (C)— the outcome of training attention and refining interpretations. The process starts a life transforming journey that takes you to the central triangle (D) that is comprised of peace, joy, and resilience—the state of heartfulness (Described more fully in Section III). Over a period of time, the state of peace, joy, and resilience gradually awakens your inner self and takes you toward self actualization. I will address individual components of these triangles in the sections that follow.

We have covered considerable ground already. In the rest of the book we will be expanding on the concepts covered in this section. Before proceeding further I wish you to revise all we have learned so far in the table below. The activity is in the form of an exercise.

Exercise 9.1. Please pause after you read each point and contemplate on it for a moment. Once you feel you have understood the concept, check mark it and then move to the next. If you are not clear, please go back and read the relevant text. You can also use these points when you teach some of these ideas to others.

Table 9.1 Summary of Part I		
Do not postpone joy	Do not postpone joy waiting for a day when life will be perfect and all your stressors will be gone	☐
Brain and its centers	Activation of the brain's lower limbic center makes you anxious, unhappy, depressed, and stressed	☐
	Activation of the brain's higher cortical center helps you be calm, happy, joyous, and resilient	☐
	The choice as to which center of the brain to activate is often yours	☐
	If you engage a part of the brain, you awaken and empower it	☐
Mind and suffering	"Total Suffering" has two main components: physical and emotional	☐
	An untrained mind multiplies emotional suffering. Mind does this by:	☐
	* Imagining several "believable" "worst case scenarios"	☐
	* Attempting "thought suppression" (usually unhelpful in the long term)	☐

What makes up your mind?	Mind is the sum total of the processes that lead to perceptions and actions	☐
	Perceptions have two components: attention and interpretation	☐
Attention (the process)	Attention latches on to threat, pleasure, or novelty (TPN)	☐
	Your outside world may often miss TPN, experiences are often repetitive (even boring); as a result you tend to fall into inattention with respect to the world	☐
	Inattention from the world pushes you into the mind	☐
	Mind harbors attention black holes that strongly draw your attention	☐
	These black holes form as a result of previous or anticipated negative experiences potentiated by rumination, imagination, and an avoidance response	☐
	Time spent within the mind may take you into an exhaustive journey into the past and future	☐
	This journey is often unpleasant because of our primary tendency to focus on the negative	☐
	While you are within the mind, the world keeps progressing at sixty seconds / minute. Days become dull, drab, and listless; you miss out on life.	☐

Interpretation (the content)	Interpretations can be guided by principles, prejudices, or preferences – the 3Ps	☐
	"Untrained" interpretations tend to be guided by prejudices and egocentric preferences	☐
	Prejudiced interpretations impair attention and engineer a stressful self-focused life	☐
The Two Steps	**Step one: Deepen your attention**	
	* Deepen your attention by training the direction, duration, and depth of your attention – 3Ds	☐
	* This takes away the attention deficit and helps you attain attention balance	☐
	* Trained attention makes it easier for you to engage with the present moment	☐
	* Training attention trains the innate attention capacity of your brain	☐
	Step two: Refine your interpretations	
	* Delay your interpretations	☐
	* Wisely choose among the 3Ps – Principles, prejudices, and preferences	☐
	* Whenever possible, base your interpretations on principles-based values and altruistic preferences rather than prejudices and egocentric preferences	☐
	* The most important values are gratitude, compassion, acceptance, forgiveness, and meaning and Purpose	☐
	* Training interpretations engages your heart, and invites greater peace and love in your life	☐

Trained right wired brain	Trained attention and refined interpretations awaken the brain's higher cortical center	☐
	An engaged and empowered higher cortical center makes it incrementally easier to deepen attention and refine interpretations	☐
Awakening (Transformation)	Trained and right wired brain, trained attention, and refined interpretations support the inner core of peace, joy, and resilience	☐
	The process leads to transformation and awakening, an advanced state wherein your ego is but vestigial and you become an epitome of peace, joy and resilience	☐

Be Kind to Yourself

I would like to address one important issue before we proceed to the next section.

Your journey and its direction are more important than reaching a destination.

I am often asked by well-meaning learners this common question, *"What if we are not able to learn or practice all the skills that you have taught us?"* My answer usually is that as long as you make a good faith attempt to learn at least some of the skills and are able to practice even 10 percent of what we discussed, you will likely benefit immensely. So long as your momentum is toward being more heartful (loving), having a deeper attention and more refined interpretations, it does not matter if you have the most perfect attention all the time. The important tenet is to nurture the inner fire of learning and growth. A small fire gets easily extinguished by a gust of wind that disturbs it; a stronger fire, on the other hand, is strengthened by the same wind. So let what distracts and stresses you fuel your efforts to get even stronger. Protect the sapling of your wisdom and effort from the gusts of wind generated by the momentum of the world and the random cattle of desire and ego that could graze on it. It is this sapling that would nourish and protect the world once it becomes a resilient tree.

Imagine driving at sixty miles per hour on a highway. Your perception of speed depends as much on your absolute speed as it does on the direction of your momentum—if you are decelerating from eighty to sixty mph you might sense your speed slower than if you are accelerating from forty to sixty. With most medical conditions, even if you are not fully recovered, as long as you move in the right direction you begin to feel better. Complete cure is often an unattainable ideal. Healing, however, is always within reach.

Unbroken focused attention throughout the day is an elusive goal that may be feasible only within the environs of a monastery. My focus is to offer a program for the fast paced modern society in which many of you live.

The process of training your brain and engaging your heart by using your mind is not easy. Mind will fight tooth and nail before allowing you to take control. Mind is fed by excessive thoughts that it wishes you to continue generating. It will need considerable initial effort on your part to tame your mind. So keep realistic expectations and do not chastise yourself if you cannot follow everything to the letter. Let the adult within you be kind to the child within you. This is a work of compassion, including self-compassion, not of judgment or prejudice. ***Be kind to the self—that is where it all starts, doesn't it?***

SECTION II: THE BRAIN AND THE MIND

Précis

An engaged and empowered higher cortical center represents the process as well as the final outcome of training
your brain and engaging your heart

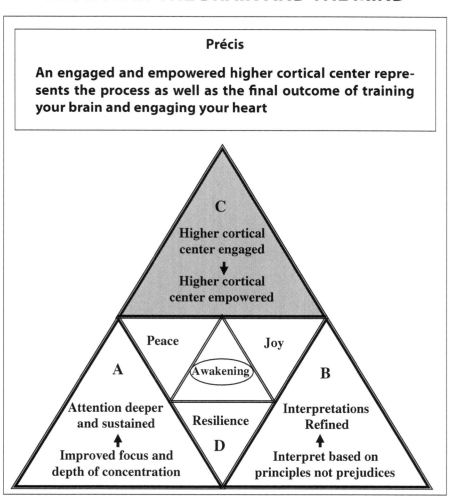

10. The Brain - Introduction

What percentage of the available options in your camcorder do you think you know well and can use any time?

1. <25%   ☐
2. 26 – 50%   ☐
3. 51 – 75%   ☐
4. >75%   ☐

There is a good chance there are several useful options you either do not know or may have never used. If you think you know >75% of the options, open your camcorder's instruction manual and see for yourself if that estimate indeed is true!

Most of us fall short when it comes to reading instruction manuals. Companies put in a great deal of effort toward creating instructions to help us quickly and efficiently learn the basic and advanced features of their products. We, however, open the box, find the power cord, plug it in, switch the "On" button, and start fumbling with the device!

As a result we do not get to know our gadgets. I am fully guilty of doing this. With most of the gadgets at our home, I know less than half of the available options. It is not because of lack of time, it is because of lack of focus. Nobody ever told me *"thou shalt read thy instruction manuals"* and on my own I never paid attention. I also may have some ego hiding in the garb of self-respect. I am a grown up adult, why should I need a piece of paper to tell me how to operate a simple washing machine?!

What happens as a result is utterly predictable. I give a vacant expression when Richa asks me to auto defrost the food and then heat it using the kitchen timer, all with a delayed start. I am never confident when I try to transfer video files from the camcorder to burn a DVD and generally am not able to make it in one smooth attempt. I even hesitate when I am asked to turn on the sub-titles while watching an international movie. In fact, I am embarrassed to accept that I do not know the majority of options in any of the gadgets we have in our home—microwave, oven, dishwasher, washer-dryer, vacuum, lawn mower—the list is embarrassingly long. I end up using only the most basic features of each of these devices, as if their technology was decades old.

What does all this have to do with the brain?

Is it possible you may be using only the most basic features of your brain?

For a moment think of your brain and the mind as an integrated machine. This machine is intelligent and incredibly complex. It has about two thousand interconnected parts, is made of about one hundred billion small units (nerve cells) that have hundreds of trillions of connections between them, all efficiently packaged within about three pounds of weight. Amazing work of art, isn't it? It took the universe fourteen billion years to transform from elementary particles to the complex circuitry of your brain.

Your brain has centers that when activated can predictably make you stressed and anxious. Conversely, your brain also has parts that when activated provide you happiness, peace, mature thinking, empathy, and long-term vision. Which part of the brain would you like to predominantly use? The overall quality of your life largely depends on the areas of your brain that functionally predominate. *And here is the best kept secret: the choice to activate a particular area of the brain largely depends on you.*

The integrated unit that comprises the brain and the mind works together with three main functionalities:
1. Input into the brain – this may be external or internal. External input is provided by all the sensory organs (eyes, ears, nose, taste buds, and skin) and the respective nerves that bring information to the brain. Internal input is provided by your thoughts and emotions, breath, and bodily sensations.
2. Processing and decision making – the information you perceive is collected and interpreted using principles, prejudices, and preferences (the 3Ps), memory, and intellect, and then considering all the possible options, used to choose one action from amongst several that are possible.
3. Output from the brain – this aspect of the brain and mind sends signals to the effector organs to carry out the action.

A good way to conceptualize brain function is that the back half of the brain directly receives the input from the sensory organs while the front half of the brain integrates this information with past memory and plans future actions. The front half of the brain is also involved in choosing the specific parts of the sensory input to pay attention to.

The brain and the mind are two intimately related entities that overlap with and constantly modify each other. It will help to consider them as tools that help you run the program of your life. The brain, as we have all learned, is a tangible part of our body. We can see the brain on CT or MRI scans, neurosurgeons operate on the brain with predictable results, we know in great details about the brain's individual parts, and are beginning to discern how they function together. The mind, that is brain's close partner and the primary frontier of human experience, however, is more elusive. Let us look at the mind a bit more to understand its functioning and imperfections. This will serve as a prelude to training our brain and developing a path out of the imperfections.

11. Mind's Imperfections

The mind is a combination of your attention, interpretation, memory, thoughts, emotions, imagination, intellect, and will. Some equate mind with its output—your thoughts. Mind is variously considered a distinct entity overlapping with the brain or having no existence of its own, primarily being an emergent property of brain activity. It will not serve our purpose here to spend too much time delving into which of these polar extremes is closer to the truth. Suffice it to say that a useful way to look at the mind is to consider it as the operating system of the brain. This operating system is the infrastructure software of the brain that manages and coordinates the activities of the brain by selecting and allocating available resources (brain centers) for a particular task. The mind also prioritizes which task to pick and which one to let go. Your programs of life (work, pleasure, play, etc.) run on this operating system. Every experience is perceived by your mind. Hence mind is the primary tool accessible to you for bringing about any change.

The mind's relationship with the hardware (brain) is interactive. The mind changes and recreates the brain, just as the brain changes and recreates the mind—both guided by the experiences you collect in your life time. You perceive and process information and express yourself in actions as a result of the activity of the mind. These processes, however, are not fool-proof; we are a good but not perfect design.

Just as the operating system in your computer is imperfect, similarly your mind also has imperfections. As we grow older these imperfections only worsen because of all the negative experiences we derive from the ego-identified world (akin to viruses, pop-ups, worms, Trojans, etc. that affect the computer as it ages). With each generation newer versions of the brain and mind arrive, slightly different from the previous one. Across the generations, however, there are two basic flaws with our untrained mind that are the genesis of much suffering:

1. *The mind is restless* – this is the source of excessive thoughts
2. *The mind carries limited wisdom (ignorance)* – this is the reason for lack of gratitude and compassion, non-acceptance, unforgive-ness, prejudice, thought suppression, faulty imagination, and egocentric preferences

Imperfection #1. The Mind is Restless

The innate nature of the mind is restlessness and a propensity to generate excessive thoughts. In Latin America this state of restlessness of the mind is aptly called *"quinhentos pensamentos"*—simultaneous five hundred thoughts. It is also called the monkey mind in some of the Buddhist traditions. Restless mind is a burden to its owner while the calm and collected mind is the spring of joy. The restless mind, very much like many of your internal organs such as your heart or liver, without training is often not in your control. You can easily get introduced to this lack of control by tracking the second hand of a watch for two minutes while trying to prevent any extraneous thoughts. You will realize that it takes considerable effort to prevent thoughts from coming and is often not possible.

Lack of control over and excessive activity of your mind may not have been much of a problem if its restlessness was intermittent, adaptive, and appropriate to the circumstances. You can predictably make your heart or lungs work harder by exercising them. In fact, intermittent increased activity of these organs is desirable and promotes good health. The mind also needs such exercise periodically. ***However, the important distinction is that the mind has a momentum problem—mind does not know when to stop.*** The mind maintains the fast momentum that it absorbs from the world or generates on its own for much longer than is desirable, a common cause of the epidemic of anxiety and sleeping difficulties in modern times. This momentum in most instances does not serve much purpose. If your heart was in this state you would have a rapid, often irregular, heart rate with potential damage to the body. The restless state of the mind also causes damage, albeit in a more subtle way.

The good news is that by purposefully training your attention, the mind's restlessness can be controlled. Even though this restlessness is often not your voluntary creation, you have the ability to slow it down. The training to brake and accelerate the mind at will provides you the important skill of *attention flexibility*. With flexibility of attention, you can direct the requisite amount of activity and calm for the mind as needed. In order to learn the skills to attain attention flexibility, it might help to know of the factors that in combination account for the restlessness of the mind.

Why is the mind restless? The mind does not like being overly restless; such a state is often not a desired conscious creation. The restlessness of the mind relates to three main reasons: effect of the world on the mind; the mind's own nature; and the mind's lack of wisdom. Let us look at these factors individually.

The world has changed dramatically in the past century, and the pace of change continues to accelerate with each passing year. This is because of several reasons, foremost among them being our excellent communication and collaboration that puts hundreds of thousands of minds working together for innovation. We are also supported by increasing intelligence over the years as postulated by the Flynn effect (Proposed by James R. Flynn, Flynn effect suggests that over the generations the average intelligence quotient test scores are rising in most parts of the world). The world's population of over six and a half billion people results in millions of people who have extraordinary intelligence because of the way intelligence is distributed in the population. Further, computers governed by Moore's law of increasingly efficient processing power are an efficient and obedient collaborator. By taking over the need to memorize and calculate, computers help us invest our brain power for creativity. This creativity may be productive or disruptive. Disruptive creativity is dangerous for the world—its most simple expression may be an elaborate Halloween prank, its more sinister expressions include computer viruses, Ponzi schemes, and intelligence invested behind the acts of terrorism.

The Internet, which virtually did not exist for the previous generation, now provides the predominant mode of communication and business. The Internet provides instant access and widespread dissemination of headlines, often at the cost of adequate research or paying attention to details. The growth in the Internet has been logarithmic. For example, in June 2008, there existed a total of sixty-three billion web pages; there were one trillion unique URLs in July 2008; and over one hundred million websites operated in March 2008.[14] The variety and options available do not help either. According to one estimate, if you go to buy a cell phone you may have hundreds of thousands of choices if you were to combine all the options available in a small store.

Each of these aspects generates extra information and uncertainty for the mind to tackle. Our mind simultaneously faces many such decisions. And if you happen to be a maximizer, this would provide a recipe for excessive sensory load and stress. The available cache memory of our mind that has a finite capacity may get overwhelmed by several simultaneous operations (open files) each needing significant capacity to run them. What happens as a result?

The sensory overload, when combined with the need to make so many choices in a limited time, increases the momentum of your life, and thus your mind. The world nudges you to conform and follow its attention style. The resulting excessive speed of your mind generates a rapid wave-form in the brain (fast beta) that over a period of time leads to fatigue, lack of sleep, anxiety, and attention deficit. The need to pay attention to the attention black holes further compounds this state. Such a momentum is also addicting. During the day you might take shots of espresso to maintain the momentum; at night you might need sedatives in an effort to break it. *We thus have become a "black coffee/sleeping pills" culture.*

The pace of life also prevents depth of attention preventing you from engaging with your life. Mahatma Gandhi aptly observed, *"There is more to life than increasing its speed."* Sometimes I wonder/dream if only we could relive the simplicity of times depicted in the *Andy Griffith Show* wherein alcoholics in Mayberry showed up on their own to be locked up when they were drunk. Or even the simple hotel menu of *My Cousin Vinny*, where there were only three choices—breakfast, lunch, or dinner!

The second reason for the restlessness of the mind is its own nature. Mind may generate excessive thoughts simply because it can do so and still run the basic operation of life. [12, 13] Researchers believe this may be adaptive, allowing continuous memory based predictions with enhanced survival value in a treacherous environment.[15] However these excessive thoughts come at a price. One price is that they influence the mind to cycle between periods of attention deficit and obsessive focus. As we experience the world, we store memories or fears of imperfections. The collective effect of these imperfections is to create feelings of sadness or anxiety. The basic instinct of the mind is to first ruminate on and then repress negative thoughts; the process generates attention black holes. We then constantly seek stimulation to prevent symptoms of sadness or anxiety from bubbling to the surface as a result of paying attention to these black holes. As a result, when our sensory experience misses out on a sufficient dose of threat / pleasure / novelty (TPN), we move quickly to something else, searching for another sensory stimulus that can keep us engaged and thereby keep the underlying hurt or anxiety in check. This forces us to jump from one thing to the next without stopping for a long enough time with any single experience—a state of attention deficit. In addition, attention deficit also has a medical (particularly genetic) component to it.

Obsessive focus originates from the proclivity of our mind to look for potential threats to keep us safe. An inordinate attention to threats is often a result of a hyperactive amygdala. In this state of stress, the breadth of our attention (our "attention bandwidth") narrows while at the same time we become hyper-focused. This increased focus however is often disorganized and haphazard—a state of hypervigilance. In the state of hypervigilance anything new or unfamiliar may seem threatening. Studies show that even observing faces of persons from another race instinctively activates the amygdala.[16, 17] No wonder we become increasingly intolerant to uncertainty and strangers.

Stress finds its origin not only from the potential threats, imperfections, and uncertainties, but also from what may be construed pleasurable, particularly if it does not belong to us. This is because of a subconscious desire to acquire everything that seems pleasurable. We begin to believe that our wholeness depends on the material possessions we can acquire—this pursuit really has no limits. The resulting E-R (expectation-reality) imbalance leads to disappointments and stress. Further, after acquiring and getting attached to the pleasurable, the desire to sustain it with related fear of loss also increases stress.

The third reason for the mind's restlessness is its ignorance. Ignorance increases uncertainty and intolerance of uncertainty. Ignorance breeds fear. I will further discuss mind's ignorance below.

Overcoming restlessness of the mind is the first step in training—breaking attention momentum and constant negative ruminations by developing a deeper sustained nonjudgmental non seeking attention and attaining attention flexibility.

Imperfection #2. The Mind is Ignorant

The second limitation of the mind is its ignorance. Ignorance is the other primary cause of suffering. Mind that feels incomplete and desires to feel complete is often ignorant of what will make it feel complete. The mind's ignorance originates from excessive ego and (self) focus that creates a sense of separation from the world. In this state, an individual's efforts are primarily directed to serve self-interests related to assuaging craving and aversion, often at the cost of others. Life force in this state is often directed to collect greater amounts of material possessions and enjoying them in hedonistic pleasure. Desire, however, sits at the leading end of achievements. This leads to senseless greed, sometimes thoughtless and dishonest actions, insatiable desires, and anger when these desires are not met. The individual stress and collective chaos in the world today is partly reflective of the ignorance of the individual and the collective mind.

Another outcome of an ignorant mind is low self-esteem. A low self-esteem originates from hearing too often from the world how we need to change to meet its standards. Sadly, often the very persons we trust to shower unconditional love on us—our life partner, parents, siblings, friends, and colleagues—are the ones who hurt our self-esteem the most. Since we often peg our identity on material accomplishments and how we are considered by others, many of us remain dissatisfied with our current state of material accomplishment and social worth. As a result, we may perceive a sense of incompleteness.

It is important to realize that material wholeness is an illusion. Perfect health and eternal life are other illusions. In the world, nothing is an absolute good. Everything is a mix of good and bad, depending on how you look at it. As Shakespeare said, *"There is nothing either good or bad, but thinking makes it so."*

Our worldly descriptors are not our identity since many of them are deterministic and create prejudice. Our real identity is our principles-based higher values. Our identity is our kind grateful compassionate disposition. Our identity is our forgiveness, spirituality, and higher meaning and purpose. If you anchor in this identity, you are closer to your true self. This is also an identity that cannot be robbed from you. This identity anchors you with a higher self-esteem that paves the way toward resilience. Your personality flowers inside out, allowing you to create a small heaven around you that travels with you wherever you go in the world.

Why is the mind ignorant? Like restlessness, the mind's limited wisdom is also not your conscious creation. Although it has taken fourteen billion years for the universe to create us, it seems we humans have arrived on the scene only very recently. The fast pace of change in the world far exceeds the ability of our brains to adapt and rewire themselves. The evolutionary processes that modify us are extraordinarily slow. The wiring of the brain depends on the genes that can only be modified in the time scales of hundreds of thousands to millions of years. Further, these processes care mostly about the survival of the species as a whole, not your individual spiritual growth or peace. Hence the (urgent) need to train our brain and engage our heart.

The focus of human life until very recently was mainly to survive the elements and reproduce in small groups. Once we developed agriculture, organized ourselves, and got industrialized we moved from the stage of bare survival to thriving. With security about food and shelter, a proportion of humanity now seeks spiritual growth. However, our brain is still wired to adapt to a world where survival and propagation of the species is the primary goal since evolution has not had the time to work its slow magic. This makes us egocentric, focusing primarily on ourselves or a small group of people we identify with. It is this instinctive egocentricity that separates us from the rest and makes us ignorant. This ignorance perpetuates if we do not make a purposeful effort to thwart it. Transcending this ignorance needs transformation of the way we interpret the world. *This is the second step—refining the interpretation.*

It is up to us

To create this transformation from bare survival to thriving to spiritual growth, our brain needs considerable training and rewiring. Since evolution cannot accomplish such elaborate rewiring in the short time span of few hundred to a few thousand years, the rewiring has to happen after we are born—using our minds. The good news is that the rewiring needed is largely functional since the basic structure is already laid down. Further, you already have all the appropriate hardware as well as the basic tool needed for this rewiring—an engaged and interested mind. All you need is a few suggestions, a structured approach you can follow, and may be a few reminders. I will try to provide those through this book.

Effecting this training and functional rewiring is well within the capacity of your minds. It is thus up to us, you and me, to create our destiny by tutoring our minds. Our transformation depends on our collective minds maturing from self-focused, ego-based living to a selfless, world-focused awareness. Fortunately for us there is help.

Principles-based skills that are now being proven by science provide a well-delineated path that can help us overcome both these limitations of the mind. I wish you to know that you have three unique gifts that work in your favor:

1.   You have control over your attention: You can choose the part of your sensory experience you attend to and the duration and depth of attention (3Ds). This helps still your mind.
2.   You have control over your interpretations: You can guide your interpretations based on any of the elements of the 3Ps (principles, prejudices, or preferences) that you choose to align yourself with. Guiding your mind by principles-based skills provides wisdom to the mind that takes away ignorance.
3.   You have control over your actions: Just like your interpretations, you can also choose to guide your actions based on any of

the elements of the 3Ps. The choice is yours: using higher-order principles, you can choose to forgive the wrongdoer; on the other hand, you can also choose to engage your prejudices and hurt the innocent.

In your mind, your attention, interpretations, and actions are integrated together to make up each unit of your experience. Each experience when integrated with the others conjoins to make up this wonderful journey that we call life. The quality and depth of your attention, interpretations, and actions depend on which elements of the 3Ps you direct your mind to apply to a particular situation. Attention helps you open your eyes, interpretation helps you make sense of what you see. The 3Ps are the lenses with which you look at the world. Let us look at them next.

(If you have read the book non stop so far it may be a good idea to pause and may be take a brief stroll. Or how about that cookie that has been waiting for you all day?!)

12. The 3Ps (Principles, Prejudices, Preferences)

Interpretations depend on your intellect, the stored database of memories, and the 3Ps. Among these, the 3Ps are the most modifiable aspects of your mind. Preferences can be guided predominantly by prejudices or principles. Refining interpretations primarily means anchoring your preferences with your principles rather than prejudices.

Principles

Principles represent the higher-order eternal laws that transcend civilizations and millennia, and promote a fair and just existence of an individual within a global family. It is these principles, applied impartially, that help an individual enjoy freedom and enable a society to thrive. In physics, the principles of gravity, relativity, and quantum mechanics are not partial—they are applicable to all the physical world there is. So are the principles that govern our lives.

The core guiding principles were beautifully spelled out by Thomas Jefferson in 1776 in the opening statement of the Declaration of Independence. He wrote, *"We hold these truths to be self-evident, that all men (and women) are created equal, that they are endowed by their Creator with certain unalienable Rights, that among these are Life, Liberty and the Pursuit of Happiness."* The second expression of guiding principles I use is based on what a patient (Cathy—I have referred to her in the prologue) said to me in the outpatient clinic, *"Fix your thoughts on what is true, and honorable, and right, and pure, and lovely, and admirable. Think about things that are excellent and worthy of praise. (Philippians 4:8, New Living Translation)*

The wisdom and richness in Jefferson's words and the beautiful lines from the Bible provide the moral fabric to our society. The most important component of these principles is that they are relational and describe your respect and acceptance of others. When anchored in these principles and using them to interpret your world, you are very unlikely to take a potentially unkind stand toward the society.

From these established and agreed upon principles you derive individual skills and values (I will call them skills as well as values since as an abstract concept they represent values, but when applied to a concrete situation they become tangible skills). In addition to principles, these values also depend on your spiritual (and religious) beliefs and past experience. Your values provide the instruction manual for your life. The higher skills and values that are a pure reflection of the transcendental principles include the attributes of gratitude, compassion, acceptance, forgiveness, meaning and purpose in life, kindness, honesty, equanimity, humility, and love. As we shall see later, it is these values that engage the brain's higher center. Guiding your life based on values that are derived from higher principles is thereby likely to promote resilience, happiness, and well-being. I appeal to you to bring these principles-based values to your attention, interpretations, and actions.

Prejudices

The second P, *prejudice,* represents a tendency to make conclusions based upon pre-existing beliefs rather than discernible facts. These are the invariant labels that prevent you from taking a fresh look. Prejudice about others often is associated with lack of kindness toward them. Prejudice generally has a negative connotation and mostly is used with respect to judgments within relationships. Prejudice jeopardizes rationality and fosters unpredictable, sometimes dangerous, behaviors in a society. Further, these prejudices may not even represent the truth. Memory researchers emphasize that our memory is not as reliable or resilient as we think. Our minds may care more about creating a good story rather than the truth, a phenomenon particularly applicable with eyewitness testimonies.

Prejudice affects your attention. If you have already decided that you are or are not going to like someone you may not pay adequate attention to the goodness in them. *Prejudice affects your interpretation.* It took us a long time to accept Galileo's assertion that earth is not at the center of the universe despite overwhelming evidence to the contrary. *Prejudice also affects your actions.* I see many patients, sometimes with serious medical diagnoses, making irrational choices about their care because of their prejudice against modern medicine. They remain handcuffed by their prejudice. As a result, they might delay treatment, increase the risk of complications, and sometimes may cause irreparable harm to themselves. ***In simple terms, prejudices force us to experience our own nervous system rather than the beautiful world around us.***

If prejudices are potentially so harmful, why do we imbibe them so easily? Prejudices may have developed because of our tendency to create heuristics or shortcuts. We develop these shortcuts all our life based on our experiences and those of others we trust. These shortcuts provide us with the ability to learn and store information in manageable packets. However, these very shortcuts when exaggerated and over-generalized generate prejudices and soak away novelty and joy from our lives. Let us look at an example.

If you accidentally touch a plant in summer with compound leaves having three pointed leaflets with the middle leaflet having a much longer stalk than the two side ones, you are likely to develop a nasty rash. This description is of poison ivy. The leaves of this plant are reddish in spring, become green during the summer, and turn into shades of yellow, orange, or red in the autumn. Once you experience this exposure in the summer, you may develop a useful heuristic, *"Leaves of three, let them be."* In other words, avoid all plants with three pointed green leaflets in the summer. *A prejudice, however, will be to avoid all green leaves in summer.* Your heuristic as well as your prejudice will serve you well to avoid poison ivy; your prejudice, however, will seriously limit your life in many other ways (Figure 12.1).

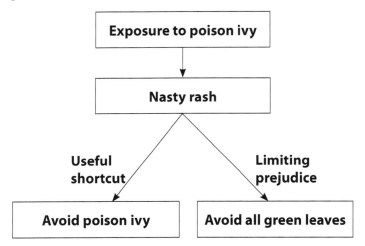

Figure 12.1 Learning useful shortcuts vs. developing limiting prejudices. Prejudices create invariant limitations that make the life dull, boring, and stressful.

Do you see how an experience taken literally and over-generalized can create a set of enslaving beliefs?

A few years ago I saw a patient in the clinic who came to obtain a refill of her antacid medication. She had run out of her medication and was complaining of occasional "stomach upset" very similar to what she had experienced prior to starting the antacid. Something about her clinical history made me uncomfortable. I still could not tell what it was, but lucky for me and her, we checked an EKG and did some blood tests. It turned out she was having a heart attack. So for the next year or so, I had a very low threshold to do EKGs and blood tests on anyone seeking refill of their antacids! My experience created within me a small prejudice that made me look at every patient needing antacid refills as a potential patient with heart problems. This was a benign prejudice, but you can see how such a prejudice can have serious consequences if the resulting actions potentially might harm others.

Your mental shortcuts collected over a lifetime provide you knowledge and make you more efficient and effective. Taken to an extreme, however, these very shortcuts become your prejudices that prevent you from engaging fully with the world. Such extreme and over-generalized beliefs are generally a product of excessive fear for the self or our loved ones. Prejudiced judgments are primarily directed to serve the self, sometimes with a risk of simultaneous harm to others. *Prejudices form because of an overdose of duality.* Excess categorization of objects, events, or persons into good vs. bad; desirable vs. undesirable; likable vs. not likable, etc. creates rigid isolating compartments. This tendency of the mind makes a person's life very limiting since the invariant beliefs cut short attention and foster a state of relative inattention with respect to the world.

Most (but not all) prejudices have a historical basis that may or may not apply to the current times. It takes some judgment and sometimes counseling from others to decide at what point your useful shortcuts have turned into prejudices. I cannot give you a more specific guidance short of saying that in most situations it will help you to prevent your prejudices from short circuiting your attention. Prejudiced attention has a high probability of pushing you into inattention, into your mind, and into a state of mindlessness. To prevent this from happening do not overgeneralize your experience and be ready to revise your interpretations based on fresh observations. Once your attention has imbibed the details of your sensory experience, interpret and act on it, to the extent possible, based on principles rather than prejudices. *It is the prejudice-based rigidity of thinking of many of our leaders, with their inability to revise interpretations and actions based on new evidence, that has led to wars and untold suffering for millions of people.*

Preferences

The third P, *preferences,* expresses your choices from among a number of possible alternatives. This choice is often based on your assessment of the value that each of the alternatives provide. The essence of this boils down to what makes you happy. The pursuit of happiness is your right as long as it does not infringe upon someone else's rights or happiness. In many instances the pursuit of happiness may be your primary goal. However, what makes you happy to a great extent depends on the guiding values of your life. This world will become a heaven if most of us abide by the values of gratitude, compassion, acceptance, forgiveness, higher meaning and purpose, kindness, honesty, equanimity, humility, and love. The farther our preferences migrate from these values, the less kind is the environment around us.

There is a good possibility that you may have some misconceptions about what will make you happy. In a study conducted to assess the effect of getting or donating small sums of money, many surveyed participants stated that they thought they would be happier if they were to receive money than to donate it. However, when the study was actually conducted, it was those who donated the money who became happier than those who received it.[18] Charity and loss both lead to loss, one leads to happiness the other does not. The study offers useful insight into why we do not engage in pro-social behavior more frequently—we do not believe that helping others is the key to our own happiness. This is an excellent example of the ignorance of the human mind.

Happiness can be virtuous or hedonistic. Hedonistic happiness focuses on self-interest and pleasure, often considering personal state of happiness as the ultimate goal, sometimes even at the cost of others' displeasure. Virtuous happiness, also called eudemonia, is a state of well-being that derives from altruistic actions, self-less work, wisdom, rationality, and having a higher meaning and purpose to one's life. Eudemonia allows sustained well-being and engages the higher cortical center. Hedonistic happiness greatly depends on material gains from the world, tends to be transient, and is often followed by a sense of incompleteness or even guilt. Recognize that the inveterate pursuit of hedonistic happiness accounts for the excess use of natural resources in the modern world. Over the long term, you are likely to be happier if you pursue predominantly eudemonic pleasure by incorporating the well-being of yours and many others in your preferences.

Broadly, the two types of preferences thus are: *altruistic preferences* and *egocentric preferences. Altruistic preferences are based on higher principles and values and thus incorporate the interest of others. Egocentric preferences are prejudice based and primarily include self-interest.*

Altruistic preferences = Principles-based
Egocentric preferences = Prejudices-based

Egocentric preferences may provide you short-term happiness; however, it is the altruistic preferences that secure long-term well-being. If your actions benefit you they please you a bit for a short time; if your actions benefit you and your family they will likely please you more and for a longer time; if they benefit you, your family, and your neighborhood, the joy will be even greater and longer. You can expand it to include all of humanity, even all life forms. Your preferences that incorporate the well-being of a large segment of the society are likely to be principles-based and not lock you into prejudice. Such preferences, their downstream actions and upstream values keep you in the state of eudemonic pleasure. It is the predominant self-focus that takes you away from higher values and toward prejudices. Egocentric self-focused preferences are a recipe for a stressful life and a fractured society.

Do not, however, play tricks with your conscience. For example, if you buy a gas guzzling vehicle because you intend to help people employed in the auto industry or if you smoke to help the tobacco industry you may be fooling yourself. In this state you camouflage your ego-based actions with a garb of selflessness. Such a state is not only immature but also dangerous because you have now created a perfect set-up to remain ignorant for a very long time.

When you make a choice, it might be good to consider all the pertinent pros and cons. For example, with tobacco use, you obtain short-term relaxation and may even help the tobacco industry; the costs, however, far outweigh these trivial benefits. Your life is shortened by fourteen years, you have about a 50 percent chance of dying because of tobacco-related illness including cancer and heart disease; and by second-hand smoking, increase the risk of asthma, ear infections, and pneumonia in your children, and cancer in others. The related societal cost is enormous. Ignorance makes you shortsighted and prevents value-based preferences.

I certainly do not wish to impress upon you that all self-focus is wrong. Most good ideas can be carried to an undesirable extreme. Selflessness does not mean living a life of deprivation. You need to feel secure and comfortable, and be reasonably well off in order to help others. Your honest pursuits to accomplish these well-meaning goals are fair and just. However, it is when self-focus is carried to the extreme and preferences only serve the self and exclude or even potentially harm the others that the problems start. Self-focus then degenerates into greed. It is to this greed I refer when I denounce self-focus in this book and elsewhere. The unethical behavior of senior leaders in several large previously well-respected companies such as Enron, Tyco, WorldCom, and Lehman Brothers among many others reflected excessive self-focus. A pathological self-focus with its result, unbridled greed, harms the economy and creates wars and terrorism. Left unregulated, human instincts drive us to incrementally increase the service of self. To prevent this degeneration from happening you have to make lifelong ongoing efforts to nurture altruistic preferences that are based on higher values.

I have summarized some of these aspects in figure 12.2 and the text that follows.

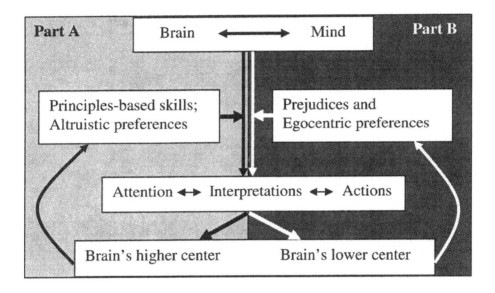

Figure 12.2 The outcome of using principles-based skills vs. prejudices—engagement of the brain's higher or lower center with respective feedbacks

1. Part A: When the brain and mind operate with principles-based skills and their offshoot, altruistic preferences—your attention, interpretations, and actions engage your brain's higher center. Such an approach facilitates resilience, happiness, and a productive life.
2. Part B: When your brain and mind operate with prejudices and their offshoots, egocentric preferences—your attention, interpretations, and actions engage the brain's lower center. Such an approach increases stress and fear and leads to an unrewarding life.

The choice to use principles based skills and altruistic preferences vs. prejudices and egocentric preferences is fully yours. This element of choice, also called *free will* by some, is unique to us humans and probably is not an option available to other animals who are guided primarily by instincts. Unfortunately, despite having this free will, our instincts of serving the self (ego) suffuse our perceptions. To disengage from these instincts requires a purposeful effort. Once you make this effort, your brain's higher center gets engaged and the process becomes self-perpetuating. You progress from being egocentric to world-centric, from stressed to resilient, from apathetic to altruistic. All these are cherished and worthy outcomes.

13. The Brain's Two Centers: Limbic and Cortical Loops

In the foregoing I have referred on several occasions to the brain's higher and lower centers. At this point I wish to take a more detailed look at these two centers. They are important because these two centers collectively contribute the most toward the quality of your attention, interpretations, thoughts, emotions, and actions. The two centers are:
1. The _limbic center,_ also called the lower limbic center / the limbic loop / or the stress loop; and
2. The _cortical center,_ also called the higher cortical center / the cortical loop / or the resilient loop.

The essence of training the brain is to increasingly engage and empower the cortical center.

The Limbic Loop

The limbic loop is your stress and worry center. All the sensory information (external from vision, sound, smell, taste, and touch; and internal from body, breath, and the mind) arrives at a central relay station in your brain called the thalamus. The thalamus collects all this information and routes it to two key areas:
1. Amygdala – Information arrives here by a short and quick route (broadband); and
2. Cerebral cortex, particularly the pre-frontal cortex – Information arrives here by a longer and slower pathway (narrow band)

The direct quick route to the amygdala, an almond-shaped nucleus in your brain, constitutes your instinctive mode of operation and allows you to react to threats. The amygdala constitutes the primary component of the limbic loop. A healthy amygdala also helps you bond and develop emotional connection. Considerable research evidence has conclusively proven the central importance of the amygdala in mediating the stress response. Studies show that the amygdala gets activated when you store memories of previous negative events and feel fearful.[19] Exaggerated amygdala activation has been shown to increase a person's vulnerability to mood disorders,[20, 21] chronic stress,[22] and post traumatic stress disorder (PTSD, a particularly severe form of stress reaction after a major emotional trauma).[23-26] The amygdala was found to be highly reactive to anxiety triggers in anxious patients,[20] particularly for long-term stressors (>21 days), which many of the modern stressors are.[27]

A peculiar mechanism in the body I have alluded to before worsens your long-term stress response once it is initiated—*the amygdala becomes more active and may even grow in response to ongoing stress.* Studies show that repeated stress causes growth of the nerve cells and their connections in the amygdala.[28, 29] *This growth of the amygdala with stress sensitizes you toward future stressors and provides the neurologic basis for the problem of stress begetting further feelings of stress.* The schematic of the limbic loop is shown in figure 13.1 with some of the research findings in the shaded text box that follows.

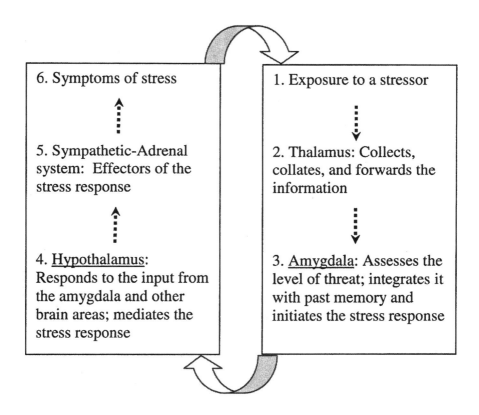

6. Symptoms of stress

5. Sympathetic-Adrenal system: Effectors of the stress response

4. Hypothalamus: Responds to the input from the amygdala and other brain areas; mediates the stress response

1. Exposure to a stressor

2. Thalamus: Collects, collates, and forwards the information

3. Amygdala: Assesses the level of threat; integrates it with past memory and initiates the stress response

Figure 13.1 The pathways of the limbic loop

* Reminder – Information in the shaded text boxes is more technical. You can skim or skip it without losing continuity.

Once the impulse reaches the amygdala and is judged to be potentially threatening, the amygdala informs the hypothalamus in the brain to generate a stress response. The hypothalamus facilitates release of hormones from a small gland at the base of the brain called the pituitary.[30] The pituitary then tells the adrenal glands (hormone producing glands that sit on top of the kidneys) to release steroid hormones. The sympathetic nervous system is also simultaneously stimulated, releasing adrenaline and noradrenaline. This is coupled with a behavioral response that increases alertness and vigilance around the stressful events. You either freeze in fright, take flight, or fight.

This response works beautifully for short-term intense stressors. Thus we use the stress response to survive most major medical illnesses, surgeries, injuries, etc. As you might imagine, the response creates a state of combat in the body and consumes tremendous energy. The response was not innately designed for long-term use, certainly not for low level chronic stressors. In modern times, however, it is for this chronic low level of stress that the stress response is mostly deployed. The result— the response turns around and damages the very body that is its source.

Parts of the brain that generate the stress response (particularly the hypothalamus) are involved in such vital functions of the body as regulation of the sleep-wake cycle, secretion of hormones, balanced functioning of the autonomic nervous system, learning, memory, feeding, immune function, and reproduction.[31, 32] When the hypothalamus gets busy defending the body, it is not left with adequate reserves to attend to these important functions. Most of these vital functions become disturbed and imbalanced by the cumulative effect of long-term readiness to fight or flight and heightened state of alertness that the stress response engenders.

Thus an ongoing perception of excess stress leads to exhaustion and causes serious deleterious effects on your immunity, memory, reproductive function, and overall well-being. You may have noted that during periods when you feel stressed you are more likely to catch upper respiratory or other infections, might become forgetful, are less desirous for intimate relationships, and have a lower threshold for getting angry or irritable.

The chemicals released in the stress response have an additional negative effect. *These chemicals disrupt the function of parts of the more mature cortical loop, particularly affecting the pre-frontal cortex and the hippocampus.* The pre-frontal cortex provides the highest level of integration for most of your decisions while the hippocampus is an area of the brain that is vital for memory. Research studies show that the stress chemicals impair the function of nerve cells in both of these areas. This impaired function partly explains why you sometimes cannot think rationally when you get angry or stressed. If allowed to persist for long, this process may cause structural damage and predispose to long-term memory loss.[33, 34]

Our default response system seems outdated with respect to the needs of the modern world. The modern world requires us to accommodate to multiple low level chronic stressors, while our response is designed to handle acute severe stresses. The insecure and relatively immature responders in this system take every little event in our life too seriously, as if the event was threatening our very existence. Our inattention and premature biased interpretations strengthen this response. We occasionally do need this response, but not in the amounts and frequency the system is wired to perform. The force this response generates locks us in an internally insecure and inflamed state (literally). Repeated exposure to stressors makes this circuit stronger. The inbuilt feedback mechanisms incrementally increase the duration and intensity of your response to future stressors.

The limbic loop in its heightened alert state generates paranoia and anger. This is the loop that has caused most of the wars and atrocities on this planet. This is the loop that mediates hatred, fear, and anxiety. Continued use of this circuit snatches away happiness from your life and may cause considerable physical damage to your brain and the body. *It is this very circuit that steals away life from your life.*

Unless you pay purposeful attention, it is this loop that you are wired to instinctively use the most. Life in this loop is a Yo-Yo, occasional spikes of pleasure followed by long and deep valleys of gloom. The calm and mature inner happiness (eudemonic happiness) eludes you in this state. If you cannot find joy within, you develop a propensity to search for joy in the external. You try to numb your feelings by various forms of addiction—to alcohol, tobacco, drugs, or to carbohydrates and fats. All these are mechanisms to escape from the present moment. A significant proportion of overweight and obesity is due to excessive activation of this circuit that leads to emotional overeating. Limbic over-activity also pre-disposes to wasteful splurging of precious resources of Mother Earth. We spend beyond our means and become insensitive to nature and others. At an individual level we pick up unnecessary debt, collectively we ravage our precious planet.

Needless to say, we need to learn to quiet this circuit. Most animals live their entire lives guided by primitive instincts—locked in their limbic loop. The life of a bunny in your backyard is mostly guided by fear. All her life, she will run away from sounds, shapes, and smells she does not find familiar and are not her food. But it is within our ability to disengage from the limbic loop and live a more fulfilling life. How blessed we are that we have such a choice, the choice to get out of this whirlpool and engage the more mature part of our brain—the cortical loop.

The Cortical Loop (Higher center)

The cortical loop is the higher center in your brain often dubbed the chief executive. The functions mediated by this part of the brain are often called the executive functions. Its main component, the pre-frontal cortex, allows concentration, sustained attention, rational thinking, long-term planning, forward thinking, impulse control, empathy, learning, and stress management. The pre-frontal cortex is thus a voice of reason within your head. Training the pre-frontal cortex allows you to postpone gratification and make better long-term business decisions.[35] If you are a busy executive, working mom, or simply have a lot going on in life, remember that it is the pre-frontal cortex of the brain that helps you negotiate complexity and novelty.

One of the important differences in the brain of humans and other animals is our well-developed pre-frontal cortex. The pre-frontal cortex provides us the uniquely human qualities and strengths and is proportionately larger in volume than any other species. The pre-frontal cortex, however, matures only by the early twenties. If you are a parent of a young child or teenager, realize that you are your child's pre-frontal cortex. They will absorb your nervous system as they grow. Research shows that when we watch self control in others, we ourselves are likely to develop greater self control.[36] It is thus extraordinarily important (almost mandatory) for you to nurture a mature and well-functioning pre-frontal cortex.

While the activity generated by your limbic loop brings desires, impulses, anxieties and fears, it is important to realize that completely silencing the limbic loop is not the answer. In fact, a weaker functioning limbic loop that decreases the feelings of anxiety and fear along with a weaker pre-frontal cortex predisposes an individual to sociopathic behavior.[37] The optimal state is thus to have a normally functioning limbic loop that generates normal desires, impulses, anxiety, and fear (the child within you) and a healthy pre-frontal cortex to provide conscience, empathy, and impulse control (the adult within you). A healthy pre-frontal cortex also reins in the limbic system from going into overdrive, allowing you to live your daily life without excessive anxiety or fear. The foregoing might give you a good insight into the importance of balance. You do need some anxiety and fear, but just like salt in your food, too little or too much is both not desirable. You need enough fear to be secure, enough desire to provide well for yourself and your loved ones, and enough ego to have a healthy self esteem. It is a trained prefrontal cortex and tamed amygdala that can help you accomplish that.

The power of the cortical loop, however, frequently goes unused—very similar to how I use gadgets in our home. A collective ignorance and apathy toward using the pre-frontal cortex is an important reason for the unrest you and I see in our world. The schematic of the cortical loop is shown in figure 13.2 below with some of the research findings in the shaded text box that follows.

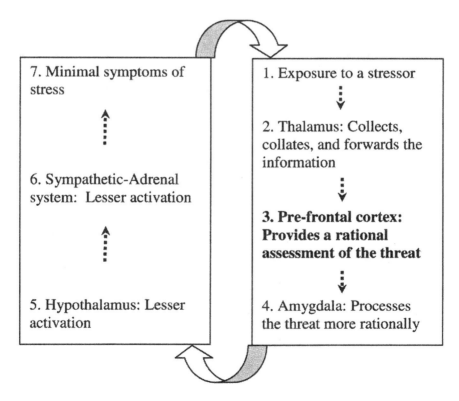

Figure 13.2 The pathways of the cortical loop

The pre-frontal cortex (PFC), often considered the CEO of your brain, is involved in such executive functions as motivation, planning, strategizing, empathy, and impulse control.[38] An engaged and empowered PFC is the central component of a transformed brain. The PFC creates a link between higher-level decision making, reward mechanisms, social interactions, capacity for empathy and altruism, and emotional regulation.[39, 40] Information that reaches the PFC is more rationally processed with a balanced attribution assigned to its significance. Better modulation of the emotional circuit (amygdala) by the PFC is one of the critical factors influencing a better capacity to function after a traumatic event.[41] Engagement of the PFC might help you overcome previous memories of fear by helping you unlearn fear and fade its memory, a process called extinction.[42, 43] This results in a more measured response unlike the response that comes from engaging primarily the limbic loop.

Neurologists consider the outer (lateral) pre-frontal cortex more related with thinking function while the inner (medial) pre-frontal cortex, including the orbito-frontal cortex, is more involved with emotional functions (heartful part of the brain). Some distinction is also drawn between the left and the right PFC, with the left PFC generally associated with well-being and fewer depressive symptoms.[44, 45] For the purpose of this text, however, we will consider the PFC as an integrated whole and will not explore such distinctions.

A closely related part of the brain is the anterior cingulate cortex (ACC). The ACC is involved in error detection and is intimately involved in the "Go, no go" decision process in the brain.[46, 47] This process depends on your ability to resolve conflicts between two choices while at the same time being flexible. The ACC also helps you prioritize your attention.

Another structure in the brain that affects stress response is the hippocampus, which works closely with the pre-frontal cortex. The hippocampus helps formation and consolidation of new memory.[48] Stimulation of the hippocampus has a potential to decrease some of the manifestations of the stress response.[49, 50] Repeated stress, particularly stress lasting for a period of time (>21 days), tends to impair hippocampus-dependent memory.[34] Early life stress reduces the number of nerve cells and their branching in the hippocampus.[33] *This might explain why chronic stress is often associated with decreased memory.*

Mediation of response by the PFC is one of the critical factors that supports an improved capacity to function after a negative event.[41] Activation of the PFC correlates with resilience. Resilience represents the personal qualities that enable you to thrive in the face of adversity.[51] In general, resilience correlates with better modulation of the limbic loop by the PFC.[52, 53] This information has been used to foster resilience, including in patients with diabetes,[54] among college students,[55] in a school setting,[56] and at the work site.[57] Positive results in these studies offer the hope that resilience as a skill can be learned and such learning has sustained positive effects. Your emotional style and propensity to experience stress is thus not set in stone—it can be changed.

Considerable research evidence suggests that a sub-optimally functioning PFC predisposes you to negative experiences. In several studies, patients with depression had a lower volume of pre-frontal cortex and hippocampus, higher volume of amygdala,[58-61] and decreased PFC function.[62] Patients with post traumatic stress disorder (PTSD) also have reduced PFC activity.[63-65] PFC also provides modulation of pain, particularly pain that is related to an uncontrolled stimulus.[66] Studies show that greater activation of the PFC in response to uncontrollable stressors leads to less pain.[66]

Like the amygdala, the PFC also shows structural changes in response to stress, and as you might expect, in the opposite direction. ***Repeated stress causes shortening of dendrites (part of the nerves) in the PFC potentially reducing its ability to modulate the function of the amygdala.***[28, 29, 67]

At this point, you are entirely justified in wondering why the refined circuitry of the cortical loop is not designed to be our default mode of operation. I also often wonder about that. The rationale for this seems simple. If a grizzly bear were charging at you, your systems should direct you to take cover, not get into an introspective thought process about why there is violence on planet earth! You also do not need forgiveness or compassion for the bear at that moment! Our default systems run by the amygdala mediated circuit prompt us to take cover and have helped us survive as a species. The world, however, has changed at a rapid pace with growing human intelligence and increased capacity for collaboration. Grizzly bears, big cats, or mammoths are no longer our neighbors. Our brains however are still wired to adapt to such challenges. Evolution takes its own sweet time to effect a change. Our default instincts that depend on the innate wiring of our nervous system, which in turn depends on our genes, will eventually change, but it might take hundreds of thousands or even millions of years. Till that time, if we are to thrive as a species, we have to train our mind and the brain so we increasingly engage and empower the cortical loop. This is well within our capacity.

We often need constant reminders if we are to cultivate a trait of constantly engaging the cortical loop. The reminders come in many ways: seeing acts of selflessness; a visit to a church, temple, synagogue, or mosque; reading a book that discusses compassion and hope; teaching these skills to others; or listening to the lives of the saints and heroes who have lived a selfless life. Fortunately in the modern world you have access to all of these. Your company of friends, books, the news you follow, the Internet sites you visit, and the quality of your attention and interpretations all have a significant effect on your ability to engage the cortical loop. On the contrary, each of these can also provide enough fodder to engage the limbic loop.

Balance between limbic and cortical loops: Most of us do not live in a monastery but in a society with its mix of challenges. Hence completely disempowering the limbic loop is not optimal. We need the excitement that limbic loop and reward centers provide to make our life interesting and full of variety. We do not need to (and should not) completely let go of *fear, desire or ego*. My suggestion for us is not to assume the benign disposition of animals in the Galapagos Islands. *What is desirable is to attain a state of balance between the limbic and cortical loops.* This balance allows appropriate caution, neither the careless and fearless disposition of a two year old, nor the excessive fear that leads to catastrophizing and panic. Similarly balanced desire avoids the two extremes of apathy and greed but is rooted in a pragmatic disposition that allows you to prosper yet not ravage the precious resources. A balance in ego keeps low self esteem as well as arrogance in check and allows confidence to flourish with readiness and humility to learn more and accept critique with grace. With balance in ego you become appropriately assertive, honest and direct, neither passive nor aggressive.

Such a balance in fear, desire and ego finds its origin in optimal balance in the activity of the limbic and cortical centers of the brain. In general, however, the proclivity of the world is to predispose us to excessive limbic system reactivity. Hence for most of us, enhancing prefrontal cortex activity and decreasing limbic activity is likely to bring us to a state of balance. Such a balance allows us to approach life's challenges with a realistically optimistic disposition. It is the cultivation of such an attitude with the other core values of gratitude, compassion, acceptance, forgiveness, and meaning and purpose that accord us the optimal balance. As a next step, let us look at how these values and their related skills modulate the activity of your limbic and cortical loops.

14. Skills, Loops, and Outcomes

Is there any research evidence to inform us how we can train ourselves to predominantly engage the pre-frontal cortex?

This question is extraordinarily significant since the answer to this question provides a scientifically valid path toward sustained happiness, peace, resilience, efficiency, focus, success, growth, and relief from stress. I have already hinted at the answer previously. A large body of scientific literature and time transcending teachings in combination provide a compelling story about how to engage the pre-frontal cortex, toward which the rest of the book will be largely devoted.

In the rest of this chapter I will try to convince you based on the available research evidence that the skills that have been shown over thousands of years to provide you peace and happiness are the very same skills that are likely to selectively engage the pre-frontal cortex. A few years ago, when I was sharing this information with a Buddhist monk who was visiting our center, his eyes sparkled as he said to his colleague, "Seems like we did not choose a wrong life after all!"

An observation of great import is that while engaging the higher cortical center brings about a positive attitudinal shift, research data that I will soon present suggests that it is this very attitudinal shift that further engages the cortical center. Thus once you initiate the shift, it perpetuates itself as shown in figure 14.1 below.

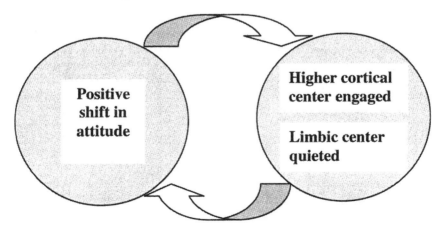

Figure 14.1 The feedback loop between a positive shift in attitude
and the engagement of the two centers

The converse is also true. With a negative shift in attitude (greater fear, depression, anger, hatred, jealousy, pessimistic self-talk), the lower limbic center gets increasingly engaged, which further predisposes to a negative attitude. This relationship is depicted in figure 14.2 below.

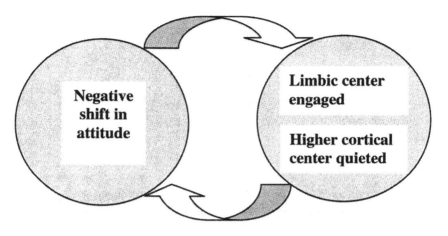

Figure 14.2 The feedback loop between a negative shift in attitude and the engagement of the two centers

The progress from living in the limbic mode to the higher cortical mode may transform several aspects of your life. It will help to directly compare the cortical and limbic modes of living. The descriptors are a bit exaggerated since most people do not live a polarized life at one end or the other. We switch the modes, often several times even in a single day. Nevertheless, it will help to compile the outcome of predominantly living in the limbic or cortical mode.

Table 14.1 Life in the limbic mode vs. the cortical mode		
Mode of living	LIMBIC MODE	CORTICAL MODE
Most active brain centers	Deep limbic system, particularly the amygdala	Pre-frontal cortex, hippocampus
Awareness	Mindless	Mindful, Heartful
Attention	Distracted, superficial, short; sometimes obsessive and hypervigilant	Focused, relaxed, altruistic, non-judgmental, in the present moment, sustained, purposeful
Interpretation	Excessive, unrefined	Balanced, refined

3Ps	Prejudices Preferences (egocentric)	Principles Preferences (altruistic)
Thoughts	Excessive, often negative	Positive and calm
Driving forces in life	Fear, greed, ego	Gratitude, compassion, acceptance, forgiveness, meaning and purpose, kindness, honesty, equanimity, humility, and love
Disease associations	Accidents[68, 69] Addictions[70] Anxiety[19] Cancer predisposition (probable)[71-73] Depression[74] Heart disease[75-78] HIV progression[79] Immunity lowered[80, 81] Increased blood clotting[82] Inflammation[83] Insulin resistance and diabetes[84] Memory impairment[85, 86] Recurrent infections[87] Sleep disturbance[88]	
Personal relationships	Strained, frequent loneliness	Close and nurturing
Quality of life	Poor	Good to excellent

Based on the evidence presented in the above table, your answer is likely to be obvious to this question:

Which mode of living would you rather choose?
1. Limbic   ☐
2. Cortical   ☐

Life in the cortical model is the truly transformed life. The reality, however, is that many of you might be *innocently* stuck in the limbic mode. I say innocently because unless you guard yourself well, this world efficiently pushes you into the limbic loop. And once you get mired in the limbic loop you might spend years, sometimes even your entire life, trapped there without even knowing it. A fairly well understood biological reason explains why it becomes difficult for you to disengage from the limbic loop. Once you enter the limbic loop, the chemicals released in the brain as a result (such as noradrenaline, corticosteroids, and corticotrophin release hormone CRH)[89, 90] further activate the limbic center and deactivate the cortical center. The brain also structurally changes to keep you in the limbic loop. The nerve cells in the limbic structures, particularly the amygdala, develop newer connections[28, 29] while the nerve cells in the pre-frontal cortex atrophy and lose their connections.[28, 29, 58-62, 67] The limbic loop thus works a bit like quick sand. The more you struggle the deeper it pulls. What a perfect set-up to keep you in suffering! I am confident Buddha and Christ would have loved to hear about these neurobiologic findings! Maybe they already knew.

Fortunately there are several time tested skills that have the potential to pull you out of the limbic loop and bring you in the cortical loop. Over the previous decade, research scientists have been systematically testing some of these skills to discern their effect on the brain using advanced imaging modalities. These imaging modalities study our brain in action and thus can assess the parts of the brain that are activated at a particular moment. The two most commonly used imaging approaches to assess brain function are the functional magnetic resonance imaging (fMRI) and positron emission tomography (PET) scan. (If you wish to know more about these imaging modalities you can find several excellent online reviews on these topics. Just Google the term fMRI or PET scan).

Next I will provide you with information (in brief) from research studies outlining the skills that help train and rightwire your brain. Remember that when you activate a certain part of the brain, you empower it. If you exercise your pectoral muscles you make them stronger. Similarly, if you practice skills that activate a particular part of the brain, you make that part of the brain stronger. Research evidence suggests that the majority of the skills I wish you to learn are associated with a selective increase in the activation of the pre-frontal cortex and other higher brain centers. *A combination of these skills might provide a perfect recipe to transform your life.* The skills with the related research evidence are summarized below.

Compassion and the brain

- In a report compiling results from eighty studies, researchers concluded that the feeling of empathy in humans is mediated by the medial pre-frontal cortex.[91]

- Further confirmation of this finding has also been obtained in patients who sustain damage to the pre-frontal cortex. Many of these patients develop a reduction in their empathic response.[92-95]

- Recipients of healing thoughts, even when separated from the healers, demonstrated increased activation in the anterior and middle cingulate area, precuneus, and frontal area.[96]

- In patients with congenital insensitivity to pain, observed pain in others was associated with activation of the anterior mid-cingulate cortex and anterior insula.[97] Further, in these patients, empathy was associated with activation of the ventromedial pre-frontal cortex in response to emotional expression of others' pain.

- A difference in brain activation pattern between empathy for ingroup vs. outgroup was observed. Ingroup empathy activated medial prefrontal cortex, while anterior cingulate cortex and bilateral insula were more activated for outgroup empathy.[98]

- In a study involving 128 children age 6 to 10 years, empathic concern and positivity empathy were associated with increased frontal cortex activation.[99]

Acceptance and the brain

- A study assessed the effect of individual differences in perceived controllability of the pain on self-reported pain perception.[66] In this study the feeling of acceptance was associated with increased activation of the pre-frontal cortex on fMRI testing.

- In a study assessing the effect of difference between believing and disbelieving a proposition using fMRI testing, rejection of a statement as false or its acceptance as true depended on processing in the medial pre-frontal cortex and the anterior insula.[100]

Meaning and the brain

- An ability to ascribe a non-emotional meaning to highly negative scenes decreased negative feelings. This process caused greater engagement of the lateral and medial pre-frontal regions and related areas of the brain, and decreased activation of the amygdala and medial orbito-frontal cortex.[101, 102]

- In a study involving recoding the meaning when switching the task from one to the next, the lateral pre-frontal cortex was shown to mediate recoding of the response meaning.[103]

- In a study testing the processing of the meaning of syllables, the left pre-frontal cortex was activated when the meaning of a syllable was being processed.[104]

Forgiveness and the brain

- In a study using functional MRI, ten volunteers made judgments of social scenarios. Forgiveness judgment activated left superior frontal, orbito-frontal and precuneus areas.[105]

- In a study involving twelve volunteers, ventromedial prefrontal cortex was found to play a central role in the forgiveness of moral transgressions involving deception.[106]

Mindfulness training and the brain

Research suggests that mindfulness training is associated with an increase in pre-frontal cortex activity. Overwhelming research evidence suggests that the converse of mindfulness, *attention deficit disorder, is caused by deficit in the activity of the pre-frontal cortex.*[107, 108]

- A disposition of mindfulness was closely associated with increased activation of the pre-frontal cortex and decreased activity of the amygdala, assessed using functional MRI imaging. The study involved twenty-seven volunteers who were asked to match facial expressions with appropriate words.[109] Higher pre-frontal cortex activation was associated with lower amygdala activity in participants high in mindfulness but not in those who were low in mindfulness.

- Mindfulness-based stress reduction (MBSR) is a well-recognized stress management program that is based on mindfulness training. Brain activity was measured in a study involving eight weeks of MBSR training and an additional four months of follow up.[110] MBSR training was associated with left pre-frontal activation on the EEG, a pattern associated with positive emotions.

Tribe and the brain

Tribe is the group of people you most closely connect with.

- In a study involving twenty-eight participants and their selected peers, interaction with friends was associated with increased activation of the pre-frontal cortex and other related areas of the brain.[111]

- Healthy social relationships were associated with healthy hypothalamic-pituitary axis function and decreased sympathetic stimulations; non-supportive interactions were associated with an opposite effect.[112]

Meditation and the brain

Several studies consistently show that meditation engages and empowers the higher cortical centers of the brain, particularly the pre-frontal cortex.

- In a study involving thirteen meditation practitioners, participants practiced meditation for four sessions of twelve minutes each and performed four sessions of a six-minute control task.[113] Brain imaging using fMRI showed that meditation was associated with increased activity in the pre-frontal cortex and anterior cingulate cortex. These changes were more evident in long-term compared to short-term practitioners.

- In a study involving sixty participants (fifty meditators), meditation experience was associated with improved performance on the Stroop test that measures executive attention, an indirect measure of pre-frontal cortex function.[114]

- In a study involving fifteen Vipassana meditators and non-meditators, mindfulness of breathing was associated with greater activation in the anterior cingulate cortex and the dorsal medial pre-frontal cortex bilaterally, compared to controls.[115]

- Pre-frontal alpha-asymmetry on resting electroencephalogram (EEG) is an indicator of emotional style. In a study testing mindfulness-based cognitive therapy (MBCT) in patients with a previous history of suicidal depression, participants were treated with MBCT (N=10) or treatment-as-usual (TAU, N=12).[116] MBCT was associated with better EEG outcome compared to TAU.

- In a study involving eight transcendental meditation practitioners, meditation was associated with increased alpha activities that mapped to the medial pre-frontal cortex and anterior cingulate cortex.[117]

- In a study involving twenty long-term practitioners of insight meditation compared to controls, meditation practice was associated with increased thickness of areas associated with attention, interoception, and sensory processing.[118] These included the pre-frontal cortex and right anterior insula with the greatest difference in older participants and those with greater meditation experience.

- A number of integrative modalities, including acupuncture, meditation, music therapy, and massage therapy were found to be associated with increased activity in the left-anterior regions of the brain and reward or motivation circuitry.[119]

- In a study involving Franciscan nuns doing verbal-based meditation, meditation was associated with increased blood flow in the pre-frontal cortex (7.1%), inferior parietal lobes (6.8%), and inferior frontal lobes (9.0%).[120] Increased blood flow is a marker of increased activity of a particular part of the brain.

- In a study assessing the neurologic correlates of the blissful state, EEG waves were assessed in meditators.[121] Blissful state in meditation was associated with increased anterior frontal activity particularly of the left pre-frontal region.

- In a study using single photon emission computed tomography with eight experienced Tibetan Buddhist meditators, meditation was associated with increased activity in the pre-frontal cortex and anterior cingulate gyrus.[122]

- In a study using fMRI, meditation was associated with increased activity in multiple brain areas including the pre-frontal, anterior cingulate cortex, and other brain areas.[123]

- In a study using MRI, higher grey matter density was noticed in lower brain stem regions of experienced meditators compared with age-matched nonmeditators.[124]   Authors speculated that this may account for some of the beneficial cardiorespiratory parasympathetic, cognitive, emotional, and immunoreactive effect of meditation.

- In a study involving 44 participants using high resolution MRI, significantly larger grey matter volumes in meditators was observed, specifically in the right orbito-frontal cortex and right hippocampus.[125]

Two conclusions emerge from the meditation studies:

1. Meditation is an effective practice to engage the pre-frontal cortex, a critical part of the cortical loop of your brain.
2. Meditation may facilitate growth of new nerve cells and thereby protect the pre-frontal cortex from the effects of aging.

Prayer and the brain

Multiple areas of the brain are involved in religious activity. These include the temporal lobe, parietal lobe, the limbic system, and the pre-frontal cortex.[126]

- In a study using fMRI imaging, contemplation of a religious image allowed the religious group to detach themselves from the experience of pain. The process specifically engaged the right pre-frontal cortex.[127]

- In another study on Franciscan nuns doing verbal-based meditation, meditation was associated with increased blood flow in the pre-frontal cortex (7.1%), inferior parietal lobes (6.8%), and inferior frontal lobes (9.0%).[120]

- In a study using functional neuroimaging, religious recitation was associated with activation of the pre-frontal, frontal, and medial parietal cortex in self-identified religious subjects.[128]

Physical exercise, diet, and the brain

Pertinent research findings showing the effect of physical exercise and diet are presented in the Appendix. Overall, the studies suggest that physical exercise and healthy diet also might improve pre-frontal cortex function.

A Word about Neuroplasticity

You might be curious if activation of the pre-frontal cortex during a particular practice is likely to be short term or may have lasting effects after that practice is stopped. The answer is that over a period of time these practices do have an effect on changing the actual structure of the brain. The simple rule is: If you engage a part of the brain, you empower it for the future. This is based on the simple principle about the brain first suggested by Donald Hebb, *"Neurons that fire together, wire together."* The attribute of the brain that makes it happen is called neuroplasticity. Hardware changes in response to the software. Active neurons increase interconnection with each other. Neuronal activity also facilitates growth of supportive tissues such as the blood vessels and other cells. This accounts for use-dependent increased blood flow and thickness of the particular areas of the brain that are used.

Neuroplasticity is often described as a dynamic process that constantly alters the neurochemical, structural, and functional components of the nervous system related to experience. This might be one of the most important components contributing to the evolutionary success of our species.[129] Neuroplasticity offers us hope that no matter how negative our past or limited our genetic endowment, we can change it for the better.

At a cellular level, neuroplasticity may be mediated by two key mechanisms—a quicker method involving changes in protein chemistry (phosphorylation) and a slower phenomenon involving change in gene expression. Phosphorylation changes neurotransmitter receptors, cell growth, and maturation. Gene expression changes proteins, ion channels, and receptors, and fine tunes neuronal function. Studies suggest that social experiences modify gene expression[130, 131] and thereby brain structure and function.[132]

Neuroplasticity partly depends on an important group of chemicals that affect the brain structure called neurotrophins. The main function of neurotrophins is to help brain cells grow and even replicate. The two important neurotrophins are the Nerve Growth Factor 1 and Brain Derived Neurotrophic Factor (BDNF), amongst which BDNF may be the most important one.[133] BDNF is expressed in multiple areas of the brain including the hippocampus and the pre-frontal cortex.[134, 135] BDNF helps the nerve cells survive and change in response to their use.[133] Studies are just beginning to emerge that BDNF is increased by physical exercise[136-138] and may also be increased by meditation.[139] Very interestingly, BDNF is decreased by a high calorie diet[140] and excessive stress.[85, 141] This decrease in BDNF provides the physiological basis for why high calorie diets and excessive stress might negatively affect brain function. Better understanding of the function of neurotrophins will likely help us understand the underlying biologic mechanisms by which stress predisposes to the loss of nerve cells in the pre-frontal cortex and hippocampus and also why stress might have a negative effect on long-term memory.

We have made considerable stride already in our understanding. At this point I would like to summarize the concepts shared so far. My desire is that you and I be on the same page as we move on to learning the specific skills.

15. The Brain and the Mind: Summary

By presenting some of the research evidence, I have tried to appeal to your good judgment and intellect as to the feasibility and value of engaging your higher cortical center. Recognize that the pre-frontal cortex functions as an integrated whole and its subdivisions are primarily to help with understanding. Further, the brain itself functions as a fully integrated unit. Distinctions between different centers or right vs. left brain are useful for understanding but their input are all combined together in generating an understanding of the world and appropriately responding to it. Both the cortical and limbic centers are activated (and needed) in response to a stressor; it is the balance in their strength and duration of activation that determines the final response. Also recognize that our understanding of brain function is presently limited; we are closer to the beginning of our exploration than the end. Hence many of the details will continue to be refined in the coming years. However, based on the review of the existing studies, I feel the overall theme seems fairly consistent and robust.

Exercise 15.1. Please pause after you read each point in the table below and ponder over it for a moment. Once you feel you have understood the concept, check mark it and then move to the next. If you are not clear, please go back and read the relevant text. I will group this summary into four parts: The workings of your mind; the workings of your brain; how you might disengage from life; how you can engage with and transform your life.

Table 15.1 Summary Table of Part II		
The workings of your mind	Mind influences all aspects of your actions and perceptions	☐
	Perceptions have two components: attention and interpretation	☐
	Attention allows you to register, imbibe and transmit the information for processing	☐
	Information so transmitted is admixed with the 3Ps (principles based values, prejudices and preferences). This leads to interpretation.	☐
	Interpretations influence your actions	☐

The workings of your brain	Brain has two groups of centers:	
	* Higher cortical center – When activated decreases stress and increases resilience	☐
	* Lower limbic center – When activated increases stress and decreases resilience	☐
	The simple rule of the brain is: If you engage a part of the brain, you empower it for the future.	
	* Greater use of the cortical center makes the cortical center stronger	☐
	* Greater use of the limbic center makes the limbic center stronger	☐
	You have a choice to engage and empower one or the other brain center	☐
	Compassion, acceptance, forgiveness, higher meaning and purpose, having a closely knit tribe, meditation, prayer, and healthy life style activate the cortical center	☐
	Experience and learning changes the brain, a phenomenon called neuroplasticity	☐
How you might disengage from life	Excessive interpretations based on prejudices and predominantly egocentric preferences make our thinking pattern excessively self-seeking	☐
	Such interpretations cut short attention. Attention thus becomes superficial and fleeting.	☐
	The resulting attention deficit and interpretation excess pushes our focus away from the world into the mind	☐

	Mind harbors attention black holes that act as attention sumps	☐
	When within the mind, we may get lost in the imperfections of past and future in a mindless state of excessive and negative thinking	☐
	Mind in this state keeps the limbic system active	☐
	Fear, anxiety, depression, stress, and ill health accompany a life in the limbic mode	☐
How you can engage with (and transform) your life again	Two important components of engaging with your life are:	
	* Train your attention by learning to focus away from the mind and increasing the depth of concentration	☐
	* Refine your interpretations by basing them on principles based values and altruistic preferences	☐
	Principles based values (and their derived skills) include – Gratitude, Compassion, Acceptance, Forgiveness, Meaning and purpose, Kindness, Honesty, Equanimity, Humility, and Love	☐
	Attention so deepened and interpretations so refined engage the higher cortical center	☐
	Inviting a tribe around you, meditation, prayer and healthy life style also engage the higher cortical center	☐
	Peace, joy, and resilience accompany this state that gradually gives way to transformation and awakening—a state of effortless presence and relaxed alertness, during work as well as play	☐

In short:

Train Your Brain and Engage Your Heart to Transform Your Life.

The next section will focus on briefly unfolding the concepts of mindfulness and heartfulness and a program we have put together encompassing both i.e. Attention and Interpretation Therapy (AIT).

SECTION III: MINDFULNESS, HEARTFULNESS & AIT

16. Mindfulness and Heartfulness

Mindfulness:

One of the most precise definitions for mindfulness was given by one of the earliest pioneers of mindfulness in the U.S., Dr. Jon Kabat-Zinn, *"Paying attention in a particular way: on purpose, in the present moment, and non-judgmentally."* A large body of research attests to this definition that cultivating mindfulness helps an individual observe and describe present-moment experiences nonjudgmentally and nonreactively.[142] Further, mindfulness is associated with improvement in psychological functioning, by reducing ruminations and emotional avoidance and improving self-regulation.

Mindfulness is bare attention, an attention that is bereft of interpretation in a state of total acceptance. Mindfulness emphasizes that the present moment is not a means to an end—it is the end in itself. Mindfulness is egoless and non-reactive awareness, a pure state of being. When mindful you carry perfect awareness of all three—observed, observer, and the process of observation. Being in the present, however, does not mean you stop thinking about the past or stop planning for the future. You still visit the past and future but only when needed and go there purposefully with your individual will in the driver's seat. Your thinking is focused and targeted; you do not drown in a deluge of thoughts. You no longer need the past for your identity or future for feeling fulfilled. When mindful, you connect with others at a deeper level, not at the level of one ego interacting with the other. Your relationships are thus secure, bonded with understanding and love.

Mindfulness can be described in many different ways. Pause for a moment to absorb each of the expressions below that describe different aspects of mindfulness.

Mindfulness is –
- Preconceptual / Prelogical
- Prior to duality
- Bare attention
- Nonjudgmental awareness
- Awareness with acceptance
- Awareness of the present as it unfolds

- Non-conceptual awareness
- Openness to novelty
- Observing, describing, and experiencing nonjudgmentally
- Prior to thoughts
- Prior to concepts
- Egoless awareness
- Total concentration
- Non-reactive awareness
- Beyond thinking
- Awareness of sameness and change
- A process as well as a goal
- Awareness of all—observer, observed, and observation
- Getting the mind unstuck
- Acting with awareness
- Non-dual experience
- Experience bereft of the self
- Non-egotistic alertness

All of the above statements point in a certain direction yet are incomplete in themselves. Mindfulness in essence is pre-logical and pre-conceptual. It is a primordial state of awareness from which all your thoughts originate. Language in the form of words or thoughts is downstream to mindfulness. Mindfulness predates language. Words can help by pointing you in a certain direction, just as a map can give you a general idea about the terrain but not the experience of the landscape—for a full experience you have to drive yourself. So take all the words written above as signposts pointing toward a general direction.

One reason for so many ways to define mindfulness is that the concept itself is so simple. The simplest entities are the ones most difficult to define. For example, how would you describe "empty space" in a few words? Or, for that matter, love? Our definitions are usually relational. Mindfulness represents the core faculty of our awareness that forms the substratum for other faculties to emerge. It has no specific reference to anything that can be perceived by our senses. Thus it is difficult to find perfect words to describe mindfulness.

The concept of mindfulness is believed to have originated from Vipassana, a form of Buddhist meditation. The word Vipassana means seeing or perceiving in a special way (Vi = in a special way; Passana = seeing or perceiving). Mindfulness training, a key component of Vipassana, provides you with an ability to see all the way through to the most fundamental nature. Mindfulness, however, is not limited to one particular tradition but is a part of most religious, spiritual, meditative, contemplative, and philosophical traditions.

Mindfulness provides the insight and clarity of awareness that helps you perceive events exactly as they happen. Mindfulness transcends science, spirituality, and philosophy—and includes all of them. Mindfulness, however, is not a religion. Considering mindfulness as belonging to a particular religion might be the same as believing that relativity belongs to Einstein or gravity to Newton. Mindfulness existed before we were able to formulate words and systematize religious thinking, and will remain unchanged despite the continued evolution of our religion and spirituality.

Heartfulness

I like to define heartfulness as, *"Practicing presence with love."* A more elaborate definition is, *"Enhancing awareness of the present moment and its contents and embodying the present moment with greater gratitude, compassion, acceptance, forgiveness, and higher meaning and purpose."*

Heartfulness recognizes that the mind was not created to be stifled and stilled. As long as we live in a material world (and not in a monastery) it would be optimal to respect the mind's need for movement. So heartfulness focuses primarily on slowing down the mind not stilling it. ***Heartfulness does not try to make the mind blank. Deep sleep although very relaxing does not lead to transformation. Heartfulness thus emphasizes on filling the mind with more of heart i.e. love.*** *Hence the focus on engaging the heart (or the heartful part of the brain). Heartfulness intends to make the brain more heartful.* Such brain and mind are resilient and can better resist the weeds of negative thoughts from growing.

In many languages, the word mind and heart have the same word *"dil."* Heartfulness thus includes a combination of the core process of the human mind i.e. attention and the core process of the human heart i.e. interpretation with love. Heartfulness has two main anchors – wisdom and love.

Among the many components of wisdom that contribute to heartfulness are recognizing and accepting the reality of suffering, finiteness, and change. Heartfulness compassionately recognizes the proclivity of the human mind to dwell excessively in the psychological time of the past and future. The vast proportion of human suffering being in these two time zones, heartfulness gently guides the human mind toward finding greater value within the present moment.

Human mind however may have spent a life time escaping from the present moment. Heartfulness thus does not "stress" the human mind by leaving it without anchors in the vast expanse of the present moment, a territory that may seem superficially unfamiliar. Heartfulness offers the anchor of love in the form of gratitude, compassion, acceptance, forgiveness, and meaning and purpose. With practice, it is possible for the mind to attain a state of total acceptance and may transcend the needs for any anchor. Heartfulness allows this process to unfold at its own pace, not necessarily setting this as a goal but only a milestone in a long journey.

Heartfulness is cheerfulness. Cultivating heartfulness allows you to carry a little heaven with you wherever you go. It allows you to nurture a cheerful heart (and brain).

A cheerful heart has a continual feast (Proverbs 15:15).

Heartfulness emphasizes the importance of attending with love, and instead of being preconceptual, prelogical or prior to duality is focused more on perceiving with love. Heartfulness does not deny the existence or non existence of thoughts, but focuses on softening the relationship with the thoughts.

The purpose of heartfulness is to guide the aspirant to an abiding state of peace and joy. Each of these are emergent properties and cannot be forcefully willed. Dance of the peacocks, natural mirthful giggle of children at play, state of flow in your work, or an experience of deep meditation; these are all emergent properties. They cannot be artificially created. They flow out spontaneously from the depth of the heart. Peace and joy also emerge from the same place. An essential ingredient required for peace and joy to emerge within human awareness, an ingredient that is a synthesis of wisdom and love and a core concept of heartfulness is altruism.

Altruism, described as a concern for the welfare of others often with selfless intention, provides the path toward heartfulness and its related states of peace and joy. Altruism recognizes the universality of suffering and finiteness. Importantly, altruism is deeply anchored in interconnectedness. Altruism thus recognizes that suffering is a common human experience, and by virtue of us being interconnected, we are affected by the suffering of the others, and importantly, have within our capacity to decrease suffering. Developing altruism and its practical application—daily kindness, is a choice we all have.

We all have the choice to embody the five essential skills to develop altruism (and thus peace and joy). The five skills are that of gratitude, compassion, acceptance, forgiveness, and meaning and purpose. A combination of these skills adds up to the universal value of love that is at the core of heartfulness. These skills and the reflections drawn from them provide an immediately available alternative to negative ruminations. *We thus do not just empty the present moment, we fill it with love—for the self and the world.* Peace, joy and resilience are a natural outcome of exercising the choice to cultivate altruism and daily kindness. It is this kindness that we should wear daily as a jewel on us. Everything that is good will naturally follow.

Don't ever forget kindness and truth. Wear them like a necklace. Write them on your heart as if on a tablet. (Proverb 3:3 NCV)

Heartfulness and Mindfulness:

You might be asking, what is the difference between heartfulness and mindfulness, if any?

Both heartfulness and mindfulness are slightly different flavors of looking at the same reality. Mindfulness, as commonly understood focuses on purposeful present moment awareness in a non-judgmental fashion. Like mindfulness, heartfulness also emphasizes on enhancing engagement with the present moment but has a more explicit focus on experiencing the present moment with greater love. Further, the present moment in heartfulness is flexible (from just this moment to an entire life time) depending on individual situation and load. In a high load situation in the midst of disruption, the present moment may be shrunk to just this second and one might live one's life one second at a time and carry only the load of this moment. On the contrary when circumstances are more favorable, the present moment can be expanded. Thus heartfulness emphasizes flexibility along with balance.

In essence, however, any difference that is perceived is only superficial. Understood deeply, mindfulness includes heartfulness and heartfulness includes mindfulness. Both emphasize that the present moment is not a means to an end—it is the end in itself. Heartfulness and mindfulness both create egoless and non-reactive awareness, a pure state of being. They are a bit like wisdom and love. At a deeper level wisdom includes love and love includes wisdom. They both overlap, almost completely. So does mindfulness and heartfulness.

I include both the constructs with the primary intention of emphasizing to you and leaving no doubt in your mind that we are not simply attempting to empty the mind, we are also focusing on enhancing presence of love with its five attributes of gratitude, compassion, acceptance, forgiveness, and meaning and purpose.

A constant practice of *"presence with love"* takes us to a state of *"prayer without ceasing."* Life, work, relationships all become a prayer. It is to such a state we wish to travel. It is a very worthy journey the important milestones on which are peace, joy, resilience, and altruism. I have attempted to give this journey a structure drawing liberally from concepts within science to develop a therapeutic approach we call the Attention and Interpretation Therapy (AIT).

17. Attention & Interpretation Therapy (AIT)

Attention and Interpretation therapy synthesizes the two steps of training attention and refining interpretations into a structured approach. The purpose of developing these skills into a form of therapy is to bring them into the scientific realm, offer them as a therapy to the patients to decrease suffering, and develop a structured approach to help learners and future teachers embody these skills. We have developed a training program in AIT with the intention to train future generation of trainers who as a first step learn to embody these principles, and with training and experience, are able to train patients and learners in this therapy.

Three essential aspects of a program offered in the 21st century for enhancing peace, joy and resilience are: incorporates the latest advances in science, particularly neurosciences; integrates the wisdom of the scriptures; and adapts to the needs and limitations of the present times. It is my humble hope that AIT offers you this combination. **In developing this therapy, I have incorporated ideas from four disciples: neurosciences, psychology, philosophy, and spirituality**—combining them with personal experiences and learning in the finest laboratory possible— clinical patient care. AIT thus addresses all the three frontiers of human experience—the brain (neurosciences), mind (psychology, philosophy) and spirit (spirituality).

The two key concepts included with respect to the *neurosciences* are: the arrangement and functions of the higher cortical and lower limbic centers of the brain; and task positive and default networks of the brain. I have covered the first component in previous chapters but have purposefully avoided describing the second concept at great lengths because it is rapidly evolving and also is a bit complex so is best understood in one-on-one or group teaching sessions. Nevertheless, I will briefly cover it here.

The latest research studies in neurosciences suggest that there is a network of neurons in the brain that host autobiographical thinking with I, me and mine as the primary focus. This network is called the "default network."[143] A healthy activity in this network may allow us to make a sense of past, present and future and may even be associated with higher intelligence.[144] However, abnormal activity and connectivity in this network, particularly when the content is predominated by past losses or future uncertainties, correlates with negative mood and may be observed in several conditions including depression, anxiety, attention deficit, stress and autism. Early result suggests that excessive activity in the default network may even be associated with a predisposition to Alzheimer's dementia.

As a broad generalization, your attention at any moment is drawn by either the task positive network or the default network. Optimal engagement of the task positive network and an ability to quiet the default network is the neuropsychological equivalent of complete and effortless focus with total immersion in the task at hand. This is a state of flow as described by the eminent psychologist Dr. Mihály Csíkszentmihályi. Research suggests that the quality of experience is not so much affected by what one is doing (work vs. leisure), but is more related to attaining this state of flow.[145] People often experience a deep sense of eudemonic happiness in this state. For such a state to materialize the optimal ingredients include: an optimal balance of familiarity and novelty in what you do; a sense of meaning and purpose; and relative freedom from the unnecessary open files in the brain (the primary source of negative ruminations). I think even a transient experience of such a state would give a shot of endorphins to the brain. It is a surefire way to improve your brain.

If you are unable to appropriately quiet the default network, then you risk developing mind wandering and as a result inattention to the present moment. In general, there are two situations when default network is excessively engaged: 1) too many open files in your mind that you cannot close;[146] or 2) not enough novelty in the world.[10] Think about when are you more likely to be lost in inward focused autobiographical thinking (also called the monkey brain). You are likely to be lost in the mind on days that are more challenging, particularly if the stressors cannot be easily resolved or are beyond control. Mind wandering is also particularly likely while cooking mashed potatoes (for the thousandth time)! Compared to mashed potatoes, if you cook some exotic tropical dish you have never made before for a special guest you adore, you would more likely be task positive.

Excess activity within the default network saps your energy and attention. Most of this time does not register in your awareness[147] and is lost time generating what I like to call *"junk food of thoughts."* Mind wandering is associated with negative ruminations, excessive planning, day dreaming, and sometimes catastrophizing. Part of training your mind and the brain is to learn how to (at least temporarily) close these extra open files. Further, this training also brings these ruminations in your awareness so they are shorter and less task impairing.[148, 149] In essence you reclaim a significant amount of lost time.[150, 151]

In *psychology* I have been influenced by the cognitive behavioral therapy model as well as acceptance and commitment therapy. Both are excellent models to help patients with a broad range of medical and psychologic conditions. I have also been inspired by the positive psychology movement and concepts within evolutionary psychology.

I believe the greatest strength of AIT is incorporation of the time transcending *spiritual* principles in the model. These include the wisdom of gratitude, compassion, acceptance, forgiveness, and meaning and purpose. AIT also includes meditation and prayer that is individualized based on learner's beliefs and preferences. The approach is secular and designed to have a broad appeal. The focus is on experience and embodying these principles rather than dogma. Further, AIT will continue to evolve with time drawing upon developments in neurosciences and related disciplines as well as enhanced understanding of psychology and spirituality. In that sense AIT is nimble and dynamic.

The goal of AIT:

There are four key outcomes we desire with AIT. These are facilitating peace, joy, resilience and altruism.

Peace, joy and resilience however do not exist in a vacuum. They travel together and are emergent properties that flow spontaneously when one has achieved an optimal balance between the higher cortical and lower limbic components of the brain, and the task positive and default network activity. They are a product of wisdom and love. Wisdom that anchors us in the reality of finiteness, suffering, and change; and love that recognizes interconnectedness, connecting us with a world much larger than our own physical being and thus instinctively fosters gratitude, compassion, acceptance and forgiveness. Such wisdom and love pave the way for a common path toward transformation through awakening brain's higher center. This path has one important milestone—the unfolding of altruism. A genuine selfless concern for the welfare of others is an essential ingredient toward individual wellness and happiness. Such a focus is also likely to enhance individual relationships and provides a strong frame work for a networked tribe.

AIT thus cares not only about the individual, but intends to train each individual as an agent of transformation. A person anchored in these principles is likely to eventually become self actualized. AIT recognizes however that perfect self actualization is a theoretical goal. Ultimately it is not the attainment of a goal that is as important. What is most vital is travelling on a path toward that goal. And also traveling like a steamer ship so you can carry a few fellow beings as you cross the river.

It is with such pure intentions and a desire to transform an individual, the society and the world that we offer AIT. In the remaining part of the book, we focus on the specific aspects of training attention and interpretation— the core components of AIT.

SECTION IV: ATTENTION TRAINING

Précis

Attention training allows you to control direction, duration, and depth of your attention (3Ds)

This is the essential first step to *train your brain, engage your heart and transform your life*

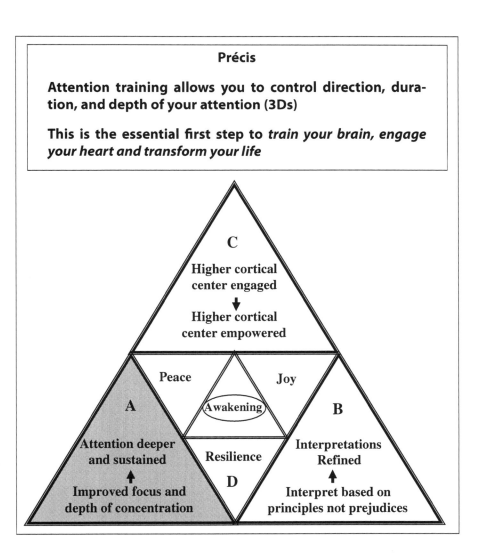

18. Attention Training: Introduction

A rusty saw and lackluster effort may double the time it takes to cut a log of wood. A sharpened edge and optimal force increases your efficiency many fold—and also the joy in your effort. The edge of the saw represents your focus; the force you apply represents your power of concentration. Focus is an ability to direct your attention to a specific aspect of your sensory experience. Concentration is the strength applied to this focus so you can sustain it. Focus and concentration imperceptibly flow into each other and together constitute your attention.

Attention is your ability to focus on a selective aspect of your sensory experience and sustain that focus for a period of time. Attention is the gateway into your mental processes. Attention is thus the primary tool you use to collect and imbibe information about the world as well as your inner environment. Your experience and recognition of beauty, truth, kindness—all depend on your ability to pay attention. You all have the power of attention but unless you train it, your attention may be deficient, superficial, and/or inflexible. Attention is highly dependent on optimal functioning of your pre-frontal cortex. Training your attention thus trains your higher cortical center.

Negativity Bias, Positivity Offset and Attention

Research suggests that the human mind has a propensity to pay greater attention to and process the bad compared to the good, a phenomenon often called the "negativity bias."[152] Bad feedback has greater impact; bad impressions are quicker to form; bad information is processed more thoroughly; distress over losing money is more than the joy in gaining money; a single strongly bad experience is difficult to compensate with even several wonderful good experiences; and negative stereotypes are easier to form. Further, the smoke detector in our brain has great propensity to pay attention to threat, a trait present even as early as 7 months of age.[4-8] Thus left unregulated and within the default mode, human mind is likely to focus more on the bad than the good with resulting lower levels of joy. This is particularly worse within the midst of challenging disruptions.

Interestingly we have a different kind of bias when focusing on the world. When disengaged from the inward focused autobiographical (I, me and mine) mode and in an environment that does not have an obvious threat, people see their surroundings positively and start engaging with it. This is often called the "positivity offset" that may compensate for the "negativity bias."

We learn from these two observations that if we can somehow train our mind to pay greater attention to the world while avoiding too many interpretations, we may be happier and have lower stress.

Since mind needs a continuous anchor, just asking it to stop generating too many thoughts is not likely to be sufficient. I have seen several patients and learners who may have spent decades searching for peace by going inwards and trying to still their mind, but with only limited progress. Mind flows like a river from past to present to future to past. It is very difficult to be in the present moment when one goes inside the mind. Further, once inside the mind, the attention black holes in the mind keep pulling you into the psychological time. **Going inwards is not the ideal first step for most of us.** It may work for a few who intrinsically have strong control on their attention but for the vast majority of us it would take a very long time.

So what is the solution? The firm anchor that is always accessible to the mind is the beautiful world that surrounds us. By learning to pay greater attention to the world, delaying judgment and paying attention to novelty, and thus decreasing the time spent in the autobiographical default mode, mind becomes increasingly stable, peaceful, and joyous. To initiate and sustain this process you have to train your attention so it is more focused on the outward rather than the inward, is deeper and sustained, and increasingly is in the present moment. The outcome of this training is that you develop a trained strong attention that is balanced and flexible. Attention training will open your world to a fresh set of alternatives so your mind is not crowded by negative ruminations.

Attention Balance and Flexibility

Two important outcomes of attention training are to develop *attention flexibility and attention balance*. Attention flexibility is your ability to change the depth and direction of attention depending on the needs of the hour. This leads to a state of *attention balance*. In a state of balance you choose the appropriate intensity and focus of your attention, neither attention deficit nor excessively focused. For example, a neurosurgeon while performing surgery needs an intense and focused attention. However, the same surgeon when in a social gathering or while reading a story to his child would have a more fulfilling experience with a relaxed and more diffuse attention while still remaining in the world. A trained attention is thus not fixed in a patterned momentum and style but can easily adapt to the environment. ***This is what you need for greater peace, joy and efficiency—to have access to different breadth and depths of attention.***

Quite commonly, however, we get locked into a pattern we have learned over the years and do not purposefully choose the direction, duration, and intensity of our attention. As a result we spend an inordinate amount of time in our mind. We bring the momentum of the workplace to our home and take the stresses of the home to our work. Attention flexibility allows you to reclaim control so you are better aware of your emotional state and environmental needs and become deliberate and responsive, not re-active. In this state a previous unpleasant experience does not limit you— you shake it away with a few deep breaths and move on to constructive actions. Just like the swans that, on emerging from the water, shake their wings once or twice and then take flight as if they never got wet!

A smoothly flowing steady stream of attention can be compared to the flow of a gentle water faucet, attention deficit and obsessive focus to the paroxysms of an ice dispenser. Converting paroxysms of attention to a smooth flow needs three key ingredients: *a purposeful effort, the right skills, and time.* Most traditions of the world have developed their unique approaches to attention training, one of them being meditation. Here I present a plan deriving wisdom from many of them and mixing those ideas with science, my own beliefs and experience, flavored with lessons I have learned in one of the most spiritually advanced place of teaching— clinical patient care.

I once heard a modern prayer: God, give me patience—but please hurry up! I fully respect this expression because it is flush with reality. I have felt that way many times and still sometimes do. I know many of you do not have weeks and months to take off to a paradise island for learning attention or meditation skills. I respect the busy-ness of yours. I know it is real; I myself live a similar life. The question I ask is, just because we are too busy can we ask God to hurry up? Can we cultivate our patience in a jiffy?

The answer I repeatedly get from within me is—probably so, but with two caveats. The caveats are that our effort should be honest and our inten-tions good and pure. It is with these good intentions that I offer what I believe is a quicker approach. I often teach it in a single session in work-shops or individually. From what I can tell based on patient feedback and a few research studies we have done so far, most of the learners are able to imbibe the ideas very quickly. On hundreds of occasions I have seen immediate and sustained drops in anxiety and stressful feelings once participants learn and start practicing these simple skills.

Among the three ingredients noted above, I trust you to bring your purposeful effort. I promise to provide the skills. With regard to time, in the initial stages I ask no extra time devoted primarily to practice. I will share with you an approach so you can embody the skills I share within your usual day. You are fully capable of doing that. Trekking over the cold Minnesota terrain in the winter months, as I watch the barren soil, I cannot help but be in awe when, come spring, this soil will be transformed into beautiful flowers and succulent fruits. If with a bit of effort and a tincture of time ordinary soil can achieve such transformation, you and I truly have infinite potential.

The two steps in training your attention capture the **3Ds** of attention. The two steps are:
*a) Find the right **D**irection of your attention; and*
*b) Find the right strategy to sustain the **D**uration and **D**epth of attention.*

Both these steps need purposeful effort. This effort, however, has to be relaxed and balanced, neither dull and slothful nor chaotic and tense. Excessive rigidity and an obsession to "get it right," may not help. It tends to create a situation akin to golfer's "yips" wherein some golfers develop an inability to complete a stroke usually during putting or chipping that is worsened by anxiety. An optimal level of flexibility and balance is needed in your attention. In order to attain an attention with optimal flexibility and balance it will help to understand the 3Ds of attention a bit more. Let us pursue that next in preparation for moving on to specific attention training exercises.

19. The three Ds: Direction, Duration and Depth of Attention

Broadly, attention can be directed within (toward the *body, breath, mind, or self*) or outside (toward the *world*). Among the four inner fields, untrained attention directed toward the mind does not (generally cannot) remain steady in the "now." This is because of two characteristics of the mind: 1) the mind has no distinct boundaries between the past, present, and future; and 2) the mind has no fixed speed. The mind's speed may range from zero miles to several light years per second. When lodged in the mind, attention thus jumps between the present, past, and future at the prevailing speed of the mind. The energy of attention gets divided and cannot engage fully with anything, certainly not with the present moment. This is similar to a leaky vessel with many holes.

Even the most adept meditators cannot consistently remain anchored in the present when they bring their attention to within their mind. This mind travel into the past and future is stressful since many of your imperfections hide in your past and most of your fears lie in the future. Your efforts to resolve them may keep you exhaustively and dreamily engaged. Attention within the mind also keeps you away from your life—you imagine instead of perceiving, think instead of feeling.

Among the other three inner domains, "self" is the most tenuous entity to define. You could call it stillness, tranquility, soul, or consciousness. During deep sleep most of our "definitions" melt away. In that state, however, I am still me and you are still you. The part of me that remains with me in the state of deep sleep can be called the "self." This true "self" is not easily accessible. Hence aligning attention with the body and the breath seems like the optimal two choices. And this indeed is what the traditions have offered over the past thousands of years. Relaxing and training with the body and the breath have been the essential beginning components of meditation training. The constant, predictable, and controllable activity that the breath provides is nicely complemented by the stability of the body. The breath and the body would be the ideal anchors for your attention training, but in the modern world they have a few limitations:

1) You have to set aside extra time to practice body or breath awareness;
2) Training in the body and breath awareness is a slow process;
3) Your breath is formless and with the eyes closed, the body is imperceptible. Hence in the initial stages, the breath and the body

may not provide the structure you need to anchor your awareness; and

4) Your body and breath are very close to, and interconnected with, the mind as shown in figure 19.1 below. In the early stages of training, if your attention is mostly with the body or the breath, you are likely to slip into the mind and then into the past and future.

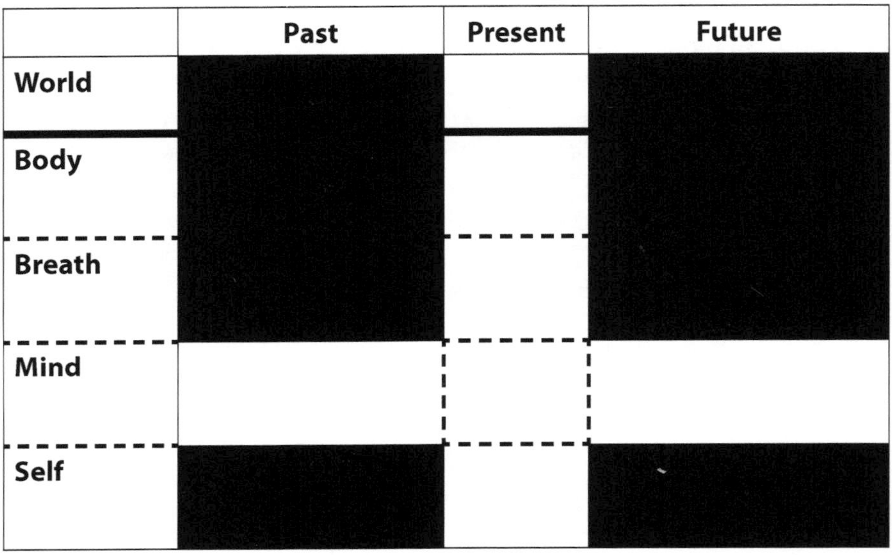

	Past	Present	Future
World			
Body			
Breath			
Mind			
Self			

Figure 19.1 The five fields of attention. Notice that while the mind has perceivable past, present, and future that are in connection with each other, the other four fields are only in the present. Also notice the porous connection between the body, breath, mind, and the self.

Figure 19.1 shows the five fields accessible to your attention. Notice that the mind has a porous border between the past, present, and future, while the world, body, breath, and self are all in the "now" bereft of any past or future. Also note that the borders between the body, breath, mind, and self are indistinct. So we will take the few first steps in attention training by keeping a focus on the world and only later come to the body and the breath. Training your attention with the world makes it much easier to use the same skills for the body, breath, and even the mind.

Because of the above reasons, *I believe that the natural first step in attention training is to anchor it to the world.* Attending to the world without mixing it with too many biased interpretations offers the path to direct experience. The world offers several advantages:

1) The world is available to you all the time—through work as well as play;
2) You attend to the world sixteen hours a day on most days;
3) The world moves at a fixed speed of sixty seconds a minute;
4) By becoming more aware of all the details of your world (home, work, and leisure), your overall knowledge and work performance may improve;
5) You need not set aside extra long hours to train yourself; and
6) You can start training right away and maintain attention flexibility all through the day.

There are two additional reasons why I prefer the world: 1) the world offers no perceptible past or future—it is only the present unfolding itself; and 2) the skills are very easy to learn, can be taught in a single short session (or with the help of a book), and thus do not need long, expensive retreats. In several instances I have found immediate and lasting results with this training even in patients who have had long-standing issues.

A Balance in Focus

Among the five domains that can hold the focus of our attention, for the reasons mentioned above, our innate tendency is to spend an inordinate amount of time with the mind. The proportion of time we may spend with individual domains on a typical mindless day is shown in figure 19.2.

Mind   **World Body Breath Self**

Figure 19.2 Distribution of attention on a typical day with the untrained mind

This proportion is particularly skewed if you have attention black holes in your mind that draw your attention. These attention sumps could be in your past or future. As a result of their presence, while your eyes and ears stay in the world your attention may not be in synchrony with them. Your attention gets split—part of the power goes toward the world, while the rest stays with the mind (Figure 19.3). This habitual multitasking leads to lack of synchrony between the senses and the mind and is one of the primary reasons we feel incomplete, hollow, and dull. Out of tune with our senses, our observations become superficial and incomplete.

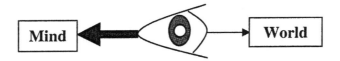

Figure 19.3 Untrained attention is split between the world and the mind. In the mindless state the bulk of the attention remains locked within the mind, decreasing your ability to pay attention to the world.

Unlike the mind, the other inner domains—body, breath, and self—are only momentarily experienced during the day. Body awareness mostly happens if the body is at dis-ease. Focus on the breath mostly occurs during breathing exercises, in meditation, or when you are short of breath. The time spent with self is mostly only when you are in deep sleep. Deep sleep is a precious entity that is systematically eroding in the present generation because of the increasing momentum of life and the resulting sleep deficit we are accumulating.

With training as your attention matures, you increase the time spent with the world while decreasing the time with your mind. For the time you are with the world you stay away from duality and categorizations to the extent possible. You delay judgments. Further, your awareness stays mostly at one place and in one time zone in synchrony with your senses. In this state your time with the self—that is the most healing time full of joy and bliss—may also expand, partly because of improvement in sleep quality and the ability to access deep sleep (Figure 19.4).

Mind   **World**   **Body Breath Self**

Figure 19.4 Distribution of attention on a typical day in the attentive state

Such a trained attention remains mostly with the world with little "attention dollars" invested in the mind (Figure 19.5). This allows purity and depth of observation and decreases premature prejudice-based interpretations. Such attention, when it chooses to be directed to the mind, uses the same force and goes into the mind purposefully without getting caught in the web of past and future. I often give the example of someone waking up at 2 AM hungry. If they go to the pantry to eat a cookie or a fruit, they do not intend to stay there. They eat a snack and are quickly back snug in their bed. Similarly when you have to travel into the psychological zone of past and future, visit there purposefully and for a short time, and then come back to the comfort of the present moment.

Figure 19.5 Trained attention is mostly with the world with little "attention dollars" invested in the mind

As you advance, the time you spend with the world proportionately increases. With further training, anything coming to attention, such as thoughts, sensations, body, breath, or self, are accepted with equal enthusiasm and without judgment. You flexibly switch between different depths and intensity of attention—a state of attention flexibility. The time spent with the mind decreases even further. Finally, your time with the self takes over all the other entities. This does not mean that you move around like a zombie, self-absorbed. It means that your definition (and realization) of self expands and goes beyond your inner self to include your body, breath, mind, and the world. You become fully self actualized. You remain relaxed and calm, yet are fully engaged, passionate and functional.

It is toward such an awareness I wish you to progress. The first step in this progress is to attain a focus so that on the whole you are less with your mind and more with the world. This constitutes the first D, direction of attention.

Duration and Depth of Attention:

Untrained attention tends to be superficial and fleeting. This nature of attention interferes with a nourishing sensory experience. The next aspect thus is to develop an attention that is sustained and deep. The three challenges that an untrained attention faces which prevent sustained and deep attention are:

1. The strong inward pull of your mind (particularly if it has attention black holes);
2. A lack of firm anchors in the world; and
3. Innately weak attention unless purposefully trained

Extra open files in the brain crowd the working memory of the brain, generate attention black holes, and provide a strong inward pull to the attention. In most situations these open files represent situations real or imagined that you may not have been able to accept. Structurally, this correlates with excessive activity of the default network of the brain.

World lacks firm anchors for many of us since most days are a repetition of the previous days. We live in the same home, travel on the same route to the same office, work with the same people, and eat mostly similar things. This familiarity makes us inattentive to the world since we cannot find much novelty around us. The reality however is that there is immense novelty waiting to be discovered. We just have to remove the dust from our eyes and start looking.

Finally, untrained attention tends to be weak, like most other trainable systems in the body such as your aerobic capacity, strength of the heart muscle etc. If you do not exercise to make your heart and lungs stronger will they become strong just with a sedentary life? Very unlikely, isn't it? Similarly attention, probably your most important tool will remain weak unless you purposefully train it. Such an attention is also inordinately directed to process threat or imperfections.[4-8]

All the three processes i.e. pull of the default network, inability to find novelty in the world around us, and an innately weak attention that focuses on threat or imperfections more than anything else, interferes with the duration and depth of attention. Training attention and refining interpretations corrects these two imbalances.

A trained attention has seven important characteristics: focused, relaxed, altruistic, non-judgmental, in-the-present-moment, sustained and purposeful. Such an attention will offer you a refreshing set of possibilities to your negative ruminations. ***Training such an attention is the single most useful skill to progress toward a transformed self actualized state.***

Forget what happened before, and do not think about the past. Look at the new thing I am going to do. It is already happening. Don't you see it? (Isaiah 43:18-19 NCV)

20. Attention Training

Attention training entails cultivating purposeful attention. This purposeful attention has the following important traits:
- It is predominantly directed toward the world
- It is flexible and balanced
- It is non judgmental
- It seeks novelty
- It is relaxed
- It is mostly in the present moment

Cultivating purposeful attention allows us to optimally engage with the world and savor it more fully. It is accomplished by purposefully loosening some of our internal maps of the world so we can immerse in it more fully. Early on in training you may have to exercise some level of deliberate control, just like you would do with physical exercise. With time the practice becomes effortless.

I will present below two broad approaches to attention training. *The two approaches are:*

1. *Joyful Attention: Delay Judgment & Pay Attention to Novelty, and Contemplate on the story*
2. *Saintly Attention: Attend with CALF (Compassion, Acceptance, Love and Forgiveness)*

One useful pearl – the primary impediment that drives us away from the present moment (even when life is going well) is our incessant tendency to plan, problem solve or engage in day dreaming, negative ruminations or just random chaotic thoughts. Decrease the tendency to constantly plan or problem solve, day dream or ruminate. It is often unnecessary and takes away the joy from your life.

Attention training will open your world to a fresh set of alternatives to negative ruminations.

1. JOYFUL ATTENTION:

DELAY JUDGMENT AND PAY ATTENTION TO NOVELTY

Remember the last time you saw a dance recital by a group of little 3-year old girls or a basketball game of young boys. It is always a source of joy to watch the little ones perform. Those are cherished and memorable moments. Do you think their performances are polished and professional or pretty chaotic? Pretty chaotic, isn't it. Then why do we enjoy them so much? I think part of the reason is that we do not negatively judge them. We accept the performance of our little ones for what it is. The very fact that they are on the stage is a reason for joy.

Now compare this experience with watching a professional football game. A very interesting study published in 2008 in the *New England Journal of Medicine* suggests that when Germans were watching their own team playing in the 2006 world cup soccer, they had upto three times the risk of a serious acute cardiovascular event while watching the game.[153] Why should an entertaining activity mutate into a life threatening event? This to my mind is related to excessive judgment invested in each move of the game. Viewers often wish to control the flow and outcome of the game by watching the television screen and are frustrated at their inability to do so. It is also related to some of their expectations not being met.

Both the experiences, watching little kids perform or watching a soccer match should ideally be a source of joy. But a lot depends on the attitude we bring to the event. If we meet the world with excessive judgment and bias, we could take the joy away even converting the experience into a potentially life threatening event. When we delay judgment we create an open receptacle for us to pay attention to novelty.

1.1 Pay Attention to Novelty
The first attention skill is to find the extraordinary within the ordinary.
Two of the most favorite toys I kept away from our daughter Gauri when she was four year old were my cell phone and pager! When she had her way, she would find options in my cell phone I never knew existed and innocently reprogram them. The cell phone was novel, interesting, and magical for her. At some point this sense of wonder about the cell phone (and the world) diminishes. I think the threshold is crossed when the accumulation of experiences and shortcuts in memory suffice to make sense of the world. While she needs this file of shortcuts and memories, she is at risk of overdoing it. If that happens she will stop finding the world novel, something that happens to most of us.

It is possible that your living room does not have anything new or novel. It is, however, equally possible that your ability to find novelty in your living room has withered. Your ability to remain in the world depends on finding novelty within boring, extraordinary within ordinary. This will help you develop the freshness of a four-year-old while maintaining the maturity of an adult. *You need to develop motivation to find novelty.*

Why am I asking you to focus on novelty and not pleasure? Among the three attributes that support your motivation (threat, pleasure and novelty, TPN), pleasant and threatening experiences are generally obvious to most. The definition of pleasant and threatening, however, is contextual, with self as the primary frame of reference. Excessive characterization of everything into the good-bad or like it-hate it model risks developing prejudices and self-focused preferences and locking us into duality. Finding pleasure independently is good but is often coupled with a desire to acquire. And if for some reason you cannot acquire what you desire, you may become angry, jealous, or stressed.

The other attribute, i.e. adequate threat perception, is important for your survival. However, the archaic mechanisms within our brain and mind exaggerate this threat and catastrophize it more than it's due. As a result, the perception of threat or intention to preserve pleasure both may create stress mediated hypervigilance. So at least in the initial steps of training we would focus on the third attribute, i.e. novelty.

Novelty is not conditioned by duality. While generally appraised in a positive sense, novelty often is value neutral. I might find something novel yet not have an intention to acquire it. *Novelty is free of judgment or prejudice.* Novelty is pure appreciation of uniqueness. An item or an event does not have to serve the self for it to be novel. You often consider something novel if it is original, contrasting, unique, exclusive, and beyond usual expectation. Is it possible you are deluged with novelty but are just failing to notice? My guess is that this is indeed the case. Let us do the exercises that follow to explore this further. **Remember one word of caution: Attention training exercise should not be attempted while driving, working with heavy machinery, or doing other such high stakes work.**

Let us begin training ourselves by paying attention to a flower (Figure 20.1).

Figure 20.1 A flower

Exercise #1. Take a quick superficial look at this flower. You might recognize this as a daisy, nothing much special or exotic about it.

Now take another look. This time bring your full attention (and patience) into looking at this flower. **Look at it with the <u>beginner's eyes</u> (or as if you designed it).** *Imagine yourself to be a flower connoisseur. Can you see that the petals are broadly arranged in two or may be even three layers? See the separation between the petals. Are they symmetrical or arranged a bit randomly? Look at each petal individually. Do you see that each petal has a unique shape and size? Do you see the lines on the surface of the petals? Jagged edges? Intensity of light reflected from the surface of the petals? Do you realize that each petal might be a unique unit and small self contained world in its own way? Systematically look at the center of the flower. Do you see the stamen? Do you see the dark spot a little off center?*

Clearly this flower is novel. There is no flower on planet earth that looks exactly like this, there never was and never will be. This novelty however will only manifest if you purposefully make this flower the entirety of your world for a brief period of time. To appreciate this novelty you may have to initially refrain from adding adjectives to your descriptors.

If we could see the miracle of a single flower clearly our life would change - Buddha

Can you bring this attention and presence to your loved ones when you are with them? *They are unique and special and precious and deserve your full attention. In reality, they are also extraordinarily novel, even if you have known them for decades. When you meet your loved ones at the beginning or end of the day, can you engage with this novelty and meet them as if you are meeting them after a long time? How do you think they will feel if you meet them with full warmth and a hundred percent of you "present" compared to just a disengaged hello?*

In an interesting study involving 32 dual-earner families with children who were videotaped for a period of time, lower stress in both husband and wife correlated with their engaged presence with each other.[154] The more they talked in the evening the lower was the level of cortisol in their saliva (a marker of stress). Still on an average they only spent <10% of their waking time alone together. So if there is one thing you can do to improve your loved one's stress and health—bring more of you in your interaction with them.

We all crave for other's attention. By providing this attention to others you can significantly enhance their (and your) quality of life. **While the amount of time you give to others is important; what is even more important is the amount of you present in that time.** *The exercise of paying attention to the novelty of the flower can be extrapolated to several experiences throughout your day. While walking in the corridor, listening to a song, having breakfast, attending a presentation—you can choose to bring your total presence in each of the experience. This brings your attention in your influence so you can train it and then deploy this pattern of attention where most needed (with your loved ones, friends, colleagues, clients, patients etc.).*

A deeper attention does not mean you obsessively notice and potentially comment on every wrinkle you see in others! The purpose is to bring your full presence in your interactions. The purpose is to practice your presence with love. By doing this you send a silent message to others that for this moment they are the most important person in the universe you wish to attend to. Such a silent message is extraordinarily healing and provides a secure bond to your relationships. It is healing not only to the others, but as you will notice when you start gifting this attention, giving such an attention provides you also with great joy.

If you wish a preview of heaven, just pay non-judgmental attention to the world around you.

At the level of your brain this pattern of deeper attention automatically delays interpretations, enhances the intensity of your sensory input, and allows you to see the world in its full brightness. Compare figure 20.2 below with figure 6.1 in chapter 6.

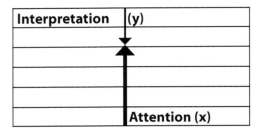

Figure 20.2 Attention and Interpretation within the brain. Upward pointing thicker arrow represents stronger engaged attention; downward pointing thinner arrow represents trained interpretations.

You use your eyes to the fullest potential and not look as if visually impaired. The process repeatedly deployed has two additional benefits: it brings your attention in your influence; and helps you disengage from and ultimately disempower attention black holes.

Training attention takes a bit of effort, sometimes a lot of effort. Initially you will have to exercise a level of deliberate control. *It seems simple to learn, but is not easy to practice.* You have to repeatedly remind yourself and pull yourself out of your head to sustain this pattern of attention. Unless you create a purposeful intention, attention black holes are likely to draw you within their folds.

I will now present this core basic concept in additional exercises to help you work toward strengthening your attention. Experience these exercises, identify the ones that you find most appealing, and incorporate them in your daily schedule. I will share one suggested schedule we have found useful with patients and learners in the next chapter.

Exercise #2. Uniqueness within the ordinary

Pick four similar looking oranges (alternately apples, apricots, plums, potatoes, cucumber, or any other medium-sized vegetables or fruits will do). Look at these oranges as if you actually created them. Carefully study how the final product turned out. Look at their shape, size, color, fragrance, surface, weight, and all the undulations on their skin. Look at the uniqueness of the "Grand Canyons" (all the dimples) inscribed on each orange's surface.

Do you think despite their superficial similarity all the individual oranges are different, unique, and special in their own way? Do you think this is true for every fruit—every tree—every human—every life form? Are you missing something by failing to notice this novelty?

Ducks floating in the pond seem like a photocopy of each other. In a group, each penguin might also look identical to the others in shape, size, and color. Yet they are all individuals, have unique personalities, have their own families, a different voice, emotions, and responsibilities. So does an ant, a grasshopper, even a ladybug. If you were to adopt two ladybugs as pets, more than likely you will give them two different names. Next time you look at any of these cute creatures, try paying attention to their individuality.

This is also true for every human being. Every one of us is unique and novel in our own way. We have our own story. It is just a chance that some stories you know and others you don't. If you pay attention to novelty in an individual, without caging too much of that into good or bad, you might be fascinated by the variety and richness that you learn. If you look for novelty you will invariably find it. A search for novelty in the ordinary will increase your depth of attention and improve your observation.

Two reasons we cannot find novelty are our prejudices and our excessive focus on the self. Our prejudices very quickly launch our invariant interpretations that prematurely stop the attention process. In this state attention acts as a filter to only bring information that agrees with our views. For example, in an interesting study involving assessment of television watching habits, viewers were observed to watch broadcasters that were likely to affirm their views rather than informing their opinion.[155] In this state true learning is extremely difficult.

Further, many of us remain either excessively self-conscious or self-absorbed. When we go to a party we remain too concerned about how we look; while giving a talk we are very invested in how we are being perceived. The excessively self-conscious state prevents us from being at our best and also takes away the fullness of experience that a party or a lecture might give. The reality is that if all of us are focused on the self, then who is paying attention to the other?

Remember that you often do not like others for who they are, but how they make you feel about yourself. Paying kind attention is the first step toward helping anyone's self esteem.

Most pleasurable events are associated with stress. In the Holmes-Rahe scale of Life Stress Inventory, vacation and holidays are rated as stressful, which is reflective of the experience many people have before, during, and after their vacation. Any party you host or attend brings an element of anxiety. This anxiety is particularly worse if you become excessively self-conscious of how you will be perceived.

Self-absorption, which ultimately leads to a selfish state, is also stressful. This is because your efforts to attract and splurge disproportionate amounts of the energy of the world, which is what you do when you are self absorbed, are often thwarted by the reality of fairness of the world over the long term. Frustration in the efforts invariably leads to stress.

The two key aspects to find novelty are thus to accept and appreciate whatever you see in its originality without too much good-bad characterization, and to temporarily forget your own agenda and immerse yourself in the experience. An ability to find novelty independent of inherent value helps greatly with the depth of attention. To find novelty, you have to let go of mind's constant tendency to plan, problem solve, over categorize and ruminate on egocentric thoughts.

Exercise 3. Unique clothes
Pick a dress of your child, grand child, or your friend's child. Look for novelty in this dress—see the cute buttons, the color patterns, appreciate the softness of cloth, the baby fragrance, and all else your senses allow you to perceive. Look at this dress as if you are an expert at designing clothes.

Exercise 4. Sea of novelty
Look around the house. Find novelty in your toothbrush; see the uniqueness in the apple you eat; find what is special about a plant, even a weed. Look with a fresh, open, and learning attitude at ordinary items in your home such as your door, windows, microwave, dishwasher, oven, furniture, beds, toothpaste, soap, and television. Each of these items has an element of uniqueness and novelty to it. Most of the things in your car, on the road, at work, or in restaurants are novel.

Would you agree that you are swimming in a sea of novelty? To appreciate this novelty you will have to delay value-based categorization. Everything is as it is—magical, unique, and precious. Even the most mundane object is a product of fourteen billion years of work of the universe and is thus novel. Finding novelty helps you respect and adore the object of your attention. Just like the objects around you, and even more so, every individual you meet has a part of him or her that is unique and novel that you can notice, admire, and learn from.

Exercise 5. Novelty in individuals
Next time you meet someone at home or work, pay extra attention to their words. Try to perceive the depth from which their expressions originate. You might find new meaning in what they say. Attend to their novelty. When looking at your loved one's eyes, try to look into their heart. Ponder over the amazing journey they may have travelled to present themselves in your life.

What you attend to expands. You will find what you look for. The more you pay attention to novelty the greater novelty you find. Once you are able to find novelty within the ordinary, you will delete the word "boring" from your dictionary. Your propensity to pay attention to the contents of the mind will also decrease.

Such an approach will help you develop a habit of trying to understand others before forcing your ideas. That will also make you more accepting. You will disassociate from being self-conscious or self-absorbed. With this attitude you will develop the instinct of approaching rather than avoiding, paying attention rather than disregarding. You will pick more details, learn more, and become incrementally enthusiastic about paying greater attention in the future. The process starts a lifelong learning program that increases your knowledge, keeps you in a relaxed attentive spirit all day long, "rightwires" your brain, and helps reduce stress.

An important reminder here—this is not a hundred meter sprint, it is a marathon. By choosing to start the program of training attention, you are delving into a life long learning program. On the surface, this seems like a simple straightforward skill. But in reality it is the most engaging (and rewarding) challenge you may have ever taken.

Young children find most things novel and thus a source of joy. Even an ordinary doll or a bunny in the backyard could create a moment of elation (though of late I find even five-year-olds getting bored—a sign of the epidemic of inattention). At some point, however, we begin creating mental shortcuts based on categorizing things into concrete boxes— good-bad, pleasant-unpleasant, desirable-undesirable, like it-hate it, and so on. These categories mostly are based on egocentric preferences and create a registry of prejudices in our mind. This process to a limited extent helps with adaptation, learning, and survival. However, when it becomes excessive, which it often does, the process leads to over-categorization. The process of over-categorizing loads us with prejudices that vitiate the purity of sensory experience and short circuits our attention. This results in interpretation overdose, biased perception, and attention deficit. If only we could transform our "partial attention" to childlike "wondrous attention" while still remaining grounded in "adult maturity." That would be wonderful, wouldn't it?

Busy as a Bee

I am sure many of you are extremely busy and stretched to the limit. Let us see if you are busier than the honeybee. Honeybees contribute about $15 billion to the U.S. economy every year. They pollinate over ninety major crops. On a typical work day a worker bee collects pollen and nectar, makes honey, stores pollen and honey, makes wax, builds the honeycomb, cleans the hive, protects the hive, keeps the hive cool, and even feeds and takes care of the little baby bees. The honeybee might make an ideal spouse! What is more, there is a fairly good chance that the one to two teaspoons of honey that she collects in her lifetime will never be used by her. She will leave it in a trust, bequeathed to the next generation or to us humans.

A bee makes about ten foraging trips every day, visiting up to one hundred flowers in each trip. Despite the one thousand unique visits each day, if you watch the bee negotiating with the flower it seems evident that the bee alights on each flower with a clear purpose—to collect as much nectar as she can in the most efficient way. Once she collects the nectar, she works with the other bees in an intimate collaborative process to facilitate evaporation of excess water that converts this nectar into honey. The honey is then stored in the hive and is used to feed the babies and the queen and also to tide over the winters. Bees also have evolved an intricate mechanism to communicate about the location of the food. A bee who chances upon an abundant source of food rushes home and starts a special dance to signal the location of food to her compatriots.[156] The direction of the dance indicates the angle from the sun; the duration of the dance provides approximate distance. After learning this information, the seekers travel on a predictable trajectory to find the food.[157] German ethologist Karl von Frisch received a Nobel prize in 1973 for describing this brilliant method of communication.

All the above activity happens in a hive of twenty thousand to eighty thousand bees. Bees do not have a level of management or police that controls them. They cannot call 911 and do not have a court system for maintaining order. I believe the basic quality that keeps the hive going is the tremendous focus and discipline that each bee maintains. Every bee keeps her head clear, her attention and flight are purposeful, and there aren't any egos or judgments. Despite all her busyness, a honeybee pays full, undivided attention to the flower she alights on. She moves from flower to flower in a disciplined and purposeful fashion. She compartmentalizes her work, is wonderful on time management skills, and is a great navigator. No wonder she accomplishes way more than we might imagine from the size of her brain and duration of her life span.

The nectar that a bee finds in flowers is the nectar of *novelty* that, if we look purposefully, we can always find in others. A purposeful search for this novelty may keep you in a relaxed attentive state all day long despite the chaos that might surround you on a typical demanding day. It turns out there is a lot we can learn from the busy bee!

Below I present four additional ideas and related skills to help your efforts toward training attention and discovering novelty that might otherwise elude the untrained eye.

1.2 Use one sensory system at a time

In the previous exercise we learned to practice deepening our attention by purposefully paying greater attention to novelty. Another way of deepening attention is to attend to the object using a two-step process in a different way. In this approach you first appreciate it with all the senses working together. As a second step you pay attention using one part of the sensory system at a time.

Exercise 6. Use one sensory system at a time
Pick an apple. Examine it as a two-step process;
Step 1 – Hold the apple in your hands and appreciate it as a whole.
Step 2 – Now appreciate the apple using your senses, one at a time.
  1. *First "look" at the apple. Attend to its shape, color, its stem, and all the marks on it. Maybe there is a sticker describing where it was produced or packaged. Appreciate the uniqueness of this apple. There is probably no other apple in the world that is identical to this one in all its attributes.*
  2. *Now engage your sense of touch and feel the apple. Feel its smoothness as well as all the corrugations and marks on its surface.*
  3. *At this point bring this apple closer to your nose and with a deep breath appreciate its fragrance. Savor this breath for a moment.*
  4. *Keep the awareness of apple in your mind, close your eyes and imagine the apple is filled with empty space. Imagine this entire space. Imagine the space gradually filling with white soothing light.*
  5. *Open your eyes, take the first bite of the apple, and close your eyes again. Feel the taste of the apple in your mouth and try to gently suck any juice that comes out of it. Once juice stops flowing chew it*

once and again enjoy the taste and suck the juice that gets released. Repeat this for a total of five chews. You can finish off the last pieces of this bite and then take the second bite of the fruit, repeating this exercise until the apple is all gone.

I wish to note two specific observations with this exercise:

1. This exercise may have introduced you to the uniqueness of the apple. You may realize that each apple has a personality of its own that is unique and precious.
2. The uniqueness can be more effectively ascertained if you use one sensory system at a time.

You can do this exercise with any other fruit or vegetable you like. Can you appreciate other aspects of your environment using one sensory system at a time? This is an excellent approach to train your attention and bring it back to the world.

1.3 Fine one new detail (FOND)

The above two exercises (paying attention to novelty and using one sensory system at a time) are excellent to practice in the quiet of a room when you are by yourself. They will also help you immediately bring focus into the present and in the world when you find yourself distracted. Mind wandering is particularly likely to happen when you have many unresolved issues and thus many files open in your head and the world around you is boring.

To make the world around you interesting, a pragmatic version of these exercises, particularly in a familiar environment, is the FOND exercise. In this approach you attend to an object at least until the point that you are able to discern at least one new detail that you did not know previously. Let us try this exercise.

Exercise 7. Find one new detail – The FOND exercise
Find four small objects that are familiar to you. If you cannot easily find four objects use the four fingers of your right hand. Straighten these fingers and first study them as a whole and individually. Now try to discern the following four new details about your fingers you may not have paid attention to previously:

- *Compare the length of the index and ring fingers, which one is longer?*
- *Does the tip of the little finger cross the second joint line of the ring finger or not quite so?*

- *Can you individually fold any of the fingers and touch the surface of the hand, while keeping the other three fingers straight? (it may not be possible to do so—the fingers are connected to each other and do not like to move alone)*
- *Now turn your hand and look at the root of the nails. Which of the nails have a semi lunar white area at the base (if any)?*

Did you learn a few new details about your fingers with this exercise?

If you picked four familiar objects such as a cell phone, pager, pen, and button on a shirt, find one detail about each object that you did not know before. For example:
- *What specific words are displayed when you turn on your cell phone?*
- *Do you have seconds displayed with the time in your pager?*
- *Is the name of the manufacturer on your pen written in italics or normal font?*
- *What is the precise color of the buttons on your shirt?*

The FOND exercise will not only make you more aware of your world, with familiarity, you are also likely to become fonder of things around you. As a result you will learn more, more easily remain out of the mind, and potentially have lower stress. FOND exercise is particularly helpful when you are in a familiar environment and is another way to make the world around you a bit more interesting.

Two words of caution here are: 1) Keep judgments away to the extent possible; 2) Do not practice this exercise and other attention exercises while driving, operating heavy machinery, or doing any other such activity that will be negatively affected by your attention being drawn away. Finally, while the exercise is designed for just one new detail, you can attempt to find any number of details you consider appropriate, may be even with the cover of this book.

Exercise 8. Pay purposeful attention to the front cover of this book. Study it carefully and try to find a few details about the cover that you may not have paid attention to earlier.

Before we go to the next exercise, think about when during the day can you seek novelty, use one sensory system at a time, or find one new detail. It is likely that you may not be able to practice such an attention pattern throughout the day. So it will help to purposefully practice these exercises at specific times (about four to eight times) during the day. Can you practice one of these approaches while getting ready in the washroom, loading the dishwasher, doing laundry, arranging clothes, eating, while watching TV, or talking to your friends or your loved ones? I will present a structured program incorporating some of these ideas in the next chapter.

1.4 Anchor on to Movement

Newton gave us three useful laws of motion. The first law, also called the law of inertia, states that, "An object at rest will remain at rest unless acted on by an unbalanced force. An object in motion continues in motion with the same speed and in the same direction unless acted upon by an unbalanced force." I believe this law is applicable not only to physical objects but also to the mind. The mind has a certain speed that is also the speed of your thoughts. The mind's speed is intimately related to the perceived speed of the world. When directed by the outside forces, the mind picks up considerable speed, and unless you slow it down, it may continue to run for considerable time. Slowing down the mind requires you to first catch up with it. It is like boarding a running train. You have to first run with the train, and once you pick a certain speed, you then hop on to it.

The training exercises we have done so far are guided to hand you back control over your attention. While the objects you attended to in these exercises are static, you move your mind into different aspects of them. Movement is important because a static mind quickly becomes restless. Mind is not used to stillness except in deep sleep. It is optimal, however, if you can control the movement of your mind and bring it to a speed that is conducive to peace. When seeking novelty, looking at the objects in two steps, using your senses one at a time, or finding one new detail, your mind moves purposefully at a speed chosen by you.

Another effective way to engage the movement of the mind is to couple the inner movement of the mind to an outer movement. A very useful tool with predictable outer movement is your clock, which we will use in the next exercise.

Exercise 9. Move your mind with the clock.
Use a clock that has a moving second hand. The clock on your computer will work great. Sit comfortably in a chair and try to remain still to the extent possible. Now track the movements of the second hand for two minutes. Do not create or follow your thoughts but if they arrive do not suppress them either. If thoughts force their way, let them in.

In your first few practices, after a few seconds or a minute or so, a barrage of thoughts will likely flow in. If you keep an attitude of being a patient observer, thoughts will gradually fade away. Increase the duration of practice as you progress and as time permits.

(Did you notice that the second hand in the clock in our laptops, every five seconds or so, pauses for a bit longer during its movement).

Among your five senses, vision and hearing register the sense of movement. Over 35 percent of the nerve fibers to the brain come from a combination of these two senses, most importantly your eyes. They attune the mind to movement since movement is the basic nature of both vision and hearing. The mind feels uncomfortable with stagnation and loves movement.

For the next exercise, I will share with you a little pearl about the behavior of the mind, particularly during meditation training—**the mind tries to do the exact opposite of what you wish it to do!** The mind is like a child. If you wish to slow down the mind in meditation it will run fast. By contrast, if you get it engaged by immersing the mind in a sensory experience, eventually it will become quiet and slow. The one essential to help it slow is to avoid prejudices and delay judgments to the extent possible. Let us try to immerse our mind in the sounds around us.

Exercise 10. Tracking the sounds
Find a room wherein you can hear some outside sounds. Close your eyes in a safe place. Bring your attention to all the sounds you hear. Allow your attention to travel to the object making the sound. For example, if you hear a car, take your attention to the engine of the car and appreciate the sound being produced. Track the sound as it moves toward or away from you. If you hear a bird, travel to its beak and appreciate the sound being produced.

You may notice after some practice that during this exercise there will be moments when your mind registers a state of calm. These are the relaxing meditative moments. The calm you experience in these moments is qualitatively similar to the calm experienced in deep meditation.

1.5 Contemplate on the Story

So far, each exercise and concept I have presented has been directed to bring your attention to the outside world. The exercise I will discuss next is an exception that is a mix of remaining with the world, yet entering the mind.

Exercise 11. An apple's journey
Hold an apple in your hand. Give it a name, say "Applina." Become fully aware
of Applina by attending to her with all your senses individually. Now look at
Applina and allow yourself to imagine her story. Right from a little insecure
blossom on a tree in an orchard, Applina has had a successful career. Take
your imagination to the orchard—to the tree, the branch, and the blossom
from which Applina started. Imagine the span of time that has elapsed be-
tween that time and now. Imagine the space that separates you from that
orchard.

The blossom was able to avoid the vagaries of the wind and rain. It also sur-
vived the onslaught of insects and any number of other threats that could
have destroyed it. Slowly the fruit evolved, from a small rancid baby apple
to now a fully grown apple of this size. When ripe, Applina was picked by a
person, labeled, stored, waxed, and then transported—probably thousands
of miles away. In her journey with her friends, she was sometimes buried and
uncomfortable, and at others on the surface and breathing fresh air. Imagine
traveling with Applina in her journey. This journey across the country may
have given Applina a few marks on her surface.

Finally having arrived at a grocery store, she was evaluated and placed for
purchase. Applina wished to be bought before she became old and perished.
Fortunately you found value in her and purchased her for the advertised
price. She is now ready to fulfill her promise, willing to sacrifice herself for
your nourishment.

Being eaten completes Applina's journey. This is exactly what she wants, but with one caveat—to be eaten with joy and presence. She has worked extremely hard all this while with one focus—to bring you nourishment. All she wants in return is that you enjoy each bite of her. This is how you pay respect to her—to each apple you eat—in fact, to everything you eat.

Every single item around you has such an amazing story that converges to one person—you. Bring your attention to all that surrounds you, take a pause, and contemplate on how each of the things have presented them-selves in your life. Things like adhesive tape, pencil, pen, paper, pager, cell phone, toys, clothes, car, and many more. Hundreds of thousands of people may have worked together to bring you simple every day items. If you cultivate an ability to introspect wisely, you may develop a skill to learn a deeper reality and pay greater attention because of a newfound respect for everything. Such attention makes everything seem special and flowers the kindness that is an inherent part of you. This is a particularly important attitude to carry for your loved ones and friends.

The fact that a particular group of friends and loved ones has manifested in your life is a miracle. If the life of the universe was one year then humans arrived on December 31 at 11:59 P.M. and almost at the last second. With the universe so big and so old, and more than six and half billion of us on planet earth, every human being who has manifested around you is a true miracle. The probability for any person to be in your life by random chance is quite small—lower than winning a big lottery. Consider every relationship, at home or at work, a true blessing, a gift that you should treasure.

With your ability to contemplate, you might realize that most people and things you encounter, you do somewhere in the middle of their journey. You meet your parents, your spouse, and your friends in the middle of their lives—you do not know their beginnings and may not know their ends. Most items in your home you know in the middle—not the beginning and probably also not the end. It is only when you pay attention to them and contemplate their story as they tell it (in words or in silence) that you can understand their unique preciousness and novelty. Most of what you own today was previously someone else's and will belong to another person after you pass it on. The purpose of knowing this is to realize the impermanence of most things in your life. This realization might allow you to appreciate everything around you even more.

To untrained attention the extremes often seem alike. Thus the apathy of someone in denial may superficially seem very similar to the calm and collected energy of a saint. It is only when you pay deeper attention, contemplate on the full story with an open mind and bring your willingness to touch the truth can you appreciate the wisdom of the calm and the words behind silence.

As we conclude joyful attention, I will share one more simple attention exercise that may help deepen your attention to your environment.

Exercise 12. Know your space
Sit in a safe place, close your eyes, and imagine walking from your office to the cafeteria (you can choose any other walk that may be appropriate to your situation). Keep your attention until you register the first twenty specific details. These could be simple things like the color of your office door, the color of your doorknob, your name plate, color of the ceiling, the sign for restroom, etc. Try and be as vivid as possible in what you see.

After completing the exercise for the first time, take the actual walk that you just tried to imagine. During this walk pay attention and memorize the details that you will bring to your awareness when you practice the exercise next time.

You can increase the number of details as you are able to cultivate deeper attention.
You can also change the scenarios if you practice this exercise regularly.

When Gauri, our daughter was two-years old she held a sharp fork in her hand. The only way she gave it back to us was when we bartered it with my cell phone, something she considered of greater value. Our attention works a bit similar. Attention latches on to the contents of the mind and will only detach if the alternative the world offers has greater value and interest. Given that the world cannot consistently and on its own provide you adequate TPN (threat, pleasure, novelty) to keep you engaged, your ability to find splendor and extraordinary within the world by infusing it with the light of novelty is likely to help you develop a deeper attention with respect to the world. These exercises help you find this novelty.

The above five exercises, i.e. seeking novelty, using one sensory system at a time, finding one new detail (FOND), anchoring on to movement, and contemplating the object or event train different aspects of your attention. They allow you to immerse in your experience, using a narrow as well as a diffuse focus. The common thread in all these exercises is that they train you to regain influence over your attention. An ability to purposefully change the 3Ds of attention offers you attention flexibility that will enable you to break free from patterned ways of paying attention (or inattention). On the whole this increases the duration and depth of your attention.

Behind the scenes as your "attention muscles" are getting stronger, you are training your higher cortical center. An added benefit also is that when you pay greater attention to the world, you pick more details and are just a more aware citizen. Further, the delayed judgment gives you enough time to activate your pre-frontal cortex. Here is how it works.

In general, when we see someone firing their amygdala (showing anger, frustration etc.), our instinct is to activate our amygdala based response. In most social situations this will lead to undesirable results. Amygdala activity inhibits pre-frontal cortex from activating preventing our higher wisdom from engaging to resolve the issue at hand. With one amygdala facing the other, the experience may not be very pleasant. If you wish to delay amygdala's firing, a very useful approach is to delay judgment, pay attention to details and particularly for our loved ones, keep an attitude of compassion and acceptance. This will give you the precious few seconds you need to engage your pre-frontal cortex, delay your instinctive counterattack, and thereby resolve the misunderstanding more adaptively. So when you train your attention to delay judgment and pay attention to novelty, you are really learning a life skill to adaptively resolve many unpleasant issues you might face in your life.

2. SAINTLY ATTENTION:

ATTEND WITH COMPASSION, ACCEPTANCE, LOVE AND FORGIVENESS (CALF)

Attending with CALF is the second component of attention training. From looking at the world with the beginner's eyes that you have done so far, you progress to developing the sight of a saint.

How do you think a saint interacts with the world? *I think they forever are sending causeless compassion, acceptance and love to every life form.* Can we cultivate such an attention? The answer is yes and is the natural next step for us—to cultivate saintly attention that is effortlessly sending out compassion, acceptance, love and (where needed) forgiveness.

To develop this attention we have to train our eyes as an organ of perception as well as of expression. Generally when we see someone, we pay attention to their physical characteristics, exclude threat, focus on how attractive they are etc. Sometimes this attention pattern has a judgmental element to it. I believe we lose precious opportunity with this attention style.

To cultivate saintly attention, spend the first half to one second of looking at someone as a precious time of sending compassion, acceptance, love and (where needed) forgiveness.

Align your mind and eyes with your heart and send them a blessing that flows from you and also through you. Your attention thus flows as a two-way process—when you see someone, as you imbibe their information, you send them a silent message of CALF. This is depicted in the figure below (Figure 20.6).

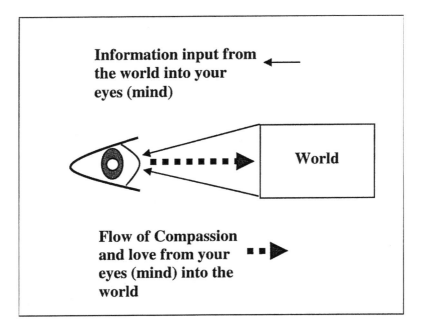

Figure 20.6 Saintly attention: Send positive energy of Compassion, Acceptance, Love, and Forgiveness (CALF) as you pay attention to the world

An efficient way of sending CALF is to send silent "bless you." Try this exercise today:

Exercise 17. The next twenty people you see, smile at them, do not while away the precious first second you look at them trying to discern if their jewellery is well matched or other such physical details. Instead, align your eyes and mind with the benevolent part of your heart and silently convey from your eyes a kind "Bless you." See how you feel at the end of this exercise.

One more way of sending a warm positive feeling to the other person is to try and focus on what you like about them within the first few seconds of your conversation.

Sending CALF to the world might benefit you in many ways:
1. You generally cannot give something you do not have. So when sending CALF to others, you generate CALF within your being;
2. When you are generating CALF within yourself, it is very difficult (almost impossible) to have negative emotions at the same time;
3. Over a period of time, people receiving your CALF begin to recognize it; a process that might have remarkably positive effect on your relationships;

4. The world is a good reflector. World keeps a small fraction of your blessings, but largely reflects back the rest to you. And if you also operate as an efficient (but not perfect) reflector, you would do the same. This might set yourself up for a very long and joyous interchange of blessings before the single quanta of energy you initiated exhausts itself. What of thousand such you might start each day? Such thoughts, expressions and related energy travels with you. This way you carry a little heaven wherever you go that transforms every experience it touches.

Benefits of Attention Training:

Your ability to sustain a deep attention in the world might have the following beneficial effects:

1) By learning to purposefully attend, you develop skills to choose attention at will;
2) Your ability to access and train different depths of attention helps you develop attention flexibility;
3) Since paying attention is a function of the pre-frontal cortex, you train your higher cortical center of the brain;
4) By anchoring attention in the world, your attention is not drawn toward the contents of your mind;
5) By anchoring attention in the world, you stop feeding energy to your attention black holes, thereby gradually disempowering them;
6) By deepening attention you delay interpretations, thus increasing the purity and depth of sensory experience;
7) You learn more about the world by paying attention; and
8) When you learn to pay attention with the exercises presented, the skills you learn may translate into other aspects of your life including improved ability to pay attention to your work, loved ones, and other aspects of daily living.

Research studies suggest that learners who actively trained attention with meditation performed better in a concentration test, were less distracted, and had better ability to focus on different perspectives.[158] Trained attention thus creates a more accurate, deeper, more efficient and flexible processing of the sensory information. These results were noted also for tasks not directly pertinent to meditation practice. Another study with attention training used mindfulness approach in military personnel prior to deployment.[159] This study suggested that attention training was associated with enhanced working memory capacity which in turn protected military personnel from stress related symptoms. Benefits in mood and better focus can be seen after as little as four sessions.[160] More research is however needed to see if these benefits sustain for a longer time.

These positive results are in contrast to results with some of the software programs for brain training that were not found to be of much help for untrained tasks. In a large study involving 11,430 participants, brain training with computerized programs while helped in the specific skills that were trained, but the skills did not transfer to untrained tasks. Thus training attention in the "real world" might be more useful.[161] More research is needed in this area.

How practical are these attention skills?

At this point you may be asking a few important questions. How should one incorporate these exercises in their daily routine? Is it practical to practice these skills for most of the day? These are very reasonable questions.

Let me clarify an important point. **You are not expected to achieve perfection in attention.** Perfect attention is possible only within the confines of a monastery or for those who do not have to juggle as many things in life as you probably have to. However, if you could pay attention just a shade more closely than you otherwise might do, that is all what is required.

It is certainly not feasible to engage each experience during the day with all the individual senses independently or try to find one new detail all the time. Such a process will hamper efficient living. A good approach may be to follow the physical exercise model. To remain physically fit, it is ideal to have a committed exercise program along with maintaining general agility through the rest of the day. Similarly you could practice paying purposeful attention to attention for a certain time during the day (the concentrative part), and then try to sustain a slightly deeper level of attention throughout the rest of the day (the diluted part). A more intense effort is needed in the first four to six weeks of training when your attention regains its tone.

The next chapter provides some ideas to translate these skills into a daily routine. It is particularly helpful and time saving to practice attention training during the gaps within your day, such as while walking in the corridor or standing in the elevator. All it takes in those times is to make an effort to stay within the world by seeking novelty, practicing FOND, using one sensory system at a time, or sending CALF (or blessings) to people you pass by. Certainly if you have some intense planning to do then it is okay to be in the mind. But in general, we tend to plan or problem solve excessively. Avoid constant planning, problem solving, day dream-ing, negative ruminations, or random chaotic thoughts. If you bring your attention into the world in the present moment and pay purposeful non-judgmental attention to the details, even a walk from your office floor to the cafeteria could be as relaxing as a stroll in the garden. Bring your pur-poseful attention for just a tiny moment longer than what you otherwise would do, and that will be enough to bring profound changes to your mind and the brain.

Let me share with you how I try to keep my attention in the world and you can choose to modify this suggestion to your own life as you see fit.

The most vulnerable moment of my day is when I wake up in the morning. If I start my day with good control of attention, then I am more easily able to carry the momentum through the rest of the day. So as soon as I open my eyes in the morning I start a simple exercise of prayerful gratitude by finding at least five things I could be grateful for this morning. Before I know it however, my mind begins to pull me. But having resolved that I would avoid planning or problem solving the first twenty minutes of the day, I bring focus to the hum of the humidifier or the AC, bring attention to my body and feeling its stiffness give it a stretch. As I step out of the bed, I try to feel the soft carpet beneath my feet. In the washroom I look at myself with kindness. While taking shower I do not allow my mind to travel to the breakfast table. Mind certainly gives it a try, less so now than it used to earlier. I try to feel the water on my head or back and pay atten-tion to the rich fragrance of the soap or shampoo. I feel connected to the river or creek from where this water may have come. Using this simple routine has significantly enhanced the joy I perceive and the focus I am able to carry during the first half of the day.

Through the rest of the day I try to maintain a purposeful attention in the world, particularly during the gaps that the day provides (such as stand-ing in an elevator, in between seeing patients, etc.). Even during a conver-sation I sometimes remind myself to bring a deeper attention toward the person I am talking to or send CALF their way.

When I feel a negative emotion related to some past or future contingen-cy over which I have no control, I try to delay judgment and find a reason and meaning (both tangible and philosophical) behind it. I have noticed that during times of setbacks, negative ruminations can be significantly de-creased by trying to send CALF or blessings to the world at that time and if possible, expanding the diameter of existence (in the larger context of the world, my personal problems are very small, described further in chapter 43).

Attention training: will these skills really work and how fast?

You might ask how these simple exercises that guide you into paying greater attention to the world can train your brain, engage your heart and transform your life.

The process of paying attention engages the pre-frontal cortex, the higher cortical center of the brain. These exercises are as simple as the gentle flow of the Colorado River in the state of Arizona. Over the last several million years, the Colorado River has slowly and diligently carved the magnificent Grand Canyon. Quite similarly, your continuous, purposeful, and gentle efforts that anchor your attention into the world and stop feeding your mind's attention black holes will slowly but surely rightwire your brain.

At first the changes are subtle and you may not even notice them. Your friends and loved ones, however, might comment on your becoming more relaxed, happy, focused, and creative. The furrows on your temples may begin to fade (if you had any); your face might seem calmer. The quality of your sleep may improve. You may feel less tired at the end of the day and be less irritable. You may become easier to amuse and please, more gregarious, and kinder. Gradually you will yourself notice the changes within. Often the first sensation is that of feeling free and light. Your desire for coffee or other stimulants starts to loosen. As you progress, you might sense spontaneous intermittent joy without the need of an exhilarating event.

How quickly can all this happen? There is an old saying in India, "the more sugar you put in, the sweeter it will get." I do believe in the 10,000 hour rule to obtain mastery in any skill, including accessing peace and joy. If we were to practice an hour a day it would take over 25 years to graduate in the attention training course. That is a long time, and is part of the reason, some of us get discouraged. How about practicing 16 hours a day? It is very possible that with a few weeks of practice you could train your attention to be relaxed, altruistic, non-judgmental, and in-the-present-moment most of the day.

The extent of benefits and how quickly you feel them depends on two key factors: the honesty of your effort and constancy of your purpose.

If you have baseline symptoms of stress, fear, or anxiety, you might notice an improvement in the very short term. It is not uncommon for me to see the beginning of these changes very quickly with underlying anxiety significantly improving within a matter of days, not to return at least for the short term. For those learners who do not have symptoms of stress or anxiety, the changes are more subtle and take longer to notice. The first observation often is your resonating with some of these ideas. The close second is you having your own ideas about how to train attention and refine interpretations. I have seldom seen anyone not obtain any benefit at all. Training attention almost always helps decrease stress and anxiety for one simple reason—it decreases your negative ruminations. Quite often however, the progress may be slower, a bit like trying to break a wall. While you may not perceive a change, the effort is surely working bit by bit.

We swim in an ocean of excessive thoughts that all but drown us. Such thoughts, particularly those with negative ruminations tend to predispose us to stress, anxiety and depressive symptoms.[162] They are also very energy intensive. We need our thoughts, but when we carry the planning and problem solving to excess, we end up with too many open files in our brain. This crowds our perceptions and is the origin of many of the maladies we face, individually as well as collectively. If you can decrease your negative ruminations and find oases through the day where you give a brake to the momentum of planning, problem solving or day dreaming, you are very likely to attain greater peace and pleasure. The joy that is within you manifests once the overpowering thoughts are decreased. An efficient way to decrease your thoughts is to turn your attention away from the mind and engage it with the world, keeping an attitude of gratitude, compassion, acceptance, and forgiveness. Try it, what is there to lose?

21. Integrating Attention Skills

Let us integrate the skills we have discussed so far to create a practical and effective program that you can incorporate in your busy life. Remember that our focus is to absorb the novelty within the world. We are intending to cultivate an attention that is focused, relaxed, altruistic, non-judgmental, in the present moment, purposeful and sustained. I will divide this training into two phases: *Train it and Sustain it.*

* Phase I: Train it – this phase may last anywhere from 4-weeks to 24-weeks depending on your starting point and how much effort you put in it. The key component is to patiently develop an aptitude to delay judgment and pay attention to novelty. A few specific skills that might help (and are described above) are:

> 1.1 Seek novelty
> 1.2 Use one sensory system at a time
> 1.3 Find one new detail (FOND)
> 1.4 Anchor on to movement
> 1.5 Contemplate on the story
> 1.6 Attend with CALF

I realize that in your busy life it may be challenging to sustain this pattern of attention all through the day, particularly in the early phase of your effort. So here is your attention prescription.

Attention Prescription:

Find four to eight times during the day wherein you can safely and effectively practice an attention that is focused, relaxed, altruistic, non-judgmental, in the present moment, sustained and purposeful. Suggested practice time is about 15-20 minutes in each session. Optimal times for such practice include – waking up in the morning, breakfast, office meeting, presentation, lunch, arriving home from work, dinner time, family time in the evening, prior to sleeping, in the church, at a party etc. Add any other time that fits in well with your schedule. In this program I do not ask you to set aside extra time for practice away from the world. Instead I suggest you integrate this attention pattern with your daily routine. *Let go of planning, problem solving, day dreams, negative ruminations or random thoughts during this time. Avoid mind wandering. Instead pay attention to your world in the present moment using skills discussed*

above. Two specific times I recommend this practice for most learners are waking up in the morning and arriving home in the evening.

In the morning start with thoughts of gratitude as suggested earlier. In the evening, as you pull your car into the garage try to forget that you are a professional. You are just a husband or wife, father or mom, son or daughter, brother or sister, or a friend. Relate to your loved ones with a genuine interest in knowing what has transpired in their lives since you last met them. You can use any of the attention skills—that of joyful attention and saintly attention mentioned previously. An excellent approach might be to start off looking at them with CALF.

Practicing this attention pattern will most likely not take any extra time from your schedule. I have discussed my wake up schedule in the previous chapter to offer you an example. It is my hope (and observation) that for the rest of the day when not actively practicing such attention, the gains you achieve spill over. So you delay judgment and pay attention to novelty just a little bit more than what you might otherwise do throughout the day.

A very good idea is to find (at least) 20 minutes during the day when you practice a relaxing exercise and simultaneously are able to practice the joyful attention. It could be a simple stroll to the park, playing with your children or grandchildren, or physical exercise. Studies show that while we may spend a fair amount of time maintaining our yard, we seldom spend any time there.[163] So if you have a yard in your home, you can practice such an attention while spending 15-20 minutes with nature.

* Phase II: Sustain it – After the initial training, your active need for formal attention training using the skills discussed above might gradually decrease as you increasingly anchor into the present moment. The need for formal practice time decreases because this becomes your innate attention pattern. The rate of progress is very individual. Our goal is to advance from transient states of calm and joy to a transformed stage wherein we sustain calm and joy most of the day. While the word "goal" may suggest a tangible end point, the progress in this training truly never ends; a journey that will continue to challenge you and is fully worthy of your time.

The exercises we have done so far help you choose the direction, depth, and duration (3Ds) of your attention while still maintaining attention flexibility. As your attention deepens, it develops greater openness and becomes more relaxed. You become more willing to invite any and all experiences. This helps you approach rather than avoid, a strategy that engages the higher cortical center and also helps you become more effective in the world. It allows every experience to walk in "as is" with acceptance and a nonjudgmental attitude. You cultivate a purposeful effort to let go of obsessive purpose. An experience becomes complete in and of itself. This is a substantial step toward transformation.

If life has offered you many challenges, it may not be easy to let go of fear. It might take you greater time to develop this openness. However, over a period of time and with practice, this becomes a way of your being; just as you learned swimming or riding a bicycle, the initial intense effort gives way to relaxed comfort and greater efficiency. It takes time and effort to reach this state. Make no attempts to hurry or force an experience in your journey. ***Hurry annihilates quality and joy in the journey.***

Instead practice presence with love. "Presence" is a state of receptivity that takes away expectations and thus a potential for disappointments. You stand in awareness, willing to take any and all experiences and re-spond to them without judgment yet with purpose. A good example of this might be the islands of presence you experience in sports such as tennis.

What does Tennis have to do with a trained brain?

The word tennis is believed to have two origins. One of the views is that it originated from the French word *tenez,* which means here or be ready. When a well-trained tennis player receives a serve s/he has to focus on the ball, allowing few if any distractions. The movement of the ball helps with engaging the mind. This allows the player to be fully in the moment. S/he has to be patient waiting for the serve, accept wherever it lands, and then respond. Every move of the game proceeds moment by moment. Mem-ory of the previous move helps, but the most important part of the game is in this very serve—here and now. ***The game of life could be played a bit like tennis, one point at a time.***

Many distracters, however, exist for the player. The cheering from admir-ers, the opponent's attitude and disposition, the current score, contents of her own mind, etc. The key to efficient play is to focus on the signal and use the noise to enrich the experience rather than being bothered by it as a distracter. This helps deepen the focus. As you advance in your depth of attention, you stop needing to cancel any noise.

The target of focus is a matter of choice. The two choices are:

1) Directed focus – here you choose to focus on a particular aspect of your sensory experience. Most of the exercises we have done so far train this type of focus.

2) Non-directed focus – you pay attention to whatever presents to your sensory experience; everything is a signal, nothing is distracting or noise. You could cultivate this attention pattern by long term sitting practice but that will entail significant time commitment. Allow this quality of your attention to develop on its own over a period of time. This will be a gift to you for a long-term disciplined practice.

As you advance in your practice, noise does not come in the way of focus; noise itself becomes the focus. Stars on a clear night do not hide the moon, they enhance her beauty. Once in this state you are meditative and relaxed all day long, no more dependent on the details of what each day brings. Stars or moon, each are special and merit your attention.

At this point I invite you to apply the skills you have learned to your everyday life. Start with one or two skills that appeal to you the most and see how you can incorporate them within your daily activities using the "attention prescription" presented above. Your ability to pay purposeful attention and engage more deeply will likely enrich your life in more ways than one. Eventually I wish you to apply these skills to most of your day. Bringing your attention to the world throughout the day keeps you in a state of diluted meditation or prayerful focus all day long. The state of concentrative practice wherein you sit and focus on a word, thought, image, breath, or prayer is important. But of even greater importance is how you keep your disposition throughout the day. If you could approach your time at home, work, and play with an attentive meditative and prayerful spirit, you might see transformational changes to your well-being and of those around you. We will come back to further discussing this state at the end of the chapter on meditation.

Once your attention strengthens and is under your greater influence, you can also consider incorporating a few attention training exercises using your body and breath. I have summarized them in Appendix II.

Mind and Metacognition

As you attain attention flexibility and are able to choose the direction, duration, and depth of attention at will, you will notice that you increasingly become self-observant. You become more knowledgeable and aware of your own thinking process. Mind gets to know the mind and starts thinking about the thought, a process called metacognition.

I generally suggest allowing metacognition to spontaneously unfold. Forcing metacognition risks pushing you back deeper into the mind. Metacognition allows you to further understand and refine your attention. It helps learning; you begin attending to attention and intention, and become aware of awareness. Your objectivity about your own thinking process improves. This enables you to question the rationality of your thoughts with greater equanimity and thus arrive closer to the truth.

The word *sapiens* in *Homo sapiens* means wisdom. Our unique wisdom separates us from the rest of the animal species. A characteristic feature of this wisdom is our ability to think about the process and content of our thoughts and as a result the power to question and modify them. I encourage you to explore this field. The experience is like two mirrors in front of each other—with infinite images possible. The thought; the thought about the thought; the thought about the thought about the thought, and so on. When you feel you are comfortable thinking about your thoughts and are able to challenge their veracity, you are getting ready for a deeper practice of attention. Such trained attention is in the service of and intimately needs refined interpretations, which constitutes the next step.

The Next Step

As the saw sharpens and has enough force applied to it, it is important that the person using the saw use it with the right intention and knowledge. You will need the right mentorship to help apply your trained attention in a gentle pro-social way toward your health and healing, and that of others. This gentleness allows your attention to sustain and will transform it from being a dry force to one that nurtures your being and helps you perform all the miracles of daily living. *This quality to your attention is provided by refined interpretations.* Attention represented the gateway; interpretations represent the content of your awareness. Refining your interpretations provides everything your attention needs for sustenance, growth, and transformation. Training attention and refining interpretations, although described as two discrete steps, should ideally be practiced simultaneously.

We will now cover in the next seven sections principles-based skills and values that can help refine your interpretations, train your brain and engage your heart to make your brain more heartful and thus transform your life. The skills that I will address include the core values of gratitude, compassion, acceptance, forgiveness, and meaning and purpose. An additional section on cultivating a tribe (relationships) follows since relationship skills are essential to flower your full potential. The first section is introductory to refining interpretations.

SECTION V: REFINING INTERPRETATIONS: INTRODUCTION

> ## Précis
>
> **Interpretations based on higher principles and values support deeper attention, engage the brain's higher center, and open the path toward peace, joy, and resilience**
>
> **Trained interpretations make the brain more heartful**

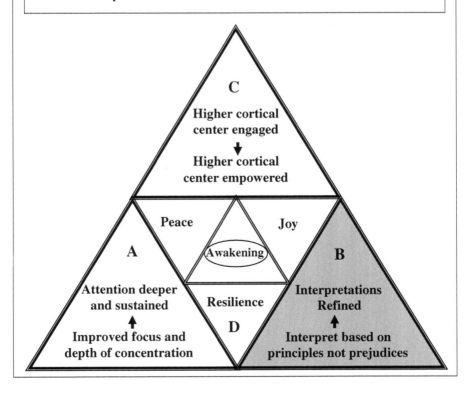

22. Refining Interpretations: Introduction

Imagine you have a cup full of nectar of life (or energy) in your heart. The fuller the cup, the better you feel and more energy you have, for yourself as well as to share. To be joyous and productive you would wish an optimal balance of withdrawals from and deposits into this cup.

The first question is what draws energy from this cup? There are two drains—the world and the self. All the responsibilities we shoulder, particularly those that feel as "onerous chores" withdraw energy from this cup. Sometimes these can be avoided, but often only to a limited extent. But there is another source of withdrawal that is even bigger. We ourselves draw down from this cup. Each of our negative thought, stressful reaction, craving and aversion empties the cup a bit. The self withdrawal has a momentum of its own and if it proceeds unregulated, our cup can get depleted very quickly. At the end of the day if you feel exhausted it is because this cup is near depleted.

Now about the deposits. The primary source of deposits are also two. World sends a few deposits, but at least in perception, not for all of us. Consider yourself extraordinarily lucky if the world around you sends consistent deposits. The most significant deposits, however, come from the self. You are your most significant depositor (as well as creditor). How do you make these deposits? Some of these deposits are related to self care, healthy diet, physical exercises, and restorative sleep. There is, however, another relatively untapped source of deposits. Your every thought of gratitude, compassion, acceptance, and forgiveness, and every action that is aligned with long term meaning makes a deposit. Meditation, prayer, sending CALF to others—these are all deposits into this cup.

Do you realize that you have the greatest influence over how full or empty is your cup. So decrease the withdrawals by changing your thinking pattern (delaying judgment, giving a positive meaning) and increase the deposits by "actively" cultivating the higher principles. Bit by bit, day by day you will notice the cup getting filled, may be even overflowing! The deposits you make with this effort (even when things are going well) will come in handy when disruptions come your way.

To fill this cup, we have so far addressed the first step that provides *gateway into* our awareness—training attention. The next step is to focus on the *content of awareness,* which entails refining interpretations by engaging the heart to make the brain more heartful (filled with love). I understand love as a combination of gratitude, compassion, acceptance, forgiveness, meaning and purpose, selflessness and interconnectedness.

Attention allows you to open your eyes and look at the world; interpretation helps process what you see. The information brought in by your trained attention needs refined processing for it to be useful and nourishing. Further, attention needs constant guidance from interpretations. This is because of two reasons—attention on its own often cannot resist the pull of the mind; and attention could be wrongly directed (such as toward an obsession or even unlawful activity). To preserve your attention, it is thus important to refine your interpretations by convincing your mind about the value of higher principles.

The Power of Thoughts

The essential ingredient that affects the content of awareness is the quality and number of your thoughts. If you were to assess your thoughts on two basic parameters, quality and number, table 22.1 illustrates the four possibilities.

Quality of thinking ⟶ — — — — — — — ↓ Number of thoughts	Negative thoughts	Positive thoughts
Few	Depressed Apathetic **A**	Attentive Mindful / Heartful Awakened **B**
Many	Anxious Angry **C**	Excited Energized Animated **D**

Table 22.1 Number and quality of your thoughts and the four types of awareness

It might help to self assess your overall disposition through the day by answering the question that follows.

Exercise 1. What percentage of your day is spent in modes represented by the four boxes?

A – Few mostly negative thoughts   _____%

B – Few mostly positive thoughts   _____%

C – Many mostly negative thoughts   _____%

D – Many mostly positive thoughts   _____%

In general, when you are anxious or angry (quadrant C) you have excessive thoughts that are often negative (the words "negative thoughts" connote thoughts that have the flavor of insecurity, loss, predominant self-focus, and excessive use of prejudices). You also have excessive thoughts when you are excited, energized, and animated (quadrant D). These states are usually in response to receiving unexpected positive energy from the world in some form. The excited state, however, is energy intensive and not sustainable over the long haul. Excited state often ends in a depressed, anxious, or even angry state if the expectations are not fully met by reality (the E-R imbalance).

Fewer thoughts alone, however, is not the answer since it won't help to have few but negative thoughts that may accompany the depressed or apathetic state (quadrant A). To arrive in quadrant B, the desirable location, you need fewer thoughts the content of which is mostly positive (positive thoughts are those that have elements of gratitude, compassion, acceptance, forgiveness, and higher meaning and purpose; generally focus on optimism and well-being; and include consideration for others). Deepened attention that decreases the number of thoughts thus needs to be coupled with refined interpretations. The additional advantage of arriving and living in quadrant B is that life in this quadrant has an elevated happiness set point. Most of us have a baseline degree of happiness toward which we tend to regress once the immediate excitement or anxiety is over. The secret for attaining greater long-term happiness is to elevate this set point, which potentially can be accomplished by deepening attention and refining interpretations.

How exactly to refine the interpretations?

You learned previously that the three attributes you mix with your sensory experience are *Principles, Prejudices, and Preferences* (3Ps). Of these three, preferences depend on the other two attributes—our portfolio of principles and prejudices interact to generate preferences. We all have a combination of principles, shortcuts, and prejudices that direct our lives. Refining interpretations entails using principles-based values and not prejudices to understand and act in the world.

Do we not know all these principles already? What is the need then to learn them? Let me take a lead from how your computer operates to answer these questions. When you buy a new computer, several programs come preloaded with it. They can be grouped into two broad categories. The first category of programs automatically activate as soon as you power up the computer for the first time. These are similar to your ingrained instincts that you are born with. The second category of programs, however, is not available in the beginning. To activate these programs, you have to actively seek them in your hard drive and purposefully run them in your system. Having activated, they go back and again sit in the hard drive but are now ready to launch any time they are needed.

These are the principles-based values that you learn in life. Some of us are fortunate enough to be effortlessly living a life engaged in the higher values. For the vast majority of us however a purposeful effort and learning is needed.

The core guiding principles that I am alluding to were eloquently spelled out by Thomas Jefferson in 1776 in the opening statement of the Declaration of Independence, which I will repeat here, *"We hold these truths to be self-evident, that all men (and women) are created equal, that they are endowed by their Creator with certain unalienable Rights, that among these are Life, Liberty and the Pursuit of Happiness."* Another lovely expression of these principles is in these words from the Holy Bible, *"Fix your thoughts on what is true, and honorable, and right, and pure, and lovely, and admirable. Think about things that are excellent and worthy of praise (Philippians 4:8, New Living Translation).* It is these principles that provide higher values and their derived skills. These values are those of gratitude, compassion, acceptance, forgiveness, higher meaning and purpose in life, kindness, honesty, equanimity, humility, and love.

The origin of prejudices is our tendency to create useful shortcuts. Shortcuts within limits are helpful for survival. However, when shortcuts cross a certain threshold, are over-generalized, and get contaminated with an inordinate focus on serving the self in exclusion of everyone else, they degenerate into prejudices. These prejudices create rigid profiles of the world—our internal maps that interrupt the process of attention by forcing a pattern of selfish thoughts and behavior. These internal maps become concretized because of our ego that gets identified with them. They prevent us from learning new things and revising our interpretations. We become effectively blind to our blind spots. A life that is mostly governed by prejudices tends to be full of stress and anxiety.

Two common attributes of prejudices are their self-focus and their tendency to categorize most entities into good-bad duality. It isn't easy to let go of good-bad duality—the tendency to assign such values is effortless, instinctive, efficient, and deeply hardwired in us. Thus asking you to completely shed your prejudices may not work and could be counterproductive. The energy that is stored within prejudices cannot be easily destroyed. It can, however, be transformed. So do not push yourself to annihilate prejudices. Instead make a consistent effort to imbibe principles-based skills. You will notice that these values will slowly replace and transform the prejudices from inside out.

Critical to your progress is to develop a willingness to loosen your internal maps and your identification with them. We need to consider a map just as what it is—simply a map—that can be edited or deleted if a newer more refined version is available. A useful entry point is to change the tendency to cling on to good-bad duality. Gratitude, compassion and acceptance help you transcend this limitation. When anchored in these three attributes you accept an experience in its purity just as it is. This fosters inner equanimity. Anchoring in higher meaning and purpose in life provides you the willpower to stay the course, particularly when an alternative option that has the elements of excessive self-focus entices you by its ability to provide immediate gratification. *Most short-term gratifications do not lead to long-term well-being.*

The decision to align your preferences and actions for long-term well-being rather than short-term gratifications is mostly in your hands. Herein is the hope for our transformation. Once you realize that our instinctive preferences are often undesirably prejudice-based, you get empowered to choose otherwise. *Preferences that are aligned with principles are the altruistic preferences.* Altruistic preferences respect the needs and values of others. With such preferences, your actions are not just for the limited self, they are for the welfare of your family, your neighborhood, your religion, your race, your state, your country, the entire humanity, all life forms. You think and act with awareness and are not limited by your instincts. You are better able to regulate your reactions to your experiences—inner as well as outer. With this transformation your definition of self expands and progressively includes larger numbers until you feel you are a citizen of the world and care about the whole.

Simultaneous with this change in your preferences and actions, one wonderful transformation happens—your brain rightwires. With gratitude, compassion, acceptance, forgiveness, and higher meaning and purpose in life, the higher center in the brain engages (we saw the research evidence of it in chapter 14). The negative thoughts of the past stored in your subconscious (amygdala) gradually wither away. The cortical center is thus empowered while the limbic center is disempowered. You become progressively free from ignorance and hardwired to live your life by these principles. You acquire wisdom and over a period of time with constancy of practice reach a state of self realization.

A self realized person is self actualized. Such a person recognizes the preciousness of the world and each individual life form, feels connected to the world through the self, derives peace and joy from this connection, has almost given up the egotist self, yet recognizes the self as the instrument to continue the path of wisdom and love. A self realized person has shed ignorance and feels complete and free. Self realization is achieved with the right balance of wisdom, love and effort and provides the optimal milieu for grace to manifest. Self realization is the goldilocks state between self abnegation and hedonism. You experience dispassion borne out of discrimination and joy out of realization of interconnectedness. In this state you enhance the experience of the present moment and its contents with greater love—a state of heartfulness. *"Do unto others as you would have them do unto you,"* is a primary guiding principle of a self realized person.

With realization and the resulting transformation, higher principles no longer remain a goal—they become a way of your life. Your eyes, nose, mouth, hands, heart, tongue, skin—all remember these principles—not just your brain and mind. In a state of true freedom you deeply love even when the feeling is not immediately reciprocated. You are freed from the limitations of the ego. You have become fully what you are capable of.

Such is the transformation. It takes time and purposeful effort. But once you cross a threshold there is no going back. The gains you achieve are written by non-erasable markers. Knowledge leads to practice and practice to habit. Effort leads to growth and growth to transformation.

A Practical Program:

One of the ways to embody higher principles is to incorporate them into a structured program. Remember that what you pay attention to expands. You will find what you look for.   Initially in training you have to actively (sometimes artificially) pay attention to the positive. It may involve exercising a level of control. With time you will instinctively start paying greater attention to the positive aspects of your life.

One approach I find particularly useful is to follow a daily theme assigning one value for each day in a weekly program. A suggested sequence is:

Monday – Gratitude
Tuesday – Compassion
Wednesday – Acceptance
Thursday – Meaning and Purpose
Friday – Forgiveness
Saturday – Celebration
Sunday – Reflection / Prayer

Let me share with you how I apply this to my life.

On Mondays I focus on gratitude. I start my day with five thoughts of gratitude and throughout the day, particularly when my attention is pulled by the default network of my brain toward autobiographical thinking, I try to actively practice gratitude. Walking among patients through the hallways on a Monday, my first thought is gratitude—for their trust and the respect they accord to our profession. Toward colleagues and fellow care providers I focus on gratitude for their kindness. I feel gratitude toward my wife for being such a good anchor for our family. I try to change my inner and outer dialog using gratitude as the central theme (see below – one helpful trick).

On Tuesdays, the day of compassion, I start my day with three thoughts of compassion, for someone I love, for someone I barely know and for someone I find difficult to love. I focus on the reality that all of us experience suffering of one form or the other and thus deserve causeless compassion from each other. This is particularly so for patients who might feel vulnerable and often have a sense of lack of control, uncertainty, or the realization of finiteness. It is thus appropriate to harbor instinctive natural compassion for everyone. A simple way I practice compassion through the day is by sending a silent "bless you" to people I happen to meet. Compassion also allows kindness to flow more easily and fully.

On Wednesdays, I focus on acceptance, primarily living the day accepting myself as I am and accepting others as they are. A commitment to acceptance delays judgment and allows time for the higher centers of the brain to engage which is particularly helpful when I process an unpleasant event. Acceptance allows me to be kind, fair and rational even in the middle of a day that may have invited chaos. Acceptance fosters inner equanimity which stops me from fighting myself and saves considerable energy to respond to the external challenge.

Thursday is the day of meaning and purpose. On this day I focus on the primary long-term meaning and purpose of my life, which is to be an agent of service and love. On Thursday, I focus more on the energy that I should send to others rather than on the energy that might or might not be coming my way. Something akin to what John F. Kennedy said, *"Ask not what your country can do for you; ask what you can do for your country."* So Thursday is the low expectation day, a day of humility. It is the day to be pleasantly surprised and excited about each packet of energy coming my way. Pleasure is easier to find if I decrease the threshold of what will make me happy.

Friday is the day of forgiveness. I start this day forgiving anyone who might hurt my feelings today. I also forgive myself for my past mistakes, known and unknown. By starting the day with the commitment of forgiveness for self and others, I am less self conscious and more accepting of any critique (with related opportunity for growth) that comes my way. If a learner has a significant hurt related to a previous transgression, I suggest we be slow and deliberate in progressing in forgiveness and focus on living just one day a week (i.e. Friday) in forgiveness.

Saturday is the day of celebration and Sunday of reflection and prayer. Celebration and prayer are related to your individual life style and beliefs so I will not go into greater specifics regarding the same. Suffice it to say that keeping a general flavor of altruism is likely to enhance peace, joy and resilience, through work as well as play.

If you keep these themes with you through the day as suggested, you will start doing ordinary things extraordinarily. Character is more determined by how you relate with the common and mundane and not particularly when the spotlight is on you.

We will discuss each of these individual skills (values) in the sections that follow. A few self affirmations I find useful to remember particularly in the morning are summarized below:

- Gratitude: I am grateful for all that this day will bring
- Compassion: I will be compassionate toward everyone I meet today; I will treat myself with kindness today
- Acceptance: Everyone I meet today I will try to accept them just as they are; I will live the day today accepting myself just as I am
- Higher Meaning: I will live the day today by the higher meaning in my life
- Forgiveness: I will try to forgive anyone who might hurt my feelings today; I forgive myself today for my past mistakes

You might ask, why not practice gratitude on Tuesday also. The purpose of providing this structure is to have a particular focus for each day and is not directed to exclude other values. In fact with practice, you will realize that each of these values converge toward the same point. They are different flavors of one core value—that of love.

Further, the suggested practice is not intended to be nerdy or to make us rigid. If you find a particular skill difficult to practice, you can substitute it for another that is easier to embody. Some learners have shared with me that they primarily practice gratitude the entire week. That is just fine. What I provide here is a roadmap. You can carve out your journey the way you like.

One Helpful Trick:

Before we immerse ourselves in each of the skills, I wish to share with you one trick I often use. The trick is not to end a sentence on a negative note but use the daily theme to give it a positive twist. For example, if I do not get a research grant funded and get a humbling review outlining all my ignorance, here is how my inner dialog might progress in three phases:

Phase I – Early response:
"Too bad I did not get the grant"
"Too bad the reviewer gave an unfavorable review"

Phase II – Quick rephrasing:
"Too bad the grant was reviewed unfavorably, but, I am grateful to the reviewer for their thorough review and for educating me" (related thought – they are not biased but are just doing their job).

"Too bad I did not get the grant, but, I hope the application that got funded was more promising than mine" (related thought – may the best team win)

"Too bad I did not get the grant, but, with all its deficiencies that now I know (but could not see earlier) may be we were not ready to do the research" (related thought – patients deserve the best)

Phase III – Final conclusion:
I am grateful for the critique
I am grateful to the reviewer for their time and effort
I am glad that learning from the critique, I will be able to improve my research design and conduct a better study
I am grateful I did not get the grant

The quicker I can go through these three phases the less my suffering. Further, this enhances my ability to learn from the experience rather than feeling dejected. In this context it is best not to be excessively self conscious or self absorbed, but learn to accept critique graciously, keeping a conviction that it is well meaning, honest, and for your good.

If you are not gracious in receiving critiques, you may stop receiving meaningful feed backs but only get a few sugar coated words, a perfect recipe for stagnation.

Notice that during the quick rephrasing phase, creative use of the word "but" and connecting it with a positive twist helps. This ability depends on how quickly you are able to quiet your amygdala and bring pre-frontal cortex on line. In fact there is good scientific basis for the "one helpful trick."

Whenever we recall a particular memory and reconsolidate it, the memory is vulnerable at that time and can be changed. At the time of recall, the memory can either be reconsolidated or weakened.[164, 165] The latter phenomenon, that scientists describe as extinction, is particularly useful to modulate the memory of fear and is hosted by the pre-frontal cortex and related brain areas.[42, 43, 166] By giving a positive twist to our memory, we tap into our brain processes to positively influence all future recalls of this memory. Being able to reappraise the challenges in a positive light could indeed be a gift to the self.

I have often been asked the basis of using this particular sequence for practice i.e. Why gratitude for Monday, compassion for Tuesday etc.? It is simple and is related to ease of practice. Almost all of us can find something to be grateful for. Most of us can also practice compassion. Acceptance is a bit more difficult, meaning takes a bit of greater effort to find and understand, and forgiveness is by far the most difficult particularly for the more serious transgressions. We wish to start with success. Hence we begin with gratitude on Mondays, which is where we will now initiate the next phase of our journey together.

SECTION VI: GRATITUDE

Précis

The only two things you may not have borrowed from the universe and are yours to share are your love and an honest thank you

Gratitude allows you to pay back in thoughts and feelings, when you cannot pay back in kind

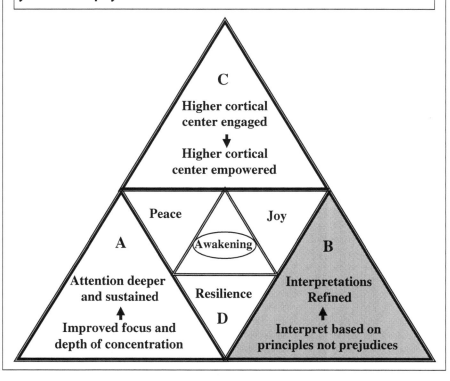

23. What is Gratitude?

A saint once sat for several years in intense meditation seeking *nirvana*. Impressed by his austerities and devoted practice, he was visited by an angel who praised his efforts. The angel, however, said she could not give him the boon of salvation since there were many who deserved to share the benefits of his efforts. Hearing this denial, the saint was disappointed since he believed he had practiced unassisted all these years. He sought an explanation. The angel gently asked the saint if he had ever thanked the rock that provided him the support as he sat, or the wind he breathed, the tree that gave him fruit, the soil that nourished the tree, the rain that nourished the soil. The list was endless. The saint realized his mistake. His ego had prevented him from recognizing and expressing gratitude for all the help he had received from uncountable elements of nature. Having learned his ignorance, he cultivated gratitude in his heart. With sincere gratitude he thanked Mother Nature and all her elements every day. His debt was eventually repaid. In time the saint was duly rewarded.

What is ordinary today was miraculous and unthinkable yesterday. Beyond the known and palpable, innumerable elements of nature are supporting your individual and our collective efforts—right from corals in the ocean to ice caps on Antarctica. Everything we receive in life is either a loan or a gift from nature. We all carry a heavy debt of the blessings bestowed upon us. Who will we borrow from to repay all this debt? Nature itself? There is, however, a precious and profound gift that exclusively belongs to us and may go unused unless we share it. That gift is our love expressed as an honest thank you. Our honest feelings of gratitude immersed in gentle humility are the primary reward the universe needs to keep providing.

A key to long-term successful relationships is a balanced exchange of energy. The energy could be in the form of tangible things appreciable by senses. The energy also could be the precious and abstract intangibles such as love, joy, and thankfulness. The simple expressions of love may provide you greater meaning than anything material. A child's hugs, smiles, and kisses more than repay for all the efforts and hard work of her parents. Gratitude as a feeling and expression is thus an effective way to reciprocate the gifts you have received and might receive in the future. Before we consider the benefits of gratitude and invite a few skills to practice gratitude would it not be appropriate to try and answer a simple question, what is gratitude and how does it differ from indebtedness?

What is Gratitude?

Gratitude is a positive emotion and represents acknowledging the blessings you have received or might receive and showing appreciation for the same. Gratitude is a combination of humility, grace, love, and acceptance. Gratitude is your moral memory. A useful distinction can be drawn between gratitude and indebtedness. In the movie *The Godfather*, Don Vito Corleone throws favors at others with the intention of making them feel indebted. He helps Enzo the baker stay in the U.S.; the baker later paid back the debt as he feigned a gun in his pocket and stood guard at the hospital entrance protecting the Don.

Indebtedness is a useful construct in business transactions. However, indebtedness may make you feel heavy; you may feel weighed down by the help you have received. It is because of this lack of distinction between indebtedness and gratitude that people perhaps find themselves uncomfortable in expressing or cultivating gratitude.

Gratitude is a much purer feeling. Gratitude is spiritual. Gratitude flows naturally, without expectations and out of love. There is no fear or hierarchy in gratitude, nor is there any desire. You do not express gratitude to get more. You show it out of pure love at being treated with grace and compassion. In research studies intention of the benefactor had considerable influence on the feelings of the recipient. As expected, favors done for unselfish reasons evoked a greater feeling of gratitude compared to selfish favors.[167]

Gratitude is not outcome dependent. It originates primarily in the intention. It is not a result of benefit, it is a positive attitude. You have gratitude not only for what people do, but simply for who they are. Thus gratitude is non-conditional. It is being thankful for every experience that life brings to you, good or bad, realizing that every experience provides you an opportunity to learn and grow.

24. Why Practice Gratitude?

The wisdom in practicing gratitude seems self-evident. However, it will help to formally collate the potential advantages of practicing gratitude in one place.

Gratitude Keeps Ego in Check

Gratitude with an attitude is no gratitude; what we need is an attitude of gratitude. An essential ingredient that supports the feeling and expression of gratitude is humility. Perception and expression of gratitude itself also makes you more humble. Humility is a true appreciation of the principle, *"all men (women and children) are created equal; they are endowed by their Creator with certain unalienable rights; that among these are life, liberty, and the pursuit of happiness."* Humility is conducive to keeping a world focus and prevents developing excessive arrogance and pride.

Recognize the difference between true internal humility and keeping ego in check because of fear or lack of control. If you leave your puppy at home and come back to find that she has torn off your sheet and created a mess you are likely to find her subdued and probably hiding beneath a bed. This behavior is not necessarily humility. She is simply fearful! Meekness that comes from loss of power or influence is not humility. True humility does not originate in fear or defeat. Humility is a sign of strength and thrives in success. Humility itself increases the chance of success.

Pride hath a fall said Shakespeare. One way to prevent a fall is to check the pride and transform it into honor and humility.

Gratitude Helps with Acceptance

I am sure your grandma must have read you stories about hidden treasures and magical kingdoms. These treasures are almost always guarded by vicious serpents, dragons, or, as in the movie *Mackenna's Gold*, by spirits and gods. Could it be that these treasures really are life's lessons that you can learn and imbibe only after you prevail over the serpents of challenges and failures? Success gives you pleasure, while failure provides the opportunity to grow. Gratitude allows you to acknowledge and accept the preciousness of both.

Untrained mind is often dominated by unsatisfied wants masquerading as needs. In this state we become oblivious of the blessings that have come our way. Gratitude allows you to recognize the blessings you have received. You ponder over the meaning and purpose that others provide to your life. Gratitude fills your cup of desire so you internally feel content. In this state you do not struggle with emptiness or its related concern of missing out on life. When feeling nourished, you are more likely to have equanimity and thus an acceptance of even adversity. Such acceptance and gratitude give you the gift of peace and joy.

You are blessed when you are content with just who you are, no more no less. That is the moment you find yourselves proud owners of everything that can't be bought (Matthew 5:5 MSG).

Gratitude Helps Healing

Over the years working with tens of thousands of patients, I have found one distinct predictor (amongst a few others) that helps me foresee which patients are likely to get better relatively sooner. It is their attitude of gratitude. The greater the appreciation I notice in a patient for the care they have received or for other little gifts of life in general, the better the effect of treatment. This deeper feeling of gratitude reflects their inner faith and acceptance.

Your gratitude is also noticed by others. I have consistently found hospital staff noticing expressions of gratitude and fondly remembering the more grateful patients. In a resource restricted world, you are likely to find greater geniality and genuine care if you harbor a feeling of gratitude and express it generously.

Gratitude Might Help You Get a Better Tip!

In an interesting study performed in an upscale restaurant in a large Northeastern city, a server wrote on the backs of the checks either nothing, "thank you," or "thank you" plus her first name.[168] The experimenters were interested in knowing if any of these strategies would change the amount of the tip. The study showed that the addition of "thank you" increased the tip percentages; personalization by adding the first name had no additional effect. By writing thank you the server sent an extra packet of energy toward her guests to which they reciprocated in kind.

In general the more thankful you are, the more reasons you will find to be thankful about. What you focus on expands, what you engage you empower. If you appreciate the love you already have you get greater love. This purpose of receiving more, however, is not purely for selfish fulfillment. The purpose is to share more with others who may not be so fortunate. When you learn to graciously share, somehow the energy finds you an optimal conduit for distributing itself.   The feeling of gratitude works as a magnet to invite the gifts of life that you can then share.

The Obstacles to Gratitude

The relative lack of appreciation for our blessings is for one simple reason—we take what we have for granted. We take our loved ones, our job, our health, our life for granted. We do not purposefully pause to contemplate on how each of the loved one and friend in our life is actually a work of a miracle. Often this unawareness is not willful, but simply instinctive. Quite often we realize the preciousness of our benedictions only when we begin to lose them. More patients quit smoking after a diagnosis of cancer, heart attack, or lung disease than on their own. It is only when the reality of finiteness touches us in the form of a serious diagnosis or some other loss that we might begin to appreciate the preciousness of each moment. One obvious purpose such a disruption serves is to act as a reminder to enhance engagement with the here and now. A moment of disruption thus is actually a moment of great opportunity that can start us on a path toward transformation.

I was once seeing a young woman in her late thirties with a diagnosis of metastatic colon cancer. I greatly respect her for her insight and resilience. One of her statements that I will never forget was, "Why do we have to wait for such a diagnosis to start thinking about these higher values?" I fully agree. We should not wait for a disruption to start the path of transformation. We should begin the journey on our own. You could call this beginning a positive disruption, wherein the ego and mind within us realize that there is more to life than running the show primarily to assuage our appetites.

Part of the reason we miss opportunities toward growth is due to our propensity to quickly revise expectations. If your lottery ticket hits a jackpot of $100 million you will be elated. However, if a few days later you learn that you are one among twenty winners, you will likely be disappointed. The drop in your imagined bank account by $95 million is too much of a jolt to let you enjoy the real $5 million! Several studies show that the intensity of negative emotions associated with loss is much more potent than the intensity of emotions associated with gain of the same entity.[169] This is often called the Endowment effect (development of a sense of entitlement to the object we acquire). Recognizing this nature of the brain and the mind and preventing ourself from revising expectations too soon might help us find greater gratitude for the everyday little things around us that we sometimes take for granted. In the words of Albert Einstein, *"There are two ways to live: you can live as if nothing is a miracle; or you can live as if everything is a miracle."* The truth is every little thing around us is a miracle; something we could be grateful for.

Also very often, desire sits at the leading edge of achievements. Our attention is often buried in figuring out what we need for continued growth, with minimal time invested in celebrating the previous and present success, and similarly little to no time applied in perceiving or expressing gratefulness for this success. There is a good biological reason for our propensity to need greater success for incremental happiness. It relates to the functioning of the reward pathways in the brain that quickly adapt to a previous reward and need incremental level of achievement to get activated.[170, 171] The wants thus become the needs.

Human mind however can also revise expectations the other way around. Over a decade ago I was caring for a very sick patient who had received a kidney transplant that was being rejected by his body. He was a very wealthy and popular businessman with many accomplishments. I was moved when, with tears in his eyes, he told me his most cherished dream of life. His dream was that for once his kidneys would produce a bladder full of urine and he could walk to the restroom to empty it. A few years of illness had drastically brought down the expectations of a previously vivacious and active man.

There is nothing around you that is not of value. The first car we bought was for $1,000; it was a dream come true. We welcomed the car in our life, applied sacrament to bless it, took pictures, and sent those pictures all around the world to proudly show to our loved ones the new addition to our family. I was enormously grateful to have my own car. The previous owner, however, may have been only too glad to get rid of what probably was of no use to him. Value is thus a relative term—I am told the value of a glass of water if served on the moon is about the same as that of an equal weight of gold. If you keep your gratitude contingent on finding material value, you may push yourself away from appreciating the everyday pleasures that fill up your life. A more generous disposition of unconditional gratitude is likely to be more rewarding.

A Few Research Studies with Gratitude

I will present a summary of information from a few research studies that have evaluated the effect of an attitude of gratitude on outcomes related to well-being and health. In general a feeling of gratitude is associated with better health outcomes.

- In a study involving Vietnam War veterans, a disposition of gratitude predicted greater daily positive mood, percentage of pleasant days, and self-esteem. Gratitude was correlated with lower risk of post traumatic stress disorder and increased daily well-being.[172]

- In studies employing interpersonal emotional training, feelings of gratitude were shown to increase individual efforts to assist a benefactor even at personal cost.[173]

- A study compared three groups of patients assigned to focus on hassles, gratitude, or neutral life events. Focusing on gratitude was noted to significantly improve well-being, particularly improved overall mood. Thus a conscious focus on blessings may help with well-being and provide emotional and interpersonal benefits.[174]

- In a series of four studies, authors found that self and observer ratings of grateful disposition were associated with well-being, better emotional health, greater pro-social behaviors, religiousness/spirituality, and less envy and materialistic attitude.[175]

- In a series of two studies investigators reported that a variety of positive mood traits were related to higher mean levels of gratitude across three weeks.[176]

To summarize the research studies, a feeling of gratitude is associated with better health outcomes including:

- Positive mood
- Better self esteem
- Lower risk of post traumatic stress disorder
- Well being

I hope the foregoing has offered you a convincing argument about the value of inviting gratitude into your life. Next we will go over a few simple practice exercises.

25. How to Practice Gratitude

The three most important aspects toward practicing gratitude are: 1) intellectually be convinced about the innumerable ways you have been blessed; 2) cultivate gratitude as a way of life; and 3) when life's challenges knock at your door, as they invariably will make sure you remember all of your blessings at that time.   Let us look at some formal exercises you can learn to invite gratitude in your daily activities.

Exercise 1. Say "thank you" in the morning
When you wake up each morning, even before you open your eyes, think of five things you could be grateful for and spend the first thirty seconds silently expressing gratitude. These could be such simple things as a soft carpet, a warm room, a good night's sleep, toothpaste, electricity in your home; or might include people around you such as your spouse, children, friends, or siblings; or even gifts of touch, vision, faith, or anything else that might come to your mind. All these are true blessings that we tend to take for granted.

Be grateful even for what might seem unpleasant. If your spouse snores, rather than focusing on the unpleasantness of the sound, try to be thankful for the breath that is giving them vitality and life. This might allow you to find meaning in it rather than keeping all your focus on the negative aspect of the sound. What you pay attention to expands. Pure and intense love is grateful for both pleasant and unpleasant.

I witnessed the transformative power of gratitude most transparently in the experience of a patient. She suffered a serious life threatening diagnosis, experienced loneliness through it, and at the same time was also under considerable financial duress.   Early in the course of her illness she experienced severe stress but with training in the two steps outlined here, over a period of few weeks, she transformed into a new evolved being. She reached a point wherein she had to sell her home to pay all her bills. When I asked her about her inner feelings, the words she spoke I will never forget. She said, *"Dr. Sood, earlier I would have mourned the loss of our home. Now I have gratitude that I at least had a home I could sell."* I deeply respect her faith and resilience. How can suffering find a place within such a resilient being?

Exercise 2. Say "thank you" during the day
At least once every day find a reason to express appreciation to someone.
You could do this by sending a card, a gift, a favorable e-mail, or just plain

heartfelt words of "thank you." If none of these are feasible on a given day, you could send a silent thank you message to them.

Be grateful for the past, the present and the future; or the material, intangible, and spiritual. Be grateful for those who help you and also those who need your help. Be grateful for life's pleasures and lessons. Say to yourself today, *"I will live my day today in gratitude for whatever this day will bring, life's pleasures or life's lessons."* See if carrying this intention makes your day a little happier.

Exercise #3: Say "thank you" at night
As you close your day prior to your sleep, find at least one thing you could be thankful for.

Exercise #4: Include gratitude in your prayer
Start and end your prayer with words of gratitude.

Exercise #5: Gratitude as a way of being
Bring your life partner into your awareness. Think of all their qualities. Be grateful for those qualities. Now think about their weaknesses. Find ways in which those weaknesses have helped you grow and become strong. Be grateful for those weaknesses. Be thankful for who s/he is. Progressively cultivate this feeling for everyone in your life. Keep gratitude as a background theme in everyday experiences. Gradually you reach a stage where you are forever anchored in gratitude irrespective of whether the world rewards you in kind or not.

I once heard someone say, "Thank God for my spouse's weakness. But for those they would have been married to someone else!"

Exercise #6: Be grateful for the future
Meditate on your loved ones and everyone else who might come into your life. Thank them unconditionally for the blessings and challenges they will bring to you in the future.

Exercise #7: Gratitude exercise with your child
Try this exercise with your children, grand children or friend's children for practicing gratitude as well as exercising their brain. Ask them to note three things they are thankful for starting from each alphabet (A to Z). For each thing or person, ask them why they feel that is important to them.

What is boring and ordinary in your life actually is vital and precious. Often, the true value of an ordinary object or a person in your life is realized only when you miss them. Do not let that happen to you. Perceive and express gratitude and spread greater love before the time comes to say good bye. You will live a happier life that way. No doubt.

SECTION VII: COMPASSION

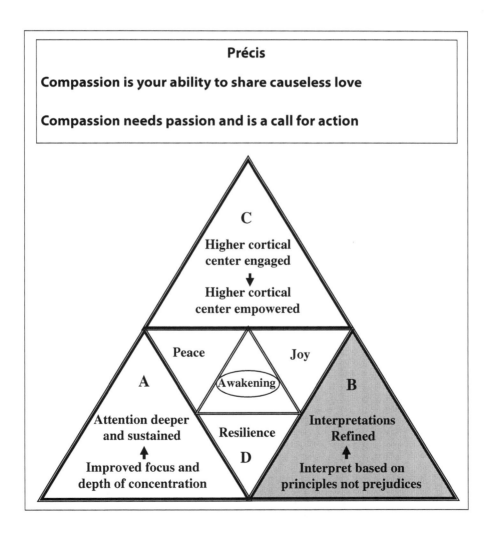

Précis

Compassion is your ability to share causeless love

Compassion needs passion and is a call for action

C
Higher cortical center engaged
↓
Higher cortical center empowered

Peace   Joy

A
Awakening   B

Attention deeper and sustained   Resilience   Interpretations Refined

↑   D   ↑

Improved focus and depth of concentration   Interpret based on principles not prejudices

26. Compassion: Concepts and Ideas

From the tiniest of birds to the strongest of men, each of them are creating and uncreating what may seem like imperfections to their own eyes. Looking at these reflections, with a constant struggle to make it better, all of them are fighting their own little battles. One force that can help ease their burden and provide wind beneath their wings is your compassion.

Compassion is the very nature of your being. When you have a headache, your entire body mounts a response to decrease your suffering. Hands come and massage the painful area. Legs walk over to get the medicine. The stomach might actually get sensitive and sore absorbing this medicine. Hands, legs, stomach, and other organs do not pause for a moment when they see the need to help—nor do they expect anything in return. You heal because your individual body parts do not consider themselves separate. They are a part of the whole that is you. The whole that is you has many parts. The whole that is this world also has many parts, with one of them being you.

We all are parts of this world, separate yet connected in many ways. Your individual pain is absorbed by the collective whole. In turn you cannot remain unaffected by others' pain and misery. Once you wake up to it, compassion seems but a natural response to all the pain and suffering in the world irrespective of its bearer. No matter how strong you are presently, you have had moments in life where you needed the grace of someone's compassion to reach here. Your moments of weakness, vulnerability, and ignorance may sometimes be within your awareness, at other times not so palpable. Weak, unwell, vulnerable, defenseless, lonely—you may have been in each of these states at some point. It is the compassion and care of others that pulled you through. What is compassion and how does it differ from empathy?

Compassion and empathy are closely related terms. Compassion (co = together; passion = strong feeling; to suffer with) is an ability to feel the suffering of others—often with a desire to help. Empathy is the capacity to understand another person's experience from within their perspective.

Compassion is a divine force within man, a manifestation of love, selflessness, and a strong intention to serve. The life of Christ and Buddha epitomized compassion. The golden rule, *"Do unto others as you would have them do unto you"* is accepted and taught in all the religions, although the expressions might be different. All but one of the 114 chapters of the Holy Quran start with the statement, "In the name of God, Most Gracious, Most Merciful." Jewish tradition talks about *Rahmana* the compassionate. The law code of Manu in Hinduism states, *"Wound not others, do no one injury by thought or deed, utter no word to pain thy fellow creatures."* Compassion is the *Karuna* of the Buddhists; *Daya* of the Hindus. Compassion is a common thread that joins all the major religions in the world including Baha'i, Buddhism, Christianity, Confucianism, Hinduism, Islam, Jainism, Judaism, Shinto, Sikhism, Taoism, and Zoroastrianism.

Compassion is a call for action

Distinguish between *attitude of compassion* and *practice of compassion*. Attitude is the general disposition you carry, while the actual practice is what you actively seek out and do every day. It is not enough to intellectually understand or feel the pain and suffering of others and do nothing. True compassion entails putting energy behind the feelings. ***Kind is as kind does.*** This needs courage, strength, and motivation. Compassion is truly a call to correct the injustice, remove pain and suffering, and bring peace to those not so fortunate within the means possible and reasonable. If, however, you cannot do anything material, you can at least include those who suffer in your prayers. Praying for others is a tangible response that finds its origin in compassion.

A feeling of compassion takes the focus away from everyday stresses experienced by the self. Putting energy behind your feeling of compassion elevates your mood. When you share your gifts and blessings, your system tells you that you have plenty. The universe then might find you a good channel to share its resources. As a result, the more you share, the more you might receive so you can share. Feelings of compassion might thus be intimately related to success.

Compassion in Medicine

A recent report suggested that care in hospitals could be more compassionate.[177] In another study on physicians starting their training, at the time of beginning their internship training, physicians exhibited less tension, depression, anger, fatigue, and confusion and more vigor, perspective, and empathic concern than general adult and college student populations. However, five months into internship these physicians developed significant worsening in depression, anger, and fatigue symptoms with associated reduction in empathic concern.[178] In a study involving observation of 264 outpatient encounters in patients with cancer, in only 29%

of the encounters were physicians noted to demonstrate empathy.[179] The good news is that it does not take too long to relearn these skills. A study with medical students and residents showed that empathy skills can be improved with a single communication skills workshop that reminds them of this essential trait.[180]

Further, once learned, empathy skills tend to stay for the long term, with the effect continuing up to three years after training.[181] Empathy skills do decline with time, however, suggesting that continuing refreshers might be needed.

Connectedness and Compassion

A precious trait within us that helps cultivate compassion is our ability to find a common ground with the other person. Developing a degree of identity and connection enhances compassion. Often even a similarity in experience and being able to identify with what the other is going through can help. In a study, participants were asked to read four separate stories and rate their empathy.[182] Self-report of prior similar experience was associated with greater empathy for the persons in the stories. Thus finding similarity with the others in any way is likely to increase empathy. In another study testing a similar phenomenon, measures of empathy for new-mothers were assessed for women who had never been pregnant vs. women who were pregnant with their first child, or who had just given birth to their first child. In this study women who just had or were experiencing having a baby had greater empathy and much better understanding of the new-mothers.[183]

In a series of three studies, greater compassion was associated with sense of similarity to weak or vulnerable others compared to strong others.[184] In a research study, greater helping intentions were observed when the participants belonged to the same cultural group compared to those not belonging to the same group.[185] Increased exposure to the target improved empathy in another study.[186] Even exposure to a single member of a stigmatized group can improve attitudes toward the group as a whole.[187] In a study involving 370 university students, feelings of empathy were assessed in response to a student describing a distressful experience.[188] Stronger empathy was reported if the student belonged to the in-group rather than an out-group university. However, if an in-group norm was activated for an out-group student, greater positive attitude developed toward the out-group student also. Finding similarity with others thus is likely to increase your compassion, an attribute we will use in the exercises below.

Another interesting observation is that empathy for ingroup vs. outgroup is associated with different brain activation patterns. Ingroup empathy activated medial prefrontal cortex, while anterior cingulate cortex and bilateral insula were more activated for outgroup empathy.[98] Further, greater medial prefrontal cortex activation (higher brain center) was associated with greater empathy and altruistic motivation. Research suggests that compassion may be a fully integrated response with its own unique neurological pathway.[189]

Several theories suggest that compassion serves the purpose of cooperation and to protect the weak and those who suffer. Compassion recognizes suffering, stimulates behavior to decrease suffering, and provides the person a deeper understanding of suffering among others.

An accurate summary of the above observations could be that to generate compassion for the others, particularly the weak and vulnerable others, it helps you to find similarity with them. *The realization that we are different arrows launched from the same bow allows compassion to naturally blossom.*

Phases of Compassion

Expression of compassion is a multiphase process with at least three distinct phases that meld into each other. The first phase is inner, wherein you develop compassionate feelings. The second phase is your ability to communicate this feeling (in words or actions), with the final phase being the ability of the receiver to accept it. A slip at any of these levels may lead to an incomplete expression of compassion.

In a study involving emergency room physicians, focus only on the physical symptoms, sub-optimal communication, and a lack of realization that patients were seeking empathy was observed.[190] Such lack of awareness of others' needs is likely to provide significant barriers in the expression of inner compassion. If the empathic feelings are not expressed and not registered, they serve very little purpose. They are like a closed book that is well preserved but never read.

Compassion can be significantly increased with training. In a study involving physicians, providing training in communication skills improved the mean measures of empathy by up to 50 percent.[191]

Universality of Suffering

It is not uncommon for me to hear patients tell me in the office, *"Doctor I am the only one who seems to be suffering, everyone else sitting in the lobby seemed okay."* There is some truth to this perception. Part of the reason we cannot see others' suffering even though we are fully aware of ours is because while we can feel our inside we can only perceive others' outside. Also our society does not promote unbridled expression of inner emotions, mostly for a good reason. The reality however is that if most of us feel this way, then suffering is truly universal, isn't it? Almost everyone you run into each day is fighting a little battle of his/her own. A vast majority of us experience negative emotions each day. So who all should you feel compassionate for? Everyone, isn't it? With active cultivation of empathy we decrease the risk of objectifying others, enhance perception of their essential humanness and as a result better recognize their suffering.[192]

Just as life is simpler if you always speak the truth, I think life is simpler if you harbor causeless compassion for everyone. This is particularly true when you find your loved ones, friends or colleagues frustrated or upset. One belief that has transformed my relationships can be scribed as, ***"An expression other than love is often a call for help."*** In fact I believe that an expression of anger or frustration almost always is a call for help. Anger, hatred, jealousy all represent an inner void not accepted. With such a void and in ignorance, we attempt to fill our own inner emptiness by trying to create emptiness in someone else. Understanding this truth has provided me numerous benefits.

I feel so much better about myself when my first reaction to someone who seems upset is that they are hurting in some way. Their frustration is not about me or them, it is some true genuine inner conflict they are not able to resolve. This belief almost always leads to a search for the reason they are hurting. More often than not I am able to find a rational explanation, even if the actual problem boils down to something that I actually goofed up! The result is lesser reactive frustration on my part and as a result more mature response; better ability to solve the primary issue at hand; more meaningful relationships; better self esteem for them and me; and in the long-term lower likelihood of their being upset again. The first step in this process is to truly believe that an *expression other than love is indeed a call for help*.

Your ability to practice this important skill critically depends on your ability to delay judgment. When faced with someone who might seem angry or upset (and thus with an active amygdala), you might instinctively launch an amygdala based response. This puts your amygdala against theirs, not a desirable combination. In contrast to amygdala that fires immediately, your pre-frontal cortex is a much more complex machinery and needs more time to activate. The real challenge is that once the amygdala fires, the resulting soup of chemicals released (Steroids, Cat-echolamines) may practically inhibit the activation of pre-frontal cortex. Hence if you wish your pre-frontal cortex to activate, you will need to buy some time. An optimal approach will be to delay judgment, pay attention to details and fully assess the situation, and thereby train your amygdala to refrain from immediate firing, except for in the most pressing circumstances.

Your compassion hides within it, your respect and love for others, and your regard for their dignity. Compassion recognizes that the journey others are treading you may have traversed before, and it was the kind compassion of unknown unseen that adjusted your sail. The wind sure changed directions, possibly multiple times—for such is the nature of the wind.

Compassion and well-being

The feeling of others' compassion toward us symbolizes being accepted by them, considered worthy and cared for, and a feeling of security and comfort. The person who receives an honest expression of compassion often has a tremendous healing experience. No wonder compassion has been associated with several positive outcomes in clinical studies that are summarized below.

• In a study that assessed the effect of asking physicians to actively practice compassion, physicians needed to spend only forty seconds longer to significantly decrease patient anxiety.[193] Compassionate care led to greater satisfaction and lesser need for ongoing health care.
• Compassionate care led to almost a one-third reduction in the number of return visits within one month in patients presenting to an emergency room.[194] The reason for this was greater satisfaction among patients receiving compassionate care.
• In a study involving 350 patients experiencing common cold, physicians were trained to provide routine care or enhanced compassionate visit. Patients experiencing more compassionate care were found to recover a day sooner compared to the other group.[195]

- In a study assessing fifty-one physician interactions with family members involving seriously ill patients in the intensive care unit, physicians showed empathy in two out of three interactions.[196] Results showed that expression of empathy was associated with greater satisfaction with communication.

- A loving kindness meditation program incorporating compassion improved low back pain in a study.[197]

- Compassion is not only good for the receiver but also for the person expressing it. In a study involving patients with rheumatoid arthritis, patients who cried easily had improved immune parameters and better outcome at one year compared to patients who did not.[198]

- In a study involving sixty-one participants, compassion meditation training was provided.[199] The study found that the duration of practice of compassion meditation was associated with improved immune parameters and lower distress in response to a standard stressor.

- An interesting area of research that supports the value of compassion is the study of non-local effects. These studies address the impact of intentionality and ability to send healing thoughts and other emotions from a distance without any physical proximity. Over 120 lab studies and eighty randomized trials have evaluated these non-local effects with half of these studies showing positive results that were statistically significant.[200] One explanation of this effect is based on quantum entanglement, a fascinating concept within quantum mechanics;[201] however, the precise mechanism of action is unclear.

To summarize the research results, compassion has been associated with the following positive outcomes:

- Satisfaction among patients that they received good care
- Decreased low back pain
- Earlier improvement in symptoms of common cold
- Improved immune parameters with arthritis
- Less pain with arthritis
- Lower stress

In chapter 14 we reviewed studies that suggested the effect of compassion on the brain's centers. Several studies consistently show that the feeling of compassion engages and empowers the pre-frontal cortex and other higher cortical centers.[91-96] In another study, experience of empathy was associated with a rise in blood oxytocin levels.[202] Oxytocin is a hormone released by the brain that mediates trust, love and attachment to others. An empathic disposition is thus likely to increase the strength of your tribe.

At this point we are ready to apply some of the principles we have learned so far into developing a few practical compassion exercises.

27. Cultivating Compassion

I will now share a few practice exercises and tips that might come in handy in your journey into compassion.

Exercise 1. Do good and forget
What do you expect in return for your acts of compassion? Check the most appropriate response.

1. A public acknowledgment ☐
2. A personal expression of gratitude by the receiver ☐
3. A reciprocal act of compassion ☐
4. No expectations; joy in the act of compassion is your return ☐

You are likely to be happiest if you picked the fourth option. ***A good deed is best forgotten by the doer with nothing expected in return.*** Consider yourself extraordinarily lucky and be pleasantly surprised if your feelings and acts of compassion are appreciated and appropriately acknowledged. Act for the sake of action; feel for the sake of feeling; and love for the sake of loving—with nothing expected in return.

If you get stuck in the desire to get recognition, you are more likely to invite disappointments. Expectation also takes away some of the purity from your compassionate actions. If you mix compassion with expectation, your act of compassion might degenerate into an ordinary deed involving energy exchange of some form.

Consider yourself blessed that you were provided the opportunity to be in the giver mode. It is only the blessed few who get an opportunity to provide selfless help. Actively search for these opportunities and do not let them go by unattended. As you help someone else, you are really helping yourself. The energy will eventually come back to you once the circle gets complete.

Exercise 2. Attitude toward compassion
How do you see your acts of compassion? Check all that apply.

1. Burden ☐
2. Load ☐
3. Drain ☐
4. Opportunity ☐

5. Energizing   ☐
6. Privilege   ☐

Compassion should be energizing and add meaning to your life. Compassion does not mean you stop caring for the self. Studies suggest that active cultivation of empathy should add an altruistic dimension to your personality without taking away your ability to care for the self.

If compassion is felt as a burden, a load or a drain on your energy, something is wrong. If you have any of these feelings, you may be experiencing *"compassion fatigue."* Compassion fatigue primarily originates from expanding your diameter and intensity of concern way beyond what your emotional strength can manage. Such an approach may degenerate compassion into catastrophizing. In general it is a good idea to cultivate compassion and love for everyone, including many you do not know. But if compassion is excessive and is not coupled with a good understanding that suffering and finiteness are ground realities for every life form, then compassion leads to non-acceptance which compounds your own suffering. Such compassion can help no one.

Unfortunately, the current state of the world offers enough opportunity for you to feel paralyzed by the misery you can find by just a few clicks on the Internet. Our brains evolved around a time when we lived in small tribes and could see suffering of only a relative few. But now with excellent communication in the world, we get inundated with graphic images and words of unimaginable suffering experienced by large groups of people. This may lead to compassion fatigue or worse still, numbing and loss of sensitivity. Research suggests that we respond much better to suffering that our brain and mind feel is manageable.[203] Reports of millions suffering tend to make us numb and emotionally paralyzed.

Excessive compassion may be far too common than a total lack of it. In a review of fifty-seven studies on compassion fatigue among cancer-care providers, compassion fatigue was found to be common and noted to have a negative impact on cancer-care providers individually as well as the whole workplace.[204] A particular aspect of compassion for others is that intense compassion may actually have the person not only understand others' suffering but also actually experience it. Synaesthesia refers to empathizing for as well as experiencing the observed or imagined pain in others as if it is their own. Scientists note that individuals with previous painful or traumatic experiences may be predisposed to such pain experience. While some of this may be unavoidable in a given individual, in general it might not be adaptive to compound suffering.[205]

Thus compassion fatigue is more likely to happen when one has personal-ly experienced suffering. Compassion fatigue is also likely in the following instances: lack of full perspective (lack of acceptance about the universal-ity of suffering); too much news; tendency to catastrophize particularly with previous negative experiences; and too broad a circle of compassion. While it is appropriate to keep a general attitude of compassion toward all, actively practice compassion only to the extent that you're emotional and physical capacity allows. As you grow and mature, you will find that you can gradually expand your capacity for compassion. If you aim to lift two hundred pounds, you may have to start with twenty and build from there. With untrained muscles, trying to lift the entire two hundred pounds could hurt you.

Protecting yourself from compassion fatigue, however, does not imply that you allow the pendulum to swing the other way. An interesting study suggested that as individuals rose in status and power, their level of compassion decreased, partly because of decreased motivation to affili-ate. It will help you to remember this possibility and protect your "higher self" as you rise up the social and professional echelons.

Exercise 3. Meditation on compassion
Sit in a safe place with your eyes closed. Draw an imaginary circle. Place your-self in that circle. Within that circle allow yourself to bring someone you think needs help and feel compassionate about. Create positive warm feelings for that person. Now with each in breath try to imagine that you are sharing their pain and suffering. With each out breath imagine sending them healing energy and love. Once you feel comfortable with this exercise, expand the diameter of your circle. Add others into the circle and repeat this exercise.

You can do this exercise with several people sharing their compassion and care with someone who may be suffering.

Exercise 4. Compassion for someone you love
Sit in a safe place with your eyes closed. Draw an imaginary circle. Place yourself in that circle. Within that circle also include someone you dearly love. Create positive warm feelings for that person.

Now focus on how the two of you are similar. At its most basic level you are both humans. You have similar biologic needs (food, breath, healthy body). You both need love, care, and security. Next find other areas of similarities. Do you have similar preferences for food? Do you both like to travel? Do you both have unique idiosyncrasies? Do you like similar clothes? Are your movie choices similar? Try to find similarities even in differences. Are you both similar in having unique preferences?

Now with each in breath imagine that you are sharing their pain and suffering. With each out breath imagine sending them healing energy and love.

The more similarities you seek and are able to find, the closer you will come to others, including your loved ones. You are then more likely to accept their uniqueness, even those aspects that so far may have seemed annoying.

Exercise 5. Compassion for someone you barely know
Sit in a safe place with your eyes closed. Draw an imaginary circle. Place yourself in that circle. Within that circle allow yourself to include someone you barely know. Create positive warm feelings for that person.

Now focus on the similarity of that person with you. We all are humans, our needs are similar (food, security, love, happiness, and sense of fulfillment). We all are ignorant at some level and wish to avoid suffering. Based on what we discussed in the previous exercise, try and find anything else that might be common between the two of you.

With each in breath imagine that you are sharing their pain and suffering (known or unknown). With each out breath imagine sending them healing energy and love.

Exercise 6. Compassion for someone you are not able to love
Sit in a safe place with your eyes closed. Draw an imaginary circle. Place yourself in that circle. Within that circle also include someone you are not able to love. This could be someone who may have hurt you in the past, at home, or at work. Try to create positive warm feelings for that person to the extent you can. Do not force yourself.

Now focus on the similarity of that person with you. We all are humans, our needs are similar (food, security, love, happiness, and sense of fulfillment). We all are ignorant at some level and wish to avoid suffering. Is there any other similarity you can find? Are they caring for at least someone, even if that someone does not include you?

With each in breath imagine you are decreasing their pain and suffering. With each out breath imagine sending them healing energy and love. If you can, forgive them just for this moment and accept them for what they are.

But do not force this feeling. Go only as far as you feel comfortable. Be open to the possibility that you might feel more compassionate toward them tomorrow than you are today.

We all are intimately interconnected to each other. At a macro level our destinies are closely intertwined. We are almost identical biologically, genetically and behaviorally. The differences are easily eclipsed by similarities.

I think it will be right to say as Meher Baba expressed that you and I does not equal just we, you and I equals one.

So let your compassion flow, just as water flows when the tap is opened, ever ready to quench the thirst of people unknown and previously unseen. This is the nature of grace. Compassion is nothing but a manifestation of your grace.

SECTION VIII: ACCEPTANCE

Précis

Internal acceptance nurtures equanimity and poise that fosters efficient external action

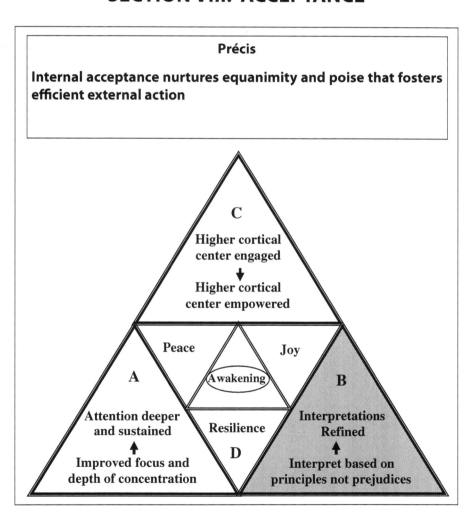

28. What is Acceptance?

I see what I am.

Our perceptions depend on the quality of our attention and how we interpret the information we receive. The greater our ingrained bias, the farther our perceptions are likely to be from the truth. Realistically, it is extraordinarily difficult to completely let go of the bias. However, here is what we can do to decrease the negative impact of bias: minimize the bias by *being more objective*; be willing to consider possibilities that do not align with preconceived notions by *being more flexible*; develop a perspective that is closer to the reality of everyday life by *nurturing wisdom to pursue truth*; and *develop willingness* to work with the imperfect, undesirable, or uncontrollable. **Acceptance is a combination of these four aspects: objectivity, flexibility, pursuit of truth, and willingness.**

What is Acceptance?

Objectivity: Acceptance is your ability to minimize bias. Acceptance is your willingness and ability to see things as they really are and not as you prefer them to be. It is an internal acknowledgement of "what is" as you prepare for the appropriate response. Acceptance entails deepening and sustaining attention, delaying interpretations and their related judgments. This enriches your sensory input providing you more time and thus more details to help you arrive at an interpretation that is closer to the truth.

Flexibility: Acceptance is an inner flexibility in your mind processes. Acceptance allows you to consider novel possibilities that may not necessarily align with your preconceived notions. This willingness offers flexibility to your thought and behavior and is critical to learning and adaptation, and to participate in a team both as a leader as well as a part of the team. Rigidity with few exceptions is a sign of ill health while flexibility is a sign of wellness and growth.

Wisdom and the pursuit of truth: Acceptance is searching for and collecting knowledge that is closer to the truth, irrespective of its desirability. Developing a model of the world and its parts that is closer to how they actually operate is likely to empower you to better describe, predict, and influence phenomenon.

Willingness: Acceptance also is (at least) temporarily becoming comfortable with the imperfect, undesirable or uncontrollable and willingness to engage with it. The purpose is to decrease negative emotional reactivity as you try to improvise, correct or adapt to the disagreeable. This is the "approach" strategy compared to "avoidance" that may disengage you from the world and increase stress and dis-ease.

Research shows that acceptance is sometimes difficult to learn, particularly if you have a predisposition to experience negative mood. This may be partly because acceptance is often confused with apathy. A common question patients and learners often ask me is, "With acceptance am I resigning myself to fate, becoming apathetic, and not doing what I should be doing?"

My response is an emphatic No. Apathy is loss of passion and hope and reflects pathological pessimism. Apathy signifies gloom, is almost sinful, and will never lead to the higher goals toward which you strive. Apathy expresses itself as listlessness and is often reflected in expressions such as, "Whatever" or "I just work here." Nothing could be further from acceptance than the feeling of apathy.

Acceptance, on the other hand, represents hope, optimism, and faith. Acceptance is making the snow man each time it snows knowing fully well that it will eventually melt when the Sun shows up. Joy is in the process of making the snow man, not in having it last forever. By becoming comfortable with the reality of imperfections, undesirable and sometimes uncontrollable outcomes, as well as finiteness, acceptance helps remove fear and fosters a deeper engagement with life. Acceptance is maintaining an inner balance so you can cultivate strength that facilitates passionate action. This passion is rooted in calm. It is this combination of passion and calm that promotes creativity and growth of the individual and the society. ***External effort powered by internal acceptance generates a strong and focused action.***

When expectations do not match reality, an internal battle often starts that leads to frustration and anger. A battle with the self can never be won. Acceptance allows you to step out of this largely unnecessary battle. This stepping out saves energy, prevents premature reactions, and helps enhance your joy. Further, by letting you see the reality and giving you greater time to respond to the situation, acceptance helps you engineer the response constructively.

A key aspect of acceptance entails recognizing that there is a limit to what you can control. The reality is whether we like it or not, often what is beyond our control is way more than what is fully within control. This realization saves you energy since you focus on the controllable aspects of your life rather than feeling despondent about the uncontrollable components. Acceptance thus helps create a realistic world model where uncertainty can be more easily accommodated. Once this is fully understood and embodied, it is immensely empowering because it diminishes our unwillingness to experience unpleasantness. This unwillingness is a significant contributor to our suffering.

A constant practice of acceptance leads one to surrender. Surrender, like acceptance, may sometimes be misunderstood. *Surrender is the ultimate feeling in optimism, a belief that the world is just and fair and that the right long-term path is to follow the principles of fairness and justice.* Surrender also entails cultivating a secure belief that the world cares about you because you are a most intimate and precious part of the creation, just like everyone else is.

Mature surrender is rooted in the deepest wisdom. Surrender recognizes that our contextual knowledge that is limited by our paradigm critically depends on our ignorance. Anything we see depends on clarity of our vision to that point but also inability to see further. This could lead to infinite regression with progressive ability to see a deeper reality. Surrender looks at this exercise with engaged amusement and recognizes its ultimate futility. The ultimate why may be unanswerable because it comes with a load of assumptions that our mind cannot easily reject. Every answer will only sprout a future question. Armed with this wisdom one learns that it is most adaptive to not peg one's peace or joy on the specifics of contextual knowledge. This breeds surrender, an offshoot of the deepest wisdom. Greatest peace may hide in relinquishing the need to know. Pick blessings not knowledge if you are given only one to choose from. *You are blessed when you are content with just who you are. That's the moment you find yourselves proud owners of everything that can't be bought (Matthew 5:5 MSG).*

I realize there are times when acceptance, as it might be understood superficially, just does not seem fair or appropriate. Many of these situations are where innocent well meaning people are faced with markedly adverse events in their lives. Optimism and faith may be severely challenged in these times and need significant strength and courage to sustain. A few approaches alone or in combination that might help you turn around the adversity and preserve some sanity include: considering disruption as your spiritual stress test; trying to find meaning in the adversity; considering adversity as a challenge rather than as punishment; expanding the world view to include imperfections; keeping the faith; reading inspirational stories; and realizing (and accepting) that there are aspects of life that are just beyond individual control. Each of these is a step toward developing acceptance.

Inner acceptance is a critical point in your journey from disruption to transformation.

29. Why Acceptance?

Imagine you have to face an event that you find challenging (e.g. giving a presentation or an interview, or hosting a party). We will use the example of giving an important presentation for this exercise, but you may substitute it for any other event that might be more appropriate for your situation. Your energy for such an event is distributed in two directions: 1) externally toward preparation for the upcoming presentation; 2) internally toward reflexive generation of anxiety about the process and outcome; attempts to suppress this anxiety; frustration at the inability to do so; decreased quality of life for the days awaiting the presentation; and once the presentation is over, ruminations on how the whole thing went focusing mostly on the negative (Figure 29.1).

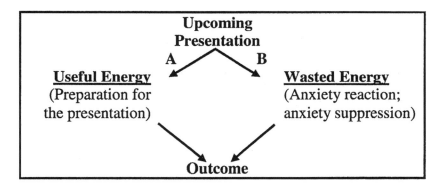

Figure 29.1 Partition of energy into useful and wasteful energy when responding to a challenge

Exercise 1. If the energy you use toward preparing for the presentation is depicted by A and for the anxiety reaction and associated phenomenon represented by B, *try and rate yourself where you stand.*

    1. A = 20%; B = 80%   ☐
    2. A = 40%; B = 60%   ☐
    3. A = 60%; B = 40%   ☐
    4. A = 80%; B = 20%   ☐
    5. A = 100%; B = 0%   ☐

If you marked 1 or 2, you are in a state of non-acceptance; 4 or 5, you have trained yourself well; 3 is somewhere in between.

Now ask yourself what parts of the variables in this specific example are in your control:

Table 29.1 Table for Exercise 1	Yes	No
1. Preparation for the presentation	☐	☐
2. Quality of your presentation	☐	☐
3. Mood of the attendees	☐	☐
4. Bias of the attendees	☐	☐
5. Working audio-visual system	☐	☐
6. Outcome of the presentation	☐	☐

There is a good chance you probably marked No for options 3-6. The outcome of your presentation depends on several variables (in this instance from 3-5) that are beyond your control. If you have no control over any of these then why sweat over them and drain your energy? The energy you spend in the generation of anxiety reaction and its downstream effects goes to waste. Often this is the more difficult part to handle than even the original issue at hand.

A slightly different approach would be to develop an internal acceptance of the outcome. It is reasonable to desire a positive outcome. However, an obsessive attachment to that outcome will create an internal chaos and impair your performance. Total apathy toward the outcome is not healthy either. Internal acceptance is the balanced middle path between chaos and apathy. With acceptance you are able to see the truth. The truth is that you have some (but limited) control over the outcome. Your control is mostly limited to your intention and effort. Variables you cannot impact, known or unknown, are best left alone and accepted. Save your energy and leave those unknowns to the element of chance or to providence. Internal acceptance of the outcome of the event blocks the ineffectual internal anxiety reaction and all its accompaniments, thereby increasing the amount of energy available to you to respond to the challenge.

Non-acceptance keeps us in a state of fight with ourselves

Who wins if you pick a fight with yourself? Certainly not you. A fight with the self can never be won. In medicine, some of the most difficult illnesses to treat are those where the body reacts against itself. Cancer and autoimmune diseases are good examples of such conditions. An attempt to neutralize such deviant cells almost always causes collateral damage to the normal cells. Our societal challenges are also similar—external wars are easier to fight; internal wars are the more difficult ones; worst are the wars where officers in the internal ranks themselves mutate into destructive enemies.

In the same vein, battle with an outside ego is much easier compared to a fight with your own mind. If you pick a fight with your own mind the fight is never likely to end. The fight goes on until one day you realize there was no reason to fight in the first place. You always had the option of not fighting this war but just were not tuned to avail it. You can step out any time and make internal peace with the imperfections. Unfortunately, oftentimes this realization comes very late in our journey. Acceptance fosters internal peace early on despite the outside imperfections. Acceptance thus helps you respond more effectively to the outside challenges.

Acceptance is a key ingredient toward happiness

We often seek a state of lasting peace, security and happiness from the world. What we do not realize, however, is that every aspect of the world is ephemeral, always changing. How can the world that itself is transient offer something that is permanent? Our youth, health, vigor, loved ones, even our dear life—everything we hold dear we will have to surrender one day. World just cannot guarantee sustained joy. Depending on the world for lasting inner peace is likely to be an exercise in futility. Trying to hold the world in hands is like trying to catch empty fog—in the end your hands are likely to be empty. Or drawing a lovely painting on flowing water. The stream will carry it away. Acceptance (both in terms of ability to see the reality, accept imperfections, seeking truth, and willingness to engage with the undesirable) helps us discipline our expectations, and guides us to seek greater joy from within. Acceptance helps us seek true gain, one that cannot be lost.

Even phenomenal success in an endeavor may not bring happiness until we truly accept our success. Let us look at an example. Imagine you receive an e-mail that you have received a surprise promotion and a pay raise. The sequence of the phases of reactions might flow something like this (Figure 29.2):

A. Non-acceptance – the initial reaction may be a feeling of anxious disbelief. You may try to cross-confirm or believe that this is some sort of a practical joke. The uncertainty in this period keeps you anxious and prevents you from celebrating the happy event.

B. Acceptance – eventually initial disbelief gives way to a brief period of acceptance. The moment you accept, happiness springs forth from inside you. This state, however, often tends to be transient and is soon followed by the next phase, that of anxietment.

C. Anxietment – the combination of anxiety and excitement comes again, this time from several unanswered, possibly presently unanswerable questions such as: Will I be able to meet the expectations of the new position? What if they find out I am not as good as they think? Will I get along with the new staff? What about work-life balance? And many more. In this state, you may again revert back to non-acceptance. Expansion of most pleasures hide the risk of increasing the zone of potential displeasure.

One more reason why success and happiness do not always travel together is because of our tendency to discount future events. If we have already mentally celebrated a future happy event, then when that future transpires in the present it tends not to be as pleasing. You may have noticed that often anticipation causes more goose bumps than the actual event. There is a good neurological basis for this since such anticipation releases more dopamine in the reward area of the brain than the actual experience.

Instead of a promotion and pay raise, you can change the specific example to any event that suits your situation e.g. learning about a new pregnancy, after being told that your cancer is in remission, being proposed by the person you love etc.

Phase	Reaction	Feeling
A. Non-acceptance	Can't believe it	Anxious
B. Acceptance	**Believe it**	**Happy**
C. Anxietment	Concerned that the gains might be lost	Anxious

Figure 29.2 Sequence of instinctive reactions in response to happy news

Our moments of happiness thus become limited only to the precious small window when we are in acceptance. This sequence is one of the primary reasons we often cannot easily access or sustain joy. Even if all the individual pieces necessary for happiness exist, they do not somehow create a cohesive whole. The essential glue to create that cohesive whole is the feeling of acceptance. By inviting inner acceptance early on and keeping it for a longer time we are likely to increase the time we feel happy and savor our good fortune (Figure 29.3).

Phase	Reaction	Feeling
A. Non-acceptance	Can't believe it	Anxious
B. Acceptance	**Believe it**	**Happy**

Figure 29.3 Sequence of more adaptive reactions in response to happy news. With training, non acceptance lasts for a shorter time bringing you greater joy.

Acceptance does not mean you will not consider the possibility that your responsibilities are likely to increase with the job promotion and your capabilities are likely to be tested with greater rigor. You certainly will. But as you celebrate this moment, you do not allow this thought to contaminate your joy and are temporarily willing to postpone the related concern. And when you revisit this concern you also keep in mind that just as you have risen to challenges in the past, you will rise again this time, may be with some additional training and support.

Things tend to be even more challenging in the not-so-positive moments. These moments often start an exhausting and resource-intensive internal dialog. The content of this dialog often has two directions: 1) Toward self – reviewing how this failure might negatively affect us; and 2) Toward others – looking at how they might have caused us to fail. Our mind tends to exaggerate both the components of this dialog. For the time we are locked in these thoughts we stay in non-acceptance (Figure 29.4). Finally exhausted, at some point we accept the reality. The moment we accept the event, even though mired with all the problems, magically an oasis of peace manifests. Research studies suggest that resolution of grief closely coincides with the acceptance of reality. This peace frees up your energy and provides a more stable platform for you to plan the next adaptive steps to transcend the misfortune.

Phase	Reaction	Feeling
Non-acceptance	Can't believe it	Denial, Anger, Anxious, maladaptive response
Acceptance	**Believe it**	**Greater peace, adaptive response**

Figure 29.4 Sequence of instinctive reactions
in response to unfavorable news

Your ability to respond to a challenging event thus depends on your ability to see the reality and accept it for what it represents. Only then can you respond effectively and also feel some peace in the midst of the challenge. When I see patients with challenging diagnoses in the clinic, I often ask this question, "Have you accepted your diagnosis?" The response to this question stratifies patients into two groups. Patients who have accepted the diagnosis are able to bring about a much more adaptive coping response compared to patients who are in non-acceptance. Non-acceptance keeps the fire of resentment, anger and frustration smoldering. This fire is energy intensive and redirects attentional resources away from useful effort.

Peace and happiness thus greatly depend on your reaction to the events of your lives; how quickly you are able to accept them and then respond to the reality. The actual event—whether it is good or bad—is important. However, of equal importance, if not greater, is the efficiency with which you can initiate a mature response. Biologically this efficiency might depend on how swiftly you are able to engage the higher center of your brain, your pre-frontal cortex. Your ability to quickly engage your prefrontal cortex can be enhanced by training.

Accepting others as they are is the most efficient approach to bring about a change in them

There is a good chance you are surrounded by people you wish were a bit different. Your spouse or friends probably are not the same as they were when you first met them. Your older parents might be changing and getting more stubborn. Your children may not always behave like the gentle angels you wish them to be. Your employees, colleagues or supervisors may not be as flexible and accommodating as they seemed to be at the first impression. A large part of your energy may be spent in efforts to bring all these "others" to a more desirable state—mostly without success. If any of this applies to you, please be comforted that you are not alone.

Part of your unhappiness certainly comes from the fact that the people around you have imperfections (just as you have). But the greater part of unhappiness comes from your desire to control and change them and frustration at your inability to do so. The more you try to change them, the greater will be your assault on their ego and the less likely they are to change. The one person who predictably listens to you and will be most willing to change at your suggestion is you. Trying to change others is an insurmountable task and one fraught with a high risk of failure or distancing yourself from your loved ones. The most efficient way you can change others is by changing yourself.

The key to open the door for change in others is with them, not you. Only they can open that door, once they are willing. They are likely to be more willing on a day they feel good about themselves. They will also listen to you more openly if they perceive your unconditional warmth toward them. What do you think is the first step to enhance their self esteem and show them your warmth? *Accept them as they are.*

The three diameters of control, influence, and lack of control

From the perspective of control, there are three aspects to your life: controllable; within influence and beyond control. There are many things definitely in your control. These include simple things like getting a dripping faucet fixed; clearing e-mail inbox; putting in a spam filter; or proposing to the person you love. But many things you have no control over. You cannot totally prevent faucets from aging and beginning to leak. You cannot prevent people from attempting to send you spam. You might charmingly propose, but there is no way to know if your offer will be accepted. A third, somewhat hazier compartment includes aspects that are within your influence. This might include for example your children's behavior, your spouse's mood, the amount and type of food you eat etc. Realize that some of the most important aspects of your life such as the choice of your parents, country of your birth or your race you have no influence or control over.

Maintaining a flexible disposition toward the controllable aspects of your life, wisely exercising your options toward elements within your influence, and letting go of the uncontrollable might be the optimal approach to handle the three compartments of your life. Controlling the uncontrollable takes away energy from controlling the controllable.

Rigidity is a sign of ill health while flexibility is a sign of health and well-being. Avoidance is also generally a sign of ill health while approach is a sign of well-being. Acceptance connotes flexibility and approach rather than rigidity and avoidance. ***Trying to control the uncontrollable and predict the unpredictable contributes significantly toward unhappiness and is wasteful of time and energy.***

Picking a fight with unpleasant weather is a waste of time. If it snows, let it be. The winter will only last so long. Summer is sure to follow. This has been the rule for as long as we can remember and will not change. We still fight with the seasons. If winter is here so be it. The seasons reflect the creative workings of Mother Nature. Welcome all of them just as they are. Do you have a choice?

Life is not a meticulous pre-planned scientific experiment with a pre-defined expected outcome. Most of what happens in the future cannot be predicted. It is better to find the future "interesting" and "novel," for that is what it is. Any other adjectives to the future are likely to be imprecise since short of time travel you will never know how it will turn out to be. It will likely be better than what you fear and not as exciting as you hope.

Every day brings a different set of experiences. In general we feel happier on days when the challenges we face fall within the domains of our life that are in our control. However, if today is the day when your challenges mostly occupy the uncontrollable compartment, instead of anger or dejection, try to find an opportunity in it. Most such days will finally be over. By accepting the unpleasant experience, trying to find meaning in it and avoiding a fight with the self, you are more likely to perserve your sanity and be more present for the days when your experiences are mostly within the controllable domain. Without true acceptance, you will continue to try and stop an oncoming train rather than joining it. ***Only after you join can you change the direction of the train—if that is what you desire.***

Acceptance allows you to learn from failures and turn them around into success

Life will always bless you with failures. World is not always going to be fair. Inequality is the very basis of creation. The important point is how you tackle your failures to transform them into success. In the midst of planning and taking actions it might help to internally accept that some of your plans will not materialize and actions will not bear fruit. In fact, sometimes it truly is a blessing that your plans did not materialize. You might only come to know years later what an opportunity it was when something you desperately wanted to achieve eluded you.

Failure is always painful. Failure, however, is much needed and the sooner it happens, the higher you are likely to go. Within failure are hidden the golden lessons to help you learn and grow. In fact one of the important attributes of many successful entrepreneurs is their early experience of failure. ***Ability to turn a failure into opportunity and advancing not only despite failures but sometimes because of failures is a hallmark of resilience.*** Resilience is an ability to learn from and grow with each change and challenge. Resilience depends on a healthy and mature strategy toward handling failure. An essential ingredient in this approach is an attitude of acceptance. With acceptance, the more you get disrupted, the greater your learning and the higher you go.[206]

Alexander Fleming's search for an anti-bacterial agent had a special meaning since he had witnessed the death of many soldiers from serious infections as a result of war wounds.[207] Fleming once noticed that his culture dishes were contaminated with a fungus. He first discarded them, but on retrieval was intrigued by a zone around a particular fungus wherein the bacteria just could not grow. Instead of fretting about his inability to grow the bacteria, he was intrigued by this observation. He explored this further, and this exploration led to the discovery of penicillin, an antibiotic that has saved hundreds of millions of lives. Fleming retained his humility despite having transformed medicine. He called all the attention he received the "Fleming Myth" and actually gave greater credit to his colleagues Ernst Chain and Howard Florey who diligently worked to convert his finding into a useful drug. Fleming was sure lucky for this "contamination." But the other skill that helped him was acceptance. He could have easily rejected his inability to culture the bacteria, got frustrated, and moved on. But true scientist that he was, he accepted the reality and tried to look behind it to understand the nature of the mechanism.

Hans Selye, the scientist who described the stress response, also achieved fame because of his ability to turn an unpredicted outcome into a powerful generalization.[208, 209] Selye, a Canadian endocrinologist, was conducting an experiment in which he injected mice with extracts of various organs. He was initially excited that he had discovered a new hormone in this experiment. He, however, noticed that every irritating substance produced the same response (stomach ulcers, swollen adrenals, and shrunken thymus). Instead of rejecting his observations and moving on to continue to search for the hormone, he interpreted all the data and came to the conclusion that the changes he saw likely represented a generic response of most animals in response to the effects of a noxious agent. He called this a stress response, a term we now understand very well. Reaching this deep insight critically depended on his ability to remove his own bias, accept his observations for what they were, and work with them to come to a meaningful interpretation.

Acceptance as a behavioral attribute has been researched in several studies with consistently beneficial results

Below I summarize some of the research findings that show the benefit of acceptance for a number of conditions. Cultivating an attitude of acceptance constitutes the core of acceptance and commitment therapy (ACT) developed by Dr. Steven C. Hayes at the University of Reno, Nevada. ACT has been tested in several clinical trials with encouraging results.[210-212]

• Acceptance and commitment therapy helped patients with diabetes achieve better control.[213]
• Soldiers caught in an avalanche coped better if they brought an attitude of acceptance compared to soldiers who refused to believe that it had happened.[214]
• Women who experienced assault had less symptoms if they used "positive distancing" (accept the next best thing to what you want) compared to "wishful thinking" (wishing that you could change the way you felt).[215]
• Acceptance and commitment and cognitive therapy facilitated better awareness in actions in addition to improvement in other variables and thereby improved symptoms of depression, anxiety, functioning difficulties, quality of life, life satisfaction, and clinician-rated functioning.[216]
• Acceptance and commitment therapy improved a multitude of symptoms in patients who had problems with marijuana dependence.[217]

- Non-acceptance of pain by others was noted to be a barrier toward patients' ability to accept their own pain.[218]

- In a study involving 378 psychology students, acceptance of the present moment and its contents and non-judgment of experiences was associated with lower risk of PTSD.[219]

- In a randomized study involving twenty-one patients with chronic pain and whiplash-associated disorders, acceptance-based strategy significantly improved pain disability, life satisfaction, fear of movements, depression, and psychological inflexibility compared to wait list control.[220] This was despite the fact that no change was observed in pain intensity. Improvement persisted for up to seven months of follow up.

- Acceptance of negative emotions associated with a stressful experience was associated with healthier heart rhythm compared to ruminating on these emotions in a study involving eighty-one volunteers.[221]

- In marital discord, emotional acceptance versus traditional behavioral couple therapy focusing on change showed a greater increase in marital satisfaction with a higher percentage of couples that improved or recovered.[222]

- In a study involving 150 participants with chronic pain, pain acceptance decreased negative emotions, activity engagement produced additional positive feelings, and a flexible disposition to adjust individual life style helped with all these processes.[223]

- In a randomized study involving thirty-one patients with generalized anxiety, increasing acceptance of inner experiences and actions in valued domains significantly decreased anxiety-related symptoms.[224] Even just using a self help book that guided participants into greater acceptance was associated with lower anxiety and better quality of life.[225]

- In a study involving forty-seven patients with tinnitus (chronic unpleasant sounds in the ear), teaching participants acceptance compared to suppression led to a greater ability of participants to focus on treatment rather than continue to be interrupted by the tinnitus.[226]

- In a study involving 106 patients with cardiac disease, illness acceptance was associated with better physical functioning and emotional well being compared to helplessness.[227]

- In a review of fifteen studies testing the effect of acceptance for improving chronic pain, it was concluded that incorporating an attitude of acceptance of the pain in general produced promising results for functioning in these patients.[228]

- Some of the other conditions helped by acceptance and commitment therapy (ACT) include:
  - Patients with drug refractory seizures;[229]
  - Symptoms of skin picking;[230]
  - Compulsive hair pulling;[231]
  - For the treatment of psychotic symptoms;[232, 233]
  - Patients with obsessive compulsive disorder (OCD) for reducing symptoms of anxiety and depression and for the treatment of compulsions;[234]
  - Depression and anxiety symptoms;[235]
  - Willingness to use appropriate pharmacotherapy;[236]
  - Symptoms associated with chronic pain (pain, depression, pain-related anxiety, disability, medical visits, work status, and physical performance).[237]

In summary acceptance has shown benefit in the following conditions:

- Diabetes control
- Coping among soldiers
- Coping among assault victims
- Depressive symptoms
- Anxiety symptoms
- Quality of life
- Life satisfaction
- Marijuana dependence
- Chronic pain
- Marital satisfaction
- Tinnitus
- Drug refractory seizures
- Skin picking
- Compulsive hair pulling

- Obsessive compulsive disorder (OCD)
- Cardiac symptoms
- Chronic pain

A common approach our mind takes when it is not in acceptance is to try and suppress the thoughts of the negative event. ***Mind does not realize that what we fight, we actually get attached to.*** *An attempt to avoid and suppress the thoughts increases the same thoughts and is mostly counterproductive as shown in several studies:*

• Attempts to suppress either emotionally neutral[235, 238-241] or intrusive thoughts[242, 243] predisposed to an increase of the same thoughts and even a later rebound of the very thoughts that were suppressed.
• Thought suppression by itself was associated with increased distress.[243, 244]
• Suppression of thoughts also tends to increase dreams related to the thoughts we are trying to suppress.[245]
• Thought suppression was associated with greater increase in heart rate and more anxiety compared to reappraisal or acceptance.[246]
• A positive confronting coping style allowed better adaptation compared to negative avoidance.[247]
• In a study involving fifty-six patients diagnosed with breast cancer, patients were found to be less likely to employ productive strategies (decision making, information seeking) and experience more symptoms if they used avoidance or felt resigned to their fate compared to confronting the issue.[248]
• Expressing anger by writing about it led to better improvement of pain and depressive symptoms in patients with chronic pain.[249]

In addition to the above clinical benefits, recall that in chapter 14 we also saw that a feeling of acceptance helps engage the brain's higher centers.[66, 100]

In the foregoing discussion I have appealed to your inner wisdom about the benefits of acceptance. I hope I have been able to give you a compelling idea about acceptance and you are enthusiastic about cultivating this skill within you. I wish to emphasize that acceptance is the hallmark of resilience, and most effective actions that bring about transformational change in our lives are rooted in acceptance.

I commonly see patients who suffer annoying symptoms not getting fully controlled with maximal medical therapy. One skill I often teach them is to improve their ability to *accept the symptom but fight the disease*. You have to save the physical and mental energy to fight the disease. For that you have to internally accept the symptoms even though they are annoying and discomforting. Once patients understand the value of acceptance, their emotional fight with the symptoms subsides. This by itself decreases the intensity of symptoms. They are now ready to fight the disease that they can clearly see separate from who they are. They thus no longer find identity in their diagnosis. They are not cancer patients, diabetics, or heart patients. They are individuals—Cathy with a history of cancer, John with a history of diabetes, Peter with a history of heart disease. The difference is subtle but important. Your ability to "look at" your medical illness knowing that you are not the medical illness is an important attribute that will help you respond to the illness, cope with the symptoms, develop an optimal healing plan, and continue to live the life of your dreams. A particular diagnosis or event is one among many shades that contribute to the mosaic of your life. Do not allow a disruption to dominate your experience. The first step toward this progress is cultivating the feeling of acceptance.

I think we are now ready to explore a few practice exercises in an effort to embody acceptance in our lives.

30. How to Cultivate Acceptance

The two most important steps toward developing acceptance are to understand what acceptance really is and be convinced of the benefits of cultivating acceptance. We have just completed these two steps. Once you understand acceptance and find it appealing, the next step is to invite acceptance into your life. Let us incorporate some of the concepts we have learned so far into practice exercises.

Exercise 1. Invited or just showed up?
Spend some time in your garden bringing your full presence. Notice all the plants. Some of them you may have planted....others came of their own volition without your specific invite.

Not every plant or blade of grass growing in your garden had your invite. On any given day your garden has both, the weeds and the flowers. You may, if you like, work extremely hard to get rid of every little weed and unwanted plant from your garden and make your garden perfectly immaculate. But then, that is all you might do all spring! And if your attention wavers even for a day or two, an irate weed might just show up. The process however has another cost. While obsessively clearing all the weeds you are likely to miss on something precious—enjoying the beautiful flowers that show up in your garden. These flowers generally do not wait for our attention to complete their journey. They are leased to us by Mother Nature only for a brief period of time.

A more balanced and flexible approach might be to divide your attention between clearing up the weeds and attending to the flowers. Remove as many weeds as you can, particularly the larger more obvious ones, and then accept that maintaining a perfect weed proof lawn is impractical, even undesirable.

When with your loved ones, focus on the blessing of togetherness. Delay judgment. Meet them each time as if you are meeting them after a long time. The first step toward a deeper engagement starts with accepting them as they are. Like the tulips this spring, your time with them is finite and generally shorter than you might imagine or like.

An important question to ask here is, are all the weeds so undesirable? Some of the weeds in our garden may be a creation of our own bias. Luther Burbank said, *"A flower is an educated weed."* Consider this possibility that weeds are just plants trying to find a safe haven in this competitive world. Maybe they are not as pretty, maybe they have more thorns. But is it possible that they are also serving a purpose in your garden? Could they be, like the healthy bacteria in our colon, preventing a more sinister weed or bug from showing up?

Sometimes you might confuse a flowering plant for a weed. I have been guilty of throwing away perfectly healthy and well-meaning plants mistaking them for a weed. On a bright and sunny day of your life you may be amazed to see how all the weeds suddenly disappear. The flowers appear in full bloom and even what seemed like weeds the other day blossom as beautiful flowers. Sun decidedly helps, but the larger part is the state of your own mind. Your garden all but remains the same. The important thing is—where are you looking?

Exercise 2. Did you preplan all the flowers this spring?
Stroll through your garden and notice all the plants, with or without the flowers. Did you know in the winter precisely which plant will blossom how many flowers and in what arrangement?

As you plan your garden, all you can do is to plant the right seeds, provide them the right nourishment, protect them from the elements, and then just wait. Your hurry or impatience will not accelerate the arrival of the sapling. Some of the seeds will oblige, others will wither away. Not all plants that are born from these seeds will find an eventual place in your garden. You are mostly thus an observer, with each plant pursuing its own journey as your co-traveler. **Breaking chrysalis open prematurely does not deliver a happy butterfly.**

We will enjoy our garden more if we do not excessively impose our preference or bias on Mother Nature and learn to appreciate the flowers that have blossomed, accepting them in their natural beauty and arrangement. It might be better to respect the decision of a plant that chose not to blossom this season and give it some more time. Further, keeping a realistic expectation that some plants will not oblige almost every season and it is often difficult to spot them ahead of time will also help. It is likely that this is how nature assures that with its limited resources, your garden and everyone else's garden has flowers blossoming each spring.

Exercise 3. Is it a source of stress or a source of joy?
List everything in the world that makes you happy today.

1. _____ ☐

2. _____ ☐

3. _____ ☐

4. _____ ☐

5. _____ ☐

6. _____ ☐

7. _____ ☐

8. _____ ☐

9. _____ ☐

10._____ ☐

Now go back and check mark those that may have been a source of stress in the past or you think could be a future stressor.

Welcome to the world that is at the same time Joyville and Stressville! In every home of this village, every nook and corner, stress abounds. But so does opportunity and joy. The two are often inseparable; when you pick one you almost always pick the other. What would you rather do? Stay passive for the fear of displeasure or embrace all your opportunities? It might help to accept and in some instances even like all that challenges you. The face might look like that of a stressor; the body, however, is that of opportunity.

Work, family, health, finances—all your challenges are also your playing ground, your life breath. How can you let them go? Life without these challenges might become boring and unproductive. Life is a beautiful mosaic with multiple colors. All these colors have their place. Do not wish any of the color away. Accept them as they are. Absolute good is an imaginary entity. Everything in the world is a combination of good and bad—it is all contextual. See how each of the colors fit together; be an observer of apparent imperfections. Try to embrace those imperfections. This is the first and most essential step toward their transformation—toward your transformation.

Like an appetizing menu, many (but not all) things in life are here for the asking. Do not place your request based on what you see on others' tables. Create your own plate based on your preferences, appetite, and palate. Make sure you keep enough servings of love and peace, not just as a dessert at the end of the dinner, but also as a part of the main course.

Exercise 4. Your very small circle of control
Answer this question by selecting Yes or No.
Which of the following in your life did you choose of your free will?

Table 30.1 Table for Exercise 4		
Which of these did you consciously choose?	**Yes**	**No**
Parents	☐	☐
Siblings	☐	☐
Country of birth	☐	☐
Race	☐	☐
Your health	☐	☐
Falling in love	☐	☐
Children	☐	☐
Children's health	☐	☐

You may have answered "No" to all or most of the above. Even falling in love—because love just happens—is not in your control. These are some of the most important things that determine the direction of your life.

As previously suggested, maintaining a balanced and flexible disposition toward the controllable, wisely exercising your options with compassion and equanimity toward elements within your influence, and letting go of the uncontrollable observing it with amusement and grace might be the optimal approach to handle the three compartments of your life.

This approach is likely to decrease anxiety about uncertainty and instill a sense of acceptance. A feeling of acceptance allows us to find islands of peace within the ocean of uncertainty that tends to be our life.

No one purposefully chooses to have a flat tire. However, if you do have one, sitting in the middle of the road lamenting and getting frustrated is not likely to help. Some things you desire and choose in life, others you are willing to accept. Incorporating the possibility of having a flat tire in your journey, not knowing when it will happen, but keeping this in mind that when it happened last time you were able to effectively tackle it, will help with the quality of your journey. Such an acceptance is also likely to decrease stress and anxiety and enhance your ability to engage and continue with exciting journeys.

Exercise 5. Wake up to the impermanence
Look at any aspect of your life—home, work, relationships, or even your own emotions. Do you think things are more likely to stay the same or change?

1. Stay the same   ☐
2. Change   ☐

Since the beginning of creation, our world is constantly changing. Change is a way of nature. Getting comfortable with change is an essential step toward inviting peace. Progress almost always entails change; every change, however, is not progress. Change could entail a loss, gain, or transformation. Loss is often the most noticeable and most hurtful change. Loss of what you hold close to your heart is usually a painful experience. It is only natural to love and be attached; these feelings form the very basis of creation.

Love, however, finds its greatest intensity when it is rooted in the acceptance of finiteness. Every moment then becomes unique, special, and precious. Finiteness is the reality. The sun has to set for the stars to twinkle. A flower has to let go of her nectar for her pollen to spread. A flower also has to wither for the fruit to come. The person you dearly love will have to go away some day. You and I will eventually surrender everything we hold dear. Try to see a world where no one ever dies—it is a pretty congested place. Know and absorb the transience of each moment, live it to the full and then let it go. Understand and then accept that you will forever face change, and this change will not always be pleasant or desirable. Your stress and grief come not from the change *per se* but your attachment and desire for permanence. The sooner you imbibe the lesson of impermanence, the quicker you will be able to access the state of joy. Do not postpone sharing your love; and do not save your love for only special moments. ***When the time comes it will be easier to say good bye when you have loved deeply and were able to express it.***

Exercise 6. Track the journey of your life
Go back down the memory lane into your life and start from the beginning of your career (point A) to now (point B). Look at two possible tracks shown below. Model 1 depicts a journey that is straight up; while model 2 shows a more zig zag course—a few steps forward a few behind.

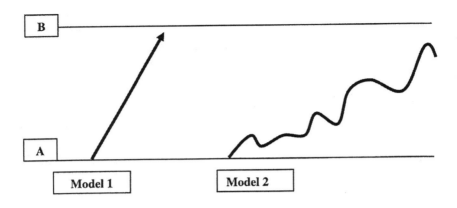

Figure 30.1 The two models of growth

Ask yourself this question:
Which model more accurately depicts your progress so far, model 1 or model 2?

In general model 2 is a more accurate depiction of our life's journey. For most of us progress comes in steps that are interspersed with a lull phase or even a step back. The step back prepares us for the next phase of progress. In general, when faced with a period of reversal it might help to nurture a long-term view, keeping in mind that each of us have our own unique path, that will likely work out over the long haul, as long as we keep the perspective that ***a step back often is a move forward***.

Life is a journey. You spend the bulk of your time traveling. Wherever you reach is a starting point for the next trip. You seldom stop at any of your destinations. Such is the nature of life. The fun part is often not the final stop but the entire journey. If you spend your journey thinking, dreaming, and worrying about the destination, you might spend your entire life never having experienced joy. Our natural instinct is to be just a bit ahead of ourselves. While taking a shower we often are mentally at the breakfast table and at the breakfast table mentally in our office. With this approach we may not show up for the bulk of our life. Accepting and engaging with the present moment will enhance our presence.

Forward and backward movements are the natural chatter ingrained within the overall journey that is only partially in your control. Accepting this variability and incorporating this into your overall model of life, you can cultivate a state of inner equilibrium that is not likely to be easily disturbed by the frequent stronger gusts and will have better resilience to withstand the occasional severe storms.

Recognize this nature of life. You are really going nowhere. All you are doing is traveling. Your commute is the end in itself. This commute is but a series of present moments stacked upon one another. So enjoy this moment here and now. Be awake as you travel. **The best way to live happily ever after is to live it in the now.** Attend to the tree, the streets, the shops, every friend waving at you as they pass by. And whenever you can afford to, stop and smell the roses.

Exercise 7. Make peace with the past.
Answer this question about your past. What is the best strategy to approach your past?

1. To observe and learn from it ☐
2. To spend a lot of time regretting the past ☐
3. To close your eyes to the past ☐

You probably chose the first option—to observe and learn from it. Your ability to observe and learn depends on acceptance of the past as it was. If your past was unpleasant, acceptance prevents the imperfections of the past from contaminating the beauty of the present. Just as roasted seeds do not germinate, a past that is accepted does not haunt and annoy us as much. Acceptance of the past stops you from feeding more energy into the negative experiences, thus disempowering the attention black holes that might be lodged in your memory.

Our mind, however, has a great propensity to excessively consult the past before allowing us to be happy in the present. The past draws attention to both happy and unhappy moments, more often the latter. We tend to judge the past based on what we know today. Past events thus might look unacceptably imperfect. The past could have been better or it could have been worse. The fact is it could not have been either. It was what it was because that is what it was meant to be. Be amused by your past without attaching too many judgments to it. Your past contributes to your current emotions; while how you feel in the future will greatly depend on your present experience.

. Accept that if you have painful memories they will not completely go away. The kernel of attention black holes will remain buried within layers of newer and fresher memories. If you send energy to these black holes by dwelling excessively on the unhappy events, they will be further empowered, fresh, and hurtful.

Develop a more accepting relationship with these memories by knowing the reality. And the reality is that these memories are like your unpleasant cousin who embarrasses you, causes you grief, won't go away—but is not vile. No point fighting him, just accept him as he is. Include in your worldview the existence of an imperfect cousin. Similarly, make peace with these unhappy memories and accept them for what they are. They cannot harm you anymore, as long as you choose to accept and transcend them. When they do however surface once in a while do not put too much energy suppressing them. Instead observe them in a detached way. The moment you start observing your feelings, you stop owning and identifying with them. The outer layers of rumination and avoidance gradually disappear from your attention black holes. Even the dark kernel in the center may be reinterpreted as you begin to find meaning in your suffering. It is then that you start learning from those memories. These negative feelings thus serve a great purpose by providing you a perfect opportunity for growth.

Exercise 8. Consider the totality of your life—material, physical, relationships, emotional, and spiritual. What percentage of your life globally is right vs. wrong?

1. Right   _____%
2. Wrong   _____%

There is a good chance that, for almost all of you, what is right is greater than what is wrong.

Our reality:

1. Right   90 %
2. Wrong   10 %

How we live if we are in non acceptance and do not actively practice gratitude:

1. Right   10 to 20 %
2. Wrong   80 to 90 %

As long as there is life, as long as we are breathing, what is right is more than what is wrong. However, we often live life perceiving just the opposite. Why not accept the right that is right and savor it. Recognize that excessive focus on the wrong is a biologically driven instinct that frequently prevents us from enjoying the glory of the present moment.

Do not let the unpleasant conceal everything else that is blessed. Life is a precious opportunity to practice goodness and experience joy. Your sad thoughts tell you that you have experienced pleasure. You can tell darkness because you have seen the light. However, our moments of blessedness, which all but fill our Garden of Eden, sometimes do not register. We move past them unconsciously and wake up only in moments wherein we are challenged. We thus might feel more stressed and unhappy than we should be, based on the reality of our life.

Do not allow your feelings of anxiety or stress to overwhelm all the goodness showered upon you. Instead of feeling that you are living a life absorbed in stress, try to look at your stress as a detached observer. As an impartial third person, you are more likely to be objective and accurate in your assessment.

Exercise 9. Islands of acceptance
Find a time and place where you feel safe and can let go of intentions. Remain in total acceptance of the past, present, and future, with no intention to judge or reason. Let go of the tendency to plan or problem solve. When your mind tends to wander, bring it back to the sensory experience in the present moment, breath, or your daily theme (gratitude, compassion, acceptance, meaning, or forgiveness) to keep your mind anchored. An ideal time to practice this would be at the time of your daily prayer or meditation or during the times you are instructed to train your attention.

See how acceptance of "what is" instills peace and brings bliss to you from your inner self. Prayer brings peace partly because when praying we are instilled with a feeling of acceptance. We accept the divine presence of our devotion, be it a thought, an image, or a word, with no judgment. However, if you bring an intention of a self focused reward into the prayer, its beauty and purity will go away. Such a prayer is often not relaxing.

With constant practice of acceptance, you might find yourself more patient, humble, compassionate, gentle, and kind. As you become more comfortable with these ego-free moments, expand them into other periods of your life.

Exercise 10. Island of mindlessness and non-acceptance
We are often not able to sustain our presence in the present moment because of living in a fast paced world that forces us to multitask. If your responsibilities ask you to take your mind in different directions at the same time, trust me you are not alone and count me also with you! This is very common with the patients I see since there is so much they have to figure out. In this state it is easy to slip back into mindless awareness

and non-acceptance. Often there is a lot going on in life that needs your attention. In fact, this may be a rule rather than an exception. I find two useful approaches in this situation: keep the perspective; and schedule some times for mindlessness.

By keeping the perspective, I mean being able to keep in mind that most of my fears are not going to come true; my hurry is mostly internal; everything I have is ephemeral and finite; suffering is universal; and a hurtful expression from someone toward me shows that they need help or hug (and not an unkind reaction).

Accepting a time for mindlessness decreases guilt and internal conflict when I have no choice but to be mindless. A prime example of this is when trying to go through security line prior to boarding a flight. Simultaneous attention is drawn toward making sure the liquids are out in the appropriate sized ziplock, the computer and shoes are placed separately, water bottle is empty, no metal is left on me, boarding ticket is in my hand, all the while making sure that our daughter is making progress, my wife does not need help, I am not delaying the person behind me, and I still maintain a smile on my face. And if all this happens when we are closing in on the boarding time and can not afford to miss this flight since it is the last flight out today and I have to see patients next morning, then this is an excellent test for all the skills we have been discussing so far!

Will you find me a bit hassled and mindless at that time? Sure you will!

In such a situation I try to take a deep breath, allow myself to be mindless, keep the perspective that missing the flight or seeming a bit clumsy to the security agent or person behind me is not the end of the world. Just as I try to be kind to the person ahead of me, very likely others are also going to understand. This approach helps decrease my stress and helps me be more efficient. As a result I generally do not set off the alarm because I forgot to take off my belt (necessitating a longer security check), or do not have to rush back because I forgot my wallet at the security. Once this ordeal is behind me, I try to not let its momentum contaminate the enjoyable walk toward the terminal.

During your routine day you can allow fifteen minutes of time wherein your mind is not held with any leash and can think unrestrained. **You could call it your "worry break" or "scheduled worry time."** In this time take your mind through all your plans and concerns and let it think what it likes to think. Use this time to address all your fears. Through the day when you find yourself worrying, note down the concern and allocate that concern to this time. If there is a lot of stuff you have to resolve, take out thirty minutes or even an hour—whatever you can dispense with and have the need for.

Since you are in acceptance of mindlessness during your "worry break," it might actually become enjoyable. This time may allow you to remain in the present moment the rest of the day. The key is that you be the driver and not allow your mind to feast on your peace. You might experience that, over a period of time, the need for this time will likely go down.

Exercise 11. Pick only the important battles, let go of the rest
Sometimes you may have a lot going on in your life. This may actually be a rule rather than an exception. It helps in such situations to pick the problems you intend to tackle and let go of those that are not worth your time. You only have a limited quota of energy, physical as well as mental. You would like to allocate it to your most significant problems that are amenable to solutions. Unless you think about it you might pick the first challenge that comes your way in the morning in a reactionary way, dissipate your energy, and not be able to focus on the most important things.

When there is a lot going on in life, categorize your challenges into one of the four quadrants as shown below (when you actually do this exercise, take out some time and draw this table on a large, full sheet of paper):

Controllable⟶ Important	Yes	No
Yes	A	B
No	C	D

Figure 30.2 The four categories of challenges

The four quadrants are:

A – Controllable and Important – These are the core challenges / issues you should be addressing. They may include important issues such as your relationship (with spouse, family, and close friends) and health.

Sometimes they also include relatively trivial issues as a flat tire or even jammed paper in your printer that may be annoying and impact your efforts short term. Ideally you should be proactive and assign issues in this quadrant well before they become a problem.

B – Not controllable but important – This is a difficult quadrant to handle and is the one that needs the greatest adapting. All important events in the past occupy this quadrant.

For the present and future events, first of all make sure that it truly is not controllable and really important. If you have done everything to ensure that, the feeling to bring here is that of *acceptance*. You will have to expand your worldview in this situation to include imperfections. Trying to find at least a hint of meaning in this, and keeping gratitude for what is controllable will also help.

I once saw a patient struggling with many medical issues including newly diagnosed breast cancer and not having a child of her own. Her heart, however, was stuck in her father's illness; he had Alzheimer's dementia and was like a two-year-old child. She could take every challenge but not the vacant look of her father's eyes. We together found some comfort in the interpretation that maybe her father wished to give her the experience of raising a child since she had no child of her own. This provided some meaning to the patient toward his and her suffering, she was able to anchor on to this meaning, find strength, accept the reality, and thereby find an island of peace.

C – Controllable but not so important – Differentiating between what is important and not so important needs delicate judgment. Keep two general ideas in mind: 1) In research studies as well as in life when we ask people what provides the most meaning to their lives, the most common answer almost always is—relationships. So have a lower threshold to keep relationship-related issues in the important quadrant. 2) Everything that is controllable has a cost to controlling it. For example, if your partner slurps while drinking tea and you do not enjoy that sound you certainly can ask him or her to change the habit! However, this will be at a cost; s/he might feel a little slighted. If you try to conform everyone to your preferences, you will begin to gradually isolate yourself. So before trying to control the controllable but not important, look at the cost. Be easy going and flexible in your preferences. Pick your battles wisely.

D – Not controllable not important – Response to the issues in this quadrant is obvious and simple but not always easy to do. Accept the issue and let it go. For example, if you find the anchor of a TV show annoying, do not let it make you angry or upset. This is not important for your life and something that you cannot easily fix. Try to reinterpret the situation. Maybe s/he is purposefully behaving that way to appeal to a certain segment of the audience. Maybe s/he is going through a tough phase of life. Most people in the world have their share of sorrows. We feel our sorrows are worse than others because we compare our inside with others' outside. Physical suffering may be seen outside; emotional suffering cannot be easily seen. Emotional suffering, however, accounts for the bulk of our suffering. This may instill a feeling of compassion within you for everyone and thereby help you accept them as they are. A perished plant in the garden, colder winter, more snow than usual, the shape of your office building, traffic on the road, the accent of your colleague—the list is endless of issues that might create micro irritation in you, yet are neither fixable and most likely not very important. Acceptance and letting go of such issues would be ideal.

I commonly go over this exercise with patients and learners struggling with many simultaneous challenges in life such as medical conditions, relationship issues, financial constraints, work-related concerns, illness in the family, etc. Misfortunes often do not come alone. It is not uncommon, however, when we sit together we can prioritize the challenges into more manageable portions and respond only to the controllable and important.

To summarize this exercise I would say—characterize your challenges and then respond to the important and controllable, use judgment for not so important and controllable, and for the rest cultivate the attitude of acceptance by modifying your worldview to also include some imperfections.

Exercise 12. Patience
Spend a day in limitless patience. Listen fully and deeply to what others have to say. Eat with patience. Be patient with your child, a forgetful employee or employer, with your spouse or loved one. Try to find wonder in each experience. Select the following choices after such an experience.

Table 30.2 Table for Exercise 12		
	Yes	**No**
Was your day more efficient than usual?	☐	☐
Did you absorb and learn more?	☐	☐

Were you more relaxed than other days?	☐	☐
Did you connect with others more deeply?	☐	☐
Did you feel more fulfilled at the end of the day?	☐	☐
Any other comments:		

The concept of time created by human imagination has enslaved us in many ways. It is interesting that an entity that has no independent existence affects our life so much. Part of this is due to how we relate with time. Time these days is measured in seconds—Internet seconds. Most information gathering occurs primarily by reading the headlines. We tend to react with the speed of an efficient web search engine. We jump to pick up the phone at the first ring, often send an instant reply to an e-mail before having thought through the details. We hear others speak but seldom are truly listening because we already ostensibly seem to know what they might have to say. The window of that momentary pause when they stop to breathe provides us the perfect opportunity to start broadcasting our thoughts! ***Most of this impatience with few exceptions is purely internal and largely unnecessary.***

Most things will come to you, if only you could wait. Make time for everything you do so you enjoy the process. Speed often is a killer of quality. Forcefully opening a bud will not make the flower bloom. There is nowhere to go once a task is over, just another task. Be with what you are doing and you will begin doing it with greater joy and to a higher perfection. It might take a few more moments. The world can wait and so can you, a few seconds for sure.

Patience is a virtue, often not inherent in us, and has to be cultivated. Practice patience in every day events. At the dining table, while loading the dishwasher, talking to your child, listening to your mom. Just be there at any and all of these times. Look in the eyes of your children as they share the experiences of their benign wonders with you. Try to feel the benevolent voice of your mother. You might find so much wonder and connection that the rest of the world ceases to exist.

Arguments and miscommunication tend to happen because of a lack of our presence, particularly heartful presence. Most people in the world at their core are kind and well-meaning. We, however, project our bias on to what they say. We then fill some of the blanks with our own prejudiced ideas and create an image that is congruent with our thinking at that time. All this might dissolve if you are able to invite patience and trust into each experience and relationship. Impatience and heartfulness are mutually exclusive of each other.

Patience as an attribute has been researched in several studies, with a general consensus that patience is associated with improved well-being and decreased risk of illness. Here is a summary of some of the studies.

- Husbands' impatience-irritability has been associated with their own and their wives' perception of marital dissatisfaction.[250] Interestingly, a husband's achievement striving or global Type A behavior was not correlated with any of these outcomes.

- Impatience and time pressure have been closely linked with increased road traffic accidents[69] and near accidents.[68]

- In young adults time urgency / impatience was associated with increased long-term risk of hypertension.[251]

- Impatience and its accompaniment anger have been associated with worse outcomes after acute heart attack.[252]

- Impatience and anger have been associated with increased progression of carotid atherosclerosis.[253]

- The Recurrent Coronary Preventive Project (RCPP) demonstrated that the addition of Type A counseling to standard cardiac counseling resulted in significant reductions in Type A behavior and in a 44 percent reduction in reinfarction in post-myocardial infarction patients.[254]

- Impatience is also associated with impaired ability to make rational decisions, with impatience being the most common reason for patients leaving the emergency department without being seen.[255]

In summary patience has been associated with the following benefits in research studies:

- Marital satisfaction
- Lower road traffic accidents
- Hypertension
- Better outcomes after heart attack
- Less progression of carotid atherosclerosis
- Lower risk of recurrent heart attack
- Ability to make more rational decisions

To conclude the section on acceptance it might help to summarize some of the lessons we learned in the exercises above. I will state them as useful pearls. The activity is in the form of an exercise. Please pause after you read each point and contemplate it for a moment. Once you feel you have understood the concept, check mark it and then move to the next pearl. If you are not clear, please go back and read the relevant text. You can also use these points when you teach some of these ideas to others.

Table 30.3 Summary of Acceptance		
Pearl #1	You may consult the past to understand the present and anticipate the future, but do not drive looking into the rearview mirror all the time. Accept what has transpired, learn from it, and move on. Make peace with the past.	☐
Pearl #2	What you see as a weed might actually be a flower. It all depends on how you are looking.	☐
Pearl #3	Your source of stress and joy are the same. If you wish away stressors, you might be wishing away your life. Look at a stressor as an opportunity.	☐
Pearl #4	Your circle of control is small. Learn to let go of trivial differences and accept people as they are. This is the best way to change them.	☐
Pearl #5	What is right about you generally trumps what might be wrong about you.	☐
Pearl #6	Impermanence is the truth of life. Everything is in a flux. The sooner you recognize and accept this reality, the earlier you are likely to find peace and progress in life.	☐

Pearl #7	Sharing your blessings is immensely pleasing and is the ultimate treasure you save for your later years.	☐
Pearl #8	Hurry is mostly internal, not external.	☐
Pearl #9	Love, acceptance, and surrender cannot be separated from each other. You love in surrender and surrender in love.	☐
Pearl #10	Carefully pick your battles in life; fix the fixable making sure that treatment is not worse than the disease; let go of and accept the non-controllable by modifying your worldview to also include some imperfections.	☐
Pearl #11	A step back may actually be a move forward.	☐
Pearl #12	A past that is accepted and used to learn useful lessons may stop being as hurtful.	☐
Pearl #13	It is okay to be mindless if you have to be…just be aware that you are mindless.	☐
Pearl #14	Some things you desire….some you may just have to accept.	☐

SECTION IX: THE MEANING & PURPOSE OF LIFE

Précis

To be religious is to have found an answer to the question, what is the meaning of life?

- Albert Einstein

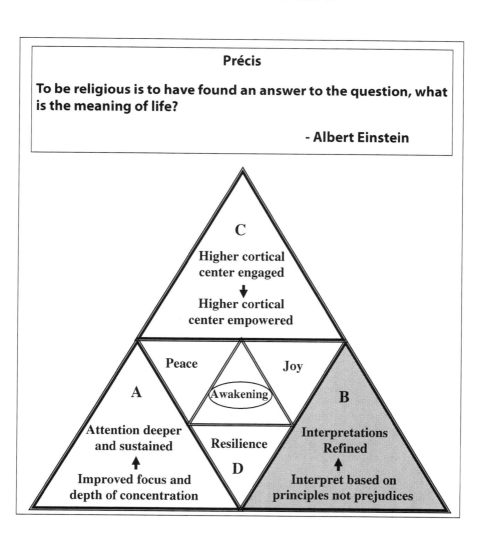

31. What is the Meaning & Purpose of Life?

Alfred Bernhard Nobel, the inventor of dynamite, got a singular opportunity—to look at his life's appraisal and still have a chance to amend it. When Nobel's brother Ludvig (who had nothing to do with dynamite) died in France, a French newspaper published his obituary stating *Le marchand de la mort est mort* ("The merchant of death is dead"). The newspaper editor confused the two brothers. The obituary stated, "Dr. Alfred Nobel, who became rich by finding ways to kill more people faster than ever before, died yesterday." On reading this report, Nobel's grief at his brother's loss turned into shocked disbelief and dismay. Nobel, who held 355 patents, never saw his work in that light and certainly did not want to be remembered that way. So seven years later, in 1895, he directed the establishment of a foundation that would honor individuals "who, during the preceding year, shall have conferred the greatest benefit on mankind." This led to the creation of what is now widely accepted as the most prestigious award in the world, the Nobel Prize, a legacy that will likely continue into perpetuity.

Nobel was lucky in many respects. Through this serendipitous feedback he was able to see the future that helped him find, in time, a true higher meaning to his life. However, it was not luck alone. Nobel's greatness was that he did not dismiss the negative press about him. He did not file a defamation lawsuit. He used this report to his advantage and created a legacy. But for his actions based on this higher meaning, he would have been just another inventor lost in the obscure pages of history books.

There is a good chance that most of us will not get such a transparent feedback about our accomplishments, certainly not in time for us to amend them. And even if we do, we may fail to recognize it. Unless we pause and purposefully contemplate on the true meaning and purpose of our life.

Suffering is pain that has no meaning. Victor Frankl noted, *"Suffering: ceases to be suffering in some way at the moment it finds meaning."* [256] The pain of childbirth, although one of the most severe pains, is accepted by millions of women the world over because of a strong sense of purpose and meaning attached to it—the gift of a beautiful baby. Minus that meaning, the pain would be equated with suffering.

So the single most precious gift you can give to yourself to decrease suffering and find joy is to find and anchor in a deep meaning and purpose of your life. *The ability to find a positive meaning is the most efficient way to extinguish the attention black holes in your mind.* A higher meaning and purpose is one of the key components to refine your interpretations. Living a life without a clear sense of purpose is like entering an unlit room and fumbling around in the dark, or randomly driving at night toward an unknown place without the headlights on. A much more efficient approach would be to pause and turn on the light so you can negotiate your path with greater clarity. This is the light of meaning.

What is this meaning and how can you find a meaning that will accord you lasting peace and happiness? Does such a meaning exist? What do the research studies show in terms of the benefit of finding meaning and purpose in life? How to find such a meaning particularly when it is threatened? These are some of the questions we shall address in this section.

What is the True Meaning in Life?

Meaning in life generally refers to the value and purpose of one's life, important life goals, and for some, spirituality.[257] Another way of looking at meaning refers to the nature of an individual's relationship and understanding of the self and the world. Meaning could span from trying to understand the world at its most expansive cosmic level to the smallest unit of existence at the quantum level. For the present, our focus is somewhere in between, at the level of the individual.

At the individual level there are two aspects of meaning:

1) Our beliefs and understanding of the world (others, circumstances, events, etc.); and
2) Our beliefs and understanding about the self (and our life).

Both these meanings converge toward the single ultimate meaning, which is the present moment. Ultimately what is most important at this very moment is what you are doing right now. The person most important at this moment is the one you are with right now.

Recognize that in the tangible world nothing has an independent and complete meaning. All our meanings are contextual. What is the comparative meaning (value) of a $20 bill for someone whose net worth runs in billions of dollars compared to a hungry orphan child who could buy months worth of food with the same money? A telephone operator at the other end of the phone may be just a voice for you but to someone else she is the precious sweetheart, a mom, a sister, a daughter. She is the epicenter of many little worlds that depend on her. Most birds in your backyard probably have hungry mouths waiting in the nest. Everyone means a lot to someone. It is just a chance that you may not be aware of their larger meaning because you are not that someone (and thus lack the full context). *But you can easily imagine yourself to be that someone.* Once you learn to look at others with the eyes of the person for whom they mean a lot—compassion, acceptance and love will automatically flow. It is a beautiful way to live.

The meaning you carry is extremely important in deciding what you do and how you feel each day. You develop this meaning over a lifetime based on what you see, perceive and imbibe, and how you think. A large proportion of this evaluation, particularly thinking may happen in your sub-conscious—below your level of awareness. An unrealistically negative evaluation is likely to provide you a biased view of the world and the self that can be very damaging in the long term. Many insensitive acts of physical and emotional violence occur within the milieu of lack of an integrated positive meaning. On the contrary, your belief that this world is just and fair, and that you are ethical, capable, and competent, is likely to improve your self-esteem, efficiency, sense of well-being and physical health, and help you pursue a path toward excellence, even greatness.

Long-term vs. Short-term Meaning

In general, most people carry two different types of meaning:

1) Long-term meaning – this is the global meaning that implies your long-term beliefs, values, and purpose/goals of life.
2) Short-term meaning – this is the situational meaning that is applicable to short-term events.

Once you pause and reflect, you may articulate an eloquent long-term meaning and purpose to your life. ***The key question is whether your short-term actions and meaning are aligned with this long-term meaning. If the two are strangers then you are likely to perceive stress.***

Short-term or situational meaning tends to be more labile and depends on changing circumstances such as relationships, health, finances, etc. You are likely to be happier if the short-term meaning of your actions is overall congruent with your long-term meaning. A lack of congruence between the situational and global meanings tends to create conflicts. For example, the simple experience of missing an exit on a highway might create a conflict and be a source of stress. This is because your goal of reaching a place is thwarted by the short-term setback of missing the exit. Resolution of this conflict can be achieved by either changing the situational meaning or the global meaning.[258] It is easier and more efficient to reappraise the situational meaning. In this example, you may not want to change the goal of trying to reach your destination, even if a bit late. However for the short term it might help to consider that had you not missed the exit you may have never noticed the interesting bookstore right around the corner or got an opportunity to spend some more time with your daughter.

Meaning is a fundamental dimension of an individual and depends on a multitude of variables that affect a person's life. These could be social, cultural, religious, philosophical, and personal values. Search for meaning is an important component of several psychological theories that describe how individuals adjust and prevail in their situation.[259-261] It is by finding meaning that individuals have climbed the heights of greatness. Meaning transformed their work and responsibilities into their prayer and calling. Just like the story of the little frail girl from Albania many of us revere.

The Little Girl from Albania

Agnes Gonxha Bojaxhiu grew up in Skopje, the capital city of Albania. Agnes, with a small, gentle frame (just four feet ten inches tall), at an early age had nurtured an ambitious fire within—the fire of compassion. She was fascinated by the lives of missionaries. She lost her father before she turned ten. By the age of twelve she was convinced that she would lead a religious life devoted to the service of others. She acted on this instinct and at age eighteen joined the Sisters of Loreto as a missionary. Initially she worked as a nun and taught English in Darjeeling (India) and later Calcutta. However, her inner self was in turmoil—she had not yet found her calling. She was constantly pained by the poverty and misery she saw around her. She longed to be a healer.

It was in September 1946 at the age of thirty-six that she experienced, "the call within the call." This call was a message that she received that she later recounted: *"I was to leave the convent and help the poor while living among them. It was an order. To fail would have been to break the faith."*[262] This call pointed her to a mission that provided her the meaning she was precisely looking for. It is the strength of this meaning that empowered the relatively unknown Agnes to face up to all the challenges that were to confront her in a foreign land thousands of miles away from home, and transform into Mother Teresa, the epitome of love and compassion who helped and inspired millions of people around the world and will continue to do so for generations to come.

We will next explore in greater details the three types of meaning. This construct will help deepen your understanding of the concept of meaning and provide specific domains for you to find a higher meaning of life. My desire is to be as practical as possible and focus on the ground realities that you and I face each day.

32. The Three Types of Meaning

The three types of meaning reflect the close emotional ties you develop; the most important goals you wish to achieve in the physical world; or your concept of spirituality. In general, across the life span, your beliefs about the world and self can be adapted to three fundamental aspects of your lives:

a) belonging (relationships);
b) doing (work or leisure activities); and
c) understanding oneself and the world (spirituality).

Pause for a second and appreciate that these three aspects—relationships, work and leisure, and spirituality capture most of what you do and experience in your life. It is within these three domains that we shall further develop the concept of meaning.

A. Meaning by Belonging

Relationships provide an identity, a sense of self to us. A question I often ask of patients I see in the clinic is: What provides meaning to your life? The most common answer is—family, mostly children or spouse. My next question then is: What is the source of your stress? The answer again is—family, mostly children or spouse. ***Our fountain of meaning, love, and also of stress often starts at the very same source—our relationships.***

Relationships are our life blood, the primary source of our joy. You may then wonder why our loved ones become the primary source of our stress. ***An important reason for this is that we do not interact with our loved ones on a day to day (short-term) basis the way we deeply feel about them.*** Our short term and long term meanings are then not aligned. We also take their presence in our life for granted and remain oblivious to the meaning they provide to us. As a result we fall short in our relationships. Love however multiplies best when it is shared.

Mother Teresa once said, *"Being unwanted, unloved, uncared for, forgotten by everybody, I think that is a much greater hunger, a much greater poverty, than the person who has nothing to eat."*

Research suggests that we as a society are slowly moving toward increasing loneliness. In a survey involving face to face interview with 1,467 adults representative of the general U.S. population, researchers found that the average number of people who are close confidants of an individual dropped from 2.94 in 1985 to 2.08 in 2004.[263] Almost one out of four (25 percent) participants stated that they had no one they could confide in. It is truly sad that while the population of the world (and the U.S.) continues to grow, we increasingly experience an inner loneliness.

Exercise 1. In the exercise below write the five closest relationships that define you as an individual. For example, I am a wife, I am a father, I am a friend, etc.

I am a _____

I am a _____

I am a _____

I am a _____

I am a _____

What you wrote above represents your primary source of joy—your inner circle. This is your oasis and cushion that nourishes and shields you on a daily basis. Later we will discuss how best to sustain and enrich this inner circle so you can thrive (and not barely survive) in it.

Beyond this inner circle there is also an important outer circle that can also be a source of great joy and sustenance. In order to be optimally effective and happy, you need a healthy relationship with both the circles, inner and outer. The outer circle includes people in your community, your town, your country, your planet. The larger the circle you draw, the more members there are in your family. As your awareness unfolds, the inner and outer circles converge, the distinctions become blurred. It is when you feel connected with your "larger family" that you can share your joy and in turn be nurtured by it. It is this connection that fills your heart with compassion, even for strangers, just as it did for Wesley.

Wesley Autrey, a New York construction worker and Navy veteran, showed extraordinary valor when he saved a nineteen-year-old film student who had fallen onto the tracks of a New York City subway train after suffering a seizure. Wesley did not know the student prior to this incident. Here is how his action was remembered in the 2007 state of the union speech: *"Three weeks ago, Wesley Autrey was waiting at a Harlem subway station with his two little girls, when he saw a man fall into the path of a train. With seconds to act, Wesley jumped onto the tracks, pulled the man into a space between the rails, and held him as the train passed right above their heads. He insists he's not a hero. Wesley says: 'We got guys and girls overseas dying for us to have our freedoms. We got to show each other some love.' There is something wonderful about a country that produces a brave and humble man like Wesley Autrey."* I agree.

B. Meaning by Doing

There are only a few things you can do day after day, week after week, month after month for years together. One of them is work. Most vacations, fun expeditions, and other leisure activities if overextended will likely eventually lose their charm. Beyond the material needs to pay your bills, work provides a sense of self-worth and meaning to your existence. This may be particularly so if your work provides an optimal change and challenge, there is opportunity to grow, you get a fair compensation, expectations are predictable, you have a sense of control, and are accorded due respect. To paraphrase Viktor Frankl, we do not need a tensionless state but rather the striving and struggling for a worthwhile goal, a freely chosen task…the call of a potential meaning waiting to be fulfilled.

Work is healing because it provides a sense of self-efficacy. Work provides you a broader perspective and a sense of control since you can make things happen. This becomes even more important when you voluntarily or involuntarily have to leave your work—an issue that will be faced by the seventy-seven million baby boomers as they begin their retirement years starting 2011.[264] The sum total of research suggests that loss of meaningful work has negative effects on health.

In a landmark Greek study, the health effects of age at retirement was evaluated in 16,827 men and women.[265] All baseline important factors that might predict survival were included in consideration. Participants were enrolled in the study between 1994 and 1999 and followed up until 2006. Results showed that in comparison to participants still employed, retirees had a 51 percent increase in all-cause death, mostly because of increased risk of cardiovascular disease. A five-year increase in age at retirement was associated with a 10 percent decrease in risk of death.

In another study across ten European countries involving 11,462 participants, among employed workers, 18 percent reported poor health, whereas this proportion was 37 percent in retirees.[266] Further, persons not having paid employment had significantly greater likelihood of having long-term illnesses such as depression, stroke, diabetes, chronic lung disease, and musculoskeletal disease. In a study involving petroleum and petrochemical industry (Shell Oil) in the U.S., the effect of early retirement on survival was assessed.[267] The study showed that participants who retired early (at age fifty-five) had a 37 percent increased risk of death compared to those who retired at age sixty-five.

Retirement also is not always associated with greater joy. In research studies retirement has not been found to be associated with increase in sports or non-sports leisure-time physical activity[268] and may be associated with weight gain, particularly in women.[269] Such effects, however, have considerable individual variability that is related to how you choose to spend your retirement time and are able to put energy behind your choices.

So how best can you make the golden years really golden? The most important aspect is to develop a sense of meaning and purpose for this phase of life. Keeping a disciplined schedule and engaging in meaningful activities wherein people or project/s depend on your attention and care will help your-self esteem, keep you healthier, and might even increase your longevity. Such meaningful work does not have to be structured or limited to a specific definition of how the work is understood. Continued engagement in any purposeful activity that provides you a sense of self-worth may obviate many of the negative effects of inactivity that comes with retirement. This is particularly so if you approach it with energy. Research shows that if you provide support to someone else, you are likely to remain healthier for a longer time. In a study involving 681 older adults, providing informal tangible support to fellow church members was associated with better health, mainly for participants deeply committed to their faith. This is a beautiful example of the synergistic effect of finding meaning by doing to support relationships, in the context of faith.[270]

A kind person is doing himself a favor....(Proverbs 11:17 ICB)

Another study evaluated the effect of financial strain on survival in late life. This study involved interview of a nationwide sample of 1500 older adults in 2001 and 2004. The study showed that providing social support to fellow church members was associated with a decreased effect of the providers' own financial problems on decreased survival. The investigator of this study (Dr. Neal Krause) made an important and apt conclusion that *"finding ways to help older adults become more involved in providing support to others at church may form the basis for developing interventions aimed at improving their quality of life."*[271]

Several years ago I had the privilege of taking care of an elderly patient, Carol, who was admitted to the hospital with heart failure and a rapid, irregular heart beat. Carol was eighty-eight years old at that time and had severe narrowing of her aortic valve (it was about as narrow as the tip of a pencil). The aortic valve regulates the flow of blood to the entire body and if it is narrow, blood flow to the body may be severely compromised. Patients with the narrow aortic valve who develop heart failure live only an average of six months unless they undergo surgery, which Carol had refused.

Understandably, I was very worried about Carol. She, however, had a luster in her eyes that I will never forget. Carol told me in her weak yet determined voice, "I am not dying anytime soon, doctor. I have several kids to take care of all over the world." Carol was the godmother of four children in Ethiopia, India, and Pakistan and was paying for their food and education from her meager income that comprised mostly of Social Security benefits. Carol also kept herself deeply engaged in their progress and was in constant touch with their care providers. This purpose gave her the energy and drive to keep going despite her illness and loneliness. The outcome was that Carol did better than most patients I have seen or heard of with her problem. She was discharged two days later and, defying all the statistics, remained active for four more years after that episode. I remain convinced that she did better than most at least partly because of the strong sense of purpose she carried with her.

You could look at what you do as a chore that you have to complete to pay the bills. *On the other hand, you could consider your work as a calling* and approach it with a drive and passion that allows you to transform your micro world in a small yet precious way. The latter approach is likely to drive away stressful feelings that sometimes come with work. People who look at their work as their calling become the agents of change. Intellect is not in short supply in this world; what we need is focus that is energized by enthusiasm. Attaching your work with something larger than you may provide it a higher meaning and is likely to help you cultivate that enthusiasm.

With this zeal, the boundaries between you and your work start getting blurred. You become your work. Mahatma Gandhi, Martin Luther King, and His Holiness the Dalai Lama represent three highly passionate individuals whose lives are known by their pursuit of a higher goal—the goal of getting justice and freedom through non-violent efforts. Their tireless work will continue to inspire future generations of visionaries and leaders. Just an inner awareness that the work you are doing is meaningful and will help a real person is enough to provide you respite from exhaustion and infuse a bolus of mental strength.

As meaning is progressively found in work, a state of connectedness develops with it. This fosters the "state of flow" where your skills and challenges are optimally matched. Work then becomes a pleasure and, despite its intensity, totally relaxing. When you reach this state, you will have found meaning through your work.

Sometimes, however, the full meaning of what you are doing may not be easily discernible, particularly in a large and complex organization. In such instances a belief in the existence of a larger meaning and maintaining a state of joyous acceptance while being absorbed in the activities of the present moment will likely bridge the time until the meaning spontaneously unfolds. The continuity and thread of our purpose is often apparent only when we look back.

Exercise 2. In the exercise below try to fill out the three most important work-related roles that you accomplish every day. For example—I am a teacher; I am a homemaker, etc.

I am a _____

I am a _____

I am a _____

Now ponder for a moment and try to find a larger meaning in what you do. For example, if you are a teacher, you provide the education and mentorship to the next generation of professionals so they can go out, succeed, help others, and further the cause of your country.

Exercise 3. In a few words describe how your work helps you, your family, community, and country.

My work helps me by –

_____

_____

My work helps my family by –

_____

_____

My work helps my community by –

_____

_____

My work helps my country by –

_____

_____

What you wrote above is the larger meaning of what you do. On a not so lucky day when you are feeling low for any number of reasons (particularly related to work), it might help to remember the larger role you fulfill. This might prop you up a little and provide you the needed energy to continue your pursuits with enthusiasm.

C. Meaning by Understanding Oneself and the World (Spirituality)

The Pew Forum on Religion & Public Life recently conducted one of the largest surveys involving over 35,000 Americans about their religious beliefs.[272] The study showed that 92 percent of Americans believe in God. The study also showed a remarkably mature and nonexclusive attitude: the majority (70 percent) believed that many religions can lead to eternal salvation. Further, most Americans have an open, non-dogmatic approach in their religious interpretation: more than two-thirds agree that there is more than one true way to interpret the teachings of their faith. One out of three surveyed stated that they receive answers to their prayer requests at least once a month and have experienced or witnessed divine healing. Spirituality is thriving in America!

Spirituality broadly relates to a combination of faith and meaning (meaning through faith). Spirituality is believed by some to provide a transcendental meaning to life, a sense of knowing that sometimes cannot be fully expressed in words. What is considered spiritual is very individual. For some, spirituality connotes one's relation with nature, for others it is work, family or community, and for still others spirituality means a relationship with God or even a metaphysical or transcendental phenomena.[273, 274]

Religion and spirituality are closely related. Religion can simply be understood as an individualized instruction manual of living. Religion represents beliefs, practices, values, and rituals that help people fulfill their spiritual needs.[275]   Many religions are associated with recognition of a higher power commonly understood as God or another exalted being.

Research studies suggest that religion/spirituality are often closely associated with meaning in life.[276-278] In the context of medical illness, spirituality acts as a cushion that allows you to use positive coping skills so you can consider the stressful event as a challenge and thereby engage with it instead of perceiving it as uncontrollable.[279]

Spirituality becomes particularly important in the midst of profound suffering such as being diagnosed with terminal cancer, losing a loved one, witnessing a natural calamity, or when severely depressed. In a research study involving patients with breast cancer, having a strong sense of meaning and purpose, and a good understanding of self and life was associated with better psychological adjustment and health status.[280] Further, the intrusive thoughts that often appear with such a diagnosis had much lesser impact on the individuals.

Eckhart Tolle in his moment of deep despair had a profound realization. He recounts his experience in his popular book, *The Power of Now: "I cannot live with myself any longer. This was the thought that kept repeating itself in my mind. Then suddenly I became aware of what a peculiar thought it was. Am I one or two? If I cannot live with myself, there must be two of me: the 'I' and the 'self' that 'I' cannot live with. Maybe, I thought, only one of them is real. I was so stunned by this strange realization that my mind stopped. I was fully conscious, but there were no more thoughts...."*[281] This spiritual experience and what followed provided Eckhart a profound realization of the meaning of life and his existence, and propelled him to share and teach what he had learned through direct experience.

Such a direct realization is unique and precious. What becomes clear from Eckhart's experience is that there might be two versions of self—contextual self and the observer self. Your contextual definitions change with each moment, sometimes for good and at other times not so good. This state of flux, the constant becoming, was recognized by the Buddha as *Anicca*—the ever changing state. A deeper understanding of this concept allows you to understand the preciousness of each moment since each moment is unique, a state of constant unfolding.

The observer self does not change and is equated by some with the spark of divinity within us (sometimes also considered the soul). According to this concept, soul represents the fundamental truth, the ultimate meaning of our existence within this world that at the macrocosmic level is connected with the supreme existence. Soul can be equated with the cloth behind the pattern. Despite the apparent differences you see in a design, the underlying cloth that provides the basis remains the same. The colors you see are but the play of light. The colors may change; the underlying cloth, however, remains the same. It is this element that might define you and remains the same all your life. The first time you open your eyes as an infant, the real you looking at the world from behind those beautiful eyes is this self; and it is this self that will look at the world when you breathe last—and at all the moments in between.

Amongst the two polar beliefs—one believing in the existence of observer self and the other stating "there is no self"—eventually it might not matter which specific belief you carry, if any. Either of these beliefs or a third or fourth one have provided peace to individuals for thousands of years. The important element is to at least contemplate these thoughts. When you think along these lines, you are likely to take a broader, mature, and more inclusive perspective toward life. If you are able to find an anchor within the true unchanging self or with the present moment or any other entity that you have faith in, such an anchor will help you take your awareness away from the daily tribulations, invite a state of calm to the inner mind, and bring lasting peace. *Such awareness over a period of time annihilates the attention black holes within the mind.*

Is such a belief or any belief necessary or helpful? Let us answer the second part of the question first. Such a belief certainly helps. For example, in a series of two studies involving 826 patients with cancer, spiritual well being (faith and a sense of meaning) were positively associated with health related quality of life.[282] So while such a belief may not be necessary it can certainly help (as long as it is not forced). Let us see what the supernatural and natural theorists opine.

Supernaturalist theories posit that a personal relationship with the spiritual element (that some might call God) is necessary to develop a comprehensive world view that is meaningful, and life might be meaningless without the existence of this spiritual element or our relationship with it. This view suggests that the divine element has a plan for each of us, the plan is meaningful, and our ability to pursue this plan would provide the ultimate meaning to our life. Fulfilling this plan provides meaning and not fulfilling this plan would be a recipe for a meaningless life. On the other hand, naturalist theories suggest that science alone can provide adequate meaning for an individual. Life in and of itself is meaningful without necessarily invoking another entity to provide meaning to it.

The basic question we face then boils down to this: Do we need an infinite principle (or God) to provide an ultimate meaning to us? The meaning that our work and relationships provide us is ever changing. Everything that provides meaning draws its meaning from something else. As Robert Nozick asks, do we then need to regress to something infinite that is all encompassing and need not go beyond itself to find meaning from anything else? If the answer is yes for you, then the belief in existence of God (however you wish to define God) and possibly an observer self is likely to help. If the answer is no, then the ultimate meaning may be the present moment, the continuous becoming. The choice of yes or no is very individual that I will leave to your own wisdom. ***Either side of the aisle can provide you peace, as long as you have a belief and spend at least some time thinking about it!***

33. Meaning: Additional Perspectives

We have thus far looked at the three core aspects of our existence—work, relationships, and spirituality. They seem like distinct entities but in reality are closely related. In your pursuit toward living a life that is true to a higher purpose, all of these merge. Self, relationships, work, and spirituality become a single whole. Differences seem meaningless. When you cannot distinguish self from any of these entities, you are living a life immersed in the deepest meaning. It is a blissful state of spontaneous peace, flow, and total contentment. In order to move along that path, it will help you to understand a few additional concepts about meaning in life.

Meaning Already Exists; You do not have to Invent the Meaning

In the movie *Jerry McGuire*, Jerry (Tom Cruise) and Dorothy (Renee Zellweger) struggle in their marriage with the ups and downs of Jerry's career. In his moment of success, Jerry finally realizes the importance and meaning of his relationship with his wife. He goes to meet her in the middle of a gathering and says, *"...But tonight, our little project, our company, had a very big night. A very, very big night. But it wasn't complete, wasn't nearly close to being in the same vicinity as complete, because I couldn't share it with you. I couldn't hear your voice, or laugh about it with you. I missed my wife. We live in a cynical world, a cynical, cynical world, and we work in a business of tough competitors. I love you. You complete me. And if I just had..."* I get touched and emotional each time I watch this scene, particularly when Dorothy stops him and expresses her modest feelings in these words, *"Shut up. Just shut up...You had me at hello. You had me at hello."*

Jerry had discovered the meaning in his relationship that already existed, but his vision wasn't previously as clear so he could not see it all this while. The same holds true for many of us. When our attention is drawn into our mind, caught within the attention black holes or otherwise, we cannot easily practice our presence with love. Our interpretations are then based on prejudices and are largely egocentric (self-focused). In this state we are likely to push joy and love away. Once our attention transforms (even for a brief moment) as it did for Jerry, we may immediately realize our priorities. If your previous actions are not in coherence with these priorities, it is time for restitution—which is what Jerry did. Do not postpone doing the right thing at this time. If you miss it now, this opportunity may not present itself again for years.

We do not have to invent the meaning. It already exists; we just have to discover it. Patients diagnosed with cancer often find a deeper meaning by developing a new attitude toward life, increased self-knowledge, and reordering of priorities.[260] This meaning was always there—just as fire is hidden in a block of wood but can only flare once all the needed ingredients are created for it to manifest. Similarly meaning can only be seen when we are able to see and think with total freedom. In this moment of realization you take off your colored glasses of judgments and bias and see the reality in its purity. It is within your ability to reach this deeper meaning without necessarily going through a life changing experience. The process, however, is not easy since it entails letting go of ego, engaging the free will and conscience, bringing unconditional gratitude, compassion, acceptance, and forgiveness and anchoring your presence in the present moment. A tall order indeed!

Meaning in Totality may not be Comprehensible

Mother Teresa spent all her adult life thousands of miles away from her home in the service of the poor and underprivileged. She is considered the embodiment of a spiritual being who truly understood the purpose of her life. Her inner thoughts, expressed in letters she had written over a sixty-year period, were recently published in a book *Mother Teresa: Come Be My Light*.[283] The world was astounded to learn that Mother Teresa struggled with spiritual meaning and experienced inner conflict and "emptiness" for most of her adult life. She wrote in September 1979 to Rev. Michael Van Der Peet, *"Jesus has a very special love for you. As for me, the silence and the emptiness is so great that I look and do not see, listen and do not hear."* Just eleven weeks later while receiving the Nobel Peace prize, she spoke, *"It is not enough for us to say, 'I love God, but I do not love my neighbor,' since in dying on the Cross, God had [made] himself the hungry one—the naked one—the homeless one."*[284] She was aware of the discrepancy between her inner conflicts and her public conduct that gave the perception that she was anchored in deep faith and a constant meditative prayer. She herself wrote in one of the letters, *"The smile is 'a mask' or 'a cloak' that covers everything."'*

Without attempting to over interpret the letters and feelings of Mother Teresa, her inner experiences despite her tireless work suggest that the totality of meaning of our life may not be easily known. Our concept of meaning reflects our present state and the paradigms in which we exist. Beyond the meaning that we can derive in the material world, it helps to keep the faith that a larger meaning exists and continue to work just as

Mother Teresa did. In my opinion, her conduct despite her inner struggles makes her work even more admirable. In some ways it reflects a true faith wherein you love the divine not even knowing if s/he exists.

In my medical school training, when I saw mice and frogs being used as "objects" in laboratory experiments, I longed to somehow whisper to them that their sacrifice indeed would serve a larger meaning and may someday help us develop life-saving medications. The meaning of our pain and suffering in this world may be a bit similar. It is possible (probably likely) that a larger meaning exists but eludes us today because of our ignorance. We will need patience and determination to keep the faith and continue a charitable disposition until the light of tomorrow enlightens us. If we can look back at our past failures with compassion and acceptance, we might discover a meaning in them that eluded us when we were experiencing the event in the "now." **The past is certainly not etched in stone.** As we learn more and find deeper meaning, the past itself sometimes changes—at least our interpretation of it. By the same token, our present also may turn out to have a different, more profound meaning that may only be discernible in the future.

The short-term loss of meaning and faith that is often experienced by the exalted saints is described by the Spanish mystic St. John of the Cross as the "dark night" of the soul.[284] At the cross, Jesus is believed to have cried in a loud voice, *"Eloi, Eloi, lema sabachthani? (My God, my God, why have you forsaken me?)"* (Mk 15:34; cf. Mt 27:46). These words of Jesus may have reflected his pain of separation; a separation that in reality did not exist. The "dark night" of the exalted beings might have a purpose—to provide comfort to us mortals by showing that it is not easy to find meaning, particularly the most comprehensive meaning. No wonder Victor Frankl noted that **the more comprehensive the meaning, the less comprehensible it is.**

Meaning Provides Joy even at the Cost of Personal Pleasure

In a series of four studies to assess the impact of personal vs. charitable (pro-social) spending on happiness, as a first step researchers asked 632 participants to rate their general happiness at baseline.[18] In this study, higher charitable spending was found to be associated with significantly greater happiness while personal spending was unrelated to happiness. As a next step investigators followed sixteen employees of a company after they received a bonus.[18] Their findings suggested that charitable spending of the bonus (buying a gift for someone else or donating to charity) and not personal spending was a predictor of increased happiness. The size of the bonus had little correlation with lasting happiness. In the third step investigators randomly assigned forty-six participants to spend ($5 or $20) on themselves or on others.[18] Participants assigned to spending the money on others reported greater happiness compared to participants who spent money on themselves. The amount again made no difference.

Finally, as a fourth step, researchers designed a clever experiment to understand why we do not engage in pro-social actions when spending as little as $5 on others can increase our happiness.[18] They asked forty participants to answer two questions: 1) what would make you happier—spending money on you or others; and 2) what would make you happier—getting $5 or $20. For both the questions participants guessed it wrong. They reported that spending money on themselves would make them happier and that $20 would make them more happy compared to $5! The results of this fourth step might explain why we do not engage much in charitable spending—simply because we do not believe it will make us happy. The truth is that charity and loss both lead to loss. Charity increases your happiness while the undesired loss does not.

Independent of the outcome of a pro-social action, the very process of such an action is meaningful and makes us happier even at the cost of personal pleasure. Ed Diener and Robert Biswas-Diener, reputed happiness researchers, note that the essence to psychological wealth is to have meaning in life along with an ability to try to achieve it and patience along the path.[285] Across all cultures, having a goal and purpose, self-respect, having a tribe and ability to meet basic needs gives happiness. Anchoring your happiness to money is a recipe for failure since money is fleeting, often not easy to earn, and can be easily taken away. This is exemplified in the melting away of individual assets of several billionaires in the year 2008, some of whom lost 80 percent to 100 percent of their net worth.[286] I hope they anchored their meaning in servicing others and not just increasing their accumulated wealth.

Meaning is Often in the Process, not in a Possible Grand Finale

Sir Edmund Hillary, the celebrated mountaineer, had a very clear vision about mountain climbing. In his opinion, *"Nobody climbs mountains for scientific reasons. Science is used to raise money for the expeditions, but you really climb for the hell of it."* The climb is a process. Reaching the summit certainly is an ecstatic event and culminates the climb; however, what needs to be enjoyed is the totality of the journey and not just the grand finale. Excessive focus on the outcome has the risk of making a person obsessive, selfish, mindless, and anxious through the climb. It is this self-focused attitude that may partially explain why a British climber was left alone to die just as about forty climbers are thought to have walked past him in their pursuit of the peak of Mount Everest.

Most summits we reach are not really our final goals. As Herbert Hoover noted, *"Just when the ends meet, somebody moves the ends."* The moment we reach a particular destination, we often begin a new journey. The period at the end of a sentence typically marks the beginning of a new sentence. There will always be greater wealth, proficiency, or fame than what you have achieved. No matter the heights you reach, greater heights exist. The purpose of this realization is not to stop the progress. The purpose is to know that the final destination is but an illusion; what is real and would provide lasting meaning is the journey. What will stay with you is the memory of the moments spent on the path. **The voyage itself may be the destination.**

The belief that life ought to be defined by a final outcome at some future point, a grand finale, tends to postpone the joy. It is the present that has the greatest power. Every moment of our experience was, is, and will be in the present. If the present lacks meaning, then it is likely that tomorrow and the day after will also be the same. The past created the meaning for today; the present is likely to define tomorrow. Sir Edmund Hillary aptly summarized his lifetime of observations in this quote, *"It is not the mountains that we conquer, but ourselves."*

Meaning That is Unique Yet Similar

The human brain with billions of neurons and trillions of connections has an almost infinite number of ways that the neurons can be interconnected. The uniqueness of these connections is caused by and in turn leads to unique thinking patterns. No wonder what superficially provides meaning seems to be very individual. This uniqueness is precious and is precisely the reason this world has such a lovely variety.

Our gift of free will allows us to be creative and provides us the means to discard, modify, and discover newer and finer paradigms. Despite the differences in means and sometimes perceptibly different short-term meaning, however, the deeper long-term meaning of different people is more similar than different.

The means we use are often related to individual beliefs and desires. These beliefs are often guided by individual preferences and skills. Werner Heisenberg said, *"What scientists observe is not nature itself, but nature exposed to our method of questioning."* Abraham Maslow most astutely noted, *"He that is good with a hammer tends to think everything is a nail."* Looking for a nail to hammer since that is the only skill you possess may be helpful for the short term. However, what will you do when all the nails run out? It is important to be able to readjust the means to a meaning.

Do not confuse meaning in life with the means you use to achieve that meaning. Meaning might remain the same even as the means keep changing. Maintaining openness to newer means fosters growth, allows diversity, and also makes it easier for you to connect with others who might seemingly be using different means. So what is the meaning that connects all our different roles?

When you are seeing patients during the day or doing some other work your identity is that of a care provider, a healer or a professional. At home or socially your role is that of a husband or wife, father or mother, son or daughter, brother or sister, or a friend. If you carry the momentum you derive from one domain to the other, you risk creating an imbalance, particularly if this becomes a habit and is excessive. The question is, in the midst of these rapidly changing roles, is there a common thread that joins it all? I think there is and **the two threads that join all the roles we play, that are the true meaning and purpose of our life are, service and love.**

Every serving of our life can be accommodated into the twin bowls of service and love. Service and love are complete in themselves. They need not regress into another purpose—service for the sake of service and love for the sake of love. A meaning so anchored instills selflessness with fearlessness and equanimity as desirable by products. Further, this meaning can never be taken away from you. While your roles in life may continue to change, no one can usurp your right to be of service and love.

Understanding the meaning of our life provides us our true identity. I think a complete transcendent identity that is not limited by space, time or any other dimensions, by relationships, nationality or any other identifier is this, **"You and I are all agents of service and love."**

To the extent we can embody the ideals of service and love in our thoughts, actions and intentions, no matter how small our role, we accomplish the ultimate meaning and purpose of our life, not in the psychological domains of past and future, but right now in the present moment.

34. Why Find Meaning & Purpose?

Henri Dunant was a relatively unknown Swiss businessman in the late 1800s. He would have remained unknown but for an inner awakening he experienced through a transformative experience—he witnessed a battle. In 1859 Dunant saw the Battle of Solferino (between the French and Austrians on June 24, 1859). This battle resulted in nearly 40,000 casualties. Dunant saw the plight of wounded soldiers with thousands of them left to die after the conflict due to lack of resources. Moved by their misery, Dunant organized emergency aid services for the Austrian and French soldiers by soliciting help from civilians. He later wrote a book about this tragedy, *Un Souvenir de Solférino* (1862; A Memory of Solferino). In this book he proposed the formation of voluntary relief societies for the prevention and alleviation of suffering in war and peacetime and also an international agreement covering the war wounded. The next year, in 1863, he founded the International Committee for the Relief of the Wounded (now called the International Committee of the Red Cross). He later continued to promote humane treatment of the prisoners of war. Dunant's work was later recognized and he shared the Nobel Peace Prize in 1901 (International Red Cross itself received the Nobel Peace Prize in 1917).

Dunant could have been another observer of war. But something inside him was shaken when he saw all the suffering. Providing relief to soldiers of war and their humane treatment became the meaning and purpose of his life. This meaning transformed Dunant from an unknown businessman into an international figure. The work he started has touched and will continue to benefit millions of lives for years to come. Oscar Schindler, who saved 1,200 lives during the time of the Holocaust, was also able to anchor his awareness toward a higher meaning that provided him a purpose beyond the service of self.

Benefits of Finding Meaning

The two primary benefits of finding meaning are:

1) *Meaning provides focus and channels your energies into a productive endeavor; and*
2) *Having a secure meaning improves your sense of well-being and helps you cope better with adversity, medical or otherwise.*

Meaning increases resilience and trains and rightwires your brain to engage its higher center.

A meaning that resonates with you focuses your energy, decreases stress, enormously improves your efficiency, and becomes your faithful companion on the path toward excellence. This focus is necessary because a cart driven by seven horses all running in random directions will go nowhere. Focused electricity when targeted through a laser beam can cut metal. I sometimes ask the audience in my presentations if anyone has a lot of free time in their lives they can spare. Never have I seen anyone raise their hands. The world is busy, we all are very busy. But often we are not focused busy. It is amazing how fast the day goes by. A few e-mails and meetings, a cup of coffee or two, some phone calls, and the day is over. Days, weeks, months, years, the entire life may pass by you if you fail to notice. One of the ways to revert this monotony is to find meaning and purpose in what you do, which in turn provides the two essential tools for excellence—focus and passion.

I intend to present next the result of research studies that have looked at the effect of an ability to find meaning on important health outcomes. In the process we will try to answer two important questions:

Q1. Does having a sense of meaning and purpose improve mental and physical health, general well-being, and quality of life?
Q2. What are the effects of finding meaning on the structure and function of the brain?

Q1. Does having a sense of meaning and purpose improve mental and physical health, general well-being, and quality of life?

The sum total of research suggests that having a sense of meaning and purpose improves individual well-being and quality of life. Below I will summarize the results of a few research studies.

- A study of 149 non-custodial grandparents evaluated predictors of their level of satisfaction.[287] The role of being a grandparent was found to be satisfying because it provided a sense of purpose and being valued in later years of life when the need for such a feeling may be the greatest.

- A study involving 122 healthy university students showed that sense of meaningfulness was associated with effective coping of past stressful life events. [288] Meaningfulness correlated with contact with self, others, and the world, whereas meaninglessness was associated with a state of alienation from self, others, and the world. Further, current sense of meaningfulness was associated with an effective coping with stressful life events of the past.

- In a survey, thirty-four torture survivors who had no history of political activity were compared with fifty-five tortured political activists. Outcome measures included assessments for measures of anxiety, depression, and post-traumatic stress disorder. Results showed that, compared with political activists, non-activists were subject to less severe torture but had higher levels of symptoms. Those interested in politics were protected by commitment to a cause and prior immunization to traumatic stress and unpredictability and uncontrollability of stressors, amongst other factors.[289]

- In a study involving elderly residents in Leganes, a city in central Spain, having a confidant was associated with a 25 percent better survival over six years.[290] In this study, lack of social participation increased risk of death by 50 percent. An important aspect of this study was that engagement in meaningful roles and providing others support was protective, while receipt of emotional support alone did not help much.

- In a study involving the survey of 931 U.S. adults post-9/11, being able to find meaning was associated with lower posttraumatic stress symptoms.[291] Finding meaning supported adjustment by reducing fears of future terrorism. Thus being able to find meaning might help even after events that negatively influence people's assumptions about security.

- In a natural experiment, one hundred Chinese immigrants who were caught in political unrest were followed up over a period of time. Those who saw past and present as interesting, challenging, and relatively satisfying were more likely to remain healthy. Those who saw their situation as threatening, frustrating, and demanding had a greater tendency to fall sick.[292]

- In a survey involving 1,012 Canadian women with a history of breast cancer, considering diagnosis of cancer as a challenge or value was associated with lower depression, lower anxiety, and better quality of life at three years follow up compared to looking at cancer as an enemy, punishment, or loss.[293]

- In a study involving 260 patients with gynecologic cancers, loss of meaning in life was associated with a higher level of depressive symptoms.[294]

- In a study involving seventy-eight patients with a previous history of breast cancer, meaning in life showed significant positive correlation with spirituality, and negative correlation with stress and distress.[295]

- In a study in Australia involving one hundred patients with cancer, social support and personal meaning were found to be related to lower psychological distress.[296]

- In a study involving seventy-four patients with recurrent cancer, having a sense of meaning in life was associated with lower distress and social dependency, and positively correlated with adjustment to illness.[297]

- In a study involving twenty-three cancer survivors, loss of meaning of life (provided by ability to work) resulted in a loss of a part of identity and satisfaction.[298] Patients missed personal challenges related to work and made efforts to compensate for those challenges with other activities that provided them meaning.

- In a study involving sixty cancer survivors, an increased sense of meaning of life (described as self-transformation by investigators) was associated with higher self-esteem and well-being compared to participants who remained stuck and did not experience this transformation.[299]

- In a study that followed twenty-four women diagnosed with breast cancer, women were followed for a period of time to understand the process of how women with breast cancer attribute positive meaning to their illness. Women were able to transform tragedy into positive meaning by reappraising life, developing a new attitude, increasing self-knowledge or self-change, and reordering their priorities.[300] Authors described the sequential four steps as encountering darkness, converting darkness, encountering light, and reflecting light.

- In a study involving 120 men with end-stage cancer, helping a patient realize meaningful existence increased satisfaction with life, self-esteem, and decreased sense of alienation.[301]

- In a study involving older adults who experienced bereavement related to spousal death, participants were followed for a four year period. Study showed that finding meaning in the death and keeping a worldview of accepting death predicted a lower level of anger. Even social support decreased anger through finding meaning in the loss.[302]

- In a study involving 270 patients with cancer, having a global meaning was associated with lower risk of depression and demoralization.[303]

- In a study involving sixty-four patients undergoing knee replacement surgery, a sense of purpose in life was associated with less anxiety, depression, negative affect, functional disability, and stiffness.[304]

- A review of forty-four studies addressing the search for meaning, evaluating meaning as an outcome measure, and also evaluating the growth enhancing aspects of cancer concluded that there is strong evidence that meaning and psychosocial adjustment to a serious illness such as cancer are closely related.[305]

The above studies mostly evaluated the impact of having a self-created innate secure meaning on outcomes. In addition, studies are also emerging that suggest that meaning-based coping can be taught and such an intervention has a positive effect on patient well-being.

- In a small study involving eighteen patients with newly diagnosed cancer within the previous three months, participants were provided a multi-component intervention that involved acknowledging the present, evaluation of the impact of previous coping methods, and a dialog on meaning in life while accepting mortality in the context of a diagnosis of cancer.[306] This intervention was associated with a significant improvement in self-esteem and a greater sense of security in facing the uncertainty of cancer.

- In a study involving emotional disclosure in relation to loss of a relative to breast cancer, setting goals that focused on relationships, personal growth, and striving for meaning in life was associated with increases in natural killer cell cytotoxicity.[307] (Natural killer cells are an important component of the body's defense against infections and cancer)

- Acceptance and Commitment Therapy (ACT) has meaning as an important component of intervention. Positive results with ACT as an intervention are summarized in the chapter 30 (Why Acceptance?).

Q2. What are the effects of finding meaning on the structure and function of the brain?

Studies are just beginning to emerge evaluating the positive effect of finding meaning on the function and structure of our brains. Studies suggest that finding meaning is associated with greater activation of the pre-frontal cortex area (central part of the cortical loop as we discussed earlier).

- An ability to ascribe a non-emotional meaning to highly negative scenes decreased negative feelings. This process caused greater engagement of the lateral and medial pre-frontal regions and related areas of the brain, and decreased activation of the amygdala and medial orbito-frontal cortex.[101, 102]

- In a study involving recoding the meaning when switching the task from one to the next, the lateral pre-frontal cortex was shown to mediate recoding of the response meaning.[103]

- In a study testing the processing of the meaning of syllables, the left pre-frontal cortex was activated when the meaning of a syllable was being processed.[104]

In summary, the following outcomes showed improvement with finding meaning and purpose in specific research studies:

- Life satisfaction
- Coping
- Anxiety
- Depression
- Post traumatic stress
- Survival
- Physical health
- Quality of life
- Self esteem
- Anger

Studies are also beginning to show that ascribing meaning to an event or outcome tends to engage the higher centers of the brain and might provide better control and more adaptive regulation of the limbic system. Only few studies have been done so far in this field and more research is needed in this area.

Having a strong sense of meaning in life may also increase your longevity! In a study involving 1361 older adults, older people who had a strong sense of meaning in life were likely to live longer compared to those who did not have such a sense.[308] This was independent of attending religious services. Thus one of the greatest gift one can give to a person is to help them discover the higher meaning and purpose of their life.

Events that predispose to suffering can not be eliminated from our life experience. However we can attempt to find meaning for the suffering. Once you are able to find a meaning that resonates with your world view, this meaning can then transform suffering. A suffering so transformed often is a pivotal point in individual's spiritual progress. Suffering thus serves a very useful purpose. Pleasure does not come with as many lessons of wisdom as suffering does.

Meaning is important in one more domain. As science progresses our concept of meaning and purpose will continue to evolve. Sequencing of the human genome, stem cell research, and synthetic biology (creating life forms in the lab) are just a few ethical dilemmas our society faces.[309] Understanding a more comprehensive meaning of all this and toward what boundaries can we push the science has to be very carefully negotiated by scientists and thought leaders who have insight into what is the meaning of life.

In the table below is a practice exercise wherein are summarized the benefits of finding meaning we have discussed thus far.

Exercise 1. Write yes or no for the potential benefits of finding meaning in life in the table below:

Table 34.1 Table for Exercise 1		
Statement	**Yes**	**No**
Do you think finding a deeper meaning has the potential to improve your focus?	☐	☐
Do you think finding a deeper meaning has the potential to improve your efficiency?	☐	☐
Do you think finding a deeper meaning has the potential to improve your well-being and decrease stress?	☐	☐
Do you think finding a deeper meaning may engage the higher center of your brain (your cortical loop)?	☐	☐
Is finding meaning within your ability?	☐	☐

Most people who are happy do not look at happiness as a primary goal. They are happy because they enjoy what they do (pre- or post-retirement), are closely bonded with their loved ones, and have a general sense of who they are and what is the purpose of their life. Happiness is a byproduct of the choices you make. If you passively let someone else choose for you, then that choice will be based on their values and not yours. Much more desirable will be to engage fully with life and write your own story yourself. The journey toward this meaning will be rewarding. T.S. Eliot summarized the outcome of this exploration in a deeply meaningful statement, *"We must not cease from exploration and the end of all our exploring will be to arrive where we began and to know the place for the first time."*

35. How to Find Meaning & Purpose

I discussed in chapter 33 the three aspects of your life (relationships, work, and spirituality) that together contribute to your sense of meaning and purpose. We will use this schematic to address specific approaches to help you find the higher meaning in life.

Relationships Rate Higher than Anything Tangible in Providing You True Meaning

In a survey of patients with cancer, patients were asked to list three to seven areas that provided the most meaning in their lives. The top three areas that were most related to meaning in life were: family (80 percent), leisure time (61 percent), and friends (55 percent). Money was rated as important by only 3 percent of the participants.[310] In another study, support of the family was reported as the strongest variable that allowed the participants to consider a negative experience as a challenge rather than punishment.[293]

Three useful ideas: Understanding three related ideas with respect to relationships may help you find and cultivate a deeper meaning. They are:

#1. The first concept relates to the *positivity:negativity (P/N) ratio*. Positivity is the positive feedback you provide to others while negativity is the negative feedback. Within a team, a ratio of five or above suggests excellent team dynamics while low performance teams often have a ratio below one. Marriages that flourish often have a high ratio (typically >5) while those that might end up in divorce have a low ratio (often <1).[311] We will come back to P/N ratio in exercise 2 below, for now just be familiar with this concept.

#2. Another interesting concept to consider in the context of relationships is the Johari model. A simple version of the Johari model is depicted below (Figure 35.1). This model reflects the extent of sharing and common understanding within a relationship. Let us take the example of you and your spouse (or friend or fiancée). The model is a 2x2 table with the columns representing aspects of your relationship that is known to you and rows representing aspects that are known to your spouse (friend or fiancée).

	Known to you	Not known to you
Known to your spouse	A	B
Not known to your spouse	C	D

Figure 35.1   Aspects of relationships known or not known
to you and your spouse (friend or fiancée)

Based on this model, your relationship has four quadrants in terms of the extent of shared information (and thus the quality of communication):
A = Known to you + Known to your spouse
B = Not known to you + Known to your spouse
C = Known to you + Not known to your spouse
D = Not known to you + Not known to your spouse

In general, in most healthy relationships, the northwest quadrant (A) is considerably bigger than the other quadrants. A large quadrant A suggests open communication and understanding. If you are open to the possibility that there is more to you than you can imagine (which indeed is a fact for all of us) and your quadrant A is smaller than it could / should be, the strategies that may help you increase its size might include: (Figure 35.2)

- Get feedback – learn the contents of quadrant B from the others. Be humble, grateful, accepting and gracious in receiving this feedback.
- Share information – share the contents of quadrant C with the others. Be open and honest in sharing the information.
- Use a third person (e.g. consultant) – learn the contents of quadrant D using a third person's perspective, such as asking a friend or taking professional help. Be kind and compassionate in sharing information with the others as a third person.

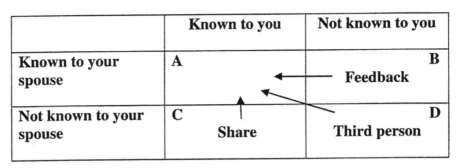

Figure 35.2   Aspects of relationships known or not known to you and your spouse. Quadrant A (the quadrant of shared information) can be expanded by sharing, feedback or asking a third person, formally or informally.

If you want deeper meaningful long-term relationships do whatever it takes to increase the size of quadrant A.

#3. The third concept is well described by Dr. Stephen Covey in his highly acclaimed book, *The Seven Habits of Highly Effective People*.[312] This is the concept of establishing and nurturing an *Emotional Bank Account* with your loved ones. An emotional bank account is the amount of trust and love built into a relationship. Every individual relationship of yours has its own account. It is difficult to maintain a high value account with every relation, friend, and colleague of yours. Practically speaking, it is impor-tant to identify the closest of your relations and friends with whom you wish to maintain a high value account while also keeping some deposits within most other relationships. Every little deposit counts toward this value. In fact, the more trivial the deposit the greater its impact. The gifts you buy for a dollar compared to an expensive gizmo may sometimes be more appreciated by your children. The feeling behind the action is what provides it with the real value. Showing understanding, meeting expec-tations, making good on promises, and being sincere in an apology are likely to enrich this account. Keeping a high P/N ratio will also make a deposit, thus fostering the long-term health of the family.

Figure 35.3 shows recent deposits in my emotional bank account with our six-year-old daughter.

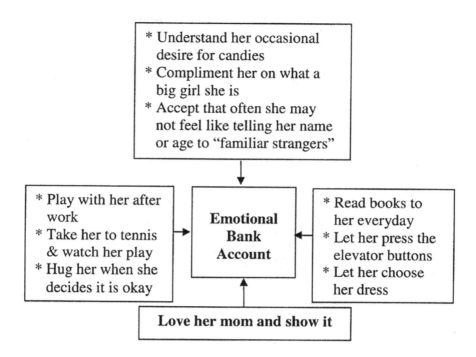

Figure 35.3 My emotional bank account
with our six-year-old daughter

I need to keep the following realities in mind with respect to this account:

1) The account needs constant deposits otherwise it depletes very fast.
2) What counts as a deposit today may not qualify anymore—it may become a basic expectation.
3) More important than buying a toy for her is my finding time to play with her.
4) I should keep most of my promises, or not make them.

The most important deposit is her perception of my love for her and my wife. I need to remember the wisdom in this wonderful quote, ***"The most important thing a father can do for his children is to love their mother (and show it)."***

Altruistic Selfishness: Most healthy relationships involve an exchange of energy, tangible or emotional. Giving energy to the system by providing support and other means sometimes provides an even greater health benefit to the self than receiving it. In that sense the best way to be

selfish is to be altruistic and selfless. There is nothing wrong with taking care of the self. But first know what is right for the self. Healthy selflessness is most beneficial to the self. In the study involving elderly residents in Leganes, a city in central Spain, having a confidant was associated with 25 percent better survival over six years.[290] In this study, the protective element was engagement in meaningful roles and providing others support and not as much the receipt of emotional support.

In a fascinating study involving eight female brown capuchin monkeys (*Cebus apella*), the monkeys were offered choice of a food reward.[313] They were offered one of two choices—a "selfish" option that provided self reward or a "pro-social" option that rewarded both the members of the pair. The study showed that monkeys systematically preferred the pro-social option provided their partner was: a) familiar, b) visible, and c) receiving rewards of equal (not greater) value. If the partner received a superior award, the pro-social behavior was reduced! Altruism thus has been observed even in non-human primates.

This altruism may originate from the potential of getting return-benefits. However, another more plausible possibility is that altruism directed toward a specific person depends on empathy. When one perceives suffering in the other, it activates shared representation and causes a similar emotional state in the observer, prompting the observer to act to decrease the suffering.[314] This directly relates to the expanded concept of the self (I suggest you to read on the fascinating information related to mirror neurons and non local effects if you wish to explore this topic further). The self could then be located beyond the physical confines of the self and include the loved ones. This expanded self prompts selfless behavior that in a sense is directed toward the self.[315] The definition of self is thus relative and evolves with the changing circumstances of your life. Elimination of this oneness of self with the others tends to negate empathy. Good deeds are sustained in the world because doing them makes you feel good.[316] Charitable actions, particularly if initiated voluntarily, are likely to activate reward (happy) areas of the brain, a process that improves the sense of well-being.[317]

The above literature suggests that your biology might consider your loved ones as an extension of self. The quality of your relationships is thus extraordinarily important for your well-being. No wonder any inkling of disapproval from your loved ones is so hurtful, as if you have been rejected by the self.

Many individuals who go through a life-changing event, particularly an unpleasant one, develop a changed perspective toward life. They become more loving, kinder, more caring, and selfless. You do not need to wait for such a reminder. Relate with your loved ones just as you deeply feel about them. Align your short term meaning with your long term meaning. Find meaning in your love. As a first step, try not to judge them; accept them as they are, in fact consider them better than they are. Johann Wolfgang von Goethe had excellent words to summarize the philosophy toward nurturing relationships, *"Treat a man as he is and he will remain as he is. Treat a man as he can and should be, and he will become as he can and should be."*

Practice Exercises: The following four exercises encapsulate some of the concepts we have discussed so far to help you find meaning within your relationships.

Exercise 1. Identify your closest relationships (including friends). Write as many as you can. Use additional sheets if necessary.

#1_____

#2_____

#3_____

#4_____

#5_____

#6_____

#7_____

#8_____

#9_____

#10_____

The loved ones you have recognized above are your most precious treasures. Through all the crests and troughs of life, it is these loved ones who will share your sorrows and joy and provide a safe cushion to your life. It is important that you nurture your relationship with them to enhance the meaning of your life.

Exercise 2. Close your eyes after you look at each name you noted above one by one and bring up your fondest memories for each person.

Keeping your feelings anchored in these memories proceed to the next exercise.

Exercise 3. Estimate your positivity/negativity (P/N) ratios for your closest relationships. For this exercise we will use the following definitions:

P/N ratio for feedbacks: (P/N^f)
       Positivity = Number of positive feedbacks
       Negativity = Number of negative feedbacks

P/N ratio for kind actions: (P/N^k)
       Positivity = Number of kind actions
       Negativity = Number of disciplining actions

Both of these are to be estimated in the previous three months and include a range of 0 to 10. Score 0 = when you provided no positive feedback and did no acts of kindness.

Score 10 = when you provided 10 such feedbacks or actions for each negative one.

If your score is >10, please mark 10 for the purpose of this exercise.

Table 35.1 An estimate of P/N ratio		
Name of the person	**P/N^f: ratio for feedbacks**	**P/N^k : ratio for kind actions**
1		
2		
3		
4		
5		
6		

7		
8		
9		
10		

Guilty as charged!! There is a good chance that you have many deeply loving relationships but may not have made efforts to keep a high P/N ratio.
What you felt in Exercise 2 is reflective of your long-term feeling about
your loved ones, while Exercise 3 more accurately reflects your short
term actions. Relationships are likely to get strained if you do not keep a
healthy P/N ratio. Remember that some of us are better at kind words and
others are more doers. Give your loved ones some leeway if they are not
able to excel in both these aspects. Men sometimes are not as good with
keeping a high P/N ratio, particularly with respect to kind (and flattering)
words. Kind words and kind actions add to your emotional bank account
with others.

*Exercise 4. Based on what you learned above, if you wish to redeem yourself
(assuming you have the need to do so, which I believe most of us do), in this
exercise write one kind thing you will do to show your appreciation of your
loved ones.* It does not have to be elaborate or expensive and could be
as simple as an unexpected phone call or an e-mail showing you remembered and cared about them. Research studies suggest that paying attention to the little things sends a message to the others that you value
them.[318] It is the little every day things that count the most.

#1_____

    Planned kind words _____

    Planned kind actions _____

#2_____

    Planned kind words _____

    Planned kind actions _____

#3 _____

    Planned kind words _____

    Planned kind actions _____

#4 _____

    Planned kind words _____

    Planned kind actions _____

#5 _____

    Planned kind words _____

    Planned kind actions _____

#6 _____

    Planned kind words _____

    Planned kind actions _____

#7 _____

    Planned kind words _____

    Planned kind actions _____

#8 _____

    Planned kind words _____

    Planned kind actions _____

#9 _____

    Planned kind words _____

    Planned kind actions _____

#10 _____

    Planned kind words _____

    Planned kind actions _____

The exercise above provides a gateway to enhancing your relationships and meaning in life. By simply becoming more aware of the meaning your loved ones provide you, you are likely to invest more energy into nurturing your relationships and in turn nourishing the self.

Let us now turn to the second important domain that could provide you meaning—spirituality.

Spirituality Could Provide Meaning for Believers and Non-believers Alike

Spirituality has a broad definition that includes one's relationship with nature, work, family, community, God, and metaphysical / transcendental phenomena.[273, 274] Finding meaning with any of the above could be considered spiritual. By that token many people who consider themselves atheists might actually be deeply spiritual. In fact, a study assessing end-of-life preferences of atheists concluded that they expressed a strong desire to find meaning in their own lives, maintain connectedness with family and friends, and appreciate the natural world through the dying experience.[319]

Spirituality and health are intimately related and are linked through many mechanisms, one of which is to provide meaning in life. Spirituality also helps by providing social support, developing a healthy relationship with the body, more healthful behaviors, decreased stress and better mood, compliance with treatments, and better coping.[320] Religion and spirituality allow you to invoke faith when you are not able to comprehend the larger meaning behind an event, particularly an unfavorable one. This faith may help you better flow with the undesirable and adverse. Further, this faith does not hinder rational thinking, but by putting brakes on the stress response allows a deeper insight to unfold. Religion often helps by invoking spirituality.[321] Spirituality is a more inclusive term and one that we will use in the exercises that follow.

Exercise 9. Based on what we discussed above, try to understand your personal spirituality by answering the next three questions:

Q1. Do you consider yourself a spiritual person? Yes / No

Q2. If yes, in what aspects of your life are you spiritual? (Check all that apply)

Relationship with nature   ☐

Attitude toward work   ☐

Attitude toward family   ☐

Attitude toward society   ☐

Faith in God   ☐

Belief in metaphysical   ☐

Others_____   ☐

Q3. *Write how you plan to deepen your spirituality*

In your relationship with nature

In your attitude toward work

In your attitude toward family

In your attitude toward society

In your faith in God

Others

The chances are that all of you care about several issues noted in question 2 of this exercise. By my definition you all are spiritual. However, sometimes this inner spirituality may not find an easy venue for expression. This exercise is to remind you and help you discover your essential spiritual nature and find greater meaning in it.

We will next turn to the third domain that provides you meaning—your work.

Work Directed Toward a Higher Purpose Provides the Deepest Meaning

Muhammad Yunus had a vision and a prayer. From modest beginnings in the village of Bathua (then in British India) to moving to the city of Chittagong (in Bangladesh) and then to Vanderbilt University as a Fulbright scholar, Yunus had seen the world. He had also held various positions as a lecturer and later head of economics at the Chittagong College in Bangladesh, assistant professor in economics at Middle Tennessee State University, member of the Planning Commission with the government of Bangladesh, and as an entrepreneur setting up his own factory. So at the age of thirty-six, while working in Bangladesh, he saw a great opportunity when he observed that very small loans could transform the life of a poor family. This provided him the opening he was seeking to be able to make a difference. While the idea was not new, it was novel enough and had the potential to create such an impact on people's lives that he pursued it with the devotion of a prayer. Despite enormous roadblocks and personal threats, he was able to carry this idea into a mission. His mission so far has helped close to eight million borrowers, loaned about U.S. $7 billion, and brought international recognition to him and the bank he established by winning a Nobel Peace Prize. Yunus energized the idea of transformation through microcredit and carried it to the next level.

Was Yunus just lucky or present at the right place at the right time? Probably yes for both. But even a more likely reason for his success is that he did not see this work as just another job or career. This was his calling, his passion, his prayer. His vision became his prayer.

It is entirely in your hands how you look at your work. No matter how mundane and uninteresting your job may be, you can squeeze a deeper meaning out of it. If you see your work as something you do just to pay your bills or for the sake of advancing your career, then you are likely to drag along. On the other hand, if you truly see your work as your prayer, you will not only infuse joy into each day, you are also likely to be more efficient, productive, and successful. Each one of us has a role to play. Whether you are a janitor or a minister, your work is precious—both are engaged in the job of cleaning; one clears the drain, the other the brain.

Another important aspect is to maintain an attitude of equanimity. Keep the desired goal in your mind, yet do not obsessively focus on the outcome. The joy is as much in the process as in the final outcome. If the process is perfected, the outcome will take care of itself. This focus on the process will likely keep you happy at work. ***Research shows that most people who are happy at work tend to be happy at home also.***

Work for money is rational and makes sense. However, while money provides the means, it cannot be the end. A lot of perils in the modern financial systems are due to money being considered the end. Money is important and serves several purposes, including providing you a better social status, greater sense of security, and more control. However, most of us do not know how much is enough *(Just when the ends meet, some-body moves the ends)*. The goal of earning money has no identified end point, is time and energy intensive, breeds stress, and takes away time from friends and family. Further, if you look at the way the world operates, all that is earned and saved can be lost within the blink of an eye.

I was once seeing a young surgeon for issues related to stress. The primary source of his stress was excessive ambition. He wished to become the most famous and accomplished surgeon in the world—and in a jiffy. We sat together and renegotiated his goals. How about keeping the primary goal of helping others? How about serving patients? How about making new discoveries to enhance patient care? The outcome may be similar, but if the intention is more altruistic than egocentric, then the path becomes less stressful. With a more altruistic approach there is lower risk of burnout and you may climb higher in career at the same time finding greater joy for the self as well loved ones around you.

Your possessions and fame are transient and ever changing. If you invest all your meaning into them, you will likely chase a moving target. The giver and receiver of the gift and the gift itself—all are transient. The action of sharing and the intention behind this action however are permanent. Find meaning in what you are able to share. Research shows that sharing and acquiring both stimulate the same pleasure centers in the brain. The good you gain in sharing always stays with you and cannot be taken back. Work that allows you to share your knowledge and skills in the service of others is a true blessing, and it will help all aspects of yours—physical, mental, emotional, and spiritual. So when you can, *Pay it forward.*

Let us explore our relationship with work in the exercise that follows. Answer this question to understand how you relate to your work:

Exercise 6. How do you see your work? Check only one option.

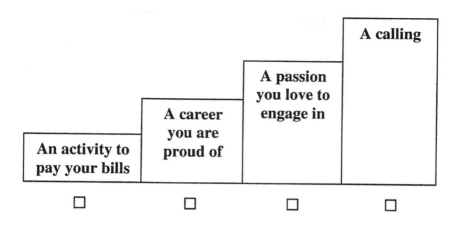

Figure 35.4 How do you see your work?

Recognize that the higher level includes the earlier ones. Thus if you consider your work as your passion, it will still be your career and pay your bills. However, work that is your passion or even your calling will provide you greater meaning.

Exercise 7. Are you enthusiastic about looking at your work in a different light? Why not think a little deeper about how your work helps others.

My work helps my family by –

_____

_____

My work helps my community by –

_____

_____

My work helps my country by –

_____

_____

Based on what you wrote above could your work be anything but your calling?

Search your heart and discover your innermost passions, talking about which brings a sparkle to your eyes. What is your unique skill that you can share with this world and make it a better place? You definitely have one. Phenomenal success comes from an ability to discover your innate talent early on and putting energy behind it. Once you get to know yourself, let nothing stop you in your pursuits. The chances are this action powered by meaning and purpose will be transformative both for you as well as for everyone around you. Purpose that is directed toward leaving the world better than you found it, a purpose that prompts you to discover at least one new truth, is profoundly meaningful.

Most happy people do not have to think about ways to find happiness. They do not live a life pondering principles of stress management. Their secret is that they have found a sense of purpose in their lives. They are problem solvers; they do not think only about the fruit that has fallen from the tree—they think about the tree, about the forest, and how all the trees relate to each other and the forest. Their lives are spent absorbed in a higher purpose. One rung at a time, they slowly climb toward greatness. They are the ones who become George Washington, Thomas Jefferson, and Martin Luther King. They eat the apple when it is served as food, but when the same apple hits them on their head—they end up describing gravity! You could easily be one of them.

36. When the Meaning is Threatened

The primary threat to meaning occurs when an interruption happens in your connection within any of the three domains—work, relationship, or spirituality. Such an interruption commonly may happen with a medical illness, but could be because of any number of events that negatively affect you such as a significant financial loss, a lay off, betrayal by a loved one, or a period of loss of faith (the dark night of St. John of the Cross).

We carry a certain set of assumptions about ourselves and the world. These assumptions include the beliefs that our world is just, fair, predictable, coherent, benevolent, and controllable. A traumatic event tends to rudely dispel such assumptions and threaten the meaning and context that had hitherto helped us operate. We respond by readjusting to a widened, possibly a more mature, worldview after such an event—our worldview now includes our experiences from the trauma. This process of readjustment takes time and changes our short-term situational meaning.[322]

Being able to find meaning in life in the context of a life stressor (e.g. a new diagnosis of breast cancer) helps with our coping strategies, feelings of inner peace, satisfaction with life, and spirituality and faith.[323] In general, an ability to ascribe a positive meaning (such as challenge or value) to a stressor is associated with lower depression and anxiety, and a better quality of life compared to ascribing a more negative meaning (enemy, loss, or punishment).[293]

Stress-related growth[324, 325] or post traumatic growth[326] (instead of post traumatic stress) is an optimistic paradigm similar to the resilience model wherein a stressful event acts as a stimulus for positive growth.[206] Indeed, even in the most challenging circumstances, such as providing care to a partner or spouse with terminal illness, an ability to find meaning has been found to create islands of positive feelings.[279] These islands serve as an oasis of respite that provides strength to be able to function and survive the ordeal.

The following two exercises are to help you understand and develop a perspective toward times when your meaning is threatened.

Exercise 1. How do you see your illness (or any other major stressor you are going through, may have gone through, or expect in the future)? Check all that apply.

1. Punishment   ☐

2. Defeat   ☐

3. Loss   ☐

4. Enemy   ☐

5. Challenge   ☐

6. Value   ☐

7. Opportunity   ☐

8. Growth   ☐

If you see your stressors as punishment / defeat / loss / or enemy, you are likely to add additional layers of emotional suffering to them. Such stressors may form the nidus for attention black holes that lodge in your mind and force you away from the wonders of your life. You can prevent such from happening using some of the approaches mentioned in exercise 2.

Exercise 2. Can you find anything positive about the stressor? Check all that apply.

1. Helped you come closer to a relative or friend   ☐

2. Gave you an opportunity to learn   ☐

3. Helped you develop a broader outlook toward life   ☐

4. Provided you an impetus to connect with your spirituality   ☐

5. Helped you cultivate greater appreciation for your blessings   ☐

6. Instilled within you the feelings of gratitude   ☐

7. Tested your resilience and thus made you stronger   ☐

8. Other_____   ☐

Being able to find meaning amidst adversity is the hallmark of resilience. On numerous occasions I have seen stress and suffering serving as a transformative event in a person's life, launching them on a deeply rewarding spiritual journey. If your suffering can serve such a purpose, some day you might find easier to accept it. I however realize that there are situations where your might feel completely at loss in your ability to find a positive meaning. I struggle with this every time I see a patient diagnosed with a serious illness. But when we sit together and speak the language of heart, more often than not we are able to squeeze out a positive meaning that provides the much needed fault in what seemed like a formidable wall of suffering.

Meaning Evolves With You

As you grow and learn, your goals and emotional ties will continue to evolve. What provides meaning today might eventually not seem so meaningful. You will change with the changing paradigms. A lot of this is adaptive. Patients with severe neurological condition find greater meaning in relationships than in their health.[327] They thus switch toward aspect of their life that is still preserved and gives them hope.

Further, partly because of our tendency to revise expectations and partly related to the nature of life, no matter how high you might reach, you will always find greater heights you could climb. The purpose of this realization is not to stop the progress. The purpose is to know that the final destination is but an illusion; what is real is the journey. What will stay with you is the memory of the moments spent on the path. Find your joy now, not in some distant omega point—your voyage itself is the destination.

The belief that life ought to be defined by a final outcome at some future point, a grand finale, tends to postpone the joy. It is the present that has the greatest power. Every moment of your experience was, is, and will be in the present. If the present lacks meaning, then it is likely that tomorrow and the day after will also be the same. Your past has created the meaning for you today. Your present that is becoming your past at each moment will define your tomorrow. Find a strong sense of meaning and purpose in this present—which indeed is a gift, a present.

Realize that means to our meaning are constantly threatened since most of them are transient. However a meaning that is anchored in service and love cannot be threatened for no one can snatch from you the right to serve and love—if not in action, at least in intention. *So identify yourself with what truly is your meaning and not just the means to that meaning.*

37. Meaning: Putting it All Together

In this final self-practice section I will put together several of the concepts we have discussed so far to assist your efforts in developing a meaning to your actions and life.

Exercise 1. What provides meaning to your life? Check all that apply

Family ☐

Friends ☐

Work ☐

Relationship with God ☐

Relationship with Nature ☐

Pets ☐

Hobbies ☐

Others_____ ☐

Exercise 2. What would you do differently (that you are not doing presently) with your loved ones, spirituality, work, and in other aspects of your life (e.g. leisure) if you were told that you have only a short time left to live?

You have just a day left:

With loved ones

_____

_____

Spirituality

_____

_____

Work

_____

_____

Others

_____

_____

You have just a month left:

With loved ones

_____

_____

Spirituality

_____

_____

Work

_____

_____

Others

_____

_____

You have just a year left:

With loved ones

_____

_____

Spirituality

_____

_____

Work

_____

_____

Others

_____

_____

Exercise 3. What would you do differently if you came to know that no one will ever know your intentions, actions, and all you achieve?

With loved ones

_____

_____

Spirituality

_____

_____

Work

_____

_____

Others

_____

_____

Exercise 4. What if your thoughts were being broadcast on the television and available for everyone to watch? How would you think differently?

About loved ones

_____

_____

Spirituality

_____

_____

Work

_____

_____

Others

_____

_____

Exercise 5. In four lines write your obituary.

_____

_____

_____

_____

Your answer to exercise 1 describes the little universe in which you operate.

Your answer to exercise 2 informs you about your priorities and how you really feel about your loved ones and others. The chances are, with little time left, you might spend more time sharing your love, care, and kindness. In the midst of an event that threatens one's survival, one of the most important thing one wishes to do is to call their loved one to say good bye and how much you love them. If this is how you deeply feel about them why not live with these feelings most of the time?

It might also be a good idea to address all the things you identified you would like to do if you were to have a finite amount of time left. There is a good chance that if you take care of these urgencies, it will take a load off your chest and give you a sense of freedom. The fact is that we all have a finite amount of time, we just do not think about it. This realization should not be a reason to become depressed; on the contrary, it should prompt you to live each moment to the fullest.

Your answer to exercise 3 (at least what you thought but may not have written!) reflects your true self. The more charitable and virtuous your core thoughts and intentions, the higher you are in your spiritual growth.

The possibility raised in exercise 4 may be anxiety provoking. One of the reasons meditation is uncomfortable is that we are made to stand face to face with our mind. Our mind generates a large number of thoughts some of which tend to be strange and do not really "belong" in our portfolio. The more you try to cultivate kindness toward others in their absence, the more likely you will achieve a state where all your thoughts could be safely broadcast. The embarrassment that some of our leaders face when they speak unkindly not realizing that the microphone is turned on speaks of their inner thoughts. A single negative statement, however, does not mean they are all bad. All it means is that they are human and still a work in progress.

Your answer to exercise 5 represents your most important achievements and dreams and your identity in this world. This also represents how you wish to be seen by others. If you wrote "a kind, loving, caring person," develop into one. If you wrote "a passionate, innovative achiever," work toward it. This is the most transparent mirror to your being. Similar to what Alfred Nobel was able to see with still some time left to mend the missteps.

Below I summarize the positive outcomes that might happen with finding and anchoring in the higher meaning and purpose of your life. This will serve as a reminder and a succinct summary for you to keep and review.

In relationship with <u>others</u> you might become more
- Loving – come closer to others
- Expressive – less inhibited in showing emotions
- Compassionate – more appreciative of others' struggles
- Kind – more willing to offer help to others
- Interdependent – more willing to offer and accept others' help
- Connected – feel greater connection with others
- Accepting – able to accept others more easily
- Forgiving – able to forgive more easily
- Charitable – more willing to contribute to social causes

In relationship with <u>self</u> you might become more
- Resilient – able to thrive despite adversity
- Optimistic – more hopeful
- Buoyant – greater ability to find new possibilities within misfortune
- Self-controlled – have better self-restraint
- Grateful – more appreciative and thankful
- Flexible – more willing to change yourself
- Effective – greater ability to make a difference
- Self-efficacious – have a better sense of control
- Equanimous – more easily able to let go
- Innovative – greater ability to invite/create newer opportunities

In work you might become more
- Purposeful – find a larger purpose
- Welcoming – look forward to work
- Passionate – more engaged and caring
- Devoted – find work as a prayer

In spirituality you might nurture deeper
- Belief – have a deeper belief that this world is just, fair, and predictable
- Faith – have a more secure faith in God
- Broadmindedness – develop greater acceptance for different faiths
- Love for nature – more appreciative and caring about the environment

The result: you will touch more lives in a positive way through your relationships, work, and spirituality.

SECTION X: FORGIVENESS

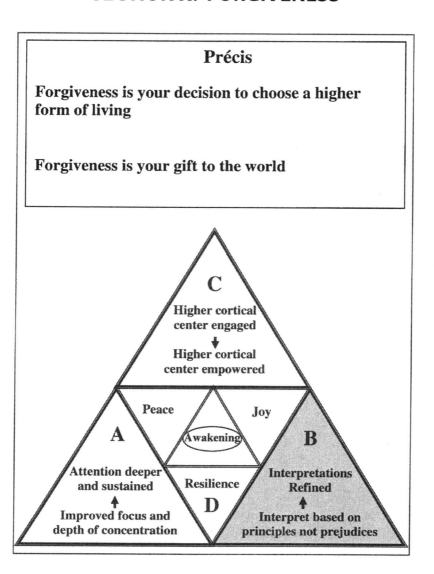

Précis

Forgiveness is your decision to choose a higher form of living

Forgiveness is your gift to the world

C

Higher cortical center engaged
↓
Higher cortical center empowered

Peace

Joy

Awakening

A

B

Attention deeper and sustained
↑
Improved focus and depth of concentration

Resilience

D

Interpretations Refined
↑
Interpret based on principles not prejudices

38. What is Forgiveness?

In the last two decades of my interactions with patients, the three most common questions I have been asked about forgiveness are:

- "If I forgive, am I not passively justifying the wrong done to me?"
- "How is forgiveness linked with my current health condition?"
- "Does an inability to forgive contribute to my stress?"

My answers to these questions are:

- Forgiveness does not mean you have to justify the wrong done to you. You may choose to forgive irrespective of whether someone does / does not deserve it. You forgive because you choose to live a higher, more fulfilling life. You forgive because you are and want to become emotionally and spiritually more mature.
- Lack of forgiveness is intimately related to many of your medical conditions. Research studies show that by practicing forgiveness, you are likely to be healthier and happier.
- Lack of forgiveness is a drain on your energy and prevents you from engaging with the beautiful present. Lack of forgiveness gets you stuck in the past and definitely contributes to stress-related symptoms.

In this section I will discuss pertinent research data that supports these three answers. I will also recapitulate the results of studies that provide a hint that forgiveness might engage your brain's higher center. I will then present some of the pearls and skills that might help you bring forgiveness into your daily life.

The above issues can be conceptualized into three specific queries:

- What is forgiveness?
- Why forgive?
- How can you learn to be more forgiving?

Let us walk together as we try to answer these queries in this section.

What is Forgiveness?

Forgiveness is a voluntary choice that you make to give up the anger and resentment despite knowing and accepting that the misconduct happened.[328-330] ***Forgiveness is your gift to others that often comes to the undeserving.*** Joseph, as described in the Hebrew Bible, was left for dead by his brothers. However, when he came back to power he forgave and embraced them even though they did not deserve his forgiveness. He chose forgiveness and his choice helped him and also helped his brothers in their journey into repentance.

In forgiveness, you choose to ascend from being reactive to becoming internally more thoughtful and loving. You can thus stamp out the feelings of hatred. Martin Luther King, Jr. said, *"Darkness cannot drive out darkness; only light can do that. Hate cannot drive out hate; only love can do that."*

You might be misinterpreting forgiveness if you think by practicing forgiveness you will have to necessarily justify, excuse, or deny the wrong. This misinterpretation often leads to a feeling that forgiveness isn't fair, particularly if you harbor significant anger or resentment. Thus forgiveness is not any of these:

- Justifying;
- Excusing;
- Condoning; or
- Denying the wrong

Forgiveness does not prevent you from taking all appropriate measures for your future safety, or even pursue a legal recourse if you have to.[331] Forgiveness does not usurp any of your basic rights.

Forgiveness, on the other hand, is a choice that you make to cultivate emotional maturity and lead a more spiritual life. Forgiveness is for you, not for the forgiven. By practicing forgiveness you become kind to yourself.

Forgiveness is your spiritual stress test. You can see your ability to truly internally forgive as a tangible milestone in your spiritual journey.

Forgiveness, however, isn't an easy skill to learn and practice. In fact, forgiveness can be mentally challenging and stressful and, particularly when the hurt is fresh, seem totally unacceptable in the short-term. Holding a grudge often provides a psychological comfort zone to its owner. Your primordial instinct might thus be to keep the grievance thriving in the sulci and gyri of your brain. To overcome this instinct, your mind will need strong convincing and your brain will need additional training. So it is very reasonable if presently you ask this question of me: Other than the fact that it sounds good, tell me doctor, why should I forgive?

39. Why Forgive?

Before beginning to answer this very important question, I invite you to pause, take a few deep breaths, and write three reasons why you think you or someone else should practice forgiveness.

1.

2.

3.

Did any of the reasons that you just wrote include one or more of the following thoughts?

- I wish to forgive because forgiveness may help me emotionally feel better
- I wish to forgive because I want to move on
- I wish to forgive because the scriptures I read eulogize forgiveness
- I wish to forgive because forgiveness may decrease my stress level
- I wish to forgive because forgiveness may help my health

The comforting fact is that all of the above statements are true. More than two thousand years after Jesus spoke the famous words, *"Father, forgive them, for they know not what they do,"* the medical research community is finally starting to discover the many practical benefits of the profound act of forgiveness. Individual researchers differ on the details, but when we put all their research together we can confidently say that forgiving others is good for a person's health. Scientific research now clearly demonstrates that voluntarily giving up bitterness toward others—without in any way excusing or justifying the wrong they have done—can significantly improve a person's blood pressure, lower the heart rate and overall stress levels, improve their sleep, and improve the body's ability to fight a wide variety of mental and physical illnesses. Further, forgiveness seals the energy drain that saps your energy and keeps you in the limbic loop. The freedom that comes from forgiveness allows you to focus on building your future by letting go of your past. This disempowers attention black holes within your mind. Forgiveness also engages the brain's higher center that may help an individual's resilience.

Further, just as the act of forgiveness is shown by scientific research to have positive health benefits, research also shows the opposite—that holding a grudge, especially over the long-term, is harmful to human health. Anger thus is like a car wreck—one causes many, sometimes far too many. While forgiveness improves measurable indicators of health, holding a grudge moves those measurements in the opposite direction, toward greater anxiety, depression, irritability, disturbed sleep, higher blood pressure, irregular heart rhythm, and even increased risk of heart attack.[332-337] Recent research suggests that anger that comes from lack of forgiveness may interact with susceptibility genes to increase cardio-vascular risk.[338] Further, anger may be medically harmful not only to the angry but also to those against which it is directed.

Anger and lack of forgiveness originate in the expectation-reality (ER) im-balance. When at the receiving end of a transgression, there is often a de-sire for just retribution. Lack of forgiveness keeps that desire alive and by itself provides a semblance of retribution. By nurturing lack of forgiveness we create a form of psychological comfort zone and carry an expectation that somehow this process will mete out justice and correct the wrong.

Harboring this anger, however, is akin to an exothermic reaction that re-leases energy. It causes considerable damage to you as its host while it may or may not hurt the person toward whom it is directed. By nurturing anger you might allow them to hurt you more than once. Anger and lack of forgiveness mutates the hurt into an attention black hole. *When angry and resentful, the imaginary trap you create to enslave the perpetrator actu-ally enslaves no one but you. Over a period of time, you become used to this prison to the extent that you might become unaware of it.* While relaxing exercises, distraction, or letting the anger out may help in the short-term, it is only by practicing forgiveness that a more permanent solution can be obtained.

Let's look in a bit more detail at the measurable health effects of forgive-ness. In recent years, scientific studies have shown that people who regu-larly practice forgiving others enjoy these benefits more often than those who don't:

Improved overall physical health

- In a research study involving interview and medical evaluation of eighty-one adults in a community, measures of forgiveness were found to be associated with improved parameters of health including physical symptoms, medications used, sleep quality, fatigue, and somatic complaints.[339] Improved mood and lower stress were closely linked with forgiveness.

- In another study involving 266 healthy undergraduates both self and other-forgiveness were associated with better perceived physical health.[340] In this study self-forgiveness was even a stronger predictor of physical health than other-forgiveness.

Improved blood pressure and cardiovascular health

- In a study involving ninety-nine participants, forgiveness was linked with overall reductions in blood pressure levels and possibly also better cardiovascular recovery from stress.[341]

- Negative thinking was associated with rapid worsening of heart and brain waves that might equally rapidly reverse with positive thinking.[342]

- In a study involving eighty-five patients with coronary artery disease, a higher self reported forgiveness was associated with lower levels of anxiety, depression, and perceived stress. Higher level of forgiveness was also associated with lower total cholesterol to HDL and LDL to HDL ratios (both at $p < 0.05$).[343]

Better psychological well-being

- In two related studies, inter-personal forgiveness and psychological well-being were found to have reciprocal relationship with both the traits supporting each other.[344]

- In another series of six studies, forgiveness was associated with four components of psychological well-being (anger, anxiety, depression, and satisfaction with life).[345]

- Patients undergoing treatment for breast cancer had less mood disturbance and better quality of life if they kept an attitude of self-forgiveness.[346]

- An attitude of forgiveness was related with lower level of back pain and psychological distress in another study involving sixty-one patients with chronic back pain.[347]

- In a study involving patients who were terminally ill with cancer, forgiveness therapy was associated with improvement in measures of forgiveness, hope, quality of life, and anger compared to no such training.[348]

Improved interpersonal relationships

- In the series of six studies noted previously, forgiveness and hostility demonstrated equivalent and inverse associations with relationship duration, and forgiveness independently accounted for relationship satisfaction.[345]

- In two other separate studies, a disposition of forgiveness improved family relationships and general family environment in the first study,[349] while forgiveness and marital quality were found to be closely related in the other study.[350]

- In a study involving eighty-seven wives and seventy-four husbands who had experienced a significant betrayal, positive forgiveness (increased understanding of one's partner and decreased anger about betrayal) was associated with several positive outcomes compared to negative forgiveness (holding a grudge and desiring revenge). These included improved marital satisfaction, stronger parenting alliance, and for wives, lower levels of children's perceived parental conflict.[351]

Improved ability to handle stress

- Lack of forgiveness was associated with long-term negative thinking and feelings that left one in a chronically aroused and stressed state.[352]

- Forgiveness along with other positive traits, including higher religiosity, spirituality, and frequency of prayer, on the other hand, were associated with a lower cortisol response in a study involving young adults.[353] Lower cortisol response is considered a marker of better control of stress.

Forgiveness and the higher center of the brain

Forgiveness and empathy awaken the higher center of your brain that facilitates resilience and allows a better control of the stress response. Promising and highly interesting results are beginning to emerge about the way forgiveness might affect your brain function. Several studies using sophisticated brain imaging show that the pre-frontal cortex activity is intimately involved in empathy and forgiveness. In a study using functional MRI, ten volunteers made judgments of social scenarios. Forgiveness judgment activated left superior frontal, orbito-frontal, and precuneus areas.[105] Similar results have been found with the feeling of empathy.[105, 354, 355] A report combining eighty different studies showed similar conclusions.[91]

A reasonable conclusion from all the research studies is that the ability to forgive other people for the hurts they have done you is associated with improved overall physical and mental health and improved relationships. Studies show that forgiveness engages the higher, more evolved areas of your brain. Engaging these areas might explain the salutary effects of forgiveness on your health. Further, these benefits will likely spill over into other aspects of your life including decisional ability, rational thinking, long-term planning, and other related executive functions.

Other reasons to forgive

There are several additional good reasons to forgive beyond what can be measured within the confines of research studies. Lack of forgiveness with the resulting resentment is often absorbed by your children. The resulting negative vibes may sap their energy. This could continue across generations unless you block this process by starting your own journey into forgiveness.

Lack of forgiveness is energy intensive while forgiveness frees up your energy. *"We can never be free unless we learn to forgive,"* said Nelson Mandela, who forgave even the person who held him a prisoner for over ten years at Robben Island. The energy available to you is limited. A large part of this energy remains locked when your mind runs the exhausting programs of unforgiveness—nurturing old grudges, replaying and reliving old hurts, and planning complicated plots for retribution. Forgiveness frees up this energy so you can focus on the future instead of dwelling on the past. Lack of forgiveness with associated ruminations gives energy to your past transgressions converting them into attention black holes. The more you ruminate on the past transgressions, the stronger their memory in your brain and farther away you are likely to get from your true masters.

Your true masters should be what provide meaning to your life; your dreams and aspirations, and not the hurts of your past.

There is an old story about a man who spent his entire life in meditation and prayer. His penance finally bore fruit and he was visited by the angels who prepared to take him to heaven. As they tried to lift him they found him too heavy, so the angels could not take him with them. The man spent the next year exercising and lost a lot of weight. But the next time they came, the angels still found him too heavy. This kept repeating for the next several years.

Finally the man lost patience and asked the angels to tell him how much more weight he had to lose, since by now he was severely undernourished. The angels then told him the secret: they were not at all concerned by his physical weight. Instead, they were weighing all the injuries and hurts that were lodged in his heart that he had not forgiven. The man got the message and used his time to cultivate forgiveness. You can imagine what happened when the angels visited him next time. Unforgiveness had kept him heavy and away from the highest place he wished to go. After unloading the extra burden, he was finally freed to feel peaceful and pursue his ultimate dream.

There is yet another reason why it is good to forgive. **You and I are being forgiven, very likely many times every day. To forgive in return only makes good common sense.** Very often the energy of forgiveness flows toward us without even our asking or knowing. By returning the favor we pass on this energy in honor of the one from whom we receive it knowingly or unknowingly every day.

There is no doubt that we all eventually will have to forgive and/or forget. Time finally will come to a halt for all of us. Past, present, and future will merge into the stillness of a single moment. All that seems real or unreal will dissolve. Everything we hold dear we will have to surrender. Great wisdom befalls us in that moment. Immediate palpability of finiteness often brings life in clear focus. It might help you to invite into the present the wisdom that might awaken in that future moment. This is the real meaning of death before dying. **How beautiful a life when you can confidently say at the end of it—I carry no grudges and have no one in this world I need to forgive!**

The benefit of forgiveness was beautifully demonstrated by the late President Ronald Reagan, after he was shot at close range in an assassination attempt. President Reagan later wrote in his diaries about the moments just after being shot: *"Getting shot hurts. Still my fear was growing because no matter how hard I tried to breathe it seemed I was getting less & less air. I focused on that tiled ceiling and prayed. But I realized I couldn't ask for God's help while at the same time I felt hatred for the mixed-up young man who had shot me. Isn't that the meaning of the lost sheep? We are all God's children & therefore equally beloved by him. I began to pray for his soul and that he would find his way back to the fold."* (The Reagan Diaries)

The anecdote vividly illustrates how President Reagan, while fighting for his life, instinctively chose forgiveness above hatred. Even as he was in significant duress, he did not need to be reminded to be forgiving. This speaks of his faith and realization of the benefits of forgiveness. Forgiveness freed his mind to focus on healing rather than the senselessness of the "mixed-up young man."

Two essential components of an approach that will help you develop a similar forgiving disposition are: 1) your conviction that forgiveness is beneficial for you; 2) specific skills in practicing forgiveness until forgiveness becomes your innate state of being.

We have spent some time talking about the benefits of forgiveness. As a next step, I will discuss pearls and exercises that will help you cultivate forgiveness skills. Prior to moving on to the pearls and exercises, let us pause for a moment and summarize all the reasons why it makes sense for you to invite forgiveness.

Exercise 1. Read through this list and check those reasons with which you agree based on what you know, feel, and may have read so far.

Table 39.1 Table for Exercise 1	
Forgiveness does not mean you justify, accept, excuse, condone, or deny the wrong	☐
Forgiveness means you choose a higher, more mature form of living	☐
Lack of forgiveness is stressful	☐
Lack of forgiveness with related anger might hurt your health	☐
Lack of forgiveness generally serves no tangible material purpose	☐
Lack of forgiveness keeps you stuck in the past and may prevent you from a deeper engagement with the present moment	☐
Lack of forgiveness drains energy	☐

Forgiveness improves several health outcomes	☐
Forgiveness helps decrease anger	☐
Forgiveness is a moral good	☐
Forgiveness frees up the mind to focus on the future	☐
Forgiveness improves relationships	☐
You are forgiven, likely several times, every single day	☐
Forgiveness engages the higher centers in your brain	☐
Eventually all of us will have to forgive and / or forget	☐
Every scripture you revere preaches the virtue of forgiveness	☐
Most of the greatest persons you admire practiced and taught forgiveness	☐

40. How to Forgive

I would like to share a few pearls that are mostly based on the results of research studies with forgiveness. Some of the pearls are also based on what appeals to basic common sense and are a part of everyday experience of yours and mine. The ideas presented will form the basis of forgiveness exercises that follow in the later part of this chapter.

Pearl #1. Consider forgiveness a lifelong process

Forgiveness is a process that progresses at its own natural, generally slow pace.[328] Trying to attain "quick fix" forgiveness is unlikely to work. Be deliberate and patient and try not to hurry yourself into forgiveness. This is particularly true for deeper hurts. When hurt in a bad way, particularly when the injury is fresh, recognize that it may be difficult or impossible for you to immediately consider forgiving the wrongdoer.

Pearl #2. It is okay to be selfish in forgiveness

Particularly for the more egregious transgression, it takes almost superhuman effort to cultivate warm and charitable feelings. It is thus okay to start by focusing on the self.[328] I call this *altruistic selfishness*. You forgive because you wish to heal, stop your pain, and disempower the person who has hurt you. In the process you may reach a point of equanimity where you are able to let go of the past and eventually start wishing well for the transgressor. This often happens simultaneously with your perspective becoming more global, where you begin to focus on essential humanness of everyone including the wrongdoer. Such a perspective is likely to percolate into other aspects of your life, bringing with it the priceless gifts of peace, joy, and freedom.

Pearl #3. Broaden your world view to include imperfections

In the eyes of a child who has never seen pain or misery, this world is nothing but a place to explore, play, and have fun. Siddhartha remained in such a carefree state until age twenty-nine, when he first saw suffering that came with illness, old age, and eventual death. This created enormous turmoil in the way he viewed the world. Siddhartha forsook everything and set out on a path to understand and transcend suffering, a path that led him to become the Buddha. It will help you to keep a broader worldview wherein, unfortunately, evil also has a place. There are people in this world that choose the path of being evil.[356] Bad things happen even to innocent and good people. If you have ever been injured, you know that evil is real and only a breath or a thought away. Incorporating a broader worldview that includes the existence of evil might allow you to better deal with the challenges of life and thereby find a more secure peace.

Lack of kindness often happens in moments when we lose self control. It may be out of anger, greed or even self defense. Sometimes we innocently hurt the very people we love the most. Keep a low threshold to forgive in such situations. We all are bound to commit mistakes. You do not punish the teeth that may have innocently bit your tongue.

Pearl #4. Try to understand others' actions

Most of your thoughts and actions can be interpreted in multiple ways. There is a good chance that none of us are either right or wrong all the time. As you mature and expand your zone of acceptance, many behaviors that might have otherwise appeared wrong may start seeming appropriate. This is because you start seeing everyone's point of view. Most behaviors and actions have a reason behind them. An ability to understand the specific reason rather than prematurely using and adding to your prejudices might help you in the path toward forgiveness. In this context it will be helpful to look at human beings as fallible and limited. Often you might find yourself at a loss as to what you would have done if you were stuck in the same situation. Remember that, *"An expression other than love is often a call for help."* The vast majority of people who seem angry or frustrated are stuck in their own attention black holes. They are fighting their personal inner battles. The purpose is not to justify but to understand. Refuse to accept the gift of their anger. Research studies show that it is easier to forgive others if you see yourself capable of committing a similar offense.[201]

Pearl #5. Consider forgiveness as an opportunity

It will help if you ask yourself this question: On the whole, has lack of forgiveness helped me or hurt me so far? If you think lack of forgiveness has not helped you and you are willing to consider the alternative, take this as an opportunity to grow rather than something that would hamper your progress. This might help propel you toward emotional and spiritual resilience. You do not have to deny the existence of negative memories. The kernel of these memories will persist. However, you can stop sending more energy toward it and prevent it from becoming an attention black hole. Accepting the negative memory by including a worldview that includes imperfections helps you make peace with it. You may find this strategy opening new doors to help you grow.

Pearl #6. Exercise the privilege to forgive as soon as you recognize the need for it

Try not to serve the stale food of unforgiveness of previous hurt as the main course of thoughts the next day. Especially for minor offences, do not let the sun set and rise again with unresolved hurts and resulting lack of forgiveness. Short-term anger directed against a wrongdoer is often appropriate and needed. However, in general the longer you ruminate about a hurt, the stronger its roots, which makes it more difficult for you to forgive.[357] It has been effectively argued that nursing a grudge is almost an addictive process that should be avoided.[358] Look deep within and try to surface the feeling of forgiveness as quickly as you recognize the need for it. This is particularly true for minor grievances. However, if this feeling simply cannot be found in this moment, then don't force it. It won't work. As long as you nurture the intention to forgive, the chances are that the freshness of tomorrow morning might take you there.

Pearl #7. Forgive gracefully without creating a burden on the forgiven

Think about a time when you may have hurt someone (deliberately or by mistake). You may have felt guilty and vulnerable in that state. You likely still feel embarrassed about your actions and would rather not be reminded of the event too many times. The same holds true for others. Reminding people repeatedly that you have forgiven them will likely make them defensive and resentful. The best approach is to not create any incremental burden or challenge for the forgiven. *He that giveth, let him do it with simplicity (Romans 12:8 KJV).* Let forgiveness not be used to show your magnanimity or virtuosity, to appease someone or, worse, to advertise how others have been wrong. Bring genuine compassion into your forgiveness.

Buddha was once attacked by a ruthless murderer named Angulimala. Angulimala used to kill his victims and make a garland of their fingers that he wore around his neck, hence his name (Anguli = finger; Mala = garland). When Angulimala met Buddha he was hoping to make Buddha his thousandth victim. However, he was stunned when instead of hatred and fear he was greeted by Buddha's compassion and causeless forgiveness. Buddha did not make any attempt to reflect on the criminal's wrongs. He only showed Angulimala the essential goodness that lay hidden within Angulimala encumbered by his detestation for mankind. This transformed Angulimala's life. Instead of assaulting Buddha he became Buddha's disciple and later a monk. Your forgiveness too might start a transformative process in someone.

Pearl #8. Forgive before others seek your forgiveness

Waiting for someone to ask for forgiveness might turn out to be a very long wait. It will only delay the moment at which you can freely begin to embrace your own destiny. Studies show that children often need an apology to be able to forgive.[359] But as a mature adult you can choose to transcend that need. It takes tremendous courage and humility for anyone to accept they were wrong. The whole life sometimes goes by trying to muster that courage. Admitting a mistake is a sign of courage but is curiously considered a sign of weakness in our society. It is fair to assume that many people do not have the emotional resources to stand up and accept their guilt unconditionally and so will not easily ask for forgiveness. Remember what we discussed earlier—forgiveness is for you, not for them.

Pearl #9. Look forward to forgiving

Do not consider forgiveness a burden, a heavy chore, or something that might take energy away from you. The truth, in fact, is the opposite. In the long run, forgiveness saves you energy. So look forward to forgiving. In fact, consider forgiveness a privilege. Often the wrong that happened may have created new and unique benefits. In this context, research studies suggest that writing about potential benefits of a negative event might allow easier forgiveness.[360]

Pearl #10. Extend your forgiveness toward what might even transpire in the future

Your ability to forgive the past is an important milestone in your journey toward happiness. As a next step, what might immunize you from future suffering will be your ability to forgive the future. Forgiving the future entails accepting your loved ones as they are right now as well as accepting them how they will be in the future. This is the greatest gift you can give them out of your compassion and love. I prefer to call it "Pre-emptive forgiveness" and regularly teach this to learners who are ready to practice it. This is particularly helpful for minor irritations within the folds of trust and love. If you can truly internally forgive and accept future annoyances that might come your way, you have in effect inoculated yourself and others against much future suffering. This does not mean you will allow indiscretions. All it means is that you will be in control of your own emotions and not allow anyone else to evoke anger or resentment within you.

Pearl #11. Praying for others increases your ability to forgive them

Research studies show that if you pray for the other person (friend or loved one) you are more likely to develop a forgiving disposition toward them.[361] So in the context of a loving relationship praying for each other might make pre-emptive forgiveness easier to embody.

Pearl #12. Prevent future situations where you may have a need to forgive

We tend to create expectations of the way this world should reward us. Often we do not share this expectation with anyone, certainly not in clear terms. Instead, our pride gets in the way—subconsciously we remain fearful that our insecure ego will be bruised if we express our desires and they are not met. Ego thus hides these desires. Despite hiding our desires, however, we carry a hope and a subtle expectation that these desires will still be fulfilled. We might even feel entitled that they eventually are fulfilled. The foregoing is a storm brewing. If you keep unexpressed lofty expectations, you might be creating a setup for disappointments and hurts. The three-part solution to prevent this from happening is:

- Lower your expectations;[358]
- Clearly communicate these expectations; and
- Keep an attitude of internal acceptance that you will not be surprised or disappointed if these expectations are not met

Pearl #13: Lower your expectations

Having lower expectations strongly correlates with experiencing greater happiness. This balances the E-R equation (expectation-reality) and is likely to lower your disappointments. For example, Denmark often ranks at or near the top of the list of the happiest places on earth based on interviews with natives of different places. A survey titled "Why the Danes are Smug" was conducted by the University of Southern Denmark in 2008.[362] Results showed that the main reason for people's happiness is their low expectations. Low expectations avert disappointments and also prevent creation of situations wherein one might find a need to forgive.

Pearl #14: Have a low threshold to seek forgiveness

Forgiveness is not just about forgiving someone. *It will also help to keep an appropriately low threshold to seek forgiveness from others if you think it is reasonable and might help.* Research studies show that when one is emotionally hurt, they are likely to experience significantly unhealthy heart rhythm and that once you express an apology, their condition remarkably improves.[363] So if your loved one is hurt for any reason, do not leave them with an unhealthy heart beat. Seek forgiveness sooner rather than later.

As we close this section and move on to practice exercises, I am reminded of the beautiful lines by Pierre Teilhard De Chardin, a French philosopher and Jesuit priest: *"Someday, after we have mastered the winds, the waves, the tide and gravity, we shall harness for God the energies of love. Then, for the second time in the history of the world, man will have discovered fire."* One of the purest manifestations of the fire of love is forgiveness—a gift bestowed to our free will that we all can multiply by giving it to others.

Practice Exercises

As you start these exercises, remember that you have to be patient with forgiveness. Forgiveness is a process—it progresses through several phases over a period of time that may sometimes take years to complete.[328]

- Early in the process, you often assess the details surrounding your hurts and begin to contemplate the possibility of forgiveness.
- Later as you decide to forgive, you might notice a decrease in negative feelings (unforgiveness reduction).
- Next, you might become neutral to the wrongdoer, feeling neither angry nor affectionate.
- In the final phase you may be able to cultivate positive feelings of empathy and warmth, wishing the other person well. This is often coupled with positive behavior. At this point you may find meaning in suffering as well as in forgiveness.[328]

Several different multi-step programs have been developed and found efficacious for enhancing forgiveness.[364-367] Even if you feel you are good about forgiving others, actively practicing these exercises might help. In a research study, clergy showed improvement in their ability to forgive after training.[368] Research with these programs shows salutary effects on physical and emotional symptoms in a variety of situations.[369] Some of the specific conditions / relationships shown to be benefited by forgiveness training include:

- Parents of adolescent suicide victims;[370]
- Substance use disorder;[371]
- Anxiety, anger, and grief in men with partners who had abortion against their wishes;[372]
- College students;[373]
- Incest survivors;[374]
- In couples to promote marital enrichment;[375]
- Anger and high levels of stress;[376]
- Elderly females who had experienced injustice;[377]
- General health and well-being;[378]
- Symptoms of anxiety and depression, and for improving self esteem;[374]
- Elevated blood pressure;[379]
- Depressive symptoms;[380]
- Anger, depression, anxiety, self-esteem, and vulnerability to drug use; [371]
- Depression and anxiety in emotionally abused women;[381] and
- Depression and physical health[382]

In summary, some of the health related benefits with learning forgiveness in research studies include:

- Lower blood pressure
- More regular heart rate
- Lower stress level
- Better sleep
- Lower physical symptoms
- Lower number of medications used
- Lower fatigue
- Less somatic complaints
- Better cardiovascular recovery from stress
- Lower cholesterol
- Better psychological well-being
- Greater satisfaction with life
- Lower level of back pain
- Longer relationship duration
- Higher relationship satisfaction
- Better marital quality
- Stronger parenting alliance
- Lower levels of children's perceived parental conflict
- Lower cortisol response (considered a marker of better stress control)

The exercises presented here are designed to introduce you to forgiveness and should not alone be relied upon for a serious transgression, for which professional help should be sought. It might help to keep the company of a kind and mature confidant who is willing to support you as you walk on the path toward forgiveness.

Exercise 1. Ponder the benefits of forgiveness
Try to assimilate and verify the truth behind the statements presented below. Consider this a mini test of your knowledge about forgiveness.

Table 40.1 Table for Exercise 1

Statement	Yes	No
Lack of forgiveness is unlikely to correct the wrong done to me	☐	☐
Harboring a grudge is stressful	☐	☐
Lack of forgiveness is a drain on my energy and prevents me from being in the present moment	☐	☐
Forgiveness has the potential to improve my physical and mental health	☐	☐
Forgiveness has the potential to improve my relationships	☐	☐
Forgiveness will help free up my mind. This will allow me to spend more time with my future dreams and aspirations.	☐	☐
Forgiveness will allow me to let go of anger and resentment so that these negative feelings no longer control me	☐	☐
Forgiveness will allow me to choose the way to respond	☐	☐

	Yes	No
I am forgiven for my mistakes, likely several times in a single day	☐	☐
Forgiveness will engage the higher center of my brain to better control the stress response and help with resilience	☐	☐

If a majority of your responses were yes, then pause for a moment and make an intelligent decision about what is better for you—to let go of anger and resentment or continue to harbor it. I need to emphasize that by letting go of anger you are in no way justifying what happened—you are only choosing to respond based on who you are (and not react to others based on their actions).

Exercise 2. Develop a good understanding of forgiveness
Evaluate these statements and make a judgment as to which ones you agree with.

Table 40.2 Table for Exercise 2

Statement	Yes	No
Forgiveness is a gift from me to others	☐	☐
I am not obligated to forgive, forgiveness is my willful choice	☐	☐
My forgiveness is often directed to the undeserving	☐	☐
By forgiveness I do not intend to forget the wrong	☐	☐
By forgiveness I do not intend to deny the wrong	☐	☐
By forgiveness I do not intend to justify the wrong	☐	☐
By forgiveness I do not intend to allow people to get away with or repeat the misconduct	☐	☐
I can stop the process of forgiveness at any point I become uncomfortable with it	☐	☐

All the correct responses in this exercise are "yes." Do you see at this point that forgiveness has the potential to help you *without* necessarily usurping any of your preferences or rights?

Exercise 3. Have you ever desired to be forgiven?
Think about a time when you may have hurt someone's feelings. Now answer these questions in a fair and objective fashion.

Table 40.3 Table for Exercise 3		
Statement	**Yes**	**No**
Did you intend to hurt their feelings?	☐	☐
If you knew your actions would hurt their feelings would you have done the same thing?	☐	☐
Does your action make you all bad?	☐	☐
Would you appreciate being forgiven?	☐	☐
Do you wish to apologize but are not able to muster enough courage at this point?	☐	☐
Would you feel relieved if they came up to you and said in a kind, friendly way they have forgiven you?	☐	☐

In all probability:

- You did not intend to hurt
- You would like to be forgiven
- You wish to apologize but are not able to collect enough courage to do so (maybe you are too embarrassed or even shy)
- You would feel relieved if you knew they have recovered and moved on

It is possible that the person who wronged you may have hurt you unintentionally, is currently repenting, but is not able to come forward and apologize. Consider what Jesus said: *"Do unto others as you would have them do unto you."* (Luke 6:31) Forgive others as you would want them to forgive you.

Exercise 4. Two options for the future
Consider these two options for your future life:
Option A – You choose not to forgive. You keep the hurt in your heart and are frequently reminded of it. In this situation you are likely to live a life controlled by the memory of the transgression, and worse still the transgressor. *Do they deserve a free rental space in your heart?* Many of your experiences are then colored by the previous hurt. Is this what you wish? In this situation you give the person a permission to hurt you repeatedly, even when you are away from them.

Option B – You choose to forgive. You decide that you wish to live your life based on your own principles rather than being dictated by someone else. You disempower the other person from constantly trespassing into your inner environment. They have no control over your life. In this situation you give yourself permission to enjoy the everyday little things in life despite the previous negative experience. You have vanquished the transgressor.

Which of these two options would you choose?

Option A	☐
Option B	☐

Exercise 5. Decide to forgive
Based on all you know and believe at this point, answer this question:

Statement	Yes	No
Have you made a decision to consider forgiveness as an option?	☐	☐

I hope you answered yes to this question.

Exercise 6. View the person / event in context
Often the event or experience is evaluated by us based on its immediate short-term personal value. Consider this scenario.

Jon, an overworked sales agent, finds it irritating that he gets the most difficult clients to work with. He is particularly upset one day because his current supervisor, Tim, always picks on him and gives him the extra work. Jon holds a grudge against Tim, considers him unreasonable, and is not particularly kind when he fills out Tim's evaluation. A few weeks later Jon receives a commendation letter from the CEO of his company along with an unexpected bonus. It turned out that Tim gave Jon the most difficult clients because he thought Jon was the best. It was Tim who recommended Jon for the bonus. Jon is happy and embarrassed at the same time.

Applying the scenario to your situation, consider the totality of circumstances. Do you think the person who hurt you purposefully intended to harm you? Was s/he fearful or stressed when s/he acted? Is s/he perhaps also suffering (e.g. from childhood abuse, work related issues, etc.)?

Now try and answer these questions:

Table 40.4 Table for Exercise 6		Yes	No	Don't know
Statement		**Yes**	**No**	**Don't know**
Is it possible that the reason you were hurt could be different from what you are thinking?		☐	☐	☐
Is it possible that the person who wronged you could have acted –	with incomplete knowledge of the facts	☐	☐	☐
	in a state of confusion	☐	☐	☐
	when stressed	☐	☐	☐
	in self-defense	☐	☐	☐
Is it possible that the anger was misdirected at you?		☐	☐	☐

None of these may be correct in your specific situation, but considering one of these possibilities has the potential to decrease your stress and begin your journey toward forgiveness. It might help to assess the totality of the situation that led to the event rather than primarily focusing on the immediate action of the perpetrator.

Exercise 7. Find meaning in suffering
Forgiveness is more difficult when we feel we have been egregiously harmed. It is easier to forgive if we can find some meaning in suffering. Almost every negative event has a potential opportunity. Many of the healthy and ethical things in life are not entirely pleasant or easy in the short-run (think about adhering to daily exercise or a low calorie diet). If you wish to progress it is important to focus on the long-term and see what lessons you can learn from the negative experience.

Write on a piece of paper any possible way that your suffering or the person who hurt you, may have actually indirectly (perhaps unknowingly) helped you.

- Is it possible that the wrong done to you may have prevented something worse that could have happened?
- Could your hurt be a wake-up call to help you work toward greater physical, mental, and spiritual resilience?

In the table below complete the two columns for your specific situation in the spirit of the suggested examples:

Table 40.5 Table for Exercise 7

The stressor	Assigning meaning
I got fired from the job	I learned new skills and found a better position
She won't let me smoke inside the house	She is helping me quit
He was mean and tested my faith	He helped strengthen my faith

Exercise 8. Find meaning in the process of forgiveness
It will be much easier to transcend your hurts if you can assign meaning to the process of forgiveness. *See if you agree with the following statements and add a few of your thoughts to the table below.*

I will be able to focus my mind better if I am able to forgive
Forgiveness will allow me to strengthen my faith
By forgiving I will be able to share a more pleasant attitude with my children.
By forgiving I will become more resilient and have better self esteem

Exercise 9. Cultivate acceptance and empathy
Once you decide to consider forgiveness, it might help to generate acceptance and empathy for the wrongdoer. This process will be helped if you:

- Minimize ruminations on the wrong that happened;
- Try and find similarity between you and the other person; and
- Try to see the good in the other person

Based on these feelings try to accept others as they are. Each one of us is unique, incomplete, and imperfect in our own way. *That is why we are Homo sapiens not Homo divine.* Every landscape, every garden has imperfections. Acceptance of these imperfections might help you enjoy the beauty that is inherent in all of us. Use some of the exercises described in the section on compassion.

Write three good things you can think about the wrongdoer:

1.
2.
3.

Recognize that developing compassion for the person who has hurt you may be enormously challenging and should not be forced. This process is greatly helped by keeping a broader, all-encompassing view of the world. In this view you recognize the imperfections, incorporate a place for evil and evil doers, and see the humanness behind everyone. Having a spiritual role model also helps with this and all other previous exercises.

I will now introduce you to some of the supportive exercises toward forgiveness.

Exercise 10. Forgiveness imagery, first exercise
On a peaceful sunny day when you are feeling good, watch a distant cloud in the sky. Collect all your hurts and park them on that cloud. See the cloud gradually float away, taking all your hurts with it. Practice deep, relaxed breathing with this exercise.

Exercise 11. Forgiveness imagery, second exercise
Collect all that you have to forgive in a folder. Realize that it is too heavy and toxic for you to keep. Forward this folder to the power you define as the creative intelligence running this planet. Let that intelligence deal with it as s/he considers appropriate. At your end, consider the job done.

Exercise 12. Release your emotions, first exercise
Write a letter to the person you intend to forgive. Put all the details about the event and state clearly why you were hurt. End the letter with a few lines specifically addressing your intention to forgive. Read this letter as if it has already been received by the person. Then shred the letter.

Exercise 13. Release your emotions, second exercise
When you are on a beach, write your grievances on the sand close to the shore and watch the waves wash the words away. Keep that imagery in mind so you can relive this experience later. This will help you consolidate the benefits. Practice relaxed deep breathing with this exercise.

Exercise 14. A day of forgiveness
If it is not easy to forgive just yet, it might help to create an island of forgiveness, a day or even an hour at a time.

Live a day of your life having forgiven everyone. Try to practice this at least once a week (Fridays are assigned days of forgiveness in our program). Say to yourself several times that day, "Today I am in bliss. My ability to forgive makes me feel healthy and happy. I carry no grudges and feel compassionate toward everyone. Whatever happened is buried in the past. I forgive, for

I have been forgiven many times." If a day is too long, practice forgiveness for just an hour.

It might help to commit to someone close to you about this exercise. This will make you externally accountable and better able to comply. If the memory of the hurt comes to you that day, postpone ruminations about it. Assign yourself to think those thoughts the next day. The joy of forgiveness might help you expand this time (from an hour to a day, to a week, and further on).

Exercise 15. Meditation on forgiveness
Take slow, deep, diaphragmatic breaths. Imagine that with each exhalation you are releasing out all your hurts, injuries, and negative feelings from your heart. Imagine that with each inhalation you are imbibing positive energy and forgiveness of the universe into your heart. In the beginning practice this meditation for five to ten minutes every day sitting in a safe and quiet place. You can increase the duration of practice as you advance.

Remember these beautiful and true words: To err is human, to forgive divine (Alexander Pope). Forgiveness raises you from being a human to the state of being divine and awakened with a life transformed.

Exercise 17. Pray for forgiveness
If you find it difficult to forgive today, do not hasten the process or force it upon yourself. Just pray that you get the strength to be able to forgive and stay with that prayer for some time. Tomorrow or day after, you will find greater strength and ability to forgive.

Now for a very important and final exercise in forgiveness:

Exercise 18. Pre-emptive forgiveness
I conducted a simple yet transforming experiment in the beginning of 2008. As a new year resolution, to a close loved one I promised unconditional forgiveness for the entire year of 2008. I resolved that everything they say or do, I will take in a positive light. This commitment enhanced our quality of life tremendously. It took away any little disagreements, judgments, miscommunications and all the other little annoyances that do not deserve to, but sometimes come in the way of fulfilling relationships. The wonderful aspect of this experiment was that later I received the same commitment from them also and we have been renewing it yearly.

Learning from my own experience and from sharing it with others, I highly recommend pre-emptive forgiveness within the context of a close loving and trusting relationship. Most minor disagreements are not worth paying attention to. If a year is too long, may be start with one day. Start your journey into pre-emptive forgiveness by praying for your loved ones. Research suggests that if you pray for your friend or spouse, it will be easier for you to forgive them.

I often tell patients and learners to just live the day today in total preemptive forgiveness. At the end of the day see if you carry a smaller burden on your shoulders. This is the perfect vaccination against much future suffering. Preemptive forgiveness does not mean you will allow indiscretions. All it means is that you will be kind to yourself, in better control of your emotions, delay judgment, do not allow amygdala to hyper-react, and train your brain to be more heartful so your brain's higher center instinctively comes on line. *This could be potentially transformative, particularly if you add to preemptive forgiveness also preemptive acceptance.*

Your forgiveness for yesterday may heal a sore that knows not its healing balm; your gift of forgiveness for tomorrow may heal a wound yet uncreated, yet as hurtful as the one experienced. If you consider forgiveness as a gift, remember that gifts are given for the joy of the present and the future, not so much the past. So gift preemptive forgiveness to your loved ones. You are thus gifting them and yourself the promise of a life with much greater joy.

SECTION XI: RELATIONSHIPS: YOUR TRIBE

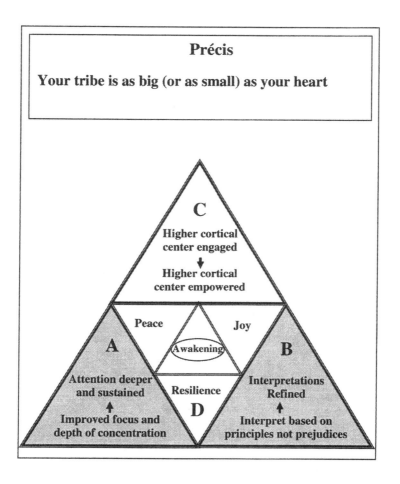

Précis

Your tribe is as big (or as small) as your heart

C

Higher cortical
center engaged
↓
Higher cortical
center empowered

Peace

Joy

A

Awakening

B

Attention deeper
and sustained

Resilience

D

Interpretations
Refined

↑
Improved focus and
depth of concentration

↑
Interpret based on
principles not prejudices

41. What is Your Tribe?

Pause for a few seconds and think about something extraordinary that you have desired all your life. It could be getting a coveted promotion, having a child, marrying your boyfriend or girlfriend, landing your dream job, winning a big lottery, or anything else that you hold very high in value... Now imagine a day in the future when this desire actually is fulfilled...

Q.1. How many friends and relatives would you call to inform about your good fortune knowing that they will be truly happy and proud when they hear about your accomplishment without an expectation of receiving any of the benefits?

1. None ☐
2. One ☐
3. Two ☐
4. Three ☐
5. Four or more ☐

These friends and relatives constitute your tribe. Consider yourself extraordinarily lucky if you have a few friends and relatives who will truly rejoice in your success. It is easier to share sorrow; the true test of friendship is the ability to share joy.

It is very important to identify your tribe so you can nurture and protect it and, most importantly, thrive in it. On the whole, however, it seems that such a tribe seems to be withering away for many of us. In a survey conducted by the National Opinion Research Center at the University of Chicago, 1,467 participants were asked questions related to their social contacts.[383] One out of four participants had no one in whom they could confide. The mean number of confidants dropped to two (from three in 1985). Several reasons are believed to account for this drop, including spending more time at work, living in suburbs, spending more time watching TV or with iPods and computers, and online social networking that fulfills the short-term needs for associating without needing a long-term committed friendship. *Our relationships thus have become a mile wide but only an inch deep.* The depth of nurturing relationships might be missing.

Part of the reason also relates to the way our society is structured. From being hunter gatherers to an agricultural and then to an industrial society, we have come to a point wherein, if we choose to, we may never need to go out of our home. Our societies are thus virtual, our greetings through e-mail cards, gifts to even neighbors delivered by online retailers. No wonder we are getting increasingly lonely.

Evolutionarily our coming together increased our chances of survival. Most vital events such as birth, death, marriage, illness, or disability need a strong fabric of the society to support an individual or a family. The help could be tangible, such as financial or medical help, or could be more symbolic, emotional, or religious. Being part of a tribe provided us a form of social insurance. This has now been effectively replaced by insurance plans of all sorts, an increased focus on individual privacy, and extreme busy-ness for all of us. As a result, while we are able to sustain ourselves without much social interactions, we lack fulfilling our emotional needs. You may buy the loveliest toys for your child, but if you are not there to play with them, those toys are of no use. A cage made of gold is still a cage. The resulting loneliness increases the sense of incompleteness and emotional insecurity in our lives.

The ideal approach will be to enjoy the benefits provided by your material and technological progress while at the same time enhancing your con-nectedness. You can achieve this by creating and sustaining a group that provides you the cushion of safety and love—your tribe.

Your own tribe is made of friends and relatives that share some of these characteristics:

1.   They accept you as you are
2.   They know you are imperfect and are okay with it
3.   They understand you
4.   They desire nothing but the best for you
5.   There is an aspect of you that they admire
6.   They are honest with you
7.   They consider your success theirs; your suffering theirs
8.   You consider their success yours; their suffering yours

There is a good chance you are surrounded by people who share these characteristics but may not have paid attention. How do you identify who truly are the members of your tribe?   In addition to Q.1. asked above, an answer to the question below might also help.

Q.2. Who among your friends and relatives can you call at two A.M. in the morning without a concern that they will be upset or judgmental? They constitute your tribe.

The fact is that at the core of your being you wish to accept everyone as they are, understand them, desire the best for them, admire their skills, be honest, and honor and rejoice in their success and empathize in their grief. This core however sometimes gets covered by egocentric dust that is sprayed on us by the fast momentum of the world. Nevertheless, if at the very core most of us are kind and compassionate, how big then is the possible membership of your tribe? The entire humanity, isn't it?

This is truly your potential. You have the potential to cultivate an awareness wherein you have an infinite square feet home—akin to the *Indra's* net. You can develop a tribe and self that has no boundaries. In weaving a heaven for everyone, you weave one for yourself.

The silo that you think encages you does not exist. Your boundaries are a creation of your limited self. The sooner you shed them in your mind, the earlier you will become free from the virtual cage created by your mind. This whole world is our home, for each of us. We all are in it together through thick and thin. The oil leak in the gulf coast will impact us also in New York or Seattle or even Minnesota. If not today, it certainly will tomorrow.

When you belong to your big tribe, your prayer includes everyone. Your every loving expression finds its way to the farthest reaches of the world and eventually travels back to you—today, tomorrow, or at some point in the future.

42. Why Develop Your Tribe?

When I am despondent or unsure, I often ask myself this question: what is the diameter of my existence this very minute?

Diameter of Existence (DOE)

By diameter of existence I mean who and what I am identifying with. Almost always I have found that my sadness, fear, or insecurity comes from too narrow a diameter of existence. Let us expand on this concept a bit.

Your identity has multiple domains as shown in figure 42.1 below. In the center sits the smiley you. Your two broadest domains are with respect to: geography (north) and shared origins (relationships / religion – south). There are several other groups that provide you an identity such as gender, work, political affiliation, sexual orientation, medical diagnosis, graduate class, school alumni, pet owners, and many more.

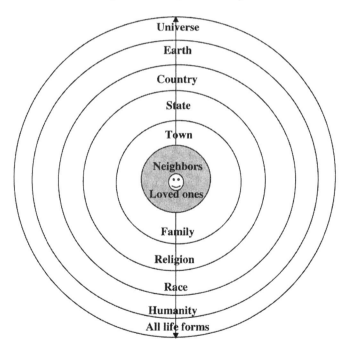

Figure 42.1. The two broadest domains of your diameter of existence with respect to geography (north) and shared origins (relationships / religion – south)

All of your identities provide you a sense of self and in combination make you feel whole, if that combination matches your ideals and expectations. These identities are also limiting. If your sense of self includes only you, then you are likely to invite much greater stress, compared to having a broader diameter of existence.

In the narrowest most limited state, which is predominantly self-focused, life is quite challenging. This is simply because all your actions are then to take care of the self. The world can only send so much energy your way. With personal failure comes despondency and frustration. While failure breeds sadness, success generates anxiety for the fear that you might not be able to maintain the momentum and preserve the gains. Self-focus generates prejudices and related egocentric preferences. This fouls your interpretations, weakens your attention, and directs your attention more toward the mind. Such a state converts a transient unhappy event into an attention black hole that may stay with you for much longer than desirable.

The panacea to overcome this state is to expand your diameter of existence. The more evolved, mature, and resilient you become, the larger your "I" and smaller the contribution of your own personal ego to it. In the northern part of the diameter, you progress from identifying with the self to neighbors, town, state, country, planet, and the whole world; in the southern part, you progress from focus on the self to loved ones, family, religion, race, all humans, and all life forms. With this expansion of diameter of your existence, your thinking matures. You rejoice in seeing others happy since their success and joy becomes yours. They are a part of your extended self. In this state you find a reason to celebrate each day, each moment.

The intelligence that runs this planet thinks not just about you or me. This intelligence cares about everyone. So when you expand your diameter of existence, you might begin thinking like this intelligence. The day your diameter of existence includes every being on this planet, you are very close to self realization. Your work would then reflect the mandate of the world. Coincidences might happen, help comes from unexpected places. Your personal concerns will start seeming small, less potent, and easier to handle. This is because in the context of the whole they seem like small, manageable perturbations. You might still do the same thing, but now with much greater ease because the perceived risk seems small and diluted.

In the long run, nature sustains an action that brings the greatest good to the greatest number. Nature protects the protectors because they are the agents of change and progress for the world at large.

Solitude – a Good Place to Visit, Not a Good Place to Inhabit

A small serving of solitude adds a desirable flavor to the salsa of our life and often is rejuvenating. Solitude allows your brain centers to regroup and provides respite from overstimulation. However, for most of us, solitude is a good place to visit for a brief period but is not an ideal place to stay—not for very long anyway. After a period of time solitude might begin to create negative emotions and impede your ability to escape from the negativity of your internal dialog. Your tribe allows you to short circuit this negative self-talk.

We have survived as a species because we were able to organize ourselves in groups that provided us identity and a blanket of security. With increasing dependence on technology and limited immediate need of each other for basic survival, we often invite loneliness without even realizing it. There was a time when several generations lived together in a family. Grandchildren played in the arms of grandparents. A lot has changed since then. The feeling of loneliness in this world is very easy to come by if you are not conscious of keeping it at bay.

Make every effort to push away the state of loneliness before it becomes a habit. A habit, good or bad, gets deeply rooted with time and is then difficult to shed. Create a tribe of yours before loneliness becomes a way of life—before you forget what it is like to be surrounded by friends and relatives you love and trust.

Transience is the Rule

Travel back in time and look at your life. Remember your first best friend, your circle of friends in high school, college, and your earlier jobs. How many of those are around you now? The chances are most of the people you have known in the past are not physically or emotionally present in your life currently. They are hiding somewhere in your photo albums, memories, and maybe a few saved cards. *Do you realize the transience of most relationships?*

Most of your relationships are ephemeral. Friends and acquaintances move on, children go off to college, and colleagues find different opportunities. This is true for the vast majority of your relationships. So realizing this transience, make the most of the time you have. Develop a more fulfilling relationship by being accepting and aware of everyone you interact with. Make time to hear what others have to say, particularly the little others, your children. That will make their day. This is how you will create islands of beautiful memories that you will be able to revisit. Parting is always painful, but more so when you have not had adequate fill of your loved ones. ***When you have loved from the depth of your heart and were able to show it, you will be more secure in saying goodbye.***

Many patients who are forced to face the reality of finiteness in terms of a life limiting diagnosis find it difficult to cope with this possibility. However, a few others take such a possibility in stride. One variable that distinguishes these two polar responses is the quality of their lives and their presence in it. Patients who have lived a fulfilling life mostly remaining present in their moments, liberally sharing their love, easy to forgive, kind and compassionate, and pursuing a higher meaning and purpose—such patients commonly find it easy to accept their finiteness. They also tend to have a larger closely knit tribe around them.

Tribe Provides Meaning to Your Life

In a series of four studies involving 643 people, researchers created the perception of social exclusion.[384] Approaches used included having a confederate refuse to meet participants after seeing their videotaped introduction or ostracizing participants in a computerized ball-tossing game. Study showed that even in the experimental setting social exclusion was associated with a reduction in global perception of life as meaningful and also a decrease in personal self worth.

Tribe provides the primary meaning and purpose to your life. In their last moments of life, I have never seen anyone reminiscing about their squeaky clean carpet or 401(k) statement. In most instances people wish to visit the memories of their loved ones or focus on spiritual thoughts.

Tribe and Medical Research

Convincing findings from research studies show that having a tribe and thriving within it improves your health and well-being. Findings from some of these studies are summarized below:

- Studies have shown that social support helps by a variety of mechanisms. These include improved depressive symptoms, perception of a better quality of life, better health care access, improved compliance with treatment, and positive effects on the immune system.[385]

- Social support helped physical health and longevity.[386]

- Higher social support was associated with lower psychosocial distress in firefighters.[387]

- In Kosovan refugees, family cohesion was associated with a lower likelihood of post traumatic stress disorder.[388]

- In elderly residents in Leganes, a city in central Spain, having a confidant was associated with a 25 percent better survival over six years. In this study, lack of social participation increased risk of death by 50 percent.[290] An important aspect of this study was that engagement in meaningful roles was protective, while receipt of emotional support alone did not help much.

- A similar study in very old Australians with ten year follow-up showed 22 percent better survival in participants with a strong network of friends compared to those without such a network.[389] Interestingly, the effect of social network with children and relatives was not so important. This study suggests that some of the effect of having a strong social network might actually be related to individual attributes that creates a network around them. These attributes themselves are likely to have a survival value.

- In a focus group study involving elderly participants, four major domains emerged as building blocks of successful aging. These were attitude/adaptation, security/stability, health/wellness, and engagement/stimulation. Amongst attitude the most important components were a positive attitude, realistic perspective, and the ability to adapt to change. Security/stability was related to living environment, social support, and financial resources. Opinions on general health/wellness were mixed. A sense of engagement, continued learning, and feeling of a purpose in life were considered important for successful aging.[390]

- In a study involving older couples over a five-year period, the impact of providing vs. receiving social support was assessed for its effect on survival. Providing social support was associated with significantly improved survival. Receiving social support alone did not impact survival when the effect of providing social support was also added to the equation. These relationships were independent of a number of additional variables including demography, personality, physical health, mental health, and marital relationship.[391]

- Belonging to a cohesive tribe and feeling that you are a member of a group has important effects on the biologic systems of your body. Loneliness was shown to increase cortisol response and fibrinogen level, both not conducive to good health.[392]

- In a study to reduce the impact of social rejection, aggression was reduced by a brief, friendly social connection with an experimenter compared to a neutral interaction. Journaling about a family member, a friend, or a favorite celebrity also helped.[393]

- Social exclusion decreased pro-social behavior, including money donated to a student fund, volunteering for lab experiments, helping after a mishap, and cooperation in a mixed-motive game. Decreased empathy as a result of isolation mediated these negative outcomes.[394]

- In a study assessing narcissistic aggression, negative behavior was completely abolished even under personal threat to the ego when participants believed that there was a similarity between them and the subjects. This similarity was projected as shared birthday or fingerprint type.[395]

- Social connection helped symptoms of depression in older adults.[396]

- Empowering and connecting elderly participants with the world by teaching them Internet use showed a trend toward lower loneliness and depression, more positive attitudes toward computers, and more confidants.[397]

> - Increased perception of rejection or social exclusion increased aggressiveness.[398]
>
> - Feeling closer to others was associated with a better ability to forgive and greater well-being.[399]

In summary, the following benefits have been shown in research studies among people having deeper more secure relationships:

- Better quality of life
- Better health care access
- Improved compliance with treatment
- Positive effects on the immune system
- Better physical health
- Increased longevity
- Lower psychosocial distress
- Lower risk of post traumatic stress disorder
- Healthier aging
- Lower stress response
- Lower depression

Recall that in the chapter on the brain and the mind we also saw that interaction with friends has been associated with increased activation of the pre-frontal cortex and other related areas of the brain,[111] and healthy social relationships have been associated with healthy hypothalamic-pituitary axis function and decreased sympathetic stimulation.[112]

There are thus several good reasons to cultivate and thrive within your tribe. We will next learn some of the principles and approaches that might help you create and nurture such a tribe.

43. How to Create Your Tribe

Creating a tribe is a bit similar to taking care of your garden. ***The three key steps in creating a garden are: seed it, feed it, and weed it.*** First you do the appropriate landscaping, take care of the soil, sow the appropriate seeds, and plant the right plants (your friends and loved ones). All this while feed your garden with water, a rich soil and fertilizers (your presence and love). You consistently maintain your garden and remain patient that one day the seeds will germinate; saplings will grow and bear flowers and fruits. You need lots of patience to let the process unfold at its natural pace; a prematurely opened bud does not deliver a happy flower. Once the garden shows the colors of green, pink and purple, to keep it pristine, you also have to regularly weed it (of miscommunications, disagreements, hurts etc.). In this entire process, the creation and sustenance of your tribe depends on one person central to your tribe—you.

Seed Your Tribe

Tribes do not get created spontaneously. Creating and nurturing your tribe will be the work of a lifetime. You will need to seed the tribe with a lot of "you." As a first step you will have to include yourself in your tribe. This sounds counterintuitive but is true. You are indeed the most important member of your tribe. If you are not "present," you might find yourself distant from everyone and everything you hold dear, even while in their physical proximity.

If you do not actively engage, your tribe stands the risk of slowly withering away. Be aware of your "presence" or lack thereof. When hearing, truly listen. When looking, truly see.

Kindness may be effortful, until it becomes effortless. Particularly kindness to the self. It is important for you to be kind to yourself and have a healthy self esteem. Your connection to yourself is the first and most critical step toward finding an anchor for you to creatively create and sustain your tribe.

Once you have arrived, you will be able to find likeminded friends who you can call at two A.M. These are the friends you will grow older with. They will share your sorrows and, most importantly, your joy. Success is only half full if you cannot share it with someone. Find all those someones and create your oasis before it is too late. These will be the prized jewels decorating your existence. They will multiply your joy and also absorb the bumps that you will most certainly encounter in your journey through life.

Some of the approaches that might help this journey are discussed next.

Use Kind Language

Language is a living being. Quite often, however, the words may belie the emotions veiled beneath them, particularly in the ambiance of formality. If you remain awake to the emotions that hide behind the words, you may be able to respond in a much better way to the core issue at hand. Sensing the emotions expressed by others needs your presence and your ability to process words in the context of other non-verbal messages.

If your loved ones choose irrational words, do not automatically react to what is spoken. Try to understand their inner feelings. *An expression other than love is often a call for help.* Maybe they had a tough day and the only reason they are irrational with you is because they trust and love you more than anyone else in the world. If you take a broad enough view, their irritation toward you may in fact be flattering. By negatively reacting to their words, you might miss the whole point.

Use the language of your heart. You can always find the right words to speak untruth yet not be literally wrong. This is not the way friendships get nurtured. If you choose ambiguous words to dodge the truth, those words might often reflect a compromise. Such words cannot be the language of your heart. Words have intrinsic energy and should be carefully chosen to be a kind reflection of your inner thought process. Be sincere in your compliments. If you are not sincere when you praise, you will likely not believe the compliments that come your way.

I once heard someone say, "A compliment a day keeps the counselor away!"

Find Meaning in an Argument

Volcanoes, angry as they are, still serve an essential function. Volcanoes release pressure from the bosom of the earth and serve a purpose—that of preventing an earthquake. Look at this value in each argument—sometimes it is your arguments that keep you together.

When in an argument remember that the particular point of contention is almost never more important than your relationship. Details of the events and their interpretations tend to be fluid. You might be looking at some of the aspects with a myopic eye. It will be kind to give others a benefit of doubt. Never let relationships sour because of trivial events. Whenever possible do not accumulate small, low-grade irritations. Do not let leaky faucets annoy you—get them fixed in time.

In an argument, do not globalize the issue. Use kind language that you can later own. By globalizing a small issue and using unkind language you are likely to increase the damage and rev up your limbic system and that of your loved one or friend. To prevent an argument take a broad look. Many things that do not make sense might seem more appropriate once you take a look at the total picture.

Try to understand others before expecting them to understand you. See details from others' vantage point—it might make a bit more sense. Consider their limitations and fears. Assume they are trying to defend themselves and not harm you.

Using these guiding principles, you may be more likely to create space for togetherness. Your boundaries will then loosen, you will be able to create a common center of gravity and not remain in your own cocoon.

If You Ever Get Critical

This is a very important issue. Be very discreet yet leave some room for uncertainty in your critique—in peace or within the scope of an argument. Also use language that focuses more on you than the other person. For example, if the coffee you are served is cold, it might be better to state something like, "I find the coffee a bit cold for my taste." You are likely to receive an accommodative response with this statement. If, however, you say, "You always serve coffee colder than it should be," what do you think you will hear? Go make your own coffee! You asked for it because you pinned down the other person in a corner and attacked his or her ego. *If you cannot be polite, be at least vague!*

Critique often reflects the past and not how things might shape up in the future. So it is ideal to focus on the future, not so much on the past, except to draw lessons from it. In the coffee example it might be even better to say, "Mostly I prefer coffee a bit warmer than what it was today. If we could warm it up a bit more in the future it might help." You certainly used more words but shifted the focus to the future where the person hearing the comment feels capable of making a change. A critique should address the issue in the kindest words and then point toward how the issue can be addressed. This is how you redirect the energy of the recipient toward a tangible solution rather than the fact that he or she was critiqued.

I also suggest following a one-minute rule. When you have to criticize someone, particularly in their absence, do it for only one minute. This might prevent you from globalizing the issue and adding extra layers of your own biases. At the end of the day you will likely feel better about yourself if you confined to facts rather than exaggerating and bad mouthing the other person.

Timing of the critique is also important. How we feel about ourselves varies from one day to the next. Accordingly, we may be more accepting of the critique at particular times or days. Try to reserve potentially unpleasant feedbacks to times when you perceive the other person is more open and receptive. We all have moments when we are more open to receive critique. Right words at the right time are a gift; right words at the wrong time can create a rift. *To everything there is a season....a time to keep silence, and a time to speak. (Ecclesiastes 3:1, 7 KJV)*

There is an old Sufi teaching that the words we speak must pass through three gates (introspections): Is it truth? Is it kind? Is it necessary? Only expressions that pass through these three gates should be spoken, particularly when we provide a critique. *Sometimes it is better to speak silence than speak words.*

When You have to say No

It is important for you to pick the size of the bite that you can easily swallow. A bigger bite is challenging to chew and could potentially be risky. In order to right size the bites of your life you sometimes will have to say No, even within your tribe. The time when you say No is one of the most delicate and vulnerable times, even within a close relationship. If not handled with great care, your No can significantly risk your relationships. Let me present an example.

You are asked by your spouse to share lunchtime on a work day. You, however, are behind and would rather work through lunch. Your response could be, "Sorry, I am too busy. Can't come today." An alternate albeit longer response might be, "I would love to share the lunch time but presently I am facing several deadlines that I have to meet. I cherish our time together and would like it to be fun and relaxed rather than hurried, so how about next Monday during lunch?" Which response do you think would you like to hear?

When someone asks a favor of you they are put in a vulnerable spot and should be handled very, very tenderly. It is your job to cushion them at that point. Even if you have no choice but to say No, in most situations the first response should be a show of enthusiasm for their suggestion. Next you can honestly and with adequate detail explain why you are not able to accept their proposal. As a third step offer the second best option that at least partly compensates for what they asked of you (assuming that is reasonable).

Do you see that your No is guarded by a Yes on both sides? That is your polite and considerate No. A No that respects the other person. The sequence is Yes-No-Yes. This is the *sandwiched No*. Like it or not, to preserve sanity you will face many occasions when you have no choice but to say No. Use No gingerly, plan how to say it, and know when to say No. This will keep your tribe healthy.

Flexible in Preferences

If within your tribe you constantly worry about how others might be judging you, you are not with them—you are only with yourself, in your head. You are either excessively self-conscious or self-absorbed. Effective communication is not possible in this state. Relationships offer the ideal ground to practice your presence and share higher values such as gratitude, compassion, acceptance, forgiveness, kindness, and love.

Make every effort to enhance peace in your circle. **One of the ways you can invite peace in your circle is by being easygoing. Be flexible in your preferences.** Learn to enjoy watching others enjoy. Try to understand, delay judgment and assume innocence. Keep the principle of assuming innocence unless proven guilty. Do not fill the blanks with negative thoughts. Either leave them blank or try to find the best possible explanation. You are more likely to be right (and happier) with this approach. Whenever possible go with the flow. If you find someone wrong from your perspective, consider the possibility that they might know something that you do not.

Memory researchers teach us that our memory is fallible and our mind may care more about creating a good story rather than the truth. Pause for a moment before you negatively judge someone based on the contents of your memory. This pause allows your prefrontal cortex to activate and provide better mentorship to the reactive amygdala. If you allow yourself to get angry based on incomplete understanding, you are creating a set-up for future embarrassment. You are also likely to lose your point and, in the long run, will have lesser ability to bring about a positive change.

P/N Ratio and Emotional Bank Account

In the section on meaning we talk about the Positivity/Negativity ratio and emotional bank account. Positivity is the positive feedback you provide to others while negativity is the negative feedback. The higher this ratio in your tribe, the more likely you are to sustain your tribe. Most teams with excellent dynamics have a ratio of >5; successful marriages also have a high ratio (typically >5) while marriages that end up in divorce have a low ratio (often <1).[311] The higher your P/N ratio, the greater the number of deposits you have made in your emotional bank account with others. Remember that the memory of the older deposits tends to fade, just like the batteries in your laptop computers. You can only draw from this account if you have made consistent and fresh deposits.

Every little act of kindness, every kind word, every expression of approval creates a deposit into this account. The little things that you do make a profound difference.

Recall the times when you have given a talk. There are two broad categories of listeners. The first type are those who maintain a gentle, approving face, remain connected, laugh appropriately, and nod their heads in the affirmative when you look at them. Such listeners bring out the best in you. The other type remains stony faced and express no expression of approval or disapproval. After giving a talk to this "tough group," you may come out confused about how you did. Experience a few talks like this and you might think about changing your job. You can bring out the best in others by being the first type of listener, by sending kind positive admiring energy.

An important aspect of P/N ratio is to remember that not everyone is good with words. Some people are kind with words, others kind with deeds, and a rare few with both. Know the traits of your friends and loved ones and be grateful for whatever comes your way—kind words, actions, or both.

Kind Words or Kind Actions?

We all have travelled a long and precious journey that is unique to us. Conditioned by this journey our individual needs are also unique. Some of us are thrilled to hear honest praise, may be this is something we missed as a child. Others really love to receive gifts, diamonds in particular! Some others appreciate any help they can get with household chores. Many others want just quality time. Some simply love chocolate! Would it not help for you to know what are the needs that your loved ones really want fulfilled?

I once had a dear colleague come to me with tears in her eyes saying her relationship with her husband was not as warm as before. They seemed to be have grown distant, something that is unfortunately all too common in our relationships. When I asked her to describe their time at home, it was all occupied by one chore after another. Together they were running their home and kids' lives perfectly. Their kitchen was squeaky clean, no dirty laundry, all bills paid on time etc. But this is all they were doing. There was no time left for quality time sitting together with no agenda. If you are asked to suggest one change to them what would be your advice? Don't you think you would suggest that they should spend 15 minutes of quality time together and may be accept a slightly imperfect kitchen?

Recognize the human nature to do even more of what we can do well. Our propensity is to overfill and over satisfy a particular need—the one we feel most capable of accomplishing. Often your loved one may be giving a different message. Listen to that message because it is a valuable feedback. If you try to fill a part of them that is totally empty, that will offer an excellent return on your investment! If you are not clear which one to choose (kind words or kind actions), start off with quality time. Try it, for I have never seen adding quality time to a relationship fail!

Be Kind to the Self

Kindness to others starts from kindness to the self. Being kind to yourself is an important ingredient that greatly helps your presence. In a study involving 2,187 participants, self-compassion was strongly associated with lower likelihood of anger, self-consciousness, and social comparison.[400] Kindness to others radiates from you once you are kind to yourself. Such kindness provides the glue that holds your tribe together.

Once a patient of mine said, "The way I treat myself, if I treated everyone else, I would have no friends left." You are your most important customer. On days of acceptance, be accepting of your self; on days of compassion, be compassionate to the self. Your self kindness is the first step toward bringing kindness to your loved ones and friends.

Cultivate Awareness of Interconnectedness

Every morning when you wake up, watch TV, use your cell phone, and sip your morning coffee, millions of people across the world have worked together to make this happen. You may not perceive this connection because you cannot easily palpate it. The fact is every being on our planet is connected with you.

The world is as small or big as you make of it. Your world could include just you, which is likely to lead you into a lonely, self-focused, and unhappy existence. Or your definition of self could be much broader, making you a patient, compassionate, and interconnected being with a reason to celebrate each day.

This world is like your own physical body; every part is connected with, and profoundly affects, the rest. You share the air, water, food, and all the other gifts of your world with everyone else. Perceive this connection. There are greater similarities between you and others than there are differences. Studies show that we share 99 percent of the DNA sequence with chimpanzees.[401] Our similarities with each other are even greater.

If I look at your and my liver cells in the microscope I will not be able to tell whether they belong to you, me or someone else. When these cells join together to create an organ such as a heart, liver, kidneys, or brain they still carry no meaning of religion, race, or nationality. When these organs develop together into a new body as a newborn, we come as an innocent human. As a newborn we cannot even tell ourselves separate from the rest of the world. It is only with the genesis of the mind and the ego that separations begin to appear that isolate us. Our similarities thus go far back in time compared to our differences. The essence of interconnectedness is to "remember" our common origins and anchor our awareness in that sharing.

In that sense, the universe is truly your extended self and all the more precious. If you wish to preserve your precious world, include as many beings as possible in your circle. Accept them as they are. The bigger the circle you draw, the larger your tribe.

Draw bigger circles.

SECTION XII: THE BEGINNING OF AWAKENING (TRANSFORMATION)

44. Meditation

Précis

Meditation is a state of deep and relaxed attention and refined interpretations that engages and empowers the brain's higher cortical center

Meditation increases your peace, joy, and resilience

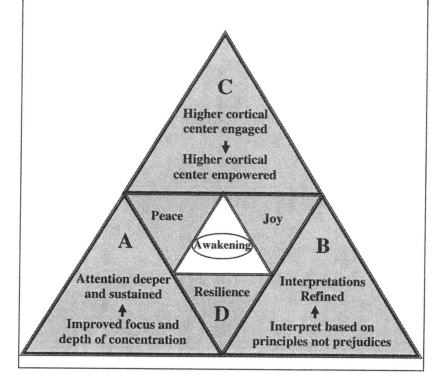

Every functioning unit of your body is supplied with nutrients to sustain itself. Every unit also has an elaborative cleaning system that dumps unnecessary, potentially toxic end products. These metabolic wastes are cleared every second of your life by venous blood, lymph channels, and other pathways. Even individual nerve cells have a system to round up all the chemicals released during transmission of a signal to avoid excitatory overdose.

However, one vital entity of yours that has no innate cleaning system is your mind. Your mind does not have a defined system to clear its waste products of "spent and toxic thoughts." Just like a sedimentary rock, the mind collects layers after layers of complex thoughts and does not pause on its own to clear itself. Sleep offers the only time that the mind comes to a partial rest, but in the modern world sleep is often inefficient, superficial, and inadequate in duration.

As a result we incrementally collect increasing number of thoughts over a lifetime; many elderly people live their life weighed down by their stored thoughts and their attendant attention black holes. There is so much baggage of the past stored in their systems that little room is left to welcome the present. This is also true of a younger generation engaged in excessive thinking. Most stressful situations can be labeled with an alternate diagnosis—*thought toxicity*.

It is important to systematically let go of this baggage if you have collected it already. It is also important to have an ongoing program to prevent this baggage from re-collecting. A useful technique to clear your mind of excessive thoughts is to cultivate a program that allows you to purposefully log off from the world for some time so you can log on again with a fresh connection. This entails reaching a state where your mind becomes calm, collected and content. This state is achieved with an effective program of meditation.

Meditation deepens your attention, refines your interpretations, engages the higher cortical center, and takes you toward peace, joy, resilience, and transformation. Meditation brings your mind in your greater influence. Mind trained by meditation starts listening to you, not as an unquestioning slave or a fear prone companion, but more as a joyous partner. This chapter outlines some of the common issues and concepts related to meditation.

To get the most benefit, a concentrative meditation program should ideally be taught in individualized sessions. Many aspects of meditation need particular attention to the state and stage of progress of an individual. On the basis of this assessment and understanding of individual goals the instructor customizes the plan that includes: teaching skills to cultivate a mind conducive to meditation, picking the right program, duration of practice, direction of focus, pace of progress, etc. Hence if you are interested in learning meditation, I recommend consulting an experienced practitioner. Here I offer a few introductory thoughts.

What do the Patients say?

Let me ask you a question that I ask many patients.

Exercise 1. Do you have a planned relaxation program that you practice on most days?

1. Yes ☐
2. No ☐

Exercise 2. If you answered yes, what does this plan comprise of?

1. Watching TV ☐
2. Reading a novel ☐
3. Going on a walk ☐
4. Talking to friends ☐
5. Playing music ☐
6. Art ☐
7. Other hobby ☐
8. Prayer ☐
9. Meditation ☐
10. Yoga ☐
11. Muscle relaxation ☐
12. Tai chi ☐
13. Qi gong ☐
14. Relaxation tape ☐
15. Deep breathing ☐
16. Biofeedback ☐

The most common answers I get are "I watch TV, I read a novel, I go on a walk, I talk to my friends, I go on vacation." Do you think these would provide adequately effective relaxation?

Watching TV or reading a novel might provide some relaxation but these are not efficient enough to counter the effect of the daily dose of thoughts. Watching TV actually might provide the seed for an additional load of thoughts.

Recall this figure that depicts the relationship between the number and quality of your thoughts and the state of your mind:

Quality of thinking→ ↓Number of thoughts	Negative thoughts	Positive thoughts
Few	Depressed state A	Mindful state B
Many	Anxious state C	Excited state D

Figure 44.1 Relationship between the number and
quality of thoughts and the state of your mind

An effective relaxation program is one that brings you to quadrant B. In true relaxation, your thought process progressively slows its momentum until you are able to reach the deepest state of calm even a moment of which is immensely relaxing. It is like being in a state of deep sleep. Beyond the ordinary, such relaxation has intensity to it. Relaxation is not just about being free of stress. It is a positive state of joy, love, peace, and bliss in their purity. It is not about just emptying the mind; it is also filling it with love. The relaxed state defragments the hard drive of your brain and gets rid of all the viruses, Trojans, pop-ups, cookies, and worms of thoughts and experiences that you may have accumulated through the day. It is like getting a car wash at the end of a dusty trip.

In addition to relaxation, such a program also trains your mind so you have greater influence in directing the content and flow of your attention. Without training we often have to put up with a mind that does not listen to us. This is the proximate cause of our stress. Would it not be nice if we could train our mind so it learns to be more relaxed and efficient at the same time?

Among the available programs that can help us toward that goal, I am biased in favor of two—meditation and prayer. I believe meditation and prayer are the two most efficient ways for you to reach a deeply relaxed state. Fifteen to thirty minutes of good practice may be adequate to counter the effect of an entire day of stress.

Before addressing what meditation actually is, I would like to answer an important and common question I am often asked—what if one cannot (or does not wish to) meditate?

What if You Cannot (or do not wish to) Meditate?

It is just fine if you cannot or do not wish to mediate. Several alternate programs, practiced with sincerity and discipline, allow you to reach a similar state of relaxation that is provided by meditation. These are listed as responses to the question above. Whether it is meditation, prayer, yoga, guided imagery, progressive muscle relaxation, tai chi, qigong, or biofeedback, the underlying principles and effects are very similar.

The three most important aspects of a relaxation program to make it work for you are:

1) Your belief that the program will help you;
2) The philosophy of the program agrees with your view of the world; and
3) You have the time and ability to practice the program.

Select the program you like and believe is feasible for you, and stay with it over the long term. Most programs will not work right away. Every skill you have acquired, whether it is swimming, cooking, or riding a bicycle, takes time to learn and master. The same is true for a relaxation program. It is important to spend some time with a program before making a switch. Most scientific studies show that the results are quite similar with any of these programs.

Consistency of practice is as important as the total duration of time devoted to a program. On a busy day even five minutes of relaxation might be rejuvenating. Ideally, however, a minimum of fifteen minutes every day would be appropriate, preferably up to thirty minutes.

What is Meditation?

This is a difficult question to answer in words since meditation is truly experiential. There are many ways to define meditation. The more words I use to describe meditation, the more likely I am going to be on a slippery slope. *Using words I can only describe the label and anticipated flavor of the wine; for the real taste you will have to open the bottle yourself.* Words create a distance between you and the experience. However, words are convenient for communication, hence I will still try. Some of the more conventional definitions of meditation given by research scientists are:

1. Meditation is a wakeful hypometabolic physiologic state.[402]
2. Meditation has five aspects that together describe the practice:[403]

- Specific and clearly defined technique
- Muscle relaxation
- "Logic relaxation"
- Self-induced state
- An anchor

Meditation encompasses a wide range of practices including the mindful awareness of a Zen practitioner, peaceful yet ecstatic state of a yogi, and constant recitation of a mantra by a TM practitioner. I cannot describe meditation in a single line; hence I will use a short paragraph.

Meditation is relaxed, non-seeking yet purposeful, and conscious attention. Meditation (*meditatito* = to contemplate) is the ability of self to dwell in self in a state of sustained attention with an aim to reach an awake and aware state. Meditation is sometimes considered an altered state of consciousness. However, it is the states of stress, depression, and anxiety that are the real altered states while the calm and peace that comes with meditation represents the natural state of our existence. Anchors that could guide you into this state include breath, soothing sound, image, body sensations, or whatever is presented to your senses in the external world. Eventually, with a systematic practice, the dependence on anchors goes away, the mind dissolves itself in pure tranquility that is your inner nature, and remains calm and peaceful throughout the day. You can see yourself separate from your body, breath, mind, and the world even as you might perceive a connection between your inner self, mind, body, breath, and the world. This perception sometimes could be as real as watching a sunset. This state can only be perceived, not fully described.

I think the last line is the most important. I may spend days, weeks, or months describing you the flavor of a popular ice cream but still not do a good job of it. Your one lick, however, would be enough for you to know exactly what it is like. Meditation is very similar. Think about a day when you woke up from a deep restful sleep on a Saturday morning after a very successful week and now have no specific agendas with the whole weekend ahead to celebrate. The kind of relaxed state you might feel does not come quite close to the relaxation experienced in deep meditation.

Meditation: the Process

The process of meditation can best be described in the form of a metaphor. Imagine a glass full of crystal clear water. Put some dirt in it and stir the water. The dirt will cloud the water and make it opaque. Water here represents the mind and dirt our thoughts. All of us arrive in the world with a pure and clear mind. However, over the years a barrage of experiences and our interpretations of them add impurities to the mind. Some of these impurities collect in chunks in the form of attention black holes. Despite the added dirt, however, there is still crystal clear water somewhere beneath the mud. How do you go about reclaiming the pure water again?

The initial two steps are:
1) Keep the glass on the table and stop stirring— you do this by training your attention so it is more joyful and not so much focused on the attention black holes; and
2) Stop adding more dirt—you do this by refining interpretations to decrease fresh load of negative thoughts

If you stop giving energy to established neuronal circuits by not using them, they tend to wither away. So the process of training your attention and refining interpretations will begin to disempower the attention black holes and clear your mind. This may be mediated by a biological process called "extinction," which entails clearing the memory of previous fears, one of the functions mentored by the pre-frontal cortex.

Meditation needs training, ideally under the tutorship of an accomplished, honest and well-meaning practitioner. A basic level of health, particularly absence of ongoing symptoms such as chronic pain, is helpful. When I see learners with symptoms that might prevent them from sitting still for a period, I often encourage them to pursue either walking meditation or prayer. Prayer offers the same benefits as meditation. Avoid superstitions, too many rituals, mysticism, and pursuit of extra powers with meditation. Also avoid day dreaming or too much association of ideas. Seeking peace, stress relief, improved focus, health benefits, and improved mood are all reasonable goals. Meditation, however, may take you to a deeper level than any of these objective benefits. To reach that state you will have to eventually let go of all your intentions—even the intention to be relaxed. In this state you almost fully dissolve your ego, have nowhere to go and nothing to seek. Prayer and meditation converge in this state.

The common non-physical impediments toward meditation are laziness, excessive enthusiasm, too much expectation, sleepiness, activity of the mind, and spiritual ego. In meditation you walk in balance between laziness and excessive enthusiasm. A calm, contained acceptance, openness to novelty, and mild positive belief might describe the optimal attitude. Too much expectation will lead to disappointment. Hope, faith, belief, and optimism are reasonable, but excessive passion and excitement may come in the way of deep relaxation.

When I first started meditation I would feel relaxed and calm at the end of the practice—mostly because I was sleeping! Sleeping is not necessarily bad, but the ideal state is that of calm alertness. Once you achieve this state gradually you will notice that your mind loses interest in excessive thinking. It is at this point that the transformation begins to happen. However, there is one more challenge you will face that has been the Achilles' heel of many traditional masters—that of spiritual ego. As you advance you might begin categorizing the world into meditators vs. non-meditators; believers vs. non-believers; anxious vs. relaxed, and so on. You might also start judging those who cannot remain calm or do not meditate. This will severely limit your progress because it will rekindle the web of judgments and prejudices.

A person does not become holy just because they meditate; many adept meditators may be wanting in core values of gratitude, compassion, acceptance, and forgiveness. More important than the daily practice of concentrative meditation is to nurture a predictably calm, relaxed, kind, gentle, compassionate and joyful disposition. True progress in meditation (and prayer) will take you along this path. Such progress leads you to selflessness and humility which promotes the feeling of compassion, not judgment. This is particularly likely if you add the flavor of faith to your meditation practice. Do not focus so much on tolerance as on acceptance. Tolerance presupposes hierarchy, acceptance is among equals. True freedom is when you can love someone even when the feeling is not immediately reciprocated. You have then transcended your ego. Ego, particularly spiritual ego, is an abyss falling into which is very easy unless you actively guard yourself against it by supporting your spiritual journey with the higher principles.

Anchors certainly help to steady the mind early in the meditation practice. The anchors used may be external or internal. They provide a convenient focus for attention. Some of the external anchors are use of sound, image, chant, etc. Internal anchors include your breath, word, or pure awareness. Gradually as you progress you move to a state of not needing the anchor. Initially the process takes effort and some intention. However, once you are beyond the clouds and at cruising altitude, deliberately letting go of strained effort and intention are likely to help. A strong intention puts the mind in overdrive and brings ego into play. When governed by these drivers, it becomes difficult for you to access the deepest states of meditation. Eventually you have to let go of intention even to be practicing good meditation; only then does the deepest relaxation blossom. You will realize that peace and tranquility is your very nature; you may have veiled it with the details of everyday living. Your underlying natural state is that of pure being—everything else is an altered state.

If your mind is active it is likely related to thoughts generated from too many open files. Stuffed with these thoughts, mind launches an escape away from the present moment. It also tries (in vain) to suppress these thoughts. A better approach is to not suppress these thoughts. You are likely to get even more attached to what you fight. Instead accept these thoughts and their related open files, gently acknowledge them and bring your focus back to your anchor. The single best way to enhance meditation practice and decrease the number of thoughts and open files is to live your day with the higher principles.

How do you know your practice is working for you? *By their fruits you shall know them (Matthew 7:16).* You become calmer, gentler, kinder, more self-less, more understanding, compassionate, more grateful and forgiving, and internally more joyous. If these changes are happening, then your practice is working for you. With progress the formal concentrative practice blends with the experience throughout the day. No distinction exists between the spiritual and worldly life; meditative spirit is present at each awake moment, even during sleep. It is with this awareness that you will be able to invite joy into every aspect of your being. This is the state of pure bliss and is the culmination of a lifetime effort of right thinking, right action, and grace.

The path toward this state is aptly summarized in this beautiful quote by Albert Einstein that he wrote in a letter in 1950 to a rabbi coping with the accidental death of his daughter, *"A human being is a part of the whole, called by us 'Universe,' a part limited in time and space. He experiences himself, his thoughts and feelings as something separated from the rest—a kind of optical delusion of his consciousness. This delusion is a kind of prison for us, restricting us to our personal desires and to affection for a few persons nearest to us. Our task must be to free ourselves from this prison by widening our circle of compassion to embrace all living creatures and the whole of nature in its beauty. Nobody is able to achieve this completely, but the striving for such achievement is in itself a part of the liberation and a foundation for inner security."*

Remaining in the awareness described by Albert Einstein in the above paragraph is the reward you get for your efforts toward training attention, refining interpretations, and thereby training your brain to transform your life.

What does the Research Show?

The effect of meditation has been tested in several hundred clinical studies. Interested reader can download the following publication for a partial compilation of all the studies: http://www.ahrq.gov/downloads/pub/evidence/pdf/meditation/medit.pdf. In chapter 14 you reviewed studies that show how meditation engages the pre-frontal cortex.

Meditative Attention

You just read Einstein's words above, *"Our task must be to free ourselves from this prison by widening our circle of compassion to embrace all living creatures and the whole of nature in its beauty. Nobody is able to achieve this completely, but the striving for such achievement is in itself a part of the liberation and a foundation for inner security."*

Meditative attention implies remaining in this awareness of **C**ompassion, **A**cceptance, **L**ove, and **F**orgiveness (**CALF**) at each awake moment. This is the saintly attention we discussed previously. Such a state creates a protective shield of CALF around you that can transform your relationships and bring healing to everyone you touch including yourself.

45. Faith, prayer and the Divine

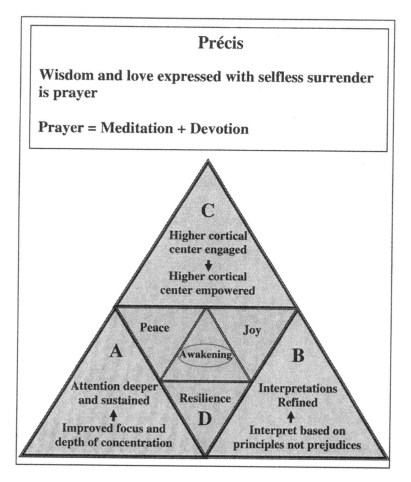

Prayer deepens your attention, refines your interpretations, engages higher cortical center, and takes you toward peace, joy, resilience, and awakening.

Divinity is an amalgamation of time, world, and self. Divinity encompasses all forms of energy—material or abstract—and all forms of concept—implicit or expressed. If you believe in your connectedness with this world, then in some way you have faith in divinity. What prevents us from connecting with divinity is our singular identification with the ever-changing contextual self. This keeps us disconnected, locked in an internal dialog and away from joy.

Use your wisdom to recognize your place. All your descriptors and relationships are precious and need to be attended to with the same devotion as a prayer. People have come into your life with a purpose—and the purpose is to bring you closer to your own divinity. When you relate with anyone, recognize that they are truly divine beings who will march with you in your journey. You do not have to search in the heavens to find divine beings and divine purpose—they are all with you right in your reach.

An attitude of prayer at each moment helps you cultivate acceptance and welcome the moment recognizing its preciousness. This attitude also allows you to give your full non-judgmental attention to the present moment. This is the path, the process, and the final outcome of a journey toward your higher purpose and potential. This is the first and also the final rung of the ladder in your journey toward awakening.

Two Ways of the World

You have a choice to believe in one of the two ways this world runs. Either there is orderliness and justice, or it is all chaotic and unpredictable. Both viewpoints are defensible, often even simultaneously. However, it does help to believe in orderliness and justice because that belief allows us to conform to a certain paradigm, making civilized life possible.

The next question is who is running this show? If there is orderliness, then it is likely that behind this orderliness is an intelligence that has put it all together and sustains it. It is also likely that this intelligence has greater awareness of reality, is more powerful, and has been around for much longer than any of us. It might help to respect and befriend this intelligence.

Divine Home

Deep within us is the seed of divinity. This is tranquility, nirvana, the source of enlightenment. In ordinary life, we have moments when we feel a sense of deep calm, have no memory of our hurts, and accept things as they are. This might happen while you watch a beautiful sunset, discover the child within you while playing with your little ones, when absorbed in creative work, or while spending time with someone you deeply love. These are truly divine heartful moments where what is outside for a brief moment brings you into the absoluteness of the present. Ego-identified mind at that moment surrenders to your inner tranquility. The joy from your tranquility then flows into the world and your whole being. Those are the most precious, peaceful, and rejuvenating moments of your life. They are the moments of the deepest prayer.

This state, however, tends not to last very long and we tend to get reengaged in the play that is life. How wonderful would it be if you could find an abode in that peaceful state while doing everything you have to do. The fact that you are able to access that state suggests that you certainly can make a home there. It is your natural state—unencumbered by the ego-run drama of this world.

The Two You

Our most peaceful moments are when we are thinking kind and selfless thoughts. When the limited self is not the center of our thinking, we have gone past the ego. No conflicts and no stresses can build up with that kind of thinking. This is how divinity operates: ever willing to bear our suffering. This is how Mother Teresa served the poor. How Gandhi moved a nation. The shift needed for attaining this is very simple—become an observer of your life.

If you watch a movie with your eyes only two inches away from the television you will not be able to watch anything. You have to distance yourself a bit. Things appear less serious from a distance, a bit lighter and easier to handle. The material problems might still remain the same, but they will be less compounded by your overreaction. This will allow you to awaken to your inner self. The moment you start watching your ego, you detach from it; ego then slows its play, even if only for a brief moment. These brief moments form the perfect bridges to link together the whole journey of life.

The Hidden Divine

For generations many or most of us have searched outside for peace and comfort, often without lasting success. We have looked with the eyes of our insecure ego scouring the world for ways to feed its insatiable appetite. It may be time to pause and reconsider. The divinity may also be within.

We all are divine. We just don't know it. Life could be defined as a journey to discover the divinity within. The paths may seem different but the general direction for all of us is similar. Everyone is facing similar struggles. When challenged, pause for a moment and look for the source of your strength within for a breath or two. Look for peace, joy and resilience hiding with the values of gratitude, compassion, acceptance, forgiveness, and higher meaning. It is these higher values that will allow you to respond to the task in a mature and effective way. Not all your challenges will, however, meet a resolution. But as long as you can see the next few hundred feet through this fog, keep driving—a few hundred feet at a time. Before you realize it you will have traveled a very long distance.

Divine not so Hidden

Find divinity expressed in everything around you. Try and connect with the divinity within your fellow beings. When you connect with others with an attitude that they are essentially divine, they will indeed rise to meet your expectations. Appeal to their goodwill. Meet them as if they are your long lost friends, which they indeed are.

Look at them with kindness. Imagine how far your loved ones have traveled to manifest into your life. It is miraculous that you are together with them. Recognize their divinity and silently bow to it. Find your own reflection in their eyes. Somewhere deep within their eyes, you are looking at yourself.

Intention Trumps Expression

People in different times have understood and described the creative intelligence differently. The word God has different connotations for us. For some God is kind and accepting; for others s/he is distant and judgmental. Words might be inadequate to fully describe this intelligence—s/he existed before we ever invented words. Using specific words is also fraught with some risk. This is because descriptors created using words tend to be divisive and create artificial boundaries amongst us. The specific words are thus less important compared to the attitude you carry.

The creative intelligence probably cares much more about how we love each other and nurture her creation than what words we use to describe her. Any name is fine as long as it is rooted in love. Words are limited and limiting. The feeling behind the words matters the most. Out of affection when I call my little daughter a pumpkin she loves it, but she balks when I mean business and formally address her with her first name.

The most precious greeting card you may have ever received likely was written by someone who was just beginning to write. Just a few irregular lines and a brief message—not entirely professional but worth its weight in gold. Perfection is needed in the feeling—a perfect feeling automatically finds a perfect expression.

It is the intention behind an action that is more important than the action itself. A dark room might be welcome to play hide and seek; while the same dark room when used to give a quiet time out to a child may not seem such a welcome place. If you preserve the purity of intention, everything else will take care of itself.

A Tool that Never Fails

A determined faith in the higher power is a God-sent help! Faith helps with acceptance when life teaches us that there are variables beyond our control that impact the outcome of our actions. Faith is also synonymous with forgiveness. Knowing that we bask in the comfort of universal compassion and forgiveness makes us grateful and brings peace. Compassion finds its origin in faith. We feel more compassionate toward each other in the name of the higher being who loves us both. Faith may also provide the highest meaning for many of us.

Faith helps us be humble and kind, allows us to develop equanimity, and instills the feeling of surrender. Faith allows us to share all our worries, desires, and negative feelings with the higher power keeping an unshakable belief that they will all eventually find a rational resolution. This belief frees up much of our "worry energy" that ordinarily might be spent in generating and controlling internal anxiety and inflammation. A strong anchor of faith thus might be the most effective tool for us to withstand the storms of life. Christ considered faith one of the most potent powers, *"…I tell you with certainty, if you have faith like a grain of mustard seed, you can say to this mountain, 'Move from here to there,' and it will move, and nothing will be impossible for you." (Matthew 17:20)*

Pray with Your Heart

Faith is often expressed in the form of prayer. Prayer is your attempt to connect and communicate with your image of the divine. Prayer is wisdom and love expressed in selfless surrender. Prayer may be simply an act of love or could have tangible goals such as seeking help or success. The first form of prayer comes from the core of your heart; the second form of prayer is that of the mind. *Prayer of the mind seeks for the mind; prayer of the heart seeks for the heart.*

Prayer mixed with ego leads to fanaticism while prayer mixed with devotion generates love. A prayer that has no goals and is a pure expression of love is a form of communication between a child and his/her father (or mother). Such prayer puts you in a state of acceptance and breeds no fear.

Such prayer allows surrender. A pure feeling and expression of surrender is the deepest form of meditation possible. This surrender finds strength in these words: *And remember, I am with you always, to the end of the age (Matthew 28:20).* While praying with total surrender, the devotee, divine, and devotion all gel into a continuum. This is the prayer of the heart. Pray with your heart. Pray with your heart even if you have to pray for the mind.

Prayer provides all the benefits of meditation. Prayer from your heart takes you to the fountain of love. This love leads to wisdom. The process of meditation often starts with wisdom. This wisdom then shows you the path of love. Prayer and meditation thus meet each other at the same point.

What does the Research Show?

Rigorous research with faith and prayer is not easy to conduct because of the strong personal beliefs of the participants as well as the researchers and the difficulty in carrying out long-term studies. Overall the results have been both positive and negative, largely a reflection of impediments toward conducting good quality studies with prayer. The research results are also confounded by the type of prayers used in the study. Further, it is difficult to control / gauge the intentionality of each participant, which may have an important bearing on the outcome.

Prayer was shown to be helpful for the following outcomes

- Weight loss intervention in overweight/obese black women.[404]
- Anxiety, pain, and spiritual health.[405, 406]
- Hospital stay and duration of fever with a bloodstream infection.[407]
- Outcome of infertility treatment with invitro fertilization.[408]
- Cardiovascular disease risk profiles in African American women.[409]
- Patients with rheumatoid arthritis. [410]
- Patients admitted to a coronary care unit.[411, 412]
- Patients with AIDS.[413]
- Older adults with improvement in survival.[414]
- Prayer as spiritual meditation helped migraine headaches better than non-spiritual meditation or muscle relaxation.[406]

Prayer was NOT shown to be helpful for the following outcomes

- Patients going for cardiac surgery.[415]
- Patients with HIV.[416]
- Recovery from open heart surgery.[417]
- Heart patients after elective catheterization or percutaneous coronary intervention.[418]
- Patient satisfaction in physician led prayer.[419]
- Children with psychiatric conditions.[420]
- Equivocal results on pain, mental health, and physical functioning.[421]
- Medical outcomes after hospitalization in a coronary care unit.[422]
- Well-being of kidney dialysis patients.[423]
- Treatment of alcohol abuse and dependence.[424]
- Mood and well-being in breast cancer survivors.[425]

Overall research on prayer shows that spiritual concerns are heightened when one is ill, and these concerns significantly influence medical decision.[426] Prayer was associated with better health status in a large study involving cancer survivors.[427] In a study involving patients with lung cancer, a higher degree of faith was associated with better response to chemotherapy.[428] The sum total of evidence suggests that religious involvement and spirituality are associated with improved health, greater longevity (by two to three years), better coping skills, less anxiety, depression, and suicide, and better health-related quality of life.[429]

Relationship with the Divine

Be preemptive in your faith. If you have faith then why not let it work for you? It almost sounds opportunistic. In reality, however, this approach will only deepen your faith. Be with your faith not just when things go wrong, but also when things are going well.

The good friends you nurture in the spring will likely stay with you when it is dark and gloomy. Long-term relationships cultivated over a period of time are the most satisfying. So is your relationship with the creative intelligence. Carefully tend to it, think about it, and invest in it. This will likely be the most important, lasting, and causeless relationship of your life.

We all need a certain anchor. Find that anchor in your faith. Meditation tends to align our thinking pattern with the object of contemplation. So meditate on God—your God. Your ego tends to create a curtain between the divine within you and the one outside. Ego separates the two lovers. Let go of your ego to reunite them. As a result the tranquility and stability that God represents will reflect into your own being. At the same time accept divinity in every representation of God—they are all one.

Standing in La Crosse, Wisconsin on the banks of the Mississippi I wonder, where is the soul of the river? Is it only at the river's origin, the midpoint, or where it meets the ocean? The answer I get is all three. The soul of the river is everywhere the river flows. ***Divinity permeates all aspect of our being. This is my faith and with this faith when I meditate, my meditation becomes a prayer.***

SECTION XII: AWAKENING (TRANSFORMATION)

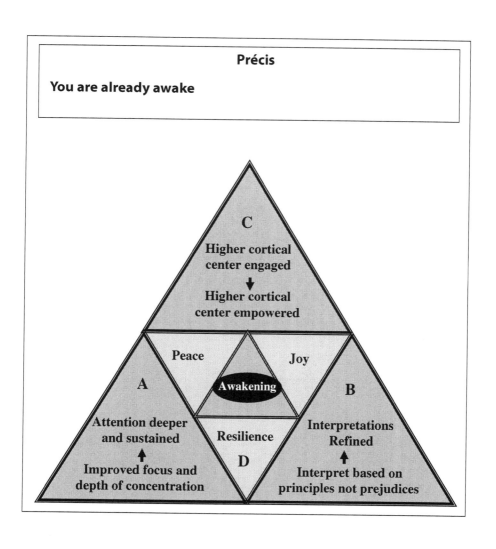

46. The Awakening (Transformation)

Three Stages of Learning

Your learning proceeds in three progressive stages:
1) Stage of ignorance;
2) Stage of knowledge;
3) Stage of transformation.

Stage of ignorance is when you do not know right from wrong. For example, with respect to interpersonal relationships, young children are often ignorant before they develop a conscience. They are well-meaning but intrinsically egocentric (self-focused). It takes many years before the pre-frontal cortex is fully developed. In fact, full maturation of the pre-frontal cortex may not happen until age twenty-five. That might explain some of your frustrations with grown-up kids who may have attained physical maturity but are still lagging behind in emotional and spiritual maturity. Adults are in the stage of ignorance in two instances. First is a small group of adults who never learn right from wrong and carry a poorly developed conscience. This is usually in the setting of medical or psychologic disorders. The larger proportion of ignorance in adults relates to their suppression of conscience by their desires created by egocentric preferences. If our eyes are closed we will see darkness. Darkness is thus not the absence of light; it is our inability to see. To remove this darkness the first step is to open our eyes and let in the light of knowledge.

The next stage is the *stage of knowledge* wherein you know the truth, but are not able to apply it consistently. There are several sub-stages within the stage of knowledge with increasing refinement of awareness, decreasing number of thoughts, and increasing peace and joy. Deepening knowledge leads to increasingly committed practice of the principles learned.

The third stage is the *stage of transformation*. **Transformation happens when your intellect finds knowledge, knowledge meets experience, you introspect on this experience, make it pragmatic and color it with empathy.** This combination of intellect, knowledge, experience, introspection, pragmatic approach and empathy adds up to wisdom. Wisdom is not mere knowing—it is knowing with all one's soul. Along the path, wisdom finds its perfect companion—love. Wisdom, love and effort create the ground work for grace to manifest. With wisdom, love, effort and grace, truth becomes an innate part of you. You do not have to think about a path that leads to peace, peace itself becomes the path. You do not have to invite joy, joy itself becomes the path. You are instinctively kind, generous, selfless, gracious, content, loving, desireless, and forgiving. You are past the stage of duality, obsessive desire, anger, greed, hatred, and jealousy. This is true realization wherein you become a reflection and source of the highest values. You reflect luminosity with such intensity that you indeed look self luminous.

I most humbly have provided you the information and skills that if practiced with sincerity will take you through higher levels of knowledge to the stage of realization. This is one among many paths. Please keep in mind that this is just a map. The beautiful journey is yours to carve based on the specifics of your life.

In the Spirit of the Buddha's Four Steps

In the spirit of Buddha's teachings, the four essential facts of life can be restated in these simple terms: there is insanity and suffering in this world; this insanity and suffering has a web of underlying causes; these causes are treatable; treatment of these causes can lead to the end of this insanity and suffering.

#1. There is Insanity and Suffering in this World

An outsider monitoring the state of mankind is likely to be amused and saddened by our behavior. We are in a true sense a split personality. Our wisdom, conscience, principles-based skills, and altruistic preferences prompt us toward one direction while the ways of the world, ego identified mind, prejudices, and egocentric preferences drive us differently.

We love most passionately yet hate and inflict torture in the most ghastly fashion. We could sacrifice our lives to save a stranger, yet kill in a moment of madness the very person we loved all our life. We invade nations because of our paranoia, and then go about rebuilding the same country. We desire to live until eternity, yet struggle with a propensity to run away from life. We love our pets, yet treat their cousins in a most cowardly and inhuman fashion. Trees soothe our senses, yet we have no qualms about devastating entire forests. We love our own homes, but do not think much before hurting our collective home, planet earth. We seem a perfect replica of Dr. Jekyll and Mr. Hyde.

We arrive in this world with an infinite potential. "Love all" is how we all start the play of our lives. However, the systems and processes that help us survive push us into duality of good-bad, loss-gain, love-hate, profit-loss, and so on. Suffering manifests in many forms. Greed, lust, anger, fear, anxiety, depression, hatred, selfishness, jealousy, excessive ego—all of these are different forms of suffering. With many of us depending on the world that is transient and ever changing to provide joy that is ever lasting, unwilling to accept loss, and the victory itself impermanent and needing constant defense, struggle and suffering seems intimately woven within the human condition.

It is not enough to state there is suffering. As a next step it is important to recognize the root cause of suffering—ignorance. This recognition constitutes the second step toward decreasing suffering.

#2. Insanity and Suffering has Recognizable Causes

Many causes, several of which are related to natural events beyond our control, propel us into suffering. The instincts of craving and aversion, self-preservation and ego that set our preferences and provide us a sense of identity are the most basic tools that help us grow past our precarious state of vulnerability as a newborn. Instincts have little to do with individual peace or enlightenment and are primarily designed to help us survive as a species. Ego that starts off with the noble intention of providing us a secure frame of reference mutates into an overinflated sense of self and leads to excessive pride, arrogance, and isolation. Suffering is thus a case of mistaken identity—mistaking ego for self. Craving and aversion that start off with the desire to help us choose wisely degenerate in greed and fear. It is in this state that ego, craving and aversion, and their primary source—ignorance contributes to suffering.

At the core of this issue is our mind's sense of feeling incomplete and a desire to feel complete. Mind however is ignorant of precisely how it can feel "whole." Untrained mind's instinct is to distance itself from aversions and seek fulfillment of its cravings—all in the service of ego. Mind does not realize that while its efforts may succeed in the short-term, they are unlikely to provide lasting success, simply because of our propensity to revise expectations and because our desires sit at the leading edge of achievements.

Further, excess ego identification and the overwhelming effects of instincts push us into a selfish existence. Our intellect also serves the agenda created by ego and instincts. In this state we become excessively prejudiced and harbor mostly egocentric preferences. These prejudices overwhelm our awareness and force us to part company with the higher principles of gratitude, compassion, acceptance, forgiveness, and meaning and purpose. Conscience, the moral substratum that is hardwired within us, finds it difficult to provide a check to an overinflated ego and the resulting fear and greed. Compassion, charity, forgiveness, and even morality, guilt, and shame are sacrificed in the process.

At the level of the mind, our instincts and ego, with the resulting self-focus, force us to pay inordinate attention to things that are unusually pleasant or threatening. This curdles minor annoyances into potent attention black holes. These black holes draw our attention away from the world into our mind in a state of inattention. Once engaged within our mind, we get lost in the imperfections of past and future, and in an attempt to resolve all of these imperfections, we find ourselves drowning in excessive thoughts. In this state we oscillate between attention deficit and obsessive focus.

This state of excessive thinking and constant engagement with the imperfections of past and future keeps us hyper-aroused, anxious, depressed, and stressed. It makes us dysfunctional, inefficient, and instills a sense of incompleteness. We thus remain chronically stressed, ego identified, and away from inner tranquility. A common feeling that accompanies this state is the feeling of fear. Fear is a potent wine that keeps the mind inebriated and away from reality. What a sad state of affairs we find ourselves stuck in, despite all the riches available to us!

Our symptoms are worsened by remaining in non-acceptance, lacking gratitude, compassion and forgiveness, and being unkind to ourselves. With excessive self-focus even within our tribe we spend little time listening. Our tribe thus tends to be loose and fractured. Feeling incomplete, we develop an unquenchable desire to seek pleasure from the material world, bringing devastation to our planet from the resulting excesses. In order to overcome the feeling of incompleteness we disengage and repeatedly escape from the present moment. We ravage our environment, engage in excessive use of resources, including excessive eating, addictions, living beyond our means (and that of the planet), and might even harbor thoughts of harm to others.

At the level of the brain such feelings are exacerbated by increasing engagement of the amygdala and related areas of our deep limbic system and the default mode network, with dampening of the oversight provided by the pre-frontal cortex. The tendency of the nerve cells in the limbic system to increase the strength of their own processes while making the higher control less and less effective perpetuates this process. We thus get stuck and might remain so for a long time, sometimes for our entire lives.

Suffering originates in a mind that is asleep and limited within the narrow confines of the barn, inhaling the stench of craving and aversion, tied by the rope of ego, ignorant of the fact that this rope is but a shadow. Locked door is an illusion. Unlimited pastures of bliss, resplendent with succulent grass and fragrance of baby flowers await it. Mind only has to shed its ignorance, make a choice, and act on this choice by cultivating the wisdom that will hold its hands and guide it toward a path out of suffering toward love and grace. These causes are surely treatable.

#3. These Causes are Treatable

The good news is that we can transcend all this insanity and suffering—many beings have done so. Look around yourself in the present time or in the past and you will find these jewels. They have recognized ignorance. Ignorance once recognized disappears. The core essence of their presence is in the acceptance of reality. Their wisdom allows them to let go of excessive craving, aversion or ego. They have inner poise and equanimity. They have a strong sense of purpose in their lives. They are kind and with compassion are ever ready to forgive. They respect all humans and all life forms. They realize the preciousness of life, of each part of creation. They are grateful for the gift of life.

The first step in transformation is to understand how we arrived here. Just as a physician has to delve deeper into the body's mechanisms to cure a medical condition and cannot base treatments only on the basis of symptoms, we need to get into the depth of understanding of the human mind. It is within the workings of the human brain and the mind that the solution is hidden.

We have overdosed ourselves with our interpretations that are preventing us from observing. Our interpretations are corrupted by our prejudices and egocentric preferences. The process creates attention black holes that sump our attention. This has come about because our ego and instincts forced us into excessive self-focus and spawned fear. Excessive use of interpretations cut short our attention and pushed us away from the world into the imperfections of the past and future lodged in our mind. *How can we change anything if we do not even show up for our life?*

If you do nothing, nothing will happen. As a result suffering will persist. Quite commonly, the realization that we have been asleep most of our lives occurs only when a life-changing experience shows us the finiteness of life and the futility of ego-driven actions. It may sometimes be very late if you wait until then to begin transformation. You have to begin right in this moment.

The first step in that transformation is for you to log back on to your life. You do this by training the 3Ds of your attention—direction, duration, and depth. You take control and at least initially purposefully direct your attention away from the mind into the world. You realize you are not your thoughts and can thus direct them at your will. As a second step you disengage from your prejudiced interpretations. You cultivate wisdom that guides you away from ignorance with its related siblings of craving, aversion, and excessive ego. This wisdom helps you understand the power of gratitude, compassion, acceptance, forgiveness, and meaning and purpose. Embodying these values disempowers your attention black holes and allows you to focus beyond the self and include the whole. You rob suffering of its continuity. Your interpretations are guided by principles-based skills and values and altruistic preferences. The process limits your desires, reduces your expectations bringing them closer to reality, and broadens the diameter of your existence. It is to this wisdom I have appealed with the intention of awakening it.

Armed with this wisdom, you can free yourself from the shackles of predominant self focus. Once free from excessive focus on the self, your desires diminish, acceptance finds a ground, and judgments, bias, and fears begin to fade. This allows you to refine your interpretations, use them less often, and increase the purity and depth of your attention. The attribute of attention flexibility pulls you away from the mind into the world. In the world you pay greater attention to novelty instead of pleasure or threat. Once out of your mind into the world and with a refined awareness, your mind automatically clears of the negative thoughts and memories (attention black holes), just as the water mixed with dirt left still on the table becomes clear in the morning. With most of the attention black holes cleared, you feel progressively lighter and freer.

You recognize that the present moment is not a means to an end—it is the end in itself. You know that real and unreal are mere definitions. Beginning and end do not have tangible time points; they repeat and are just representative of an exchange of energy that has been happening and will continue to happen for a very long time. Often this reality is not perceived because of the constant change we experience in our mind. A firm anchor in the present moment allows you to look at the substrate behind the existence and see the unreality of duality. You begin to see how noumenon (the way it is) and phenomenon (the way it seems) are connected. The co-existence of complexity and emptiness is a source of great amusement to the awakened.

At the level of the brain this process helps re-establish a higher order control of the deep limbic system. The amygdala becomes quiet while the pre-frontal cortex awakens. You are more often task positive than in the default mode. Brain becomes more heartful.

You realize that for all of us ego finally has to dissolve and our physical being will surrender to nature. There is no doubt that you will face a time when time will finally come to a halt, when past, present, and future merge into the stillness of a single moment. Everything you hold dear you will have to surrender. There are two ways you can allow the ego to dissolve. In the first path, you let nature take its course from outside. This path for many is riddled with significant suffering. **The other way is to dissolve the ego from inside by cultivating wisdom and love.** This path offers possibility of abiding peace and immense joy. I have attempted to map one possible path for you to dissolve your ego from inside by developing wisdom and love. It is through training your brain, engaging your heart and thus transforming your life.

Once you launch onto this path there is no looking back. You progress and no longer remain ego-, family- or ethno-centric; you become world-centric. This is the transformed awakened life. This is the realization or nirvana.

#4. Treatment can Cure Suffering

Science has shown in thousands of studies that sincere training toward cultivating deeper attention and more refined interpretations is possible and very beneficial. Gratitude, compassion, acceptance, forgiveness, and meaning and purpose—all of these qualities can train our brain and transform our life. These values engage the higher center of your brain. Cultivating and embodying each of these higher values is a choice you all have.

Once your brain's higher center awakens you are able to look beyond the confines of the existing paradigm. You get beyond the influence of limited instincts and prejudices of the mind and intellect. With better regulation of fear, the mind becomes anchored in the non-judgmental present, no longer needing to generate excessive or negative thoughts. You march away from ignorance toward wisdom and ultimately toward transformation. As your brain trains and mind awakens, observation leads to direct knowledge and realization; there is no need for interpretation. You do not seek a path toward peace, **peace itself becomes the path.**

You start seeking the true gain in your life. A true gain is one that cannot be lost. You realize that every material gain you will have to surrender one day—be it your health, youth, vigor, loved ones, even your dear life. You do not barter spiritual gain for any of these. You do not short change yourself. You look at each of your material endowments as your tools to progress on the path toward transformation—a gain that is permanent.

As you progress along this path, you might experience higher states of awareness that go beyond the paradigm of science. You access and stay with your essence bereft of the numerous titles and layers of thoughts that accumulate in your life. This is your ipseity, your core unchangeable self. Let us call it consciousness. Consciousness is the most refined form of self-awareness that is effortlessly anchored in the present moment. Consciousness however hides if the lake of the mind remains dirty with excessive thoughts. Consciousness exists beyond the paradigm of time and duality, always in the "now." The deeper spiritual connotation of consciousness equates it with a higher, super, or cosmic consciousness (Buddha or Christ consciousness). This is the spiritually awakened state where you become fully aware of the reality. This is the state of total surrender that takes away all the ignorance. You become aware of how the separation of thoughts and energy into the knower and knowable creates the sense of I, me or mine in what is essentially one mass of consciousness. The seeds may seem different but they all come from the same tree.

The unfolding consciousness finds sustenance in such a trained brain, engaged heart and realized mind that leads you into unconditional gratitude, compassion, acceptance, forgiveness, kindness, humility, patience, and devotion toward all. You become fully what you are capable of. An essential aspect of teachings in many faiths is that the potential for this transformation exists within all of us but is covered by the dust of hatred, anger, desire, greed, envy, and fear.

At a more subtle level beings anchored in this state derive continuous nourishment from their inner stillness. The heaven they experience within themselves is manifest in the world around them. These are celestial beings. It does not matter what religion they belong to and which form of God they follow—if any. They belong to God and God belongs to them. God evolves with them and preserves their preciousness. Their thoughts are Her commandment; just as Her thoughts are their commandment. The hope for curing insanity and suffering on our planet is for each of you to pursue a path that leads your brain and the mind toward the awakening that characterizes these beings. *The hope is for each of you to train your brain, engage your heart, and transform your life.*

What separates you from your highest meaning is also what connects you to it. Suffering may have fashioned a separation between you and your awakened self, however, it is the same suffering and your effort to transcend it that may prompt your journey into transformation. Suffering has guided countless realized souls; it could also do for you. You just have to take the first few steps.

The creation of space and time has fashioned a separation between you and your inner stillness. This separation is nowhere else but in your mind. Science and spirituality are applicable to the whole—they remain unchanged, it is only your understanding that changes with time. As you learn or unlearn, the destination and journey merge with each other. Each point on the journey is a destination—for you already are there. You are just unaware. ***You are already awake.***

Healing Our Planet: An Appeal

Our planet needs to heal. We have been inflicting a lot of wounds on her. We have abused her physically as well as emotionally. We have cut down forests, destroyed nature, melted glaciers, and brought havoc to the environment. We have been unkind to ourselves, to others, and to the animals. This cannot continue if we are to make this planet our home for the long term. This is not how we should treat our home. Earth will not tolerate us in the current form. We deeply depend on her kindness toward us. To access that kindness we ourselves have to cultivate the kindness that is inherently a part of our being.

The universe has spent fourteen billion precious years in creating you. You are infinitely more capable than you can ever imagine. You definitely have the ability to bring about your transformation. The onus of your growth and healing and that of planet earth rests with you. You can get out of this quicksand that has developed around you.

The path that leads toward peace and inner stillness will take you away from prejudiced interpretations and egocentric preferences. The short-term gratification derived from a predominant self focused disposition that is driving this world is too risky. It is like having a five-year-old drive your car while you sit as a passenger, the untrained mind and brain's lower center being the child and your awake self and brain's higher center the passenger.

You need your mind guided by brain's lower center as your assistant, not as your master. Instinctively operating an untrained mind colluding with ego has made you an automatic reactive being. You need to turn that around and take on a different journey. Drive you have to—that is the nature of life, so why not drive in the right direction? The milestones on the journey are well defined. You can find them easily if you listen to the teachings of saints and seers from all the religions. Scientists are now con-firming in their laboratory what the masters have taught for thousands of years. These teachings are in the form of metaphors; the noble truths; the shlokas; the sutras; the devotional prayers; the hymns; the poems; the parables; the psalms, and many more. *While expressions may be differ-ent, the message stays the same.*

A constant engagement with the present will prevent you from drowning within your mind and will help you stay with the ever replenishing fresh-ness of the world. Internal acceptance of what is, was, and might be, will allow you to generate a mature response to everyday challenges. For-giveness of the past and finding a meaning and purpose to your life will help you remain peaceful as you strive to rise to your highest potential. Perception of a deep connection with everyone will help you come out of the feeling of loneliness and develop a sense of ownership and union. Gratitude will prepare you to receive more by creating an even exchange of energy and will fashion an ambiance of humility amidst the feeling of plenty. Closely knit tribes will provide an internally sound structure to your society that will prevent any fracturing with the stresses brought by outside forces. Compassion will foster sharing amidst feeling of equality while daily acts of kindness will create a charitable disposition without fueling the growth of ego. Equanimity will help you transcend your cravings so you can find joy in the lovely spring as well as in the cold winter. All this is possible if you train your brain and engage your heart and thereby influence your attention to arrive and stay in the now experiencing your now with greater love and presence.

The journey that takes you away from prejudices and toward higher principles will take you toward ever lasting joy. This is the path that will help you awaken to your highest purpose and potential. The milestones seem very well defined; the path is well laid out; the destination feels palpable. It is nowhere else but right here. You just have to show up.

The solution and permanent cure for the unrest in this world is six and a half billion souls marching to a single destination—the state of transformation, awakening and realization. This is what God dreams everyday. This is the purpose of Her creation.

Mother Earth needs a critical mass of human beings who are not just humans but are truly awakened divine beings anchored in their beingness. We all have the potential to reach that state by engaging our heart and awakening the higher centers in our brains. We need to transform ourselves into a nobler, more resilient state. We have to awaken the Buddha, the Christ, and the Krishna within us.

Mother Earth needs the being within you to awaken—now more than ever. Are you ready?

Appendix I – Train Your Brain Engage Your Heart Transform Your Life: Tools and Tips

This appendix offers a broad summary of the skills discussed throughout the book and also offers structure of a program you could follow to bring these skills to your life. Summarized below are the essential elements of what I have shared previously. *We will first look at the overall theme, then the specific practices and finally look at some helpful details.*

Overall Theme:

Tool #1: Training Attention: Attention training has two components –
1. Joyful Attention: Savor the world by delaying judgment and paying attention to novelty. Several specific approaches related to this skill are described in chapter 20.
2. Saintly Attention: Look at the world with CALF (Compassion, Acceptance, Love and Forgiveness).

Tool #2: Refining Interpretations: Refining interpretations has three components –
1. Decrease prejudices and be open for a fresh perspective.
2. Give yourself a break (actually many breaks) from the constant planning and/or problem solving tendency of the mind.
3. Enhance your focus on gratitude, compassion, acceptance, higher meaning, and forgiveness.

Tips for Daily Practice:

Tool #1: Training Attention:

1. Joyful Attention:

    1.1. Pick four to eight preferred times to practice joyful attention for 15-20 minutes each. Some of the suggested times this could be practiced are:
- Waking up
- Breakfast
- Meeting
- Lunch
- Presentation
- Exercise
- Play

- At the airport
- Shopping
- Party
- Arriving home
- Dinner
- Bed time
- Other times based on your individual life style

1.2. The five specific approaches to practice joyful attention described in Chapter 20 are: Pay attention to novelty; use one sensory system at a time; find one new detail; anchor on to movement; and contemplate on the story

1.3. Rest of the day (when not actively practicing joyful attention) try to deepen attention by delaying judgment just a little bit more than what you might otherwise do.

1.4. Joyful Attention Score – You can add the number of times you were able to practice joyful attention. This is your joyful attention score for the day.

2. Saintly Attention: Attend with CALF several times during the day.

2.1. A simple way to practice CALF is to send a silent "Bless you" to people you meet (friends and strangers alike), particularly the first time you see them during the day.

2.2. CALF score – You can add the number of times you were able to practice CALF. This is your CALF score for the day. Since it is sometimes not easy to calculate a precise CALF score for each day, an approximate score (such as greater than 10 or 20) would suffice.

Tool #2: Refining Interpretations:
An effective strategy to incorporate higher principles in your life is to focus on one daily theme. A suggested schedule that we follow is noted below (also described in Chapter 22):

Monday – Gratitude
Tuesday – Compassion
Wednesday – Acceptance
Thursday – Higher Meaning
Friday – Forgiveness
Saturday – Celebration

Sunday – Reflection / Prayer

This theme is flexible. For example, if you prefer you can choose to focus primarily on gratitude on Friday or any other skills that are discussed. Having a structure helps provide a particular focus for each day. The purpose is not to exclude other values. You will realize with practice that each of these values converge toward one core value—that of love.

Helpful Details:

Here I will present a few specific ideas we have found useful toward incorporating these skills into daily life.

Tool #1: Training Attention:

A few specific ideas that I have found useful, particularly when beginning to train attention are summarized below.

- **Beginner's eyes** – Look at an object (even a familiar object) with a completely open mind as if looking at it for the first time. Each object around you would thus be novel, unique and precious.

- **Designer's eyes** – Look at the object as if you personally designed it. The purpose is not to look with hypervigilant critical focus, but with appreciative admiring eyes.

- **Meeting after a long time** – Meet your loved ones as if you are meeting them after a long time. Thus at the end of the day when you meet your spouse, instead of sharing just a Hi and then getting absorbed in your world, pull yourself out into their presence and make a purposeful effort to get a slice of their life. This will be much more enjoyable compared to playing the momentum of your work or activities in your mind. When listening to your loved ones try not to multitask.

- **Bless you** – To the first 20 people you meet during the day, send a silent "bless you" from your eyes. You do not have to say anything; just convey this warm message from your eyes. See how you feel at the end of the morning.

- **Call for help** – When a loved one or colleague seems frustrated, upset or even angry, remember that in most situations it will not help to react adversely to it. It is best to remember that, *"An expression other than love is often a call for help."*

Tool #2: Interpretation –

A few specific themes that might be useful with respect to the concepts within interpretation are summarized below.

1. Gratitude –

Morning thought: I am grateful for whatever this day will bring, life's pleasures or life's lessons

Additional concepts related to gratitude:

* Gratitude as a first thought in the morning
  * Gratitude for the past, present and future
  * Gratitude for those who help me and those who seek my help
  * Gratitude for material, intangible, and spiritual
  * Gratitude for life's pleasures as well as life's lessons

* Gratitude during the day & as a last thought at the end of the day
  * Recognize and acknowledge kindness
  * Recognize life's blessings in the daily miracles
  * Recognize life's blessings in the daily challenges

Gratitude as a way of being: Grateful for the gift of the present moment; Gratitude as a background state

2. Compassion –

Morning thought: I will be compassionate toward everyone I meet today

Additional concepts related to compassion:

* Find connectedness with others
* Recognize the universality of pain, loss and suffering
* Practice compassion with nothing expected in return
* Avoid compassion fatigue (keep the perspective)
* Meditation on compassion
  * Include others in your circle
  * Find similarity with others
  * Intend to decrease pain and suffering

3. Acceptance –

Morning thought: Everyone I meet today I will accept them just as they are; I will accept myself today just as I am

Additional concepts related to acceptance:

* Develop Objectivity, Flexibility, Pursuit of Truth, and Willingness
* Understand universality of finiteness, suffering, change, and interconnectedness
* Live with confidence (faith) and optimism
* Understand circles of control, influence and lack of control
* One minute rule – if you have to criticize someone, limit that critique to one minute
* Understand link between acceptance and happiness
* Stop and smell the roses
* Accept others just as you wish to be accepted
* Know that a step back often is a move forward
* Know that some things you desire…some you are willing to accept
* Keep realistic expectations
* As long as you live, what is right about you trumps what is wrong about you
* Put greatest effort in what is important and controllable
* You may occasionally need islands of mindlessness

4. Meaning and Purpose –
Morning thought: I will focus today on the long-term meaning and purpose of my life

Additional concepts related to forgiveness:

* Understand the three key components of meaning:
  Relationships; Work; Spirituality
* Understand short-term vs. long-term meaning and the importance of aligning them
* Relationships – Understand your tribe; Positivity Negativity ratio; Enhance your power to listen; Broaden zone of acceptance; Know that others could be right even if they think different
* Work – Balance work and leisure; Consider your work your calling; Become more comfortable with uncertainty
* Spirituality – Understand different definitions of spirituality; discover your own spirituality
* Understand the meaning (value) of disruptions

5. Forgiveness –
Morning thought: I forgive for today anyone who might hurt my feelings; I forgive for today all my mistakes of the past, known and unknown

Additional concepts related to forgiveness:

* Understand what is forgiveness
  * It is not condoning, denying, justifying, excusing
  * It is a voluntary choice, for you, to live by your principles

* Understand reasons for forgiveness
  * Forgiveness improves several health outcomes
  * Forgiveness helps decrease anger
  * Forgiveness is a moral good
  * Forgiveness frees up the mind to focus on the future
  * Forgiveness improves relationships
  * We are forgiven, likely several times, every single day
  * Eventually all of us will have to forgive and / or forget
  * Every scripture we revere preaches the virtues of forgiveness
  * Most of the greatest persons we admire practiced (or practice) and taught (or teach) forgiveness

* Understand pearls related to forgiveness
  * Pearl #1. Consider forgiveness a lifelong process
  * Pearl #2. It is okay to be selfish in forgiveness (altruistic selfishness)
  * Pearl #3. Broaden your world view to include imperfections
  * Pearl #4. Try to understand others' actions
  * Pearl #5. Consider forgiveness as an opportunity
  * Pearl #6. Exercise the privilege to forgive as soon as you recognize the need for it
  * Pearl #7. Forgive gracefully without creating a burden on the forgiven
  * Pearl #8. Forgive before others seek your forgiveness
  * Pearl #9. Look forward to forgiving
  * Pearl #10. Extend your forgiveness toward what might even transpire in the future
  * Pearl #11. Praying for others increases your ability to forgive
  * Pearl #12. Prevent future situations where you may have a need to forgive
  * Pearl #13: Lower your expectations
  * Pearl #14: Have a low threshold to seek forgiveness

* Understand that we all desire to be forgiven
* Understand difference between willful and innocent mistakes
* Understand that the harm done to you may have helped you
* Understand the value of compassion and acceptance
* Practice forgiveness imagery if needed
* Develop pre-emptive forgiveness

An important final point: To incorporate these skills into your daily life think of three things to do: Read (about these ideas); Discuss (these ideas with like minded people); and Practice (embody these ideas into your daily life). Knowledge thereby becomes action and action becomes habit.

APPENDIX II – Breath and the Body

Breath offers an excellent tool for cultivating a deeper attention. The limitations I mentioned in the section on Attention are minor and are applicable mostly in the initial stages. In fact, some of the limitations might indeed be strengths. A few reasons why breath offers an excellent tool to help train your attention include:

1) Breath is always available;

2) Breath is rhythmic and the rate can be changed at will, allowing an individual to join the breath at a personally chosen rate that feels comfortable;

3) Paying attention to the breath relaxes the mind;

4) Relaxed breath has several positive health-related effects;

5) Breath can be made increasingly subtle and your attempt to continue to appreciate its subtle state trains your senses;

6) Breath reflects the state of impermanence, one cycle merging into the next, just as life might be;

7) Breath does not have a form or structure. This lack of structure, while initially an impediment, is later helpful as it allows you to become comfortable with uncertainty;

8) You share the breath with others—what you exhale others inhale and *vice versa*. Breath thus connects you with others in a tangible way. Most animals and plants breathe, and a focus on breath may remind you of your intimate connection with them. In fact, the whole world joins together in collective breathing at each moment.

The primary limitation with breath is that in the initial stages you have to take extra time away from your busy day to practice breathing exercises. Further with no previous attention training, focus on the breath can easily take you inward into the mind and back into the attention black holes. Thus it might be optimal to use breath as an anchor only after your attention has somewhat stabilized and toned up using the world as the initial focus.

There are many ways of attending to breath. They start from simple breath awareness to deeper states of meditation. The simpler the technique, the greater is the likelihood that you will be able to do it for the long term. Throughout the practice try to practice diaphragmatic breathing. One good way to practice breathing exercises is to imagine filling a cup with water when you inhale. Just as the cup fills from the bottom up, you fill your lower lungs and then the upper lungs by expanding your belly and moving your diaphragm. You could even gently keep your hands on the belly and pay attention to their movement during inhalation. During exhalation, just as the cup empties from top below, empty the upper lungs first and then the lower lungs. If any of this seems confusing, just take deep and slow breaths in a way that feels comfortable to you.

The first exercise I share will guide you to observe your breath at a static point, the tip of your nose. In this exercise practice your skills to be an impartial witness.

Exercise 1. Breath awareness 1
1. *Sit in a comfortable, dimly lit, quiet, and safe place with your eyes closed. You can choose any posture you like other than lying down on the bed (you might go off to sleep). Also avoid doing this exercise immediately post meal.*
2. *Spend the first two minutes paying attention to all the sounds you hear in the environment. Allow your awareness to travel to the source of the sounds. Try to avoid making any judgments about the sounds.*
3. *At this point, gradually settle your awareness and bring it to your breath.*
4. *Practice deep, slow, diaphragmatic breathing for the duration of the exercise.*
5. *Adapt a breathing rate and depth that feels comfortable.*
6. *Visualize your breath at the tip of your nostril. Feel the subtle, cool breath as it flows in and a warm, cozy breath as you breathe out.*
7. *Keep your attention at the tip of the nostril for the next few minutes watching the inward and outward flowing breath.*
8. *Now allow your breath to become subtle until you reach a point when you just about not feel the flow.*
9. *Keep your awareness rested on the tip of the nostril with this subtle breath for the next few minutes.*
10. *Continue this exercise for as long as you like, at least for ten minutes.*

In the next exercise we will track the movement of the breath.

Exercise 2. Breath awareness 2
1. *Sit in a comfortable, dimly lit, quiet, and safe place with your eyes closed. You can choose any posture you like, other than lying down on the bed (you might go off to sleep). Also avoid doing this exercise immediately post meal.*

2. *Spend the first two minutes paying attention to all the sounds you hear in the environment. Allow your awareness to travel to the source of the sounds. Try to avoid making any judgments about the sounds.*
3. *At this point, gradually settle your awareness and bring it to your breath.*
4. *Practice deep, slow, diaphragmatic breathing for the duration of the exercise.*
5. *Adapt a breathing rate and depth that feels comfortable.*
6. *Visualize your inhaled breath traveling from the tip of your nostril to the farthest reaches of your brain (upper body).*
7. *Now visualize your exhaled breath traveling from your brain out to the tip of the nose.*
8. *Visualize your inhaled breath traveling from the tip of your nostril to the farthest reaches of your legs (lower body).*
9. *Now visualize your exhaled breath traveling from your legs out to the tip of the nose.*
10. *Repeat this exercise for as long as you like, at least for ten minutes.*

There are many variants possible to the breathing exercises and you are welcome to change and adapt them the way you like. It might help to work with a well-trained yoga teacher if you wish to learn the more advanced techniques. One simple variation is to pay attention to the movements of the abdominal wall instead of the tip of the nose. Another common approach is to pay attention to the pause between the inhalation and exhalation.

The next exercise I wish you to learn is to focus on body awareness. Your body offers an excellent focus for attention that is always available and enjoys the relaxation that comes with paying attention.

Exercise 3. Body awareness in six breaths
1. *Sit in a comfortable, dimly lit, quiet, and safe place with your eyes closed. You can choose any posture you like, other than lying down on the bed (you might go off to sleep). Also avoid doing this exercise immediately post meal.*
2. *Spend the first two minutes paying attention to all the sounds you hear in the environment. Allow your awareness to travel to the source of the sounds. Try to avoid making any judgments about the sounds.*
3. *At this point, gradually settle your awareness and bring it to your breath.*
4. *Practice deep, slow, diaphragmatic breathing for the duration of the exercise.*

5. *Adapt a breathing rate and depth that feels comfortable.*
6. *Take a deep breath as you bring your awareness to your head. Imagine your brain filling up with soothing white light. Gradually exhale this breath.*
7. *Take a deep breath as you bring your awareness to your face and neck. Imagine your face and neck filling up with soothing white light. Gradually exhale this breath.*
8. *Take a deep breath as you bring your awareness to your chest. Imagine your chest filling up with soothing white light. Gradually exhale this breath.*
9. *Take a deep breath as you bring your awareness to your belly. Imagine your belly filling up with soothing white light. Gradually exhale this breath.*
10. *Take a deep breath as you bring your awareness to your arms and legs. Imagine your arms and legs filling up with soothing white light. Gradually exhale this breath.*
11. *Take a deep breath as you bring your awareness to your entire body. Imagine your entire body filling up with soothing white light. Gradually exhale this breath.*
12. *Continue this exercise for as long as you like and feel comfortable. Preferred duration is ten sets, which will take about ten minutes.*

A common variation of this exercise is to focus only on the body part rather than including body and breath. I prefer to combine the two; it helps to keep the deep breathing exercise as a background for most relaxation practices.

There are countless variations to breath and body exercises. The key is to keep the exercises simple, do enough repetitions, and persevere with the practice. Pick only a few exercises for daily practice so your time commitment is realistic. As you learn and experience these exercises, keep the clarity of your primary goal. It is to cultivate a deeper attention. With this attention extraneous thoughts will automatically settle. As you progress along this path, you will become your own teacher and find newer ways to develop your attention.

Appendix III – Physical Exercise

I am commonly asked questions related to lifestyle that promotes well-being. Herein I summarize the gist of what I generally share about exercise along with pertinent research information. Please refer to additional texts if you wish additional more prescriptive information.

A healthy body and healthy mind go together. Exercise, healthy eating, self care, and adequate sleep are essential to cultivating a healthy body and independently have a considerable positive effect on your brain function.

Self Care

Your body is the outward manifestation of your inner being in this world and is one of your most valuable possessions. Your body is a sacred temple. Take good care of your physical body.

Tend to yourself like you tend your garden. Spend a few minutes daily. Enjoy doing it. Once in a while it is okay to pamper yourself with a massage or manicure. The time spent in self care is your time, is very healing, and works wonders for your personal and spiritual progress. This time will go a long way in your discovery of the beautiful, precious, and limitless that is hidden in you.

With respect to exercise I wish to share a few perspectives and then present the research evidence showing the beneficial effect of exercise on the brain.

Active Body Relaxes the Mind

Exercise is an excellent stress reliever, allowing you to discharge pent-up adrenaline. Exercise is relaxing and energizing and improves the mood. Exercise puts you in a positive self-care mode and takes your mind away from daily stresses. Experiencing a good workout is synonymous with health and positivity.

Group exercise such as in a gym might bring about the feeling of being engaged in a productive activity with each member working toward a similar goal. Such group effort is generally relaxing and creates a warm feeling of togetherness.

Fun and Play Will Help the Exercise Stay

Exercise often entails repetition of the same activity and thus tends to become boring, which leads to poor adherence. It is essential to have a component of fun with any exercise program. Partnering with a member of your tribe might increase the likelihood of continuing your practice, and as a secondary benefit strengthen your tribe.

Consider your time of exercise as a time for rejuvenation. A successful exercise program needs to engage the mind as well. Consider physical exercise as an exercise of the body as well as of the mind. Research studies that we will soon see show that physical exercise helps not only the body but also the mind by improving memory capacity and increasing levels of nerve regenerating chemicals in the blood.[136-138] Physical activity also enhances mood, self-esteem, and overall well-being.[430-432]

One of the ways to get the mind engaged in exercise is to practice joyful attention while exercising. Being aware of your body, breath, posture, and movement while exercising might be a wonderful approach. This will also be relaxing and could be an excellent preparation for concentrative meditation practice.

Is One Exercise Better than the Other?

The precise regimen of exercise is very individualized and depends on personal capacity and resources, among other variables. The program might range from a short, gentle five-minute walk to running several miles a day. It is important to carefully pick the program that you can practice over the long term. Walking might be ideal for you, so could be bicycling, swimming, or jogging. Taking the help of a professional in the early stages is likely to be beneficial, often necessary to ensure safety and select the appropriate regimen.

If you have symptoms of fatigue because of a medical condition or de-conditioning then it will be important to start low and go slow. Forcing yourself to exercise for thirty minutes would be like flogging a tired horse. Exercise is meant to be fun and not torture. Divide your exercise into six sessions of five minutes each and gradually build from there. If five minutes is too long, go to four, three, or even two minutes. Listen to your body and meet it where it currently is and then gently nudge it to go up the ladder.

What About Being Active Throughout The Day?

In addition to running on the treadmill or a stroll in your neighborhood, maintaining activity throughout the day might be as important as a concentrative workout. Consider exercise as meditation for the body. A fifteen-minute meditation practice alone is unlikely to be transformative; the greatest progress comes if you are able to maintain a diluted state of meditation all through the day. Similarly your overall pattern of activity throughout the day might be as or more important than the workout in the gym.

Maintaining activity all through the day, also called NEAT (Non Exercise Activity Thermogenesis) by researchers, is shown to have a strong effect on body weight and overall energy balance.[433] So wherever possible choose the option that allows you to move your body even if it entails parking a bit away from your office or walking up the stairs rather than taking the elevators.

Exercise and The Brain: Research Evidence

Exercise not only helps the physical body but in several research studies has also shown positive effects on brain function. The salutary effects of exercise also include an increase in a nerve growth factor (BDNF) that is associated with increased growth of the pre-frontal cortex.

The effect of exercise has been assessed in two broad groups of studies. The first group of studies are where patients are observed in their natural environment without any interference from the researchers. Several such large population-based studies have assessed relationship between exercise habits and brain function. These studies have shown that physical exercise is associated with improved brain function. The four most prominent of these studies include the Nurses' Health Study (18,766 participants),[434] Honolulu-Asia Aging Study (2,257 participants),[435] Group Health Cooperative Study (1,740 participants),[436] and Cardiovascular Health Cognition Study (3,375 participants).[437]

The second group of studies is clinical trials where investigators divide patients into two or more sets. One set of patients is instructed to exercise while the other set is observed without any such instruction. In clinical trials also exercise has shown benefit for improving brain function. In a study published in the prestigious *Journal of American Medical Association* 170 participants with memory problems not amounting to a clinical diagnosis of dementia (severe memory loss) were enrolled.[438] These were followed for up to eighteen months. The study showed modest improvement in memory function with physical exercise. A compilation of several studies in the form of a meta-analysis has also been completed by the prestigious Cochrane collaboration. This review shows that the beneficial effects of exercise in patients with an established diagnosis of dementia are not yet conclusive;[439] however a compilation of eleven clinical trials in older adults without dementia suggested that exercise improves memory function.[440] Exercise might also help vocabulary learning. In a small study with twenty-seven healthy volunteers, vocabulary learning was found to be 20 percent faster after intense physical exercise as compared to low impact exercise or a period of rest.[441]

The effect of exercise on the brain function using fMRI or other related methods is just beginning to be studied. In one study it was demonstrated that an increase in cardiovascular fitness resulted in increased activity in the pre-frontal cortex and related areas of the brain.[442] Exercise has also been associated with an increase in the level of nerve growth factor (Brain Derived Neurotrophic Factor, BDNF) in the body that has been shown to help the growth of pre-frontal cortex nerve cells suggesting a mechanism by which exercise might positively change the brain.[443-445] In a study involving fifteen healthy subjects, acute physical exercise was shown to increase BDNF as well as cognitive function.[137]

In addition to memory function, physical exercise also improves the symptoms of depression and anxiety and overall well-being.[446, 447] No matter how you look at it, exercise offers several benefits for the body, the brain, and the mind.

A related question is does your mind affect your adherence to exercise? Emerging data suggests that higher disposition toward mindfulness and acceptance enhances adherence to exercise. Thus skills we discussed in this book might help you sustain your pursuit toward better physical health.[448]

Appendix IV - Diet

One of the most common questions I am asked is: What should I eat to remain healthy? My honest answer is: Although we know a bit about diet, we still do not know a lot. For example, we do not know which (if any) of the popular diets will offer the best long-term benefits; what is the role of dietary supplements; what is the recommended daily intake of micronutrients individualized to your particular situation; and many more such questions.

Overall, however, a consistent pattern seems to emerge about the effect of diet on brain function. Here I will present some of the research evidence supporting dietary advice for brain health. This is a moving field, so continue checking with your physician or dietician for advice specific to your situation.

Remember this important pearl: A diet that is good for your brain is also likely to be good for your heart, your blood vessels, your kidneys, your joints, your liver, your bone, your muscles, your lungs, your eyes, your intestines, and to prevent cancer.

This is for one simple reason—your body's cells, although different in many ways, are still more similar than they are different. They still "remember" their origins from a single cell. Your body is the perfect replica of the "whole." Each cell has her own destiny, yet they are all intimately interconnected and closely work together for a single purpose—to serve you. It is thus no surprise that in general what is good for one part of the body is also good for the other.

In developing a schematic toward a healthy diet, it is important to recognize that there are three aspects to a diet:
1. *What you eat;*
2. *How much you eat; and*
3. *How you eat it.*

What You Eat and How Much You Eat

As an initial step, let us address the first two aspects of your diet. Food provides you with the energy and raw materials that your body uses to build and sustain itself. So what you eat has a profound effect on you. Some of the well-accepted ideas for healthy eating include: taking adequate servings of fruits and vegetables, avoiding sources of saturated fat and eliminating trans fat, minimizing intake of refined sugars, eating fresh wherever possible, avoiding stimulants, and taking adequate amounts of fluids. Let us look at some of the research evidence:

Caloric restriction in general facilitates improved nerve cell function and increases chemicals in the brain that facilitate growth of nerve cells particularly in the pre-frontal cortex. Thus excess caloric intake was found to decrease the ability of nerve cells to grow[449] while dietary restrictions increased nerve growth factors.[450, 451] A high fat diet with dextrose decreased nerve growth factors in the pre-frontal cortex and hippocampus and was associated with impaired learning in laboratory animals.[140, 452]

Caloric distribution is also important for optimal brain function. For example, skipping breakfast decreased clear thinking;[453] healthy breakfast facilitated better mental function and more positive attitude;[454, 455] big meals (high energy content) decreased concentration;[456] while between meal small snacks improved memory.[457, 458]

Food additives have generally been associated with negative effect on brain function, although the associations are not conclusive. Artificial preservatives and dyes have been linked with attention deficit;[459, 460] aspartame has been associated with seizures[461] and worsened depression.[462] In an interesting and famous application of this information at the Appleton Area School District in Wisconsin, a total educational program was introduced. This comprised of removal of soda machines, improved breakfast and lunches, fitness classes, and several other interventions (shorter class periods, a low student to staff ratio, a full-time professional therapist, school social worker, and police school liaison). The combined intervention had a remarkable effect on a number of outcomes.[463] These included an increased ability to concentrate in the school setting; increased attendance; fewer disciplinary referrals; less moodiness and more calmness, ability to think more clearly, objectively, and rationally; fewer health complaints, i.e. headaches, stomach aches, general malaise; reduced feeling of hunger in mid-morning and/or mid-afternoon; and increased practice of good nutrition outside of school. While the precise contribution of nutritional intervention may not be easy to discern, I think it added significant value to the program.

Coffee has been associated with improved focus but also is known to cause anxiety;[464, 465] tea, on the contrary, has a lower propensity to cause anxiety despite similar benefits as coffee for improving focus.[466] Tea has been associated with relaxation likely because of a compound called theanine in the tea.[467] Theanine in tea has also been thought to be protective of nerve cells.[468]

Specific **macronutrients** have interesting effects on brain function. For example, while high carb food has been associated with a calming effect,[469] eating a high carbohydrate lunch predisposed to fatigue and afternoon drowsiness.[470] The brain is also affected by intake of proteins since several amino acids act as neurotransmitters. Studies have shown that use of S-Adensoyl-L-Methionine is associated with improvement in depression equal to the effect of tricyclic antidepressants, a prescription medication.[471] Another amino acid, tryptophan, has been found to help sleep[472] and symptoms of depression in a few studies.[473]

Dietary fat has a particularly significant effect on the brain. The brain is 60 percent fat, thus the quality and amount of fat intake affects brain structure and function. The greatest impact has been with the intake of *omega-3 fatty acids.*

Omega-3 fatty acid deficiency has been associated with several neurologic and psychiatric abnormalities including attention deficit, dementia, depression, bipolar disorder, schizophrenia, and dyslexia.[474, 475] Omega-3 fatty acids are involved in the synthesis of membranes of the cells and thereby help the overall health of the cells, decrease inflammation, and elevate the level of nerve growth factors.[476]

Several studies have shown the beneficial effect of omega-3 fatty acids on brain function, particularly in children. Thus omega-3 fatty acid supplementation improved cognitive deficits in children with developmental disorders;[477] children born to mothers receiving cod liver oil during pregnancy and for the first three months of breast feeding had better mental processing at four years;[478] a nutritional drink including DHA (a type of omega-3 fatty acid) improved test scores in children in Indonesia and Australia.[479] Consumption of greater amounts of omega-6 compared to omega-3 has been associated with greater decline in mental function in patients with Alzhiemer's disease.[480] In patients with very mild Alzheimer's disease, omega-3 fatty acid consumption led to slower cognitive decline.[481] Other clinical trials in adults have been associated with mixed results. Omega-3 fatty acid supplementation has also been associated with improved depression.[482] In contrast to consumption of omega-3 fatty acid, intake of trans and saturated fat has a deleterious effect on brain function.[483, 484]

Micronutrients have also been associated with effect on brain function. Iodine deficiency might be the most common cause of preventable brain damage in the world.[485] Iron deficiency is associated with memory[486] and mood problems[487] that improve with treatment.[488, 489] Magnesium deficiency is associated with mood disorders and stress[490] that might improve with supplementation.

Vitamins are also intimately involved in brain function. Thiamine deficiency is associated with brain dysfunction that might improve with supplementation.[491] Niacin deficiency causes a medical condition called pellagra that has dementia and depression as prominent components. Pyridoxine overdose can cause neurologic problems. Folate deficiency can cause depression and impaired memory,[492] while folate supplement might augment anti-depressant therapy[493] and prevent memory decline.[494] Vitamin B12 and vitamin E deficiency can cause several nervous system abnormalities. Vitamin D may preserve brain function in the elderly.[495]

Anti-oxidants are becoming increasingly popular for protecting brain function. The brain receives 20 percent of the blood flow while it only constitutes 2 percent of body weight. Since the brain has a high amount of oxidizable materials (polyunsaturated fatty acids), use of anti-oxidants to protect the brain seems biologically rational. Preliminary studies are supportive but not conclusive. For example, flavonoids that are present in the herb *Ginkgo biloba*, dark chocolate, red wine, and citrus fruits may be helpful for decreasing cognitive decline in early studies.[496] Alpha lipoic acid slowed cognitive decline in a small trial in patients with Alzheimer's disease.[497] Vitamin E might slow cognitive decay in the elderly according to a large national survey, but in higher doses may not be a safe supplement.[498] Curcumin, a widely used spice in India, might lower the risk of Alzheimer's disease.[499]

In a comprehensive review of this topic, dietary intake of the following was related to a lower risk of Alzheimer's disease: Antioxidants, vitamins B6, B12, and folate, unsaturated fatty acids, fish, mild to moderate alcohol intake, and Mediterranean diet.[500] Prospective clinical trials (that are the more definitive study), however, have yet to confirm those findings.

In summary based on the present research, the following dietary approach might help brain health:
- Caloric restriction
- Taking a healthy breakfast
- Avoiding food additives

- Drinking tea
- Avoiding refined carbohydrates
- Avoiding saturated fat and eliminating trans fat
- Taking healthy fat, particularly omega-3 fatty acids
- Avoiding micronutrient deficiency, particularly iodine and iron
- Preventing vitamin deficiencies by eating a healthy diet
- Taking a diet with a good dose of anti-oxidants, particularly fresh fruits
- Considering curcumin, flavonoids, and other anti-oxidants in individual cases

How You Eat It

In addition to nourishing your body, food also nourishes your mind. The effect of the state of mind on eating is a relatively less capitalized approach toward preventing weight gain. Studies show that if we eat primarily for our hunger and nourishment we are likely to lose weight. However, we often engage in emotional eating to soothe our minds. This is an important issue because simple educational programs and putting more information on food labels is turning out to be an ineffective intervention for preventing weight gain. What we need is to recruit our higher order self-regulating mechanism wherein people are in greater touch with their body's needs, have better capacity for emotional regulation, and thus do not need to eat more to feel better.

Currently every third child born in the U.S. is likely to develop diabetes.[501] It is perhaps for the first time now that a child born in 2009 will likely have a lower life expectancy than the current life expectancy. With smoking rates down from approximately 60 percent in the 1960s to currently approximately 20 percent, the main challenge we will face in the future is overweight and obesity. In order to understand the importance of the mind in eating, let us understand the two primary reasons why you eat. They are the homeostatic vs. non-homeostatic reasons.

Homeostatic eating is normal physiological eating that we do everyday in order to optimally nourish our bodies. This eating is coordinated by the hypothalamus, which as we saw is an intimate part of the limbic and cortical loops.[502] The hypothalamus is the converging site where the majority of the neural and chemical inputs converge to affect our eating. We evolved around pressures to save us from starvation.[503] The caloric plenty of modern times is only a recent phenomenon. The mechanisms of the hypothalamus thus have a more secure lower set point—we are designed to maintain our weight above this set point. An upper set point, however, is not well inscribed in our genetic code. This inherent genetic predisposition to obesity[504] has now been challenged by the twin problems of easy availability of inexpensive, well-advertised, calorie-dense palatable foods and increasing stress in the society prompting us to eat for non-homeostatic reasons. No wonder we are facing the overweight epidemic.

Non-homeostatic eating is psychological hunger. Despite a state of energy balance, restricting intake of palatable foods may produce "perceived deprivation".[505] There are two areas of the brain that are involved in this non-homeostatic eating. These are the structures of the *limbic loop and the reward centers*. Activation of the limbic loop with stress increases eating behavior. Specific sensory attributes of food items such as cream and sweet affect the amygdala and also the pre-frontal cortex.[506] Thinking about the food also activates the amygdala.[507] Reward centers (centers that make you feel good) of the brain are also intimately involved in eating. When you put sweet or creamy foods in your mouth you stimulate these centers.[508] Activation of the reward centers has a widespread effect on multiple areas of the brain including the pre-frontal cortex and the limbic system.[509, 510] Eating pleasurable food directly also activates the pre-frontal (orbitofrontal) and cingulate cortex.[511] Non-homeostatic eating easily overwhelms the homeostatic eating. Declining a sumptuous dessert even when you are full needs extraordinary self-control. In fact according to a few researchers, obesity might qualify as a brain (or mind) disorder.

Eating and thinking share a lot in common. Both these are critical to our survival and thus have widespread and shared representation in the brain centers. Thus brain areas involved in these processes include the pre-frontal cortex, cingulate, insula, nucleus accumbens, ventral pallidum, amygdala, hippocampus, hypothalamus, and ventral midbrain. No wonder there is one thing we never forget—where is that delicious cookie kept in the house!

This is not only true for humans but also applies to animals. Such a small insect as a honeybee has evolved a complex and well-rehearsed mechanism to transfer information about where food is available. The informer bee dances to show the location and abundance of food.[156] The angle from the sun indicates the direction of the dance and duration signifies distance. After learning this information, the recruits travel on a predictable trajectory whether or not they are displaced from their initial position.[157]

There is one more problem. ***Eating is an automatic behavior.*** Very similar to thinking, which is a background activity that just happens beyond our conscious control, eating is also an automatic behavior beyond our conscious control.[512] An automatic behavior is one that is unintentional, uncontrolled, goal independent, purely stimulus driven, efficient, and fast.[513] Several lines of very interesting research support this contention. For example, the following were the conclusions drawn from some of the research studies:

- The bigger the portion served, the more we eat.[514, 515]
- We tend to eat whatever is available at arm's length.[515, 516]
- We stop eating not because we are full, but because—all the food is gone OR no more time is left to eat OR the TV program we were watching is over![517]
- The more pleasurable the context of eating, the more we eat.[518]
- We eat what we see others eating.
- People eating larger portions do not believe they have eaten more / and may not even feel fuller
- If we are asked to restrain our eating our thinking capacity goes down.[519, 520]
- The result is that we eat the most visible, most available, least expensive, most sugary, most fatty, most calorie dense foods… Pizza, french fries, soft drinks, and salty snacks have shown the maximum increase in sales in the last twenty-five years.[521]

An interesting study recently suggested that what we eat impacts several non eating related behaviors.[522] For example, just an unconscious exposure to fast food symbols increased participants' reading speed and focus on saving time. Such exposure also decreased people's willingness to save with greater focus on the short term. Thus fast food may have additional unconscious influences beyond its direct impact on eating.

Automatic and fast eating without paying attention to what you are eating takes away enjoyment from the eating process and often leads to overeating. This pattern of eating does not provide adequate contentment and leaves us mentally hungry and unfulfilled. This might make you hover in front of the refrigerator craving that extra dessert even when your stomach is full. In a study with overweight children, slowing the pace of eating using a pacing device called mandometer was associated with significant weight loss.[523]

A good approach is to bring your benign presence and joy to your eating. I have a few suggestions:

- **Appreciate your hunger**
- **Calm your emotions**
- **Transition into the meal gradually (possibly starting with a simple ritual)**
- **Attend your food with all the six senses (five senses + the mind)**
- **Be respectful for the food and its preparers**
- **Slow down**
- **Savor the first five bites by taking them slowly and mindfully**
- **Transition out of the meal gradually (possibly ending with a simple ritual)**

The eating program we teach to learners has the following components:

1. Stocking up – Purposeful and conscious shopping, go with a full stomach, decide prior to shopping what you are going to buy, read food labels
2. Cooking – choose healthy options, avoid saturated fat, increase fruits and vegetables
3. To eat or not that is the question – learn common eating triggers, true vs. false hunger (craving, emotion), learn skills to control false hunger
4. Serving size and appearance – use a smaller plate, avoid force feeding self and others, in a buffet do not try to get your money's worth, make your meal plate visually appealing
5. Joy and presence – slow down, enjoy food as if eating after a long time, ask yourself a few questions (which meal is the most mindless? any favorite place I overeat? can I use a few tricks like – trying dessert first, eating as if in a formal setting, eating with the wrong hand, using an awkward spoon, using a small spoon etc.), savor your food
6. Optimally full – learn common stopping triggers, be full not bloated
7. Meaning and purpose – ponder over the meaning of food and eating
8. Journaling – journal about the diet and pattern of eating

The plate of food that is in front of you is truly a miracle. The individual components in it may have traveled thousands of miles and entailed collaboration of millions of workers. As you start eating, spend a few seconds looking at your food with kindness and bless the food. This will create positive energy and prepare you to get more nourishment from what you eat.

References

1. Duman RS. Neuronal damage and protection in the pathophysiology and treatment of psychiatric illness: stress and depression. *Dialogues Clin Neurosci.* 2009;11(3):239-255.
2. Borders A, Earleywine M, Jajodia A. Could mindfulness decrease anger, hostility, and aggression by decreasing rumination? *Aggress Behav.* Jan-Feb;36(1):28-44.
3. Frewen PA, Dozois DJ, Joanisse MF, Neufeld RW. Selective attention to threat versus reward: meta-analysis and neural-network modeling of the dot-probe task. *Clin Psychol Rev.* Feb 2008;28(2):307-337.
4. Yang E, Zald DH, Blake R. Fearful expressions gain preferential access to awareness during continuous flash suppression. *Emotion.* Nov 2007;7(4):882-886.
5. Peltola MJ, Leppanen JM, Palokangas T, Hietanen JK. Fearful faces modulate looking duration and attention disengagement in 7-month-old infants. *Dev Sci.* Jan 2008;11(1):60-68.
6. Milders M, Sahraie A, Logan S, Donnellon N. Awareness of faces is modulated by their emotional meaning. *Emotion.* Feb 2006;6(1):10-17.
7. Peltola MJ, Leppanen JM, Vogel-Farley VK, Hietanen JK, Nelson CA. Fearful faces but not fearful eyes alone delay attention disengagement in 7-month-old infants. *Emotion.* Aug 2009;9(4):560-565.
8. Peltola MJ, Leppanen JM, Maki S, Hietanen JK. Emergence of enhanced attention to fearful faces between 5 and 7 months of age. *Soc Cogn Affect Neurosci.* Jun 2009;4(2):134-142.
9. Kane MJ, Brown LH, McVay JC, Silvia PJ, Myin-Germeys I, Kwapil TR. For whom the mind wanders, and when: an experience-sampling study of working memory and executive control in daily life. *Psychol Sci.* Jul 2007;18(7): 614-621.
10. Mason MF, Norton MI, Van Horn JD, Wegner DM, Grafton ST, Macrae CN. Wandering minds: the default network and stimulus-independent thought. *Science.* Jan 19 2007;315(5810):393-395.
11. Zoellner T, Maercker A. Posttraumatic growth in clinical psychology - a critical review and introduction of a two component model. *Clin Psychol Rev.* Sep 2006;26(5):626-653.
12. Buckner RL, Vincent JL. Unrest at rest: default activity and spontaneous network correlations. *Neuroimage.* Oct 1 2007;37(4):1091-1096; discussion 1097-1099.
13. Raichle ME, MacLeod AM, Snyder AZ, Powers WJ, Gusnard DA, Shulman GL. A default mode of brain function. *Proc Natl Acad Sci U S A.* Jan 16 2001;98(2):676-682.
14. http://en.wikipedia.org/wiki/World_Wide_Web. Accessed December 21st, 2008.

15. Bar M. Predictions: a universal principle in the operation of the human brain. Introduction. *Philos Trans R Soc Lond B Biol Sci.* May 12 2009;364(1521): 1181-1182.

16. Hart AJ, Whalen PJ, Shin LM, McInerney SC, Fischer H, Rauch SL. Differential response in the human amygdala to racial outgroup vs ingroup face stimuli. *Neuroreport.* Aug 3 2000;11(11):2351-2355.

17. Lieberman MD, Hariri A, Jarcho JM, Eisenberger NI, Bookheimer SY. An fMRI investigation of race-related amygdala activity in African-American and Caucasian-American individuals. *Nat Neurosci.* Jun 2005; 8(6):720-722.

18. Dunn EW, Aknin LB, Norton MI. Spending money on others promotes happiness. *Science.* Mar 21 2008;319(5870):1687-1688.

19. Schulkin J. Angst and the amygdala. *Dialogues Clin Neurosci.* 2006;8(4): 407-416.

20. Charney DS. Neuroanatomical circuits modulating fear and anxiety behaviors. *Acta Psychiatr Scand Suppl.* 2003(417):38-50.

21. Schwartz CE, Wright CI, Shin LM, Kagan J, Rauch SL. Inhibited and uninhibited infants "grown up": adult amygdalar response to novelty. *Science.* Jun 20 2003;300(5627):1952-1953.

22. McEwen BS. Central effects of stress hormones in health and disease: Understanding the protective and damaging effects of stress and stress mediators. *Eur J Pharmacol.* Apr 7 2008;583(2-3):174-185.

23. Birbaumer N, Grodd W, Diedrich O, et al. fMRI reveals amygdala activation to human faces in social phobics. *Neuroreport.* Apr 20 1998;9(6): 1223-1226.

24. Rauch SL, van der Kolk BA, Fisler RE, et al. A symptom provocation study of posttraumatic stress disorder using positron emission tomography and script-driven imagery. *Arch Gen Psychiatry.* May 1996;53(5):380-387.

25. Rauch SL, Whalen PJ, Shin LM, et al. Exaggerated amygdala response to masked facial stimuli in posttraumatic stress disorder: a functional MRI study. *Biol Psychiatry.* May 1 2000;47(9):769-776.

26. Stein MB, Goldin PR, Sareen J, Zorrilla LT, Brown GG. Increased amygdala activation to angry and contemptuous faces in generalized social phobia. *Arch Gen Psychiatry.* Nov 2002;59(11):1027-1034.

27. Conrad CD, LeDoux JE, Magarinos AM, McEwen BS. Repeated restraint stress facilitates fear conditioning independently of causing hippocampal CA3 dendritic atrophy. *Behav Neurosci.* Oct 1999;113(5): 902-913.

28. Mitra R, Jadhav S, McEwen BS, Vyas A, Chattarji S. Stress duration modulates the spatiotemporal patterns of spine formation in the basolateral amygdala. *Proc Natl Acad Sci U S A.* Jun 28 2005;102(26):9371-9376.

29. Vyas A, Mitra R, Shankaranarayana Rao BS, Chattarji S. Chronic stress induces contrasting patterns of dendritic remodeling in hippocampal and amygdaloid neurons. *J Neurosci.* Aug 1 2002;22(15):6810-6818.

30. Rivier C, Vale W. Modulation of stress-induced ACTH release by corticotropin-releasing factor, catecholamines and vasopressin. *Nature.* Sep 22-28 1983;305(5932):325-327.

31. Croiset G, Nijsen MJ, Kamphuis PJ. Role of corticotropin-releasing factor, vasopressin and the autonomic nervous system in learning and memory. *Eur J Pharmacol.* Sep 29 2000;405(1-3):225-234.

32. Richard D, Lin Q, Timofeeva E. The corticotropin-releasing factor family of peptides and CRF receptors: their roles in the regulation of energy balance. *Eur J Pharmacol.* Apr 12 2002;440(2-3):189-197.

33. Brunson KL, Eghbal-Ahmadi M, Bender R, Chen Y, Baram TZ. Long-term, progressive hippocampal cell loss and dysfunction induced by early-life administration of corticotropin-releasing hormone reproduce the effects of early-life stress. *Proc Natl Acad Sci U S A.* Jul 17 2001;98(15):8856-8861.

34. McEwen BS. Stress and hippocampal plasticity. *Annu Rev Neurosci.* 1999;22:105-122.

35. McClure SM, Laibson DI, Loewenstein G, Cohen JD. Separate neural systems value immediate and delayed monetary rewards. *Science.* Oct 15 2004;306(5695):503-507.

36. vanDellen MR, Hoyle RH. Regulatory accessibility and social influences on state self-control. *Pers Soc Psychol Bull.* Feb;36(2):251-263.

37. Glenn AL, Raine A. The neurobiology of psychopathy. *Psychiatr Clin North Am.* Sep 2008;31(3):463-475, vii.

38. Spinella M. Self-rated executive function: development of the executive function index. *Int J Neurosci.* May 2005;115(5):649-667.

39. Dolan RJ. Emotion, cognition, and behavior. *Science.* Nov 8 2002;298(5596): 1191-1194.

40. Rilling J, Gutman D, Zeh T, Pagnoni G, Berns G, Kilts C. A neural basis for social cooperation. *Neuron.* Jul 18 2002;35(2):395-405.

41. Herry C, Garcia R. Prefrontal cortex long-term potentiation, but not long-term depression, is associated with the maintenance of extinction of learned fear in mice. *J Neurosci.* Jan 15 2002;22(2):577-583.

42. Morgan MA, Romanski LM, LeDoux JE. Extinction of emotional learning: contribution of medial prefrontal cortex. *Neurosci Lett.* Nov 26 1993;163(1): 109-113.

43. Quirk GJ, Russo GK, Barron JL, Lebron K. The role of ventromedial prefrontal cortex in the recovery of extinguished fear. *J Neurosci.* Aug 15 2000;20(16):6225-6231.

44. Sutton SK, Davidson RJ. Prefrontal brain electrical asymmetry predicts the evaluation of affective stimuli. *Neuropsychologia.* 2000;38(13):1723-1733.

45. Urry HL, Nitschke JB, Dolski I, et al. Making a life worth living: neural correlates of well-being. *Psychol Sci.* Jun 2004;15(6):367-372.

46. Isomura Y, Ito Y, Akazawa T, Nambu A, Takada M. Neural coding of "attention for action" and "response selection" in primate anterior cingulate cortex. *J Neurosci.* Sep 3 2003;23(22):8002-8012.

47. Modirrousta M, Fellows LK. Dorsal medial prefrontal cortex plays a necessary role in rapid error prediction in humans. *J Neurosci.* Dec 17 2008;28(51):14000-14005.

48. Lisman JE, Otmakhova NA. Storage, recall, and novelty detection of sequences by the hippocampus: elaborating on the SOCRATIC model to

account for normal and aberrant effects of dopamine. *Hippocampus.* 2001;11(5):551-568.

49. Herman JP, Ostrander MM, Mueller NK, Figueiredo H. Limbic system mechanisms of stress regulation: hypothalamo-pituitary- adrenocortical axis. *Prog Neuropsychopharmacol Biol Psychiatry.* Dec 2005;29(8):1201-1213.

50. Saphier D, Feldman S. Effects of septal and hippocampal stimuli on paraventricular nucleus neurons. *Neuroscience.* Mar 1987;20(3):749-755.

51. Connor KM, Davidson JR. Development of a new resilience scale: the Connor-Davidson Resilience Scale (CD-RISC). *Depress Anxiety.* 2003;18(2):76-82.

52. Davidson RJ. Affective style, psychopathology, and resilience: brain mechanisms and plasticity. *Am Psychol.* Nov 2000;55(11): 1196-1214.

53. McEwen BS. Physiology and neurobiology of stress and adaptation: central role of the brain. *Physiol Rev.* Jul 2007;87(3):873-904.

54. Bradshaw BG, Richardson GE, Kumpfer K, et al. Determining the efficacy of a resiliency training approach in adults with type 2 diabetes. *Diabetes Educ.* Jul-Aug 2007;33(4):650-659.

55. Steinhardt M, Dolbier C. Evaluation of a resilience intervention to enhance coping strategies and protective factors and decrease symptomatology. *J Am Coll Health.* Jan-Feb 2008;56(4):445-453.

56. Ruini C, Belaise C, Brombin C, Caffo E, Fava GA. Well-being therapy in school settings: a pilot study. *Psychother Psychosom.* 2006;75(6): 331-336.

57. Waite PJ, Richardson GE. Determining the efficacy of resiliency training in the work site. *J Allied Health.* Fall 2004;33(3):178-183.

58. Frodl T, Meisenzahl EM, Zetzsche T, et al. Larger amygdala volumes in first depressive episode as compared to recurrent major depression and healthy control subjects. *Biol Psychiatry.* Feb 15 2003;53(4): 338-344.

59. Sheline YI, Gado MH, Kraemer HC. Untreated depression and hippocampal volume loss. *Am J Psychiatry.* Aug 2003;160(8):1516-1518.

60. Sheline YI, Sanghavi M, Mintun MA, Gado MH. Depression duration but not age predicts hippocampal volume loss in medically healthy women with recurrent major depression. *J Neurosci.* Jun 15 1999;19(12):5034-5043.

61. Drevets WC, Price JL, Simpson JR, Jr., et al. Subgenual prefrontal cortex abnormalities in mood disorders. *Nature.* Apr 24 1997;386(6627): 824-827.

62. Drevets WC. Neuroimaging studies of mood disorders. *Biol Psychiatry.* Oct 15 2000;48(8):813-829.

63. Bremner JD, Staib LH, Kaloupek D, Southwick SM, Soufer R, Charney DS. Neural correlates of exposure to traumatic pictures and sound in Vietnam combat veterans with and without posttraumatic stress disorder: a positron emission tomography study. *Biol Psychiatry.* Apr 1 1999; 45(7):806-816.

64. Phan KL, Britton JC, Taylor SF, Fig LM, Liberzon I. Corticolimbic blood flow during nontraumatic emotional processing in posttraumatic stress disorder. *Arch Gen Psychiatry.* Feb 2006;63(2):184-192.

65. Shin LM, Wright CI, Cannistraro PA, et al. A functional magnetic resonance imaging study of amygdala and medial prefrontal cortex responses to overtly presented fearful faces in posttraumatic stress disorder. *Arch Gen Psychiatry.* Mar 2005;62(3):273-281.

66. Salomons TV, Johnstone T, Backonja MM, Shackman AJ, Davidson RJ. Individual differences in the effects of perceived controllability on pain perception: critical role of the prefrontal cortex. *J Cogn Neurosci.* Jun 2007;19(6):993-1003.

67. Radley JJ, Rocher AB, Miller M, et al. Repeated stress induces dendritic spine loss in the rat medial prefrontal cortex. *Cereb Cortex.* Mar 2006; 16(3):313-320.

68. Karlberg L, Unden AL, Elofsson S, Krakau I. Is there a connection between car accidents, near accidents, and type A drivers? *Behav Med.* Fall 1998; 24(3):99-106.

69. Nabi H, Consoli SM, Chastang JF, Chiron M, Lafont S, Lagarde E. Type A behavior pattern, risky driving behaviors, and serious road traffic accidents: a prospective study of the GAZEL cohort. *Am J Epidemiol.* May 1 2005;161(9):864-870.

70. Feldner MT, Babson KA, Zvolensky MJ. Smoking, traumatic event exposure, and post-traumatic stress: a critical review of the empirical literature. *Clin Psychol Rev.* Jan 2007;27(1):14-45.

71. Antoni MH, Lutgendorf SK, Cole SW, et al. The influence of bio-behavioural factors on tumour biology: pathways and mechanisms. *Nat Rev Cancer.* Mar 2006;6(3):240-248.

72. Duijts SF, Zeegers MP, Borne BV. The association between stressful life events and breast cancer risk: a meta-analysis. *Int J Cancer.* Dec 20 2003; 107(6):1023-1029.

73. Heffner KL, Loving TJ, Robles TF, Kiecolt-Glaser JK. Examining psychosocial factors related to cancer incidence and progression: in search of the silver lining. *Brain Behav Immun.* Feb 2003;17 Suppl 1:S109-111.

74. Monroe SM, Simons AD. Diathesis-stress theories in the context of life stress research: implications for the depressive disorders. *Psychol Bull.* Nov 1991;110(3):406-425.

75. Dong M, Giles WH, Felitti VJ, et al. Insights into causal pathways for ischemic heart disease: adverse childhood experiences study. *Circulation.* Sep 28 2004;110(13):1761-1766.

76. Krantz DS, McCeney MK. Effects of psychological and social factors on organic disease: a critical assessment of research on coronary heart disease. *Annu Rev Psychol.* 2002;53:341-369.

77. Li J, Hansen D, Mortensen PB, Olsen J. Myocardial infarction in parents who lost a child: a nationwide prospective cohort study in Denmark. *Circulation.* Sep 24 2002;106(13):1634-1639.

78. Kivimaki M, Virtanen M, Elovainio M, Kouvonen A, Vaananen A, Vahtera J. Work stress in the etiology of coronary heart disease - a meta-analysis. *Scand J Work Environ Health.* 2006;32(6):431-442.

79. Leserman J, Petitto JM, Gu H, et al. Progression to AIDS, a clinical AIDS condition and mortality: psychosocial and physiological predictors. *Psychol Med.* Aug 2002;32(6):1059-1073.

80. Miller G, Chen E, Cole SW. Health psychology: developing biologically plausible models linking the social world and physical health. *Annu Rev Psychol.* 2009;60:501-524.

81. Segerstrom SC, Miller GE. Psychological stress and the human immune system: a meta-analytic study of 30 years of inquiry. *Psychol Bull.* Jul 2004;130(4):601-630.

82. Thrall G, Lane D, Carroll D, Lip GY. A systematic review of the effects of acute psychological stress and physical activity on haemorheology, coagulation, fibrinolysis and platelet reactivity: Implications for the pathogenesis of acute coronary syndromes. *Thromb Res.* 2007;120(6):819-847.

83. Steptoe A, Hamer M, Chida Y. The effects of acute psychological stress on circulating inflammatory factors in humans: a review and meta-analysis. *Brain Behav Immun.* Oct 2007;21(7):901-912.

84. Innes KE, Vincent HK, Taylor AG. Chronic stress and insulin resistance-related indices of cardiovascular disease risk, part 2: a potential role for mind-body therapies. *Altern Ther Health Med.* Sep-Oct 2007;13(5):44-51.

85. Parker JF, Bahrick LE, Fivush R, Johnson P. The impact of stress on mothers' memory of a natural disaster. *J Exp Psychol Appl.* Sep 2006;12(3):142-154.

86. Gomes LM, Martinho Pimenta AJ, Castelo Branco NA. Effects of occupational exposure to low frequency noise on cognition. *Aviation, Space, and Environmental Medicine.* 1999;70(3 Pt 2):A115-118.

87. Pereira DB, Antoni MH, Danielson A, et al. Stress as a predictor of symptomatic genital herpes virus recurrence in women with human immunodeficiency virus. *J Psychosom Res.* Mar 2003;54(3): 237-244.

88. Kim EJ, Dimsdale JE. The effect of psychosocial stress on sleep: a review of polysomnographic evidence. *Behav Sleep Med.* 2007;5(4):256-278.

89. Akana SF, Chu A, Soriano L, Dallman MF. Corticosterone exerts site-specific and state-dependent effects in prefrontal cortex and amygdala on regulation of adrenocorticotropic hormone, insulin and fat depots. *J Neuroendocrinol.* Jul 2001;13(7):625-637.

90. Roozendaal B. 1999 Curt P. Richter award. Glucocorticoids and the regulation of memory consolidation. *Psychoneuroendocrinology.* Apr 2000; 25(3):213-238.

91. Seitz RJ, Nickel J, Azari NP. Functional modularity of the medial prefrontal cortex: involvement in human empathy. *Neuropsychology.* Nov 2006;20(6):743-751.

92. Eslinger PJ. Neurological and neuropsychological bases of empathy. *Eur Neurol.* 1998;39(4):193-199.

93. Shamay-Tsoory SG, Tomer R, Berger BD, Aharon-Peretz J. Characterization of empathy deficits following prefrontal brain damage: the role of the right ventromedial prefrontal cortex. *J Cogn Neurosci.* Apr 1 2003;15(3):324-337.

94. Spinella M. Prefrontal substrates of empathy: psychometric evidence in a community sample. *Biol Psychol.* Dec 2005;70(3): 175-181.

95. Shamay-Tsoory SG, Aharon-Peretz J, Perry D. Two systems for empathy: a double dissociation between emotional and cognitive empathy in inferior frontal gyrus versus ventromedial prefrontal lesions. *Brain.* Oct 29 2008.

96. Achterberg J, Cooke K, Richards T, Standish LJ, Kozak L, Lake J. Evidence for correlations between distant intentionality and brain function in recipients:

a functional magnetic resonance imaging analysis. *J Altern Complement Med.* Dec 2005;11(6):965-971.

97. Danziger N, Faillenot I, Peyron R. Can we share a pain we never felt? Neural correlates of empathy in patients with congenital insensitivity to pain. *Neuron.* Jan 29 2009;61(2):203-212.

98. Mathur VA, Harada T, Lipke T, Chiao JY. Neural basis of extraordinary empathy and altruistic motivation. *Neuroimage.* Jul 15;51(4): 1468-1475.

99. Light SN, Coan JA, Zahn-Waxler C, Frye C, Goldsmith HH, Davidson RJ. Empathy is associated with dynamic change in prefrontal brain electrical activity during positive emotion in children. *Child Dev.* Jul-Aug 2009;80(4):1210-1231.

100. Harris S, Sheth SA, Cohen MS. Functional neuroimaging of belief, disbelief, and uncertainty. *Ann Neurol.* Feb 2008;63(2):141-147.

101. Ochsner KN, Bunge SA, Gross JJ, Gabrieli JD. Rethinking feelings: an FMRI study of the cognitive regulation of emotion. *J Cogn Neurosci.* Nov 15 2002;14(8):1215-1229.

102. Ochsner KN, Ray RD, Cooper JC, et al. For better or for worse: neural systems supporting the cognitive down- and up-regulation of negative emotion. *Neuroimage.* Oct 2004;23(2):483-499.

103. Brass M, Ruge H, Meiran N, et al. When the same response has different meanings: recoding the response meaning in the lateral prefrontal cortex. *Neuroimage.* Oct 2003;20(2):1026-1031.

104. Sharp DJ, Scott SK, Wise RJ. Monitoring and the controlled processing of meaning: distinct prefrontal systems. *Cereb Cortex.* Jan 2004;14(1):1-10.

105. Farrow TF, Zheng Y, Wilkinson ID, et al. Investigating the functional anatomy of empathy and forgiveness. *Neuroreport.* Aug 8 2001; 12(11):2433-2438.

106. Hayashi A, Abe N, Ueno A, et al. Neural correlates of forgiveness for moral transgressions involving deception. *Brain Res.* May 21;1332:90-99.

107. Arnsten AF. Fundamentals of attention-deficit/hyperactivity disorder: circuits and pathways. *J Clin Psychiatry.* 2006;67 Suppl 8: 7-12.

108. Brennan AR, Arnsten AF. Neuronal mechanisms underlying attention deficit hyperactivity disorder: the influence of arousal on prefrontal cortical function. *Ann N Y Acad Sci.* 2008;1129:236-245.

109. Creswell JD, Way BM, Eisenberger NI, Lieberman MD. Neural correlates of dispositional mindfulness during affect labeling. *Psychosom Med.* Jul-Aug 2007;69(6):560-565.

110. Davidson RJ, Kabat-Zinn J, Schumacher J, et al. Alterations in brain and immune function produced by mindfulness meditation. *Psychosom Med.* Jul-Aug 2003;65(4):564-570.

111. Guroglu B, Haselager GJ, van Lieshout CF, Takashima A, Rijpkema M, Fernandez G. Why are friends special? Implementing a social interaction simulation task to probe the neural correlates of friendship. *Neuroimage.* Jan 15 2008;39(2):903-910.

112. Seeman TE, McEwen BS. Impact of social environment characteristics on neuroendocrine regulation. *Psychosom Med.* Sep-Oct 1996;58(5):459-471.

113. Baron Short E, Kose S, Mu Q, et al. Regional Brain Activation During Meditation Shows Time and Practice Effects: An Exploratory FMRI Study{dagger}. *Evid Based Complement Alternat Med.* Oct 27 2007.

114. Chan D, Woollacott M. Effects of level of meditation experience on attentional focus: is the efficiency of executive or orientation networks improved? *J Altern Complement Med.* Jul-Aug 2007;13(6):651-657.

115. Holzel BK, Ott U, Hempel H, et al. Differential engagement of anterior cingulate and adjacent medial frontal cortex in adept meditators and non-meditators. *Neurosci Lett.* Jun 21 2007;421(1):16-21.

116. Barnhofer T, Duggan D, Crane C, Hepburn S, Fennell MJ, Williams JM. Effects of meditation on frontal alpha-asymmetry in previously suicidal individuals. *Neuroreport.* May 7 2007;18(7):709-712.

117. Yamamoto S, Kitamura Y, Yamada N, Nakashima Y, Kuroda S. Medial prefrontal cortex and anterior cingulate cortex in the generation of alpha activity induced by transcendental meditation: a magnetoencephalographic study. *Acta Med Okayama.* Feb 2006;60(1): 51-58.

118. Lazar SW, Kerr CE, Wasserman RH, et al. Meditation experience is associated with increased cortical thickness. *Neuroreport.* Nov 28 2005; 16(17):1893-1897.

119. Esch T, Guarna M, Bianchi E, Zhu W, Stefano GB. Commonalities in the central nervous system's involvement with complementary medical therapies: limbic morphinergic processes. *Med Sci Monit.* Jun 2004; 10(6):MS6-17.

120. Newberg A, Pourdehnad M, Alavi A, d'Aquili EG. Cerebral blood flow during meditative prayer: preliminary findings and methodological issues. *Percept Mot Skills.* Oct 2003;97(2):625-630.

121. Aftanas LI, Golocheikine SA. Human anterior and frontal midline theta and lower alpha reflect emotionally positive state and internalized attention: high-resolution EEG investigation of meditation. *Neurosci Lett.* Sep 7 2001;310(1):57-60.

122. Newberg A, Alavi A, Baime M, Pourdehnad M, Santanna J, d'Aquili E. The measurement of regional cerebral blood flow during the complex cognitive task of meditation: a preliminary SPECT study. *Psychiatry Res.* Apr 10 2001;106(2):113-122.

123. Lazar SW, Bush G, Gollub RL, Fricchione GL, Khalsa G, Benson H. Functional brain mapping of the relaxation response and meditation. *Neuroreport.* May 15 2000;11(7):1581-1585.

124. Vestergaard-Poulsen P, van Beek M, Skewes J, et al. Long-term meditation is associated with increased gray matter density in the brain stem. *Neuroreport.* Jan 28 2009;20(2):170-174.

125. Luders E, Toga AW, Lepore N, Gaser C. The underlying anatomical correlates of long-term meditation: larger hippocampal and frontal volumes of gray matter. *Neuroimage.* Apr 15 2009;45(3):672-678.

126. Saver JL, Rabin J. The neural substrates of religious experience. *J Neuropsychiatry Clin Neurosci.* Summer 1997;9(3):498-510.

127. Wiech K, Farias M, Kahane G, Shackel N, Tiede W, Tracey I. An fMRI study measuring analgesia enhanced by religion as a belief system. *Pain.* Oct 15 2008;139(2):467-476.

128. Azari NP, Nickel J, Wunderlich G, et al. Neural correlates of religious experience. *Eur J Neurosci.* Apr 2001;13(8):1649-1652.

129. Kempermann G, van Praag H, Gage FH. Activity-dependent regulation of neuronal plasticity and self repair. *Prog Brain Res.* 2000;127:35-48.

130. Sabatini MJ, Ebert P, Lewis DA, Levitt P, Cameron JL, Mirnics K. Amygdala gene expression correlates of social behavior in monkeys experiencing maternal separation. *J Neurosci.* Mar 21 2007;27(12):3295-3304.

131. Vicentic A, Francis D, Moffett M, et al. Maternal separation alters serotonergic transporter densities and serotonergic 1A receptors in rat brain. *Neuroscience.* Jun 19 2006;140(1):355-365.

132. Cicchetti D. The impact of social experience on neurobiological systems: illustration from a constructivist view of child maltreatment. *Cognitive Development.* 2002;17:1407-1428.

133. Hennigan A, O'Callaghan RM, Kelly AM. Neurotrophins and their receptors: roles in plasticity, neurodegeneration and neuroprotection. *Biochem Soc Trans.* Apr 2007;35(Pt 2):424-427.

134. Huntley GW, Benson DL, Jones EG, Isackson PJ. Developmental expression of brain derived neurotrophic factor mRNA by neurons of fetal and adult monkey prefrontal cortex. *Brain Res Dev Brain Res.* Nov 20 1992;70(1):53-63.

135. Webster MJ, Herman MM, Kleinman JE, Shannon Weickert C. BDNF and trkB mRNA expression in the hippocampus and temporal cortex during the human lifespan. *Gene Expr Patterns.* Oct 2006;6(8):941-951.

136. Adlard PA, Cotman CW. Voluntary exercise protects against stress-induced decreases in brain-derived neurotrophic factor protein expression. *Neuroscience.* 2004;124(4):985-992.

137. Ferris LT, Williams JS, Shen CL. The effect of acute exercise on serum brain-derived neurotrophic factor levels and cognitive function. *Med Sci Sports Exerc.* Apr 2007;39(4):728-734.

138. Vaynman S, Ying Z, Gomez-Pinilla F. Hippocampal BDNF mediates the efficacy of exercise on synaptic plasticity and cognition. *Eur J Neurosci.* Nov 2004;20(10):2580-2590.

139. Doraiswamy PM, Xiong GL. Does Meditation Enhance Cognition and Brain Longevity? *Ann N Y Acad Sci.* Sep 28 2007.

140. Kanoski SE, Meisel RL, Mullins AJ, Davidson TL. The effects of energy-rich diets on discrimination reversal learning and on BDNF in the hippocampus and prefrontal cortex of the rat. *Behav Brain Res.* Aug 22 2007;182(1):57-66.

141. Mitoma M, Yoshimura R, Sugita A, et al. Stress at work alters serum brain-derived neurotrophic factor (BDNF) levels and plasma 3-methoxy-4-hydroxyphenylglycol (MHPG) levels in healthy volunteers: BDNF and MHPG as possible biological markers of mental stress? *Prog Neuropsychopharmacol Biol Psychiatry.* Nov 17 2007.

142.   Baer RA. Self-Focused Attention and Mechanisms of Change in Mindful-ness-Based Treatment. *Cogn Behav Ther.* Aug 20 2009:1.

143.   Andrews-Hanna JR, Reidler JS, Huang C, Buckner RL. Evidence for the De-fault Network's Role in Spontaneous Cognition. *J Neurophysiol.* May 12.

144.   Song M, Liu Y, Zhou Y, Wang K, Yu C, Jiang T. Default network and intel-ligence difference. *Conf Proc IEEE Eng Med Biol Soc.* 2009;2009:2212-2215.

145.   Csikszentmihalyi M, LeFevre J. Optimal experience in work and leisure. *J Pers Soc Psychol.* May 1989;56(5):815-822.

146.   Smallwood J, Fitzgerald A, Miles LK, Phillips LH. Shifting moods, wan-dering minds: negative moods lead the mind to wander. *Emotion.* Apr 2009;9(2):271-276.

147.   Schooler JW. Re-representing consciousness: dissociations between experi-ence and meta-consciousness. *Trends Cogn Sci.* Aug 1 2002;6(8):339-344.

148.   Smallwood J, McSpadden M, Schooler JW. When attention matters: the curious incident of the wandering mind. *Mem Cognit.* Sep 2008;36(6): 1144-1150.

149.   Christoff K, Gordon AM, Smallwood J, Smith R, Schooler JW. Experi-ence sampling during fMRI reveals default network and executive sys-tem contributions to mind wandering. *Proc Natl Acad Sci U S A.* May 26 2009;106(21):8719-8724.

150.   Smallwood J, McSpadden M, Schooler JW. The lights are on but no one's home: meta-awareness and the decoupling of attention when the mind wanders. *Psychon Bull Rev.* Jun 2007;14(3): 527-533.

151.   Smallwood J, Fishman DJ, Schooler JW. Counting the cost of an absent mind: mind wandering as an underrecognized influence on educational performance. *Psychon Bull Rev.* Apr 2007;14(2): 230-236.

152.   Baumeister RF, Bratslavsky E, Finkenauer C. Bad is stronger than good. *Re-view of General Psychology.* 2001;5(4):323-370.

153.   Wilbert-Lampen U, Leistner D, Greven S, et al. Cardiovascular events dur-ing World Cup soccer. *N Engl J Med.* Jan 31 2008;358(5):475-483.

154.   Campos B, Graesch AP, Repetti R, Bradbury T, Ochs E. Opportunity for in-teraction? A naturalistic observation study of dual-earner families after work and school. *J Fam Psychol.* Dec 2009;23(6): 798-807.

155.   Powers S, el-Nawawy M. Al-Jazeera English and global news networks: clash of civilizations or cross-cultural dialogue? *Media, War & Conflict.* 2009;2(3):263-284.

156.   von Frisch K. *Dance language and orientation of bees.* Cambridge, Massa-chussetts: Harvard University Press; 1967.

157.   Riley JR, Greggers U, Smith AD, Reynolds DR, Menzel R. The flight paths of honeybees recruited by the waggle dance. *Nature.* May 12 2005;435(7039):205-207.

158.   Hodgins HS, Adair KC. Attentional processes and meditation. *Conscious Cogn.* Apr 27.

159.   Jha AP, Stanley EA, Kiyonaga A, Wong L, Gelfand L. Examining the protec-tive effects of mindfulness training on working memory capacity and af-fective experience. *Emotion.* Feb;10(1): 54-64.

160. Zeidan F, Johnson SK, Diamond BJ, David Z, Goolkasian P. Mindfulness meditation improves cognition: evidence of brief mental training. *Conscious Cogn.* Jun;19(2):597-605.

161. Owen AM, Hampshire A, Grahn JA, et al. Putting brain training to the test. *Nature.* Apr 20.

162. Deyo M, Wilson KA, Ong J, Koopman C. Mindfulness and rumination: does mindfulness training lead to reductions in the ruminative thinking associated with depression? *Explore (NY).* Sep-Oct 2009;5(5):265-271.

163. http://www.nytimes.com/2010/05/23/science/23family.html?hpw=&pagewanted=all. Accessed June 1st, 2010.

164. Bevilaqua LR, Medina JH, Izquierdo I, Cammarota M. Reconsolidation and the fate of consolidated memories. *Neurotox Res.* Dec 2008;14(4): 353-358.

165. Eisenhardt D, Menzel R. Extinction learning, reconsolidation and the internal reinforcement hypothesis. *Neurobiol Learn Mem.* Feb 2007;87(2):167-173.

166. Herry C, Ferraguti F, Singewald N, Letzkus JJ, Ehrlich I, Luthi A. Neuronal circuits of fear extinction. *Eur J Neurosci.* Feb;31(4): 599-612.

167. Tsang J. The effects of helper intention on gratitude and indebtedness. *Motivation and Emotion.* 2006;30(198-204).

168. Rind B, Bordia P. Effect of server's "Thank you" and personalization on restaurant tipping. *Journal of Applied Social Psychology.* 1995;25:745-751.

169. Kahneman D. Experiences of collaborative research. *Am Psychol.* Sep 2003;58(9):723-730.

170. Schultz W. Behavioral dopamine signals. *Trends Neurosci.* May 2007; 30(5):203-210.

171. Kobayashi S, Pinto de Carvalho O, Schultz W. Adaptation of reward sensitivity in orbitofrontal neurons. *J Neurosci.* Jan 13;30(2): 534-544.

172. Kashdan TB, Uswatte G, Julian T. Gratitude and hedonic and eudaimonic well-being in Vietnam war veterans. *Behav Res Ther.* Feb 2006; 44(2):177-199.

173. Bartlett MY, DeSteno D. Gratitude and prosocial behavior: helping when it costs you. *Psychol Sci.* Apr 2006;17(4):319-325.

174. Emmons RA, McCullough ME. Counting blessings versus burdens: an experimental investigation of gratitude and subjective well- being in daily life. *J Pers Soc Psychol.* Feb 2003;84(2):377-389.

175. McCullough ME, Emmons RA, Tsang JA. The grateful disposition: a conceptual and empirical topography. *J Pers Soc Psychol.* Jan 2002; 82(1):112-127.

176. McCullough ME, Tsang JA, Emmons RA. Gratitude in intermediate affective terrain: links of grateful moods to individual differences and daily emotional experience. *J Pers Soc Psychol.* Feb 2004;86(2):295-309.

177. Kmietowicz Z. Care in hospitals often lacks compassion, says report. *BMJ.* 2008;337:a2821.

178. Bellini LM, Baime M, Shea JA. Variation of mood and empathy during internship. *JAMA.* Jun 19 2002;287(23):3143-3146.

179. Pollak KI, Arnold R, Alexander SC, et al. Do patient attributes predict oncologist empathic responses and patient perceptions of empathy? *Support Care Cancer*. Oct 18 2009.

180. Fernndez-Olano C, Montoya-Fernndez J, Salinas-Snchez AS. Impact of clinical interview training on the empathy level of medical students and medical residents. *Med Teach*. May 2008;30(3): 322-324.

181. Poole AD, Sanson-Fisher RW. Long-term effects of empathy training on the interview skills of medical students. *Patient Couns Health Educ*. 3d Quart 1980;2(3):125-127.

182. Eklund J, Andersson-Straberg T, Hansen EM. "I've also experienced loss and fear": Effects of prior similar experience on empathy. *Scand J Psychol*. Aug 12 2008.

183. Hodges SD, Kiel KJ, Kramer AD, Veach D, Villanueva BR. Giving birth to empathy: the effects of similar experience on empathic accuracy, empathic concern, and perceived empathy. *Pers Soc Psychol Bull*. Mar;36(3):398-409.

184. Oveis C, Horberg EJ, Keltner D. Compassion, pride, and social intuitions of self-other similarity. *J Pers Soc Psychol*. Apr;98(4):618-630.

185. Sturmer S, Snyder M, Kropp A, Siem B. Empathy-motivated helping: the moderating role of group membership. *Pers Soc Psychol Bull*. Jul 2006;32(7):943-956.

186. Marangoni C, Garcia S, Ickes W, Teng G. Empathic accuracy in a clinically relevant setting. *J Pers Soc Psychol*. May 1995;68(5): 854-869.

187. Batson CD, Polycarpou MP, Harmon-Jones E, et al. Empathy and attitudes: can feeling for a member of a stigmatized group improve feelings toward the group? *J Pers Soc Psychol*. Jan 1997;72(1): 105-118.

188. Tarrant M, Dazeley S, Cottom T. Social categorization and empathy for outgroup members. *Br J Soc Psychol*. Nov 7 2008.

189. Goetz JL, Keltner D, Simon-Thomas E. Compassion: An evolutionary analysis and empirical review. *Psychol Bull*. May;136(3):351-374.

190. Lin CS, Hsu MY, Chong CF. Differences between emergency patients and their doctors in the perception of physician empathy: implications for medical education. *Educ Health (Abingdon)*. Jul 2008;21(2):144.

191. Bonvicini KA, Perlin MJ, Bylund CL, Carroll G, Rouse RA, Goldstein MG. Impact of communication training on physician expression of empathy in patient encounters. *Patient Educ Couns*. Dec 9 2008.

192. Fiske ST. From dehumanization and objectification to rehumanization: neuroimaging studies on the building blocks of empathy. *Ann N Y Acad Sci*. Jun 2009;1167:31-34.

193. Fogarty LA, Curbow BA, Wingard JR, McDonnell K, Somerfield MR. Can 40 seconds of compassion reduce patient anxiety? *J Clin Oncol*. Jan 1999;17(1):371-379.

194. Redelmeier DA, Molin JP, Tibshirani RJ. A randomised trial of compassionate care for the homeless in an emergency department. *Lancet*. May 6 1995;345(8958):1131-1134.

195. Rakel DP, Hoeft TJ, Barrett BP, Chewning BA, Craig BM, Niu M. Practitioner empathy and the duration of the common cold. *Fam Med*. Jul-Aug 2009;41(7):494-501.

196. Selph RB, Shiang J, Engelberg R, Curtis JR, White DB. Empathy and Life Support Decisions in Intensive Care Units. *J Gen Intern Med.* Jun 24 2008.

197. Carson JW, Keefe FJ, Lynch TR, et al. Loving-kindness meditation for chronic low back pain: results from a pilot trial. *J Holist Nurs.* Sep 2005;23(3):287-304.

198. Ishii H, Nagashima M, Tanno M, Nakajima A, Yoshino S. Does being easily moved to tears as a response to psychological stress reflect response to treatment and the general prognosis in patients with rheumatoid arthritis? *Clin Exp Rheumatol.* Sep-Oct 2003;21(5): 611-616.

199. Pace TW, Negi LT, Adame DD, et al. Effect of compassion meditation on neuroendocrine, innate immune and behavioral responses to psychosocial stress. *Psychoneuroendocrinology.* Oct 3 2008.

200. Joans WB, Crawford CC. *Healing, Intention and Energy Medicine.* New York, NY: Churchill Livingstone,; 2003.

201. Radin D. *Entangled Minds.* New York, NY: Paraview,; 2006.

202. Barraza JA, Zak PJ. Empathy toward strangers triggers oxytocin release and subsequent generosity. *Ann N Y Acad Sci.* Jun 2009;1167:182-189.

203. Slovic P. "If I look at the mass I will never act": Psychic numbing and genocide. *Judgment and Decision Making.* 2007;2(2):79-95.

204. Najjar N, Davis LW, Beck-Coon K, Carney Doebbeling C. Compassion Fatigue: A Review of the Research to Date and Relevance to Cancer-care Providers. *J Health Psychol.* Mar 2009;14(2):267-277.

205. Fitzgibbon BM, Giummarra MJ, Georgiou-Karistianis N, Enticott PG, Bradshaw JL. Shared pain: from empathy to synaesthesia. *Neurosci Biobehav Rev.* Mar;34(4):500-512.

206. Richardson GE. The metatheory of resilience and resiliency. *J Clin Psychol.* Mar 2002;58(3):307-321.

207. Bankston J. *Alexander Fleming and the Story of Penicillin*: Mitchell Lane Publishers 2001.

208. Selye H. THE SIGNIFICANCE OF THE ADRENALS FOR ADAPTATION. *Science.* Mar 5 1937;85(2201):247-248.

209. Selye H, Horava A. Stress Research. *Science.* May 8 1953;117(3045):509.

210. Hayes SC, Luoma JB, Bond FW, Masuda A, Lillis J. Acceptance and commitment therapy: model, processes and outcomes. *Behav Res Ther.* Jan 2006;44(1):1-25.

211. Powers MB, Zum Vorde Sive Vording MB, Emmelkamp PM. Acceptance and Commitment Therapy: A Meta-Analytic Review. *Psychother Psychosom.* Jan 14 2009;78(2):73-80.

212. Pull CB. Current empirical status of acceptance and commitment therapy. *Curr Opin Psychiatry.* Jan 2009;22(1):55-60.

213. Gregg JA, Callaghan GM, Hayes SC, Glenn-Lawson JL. Improving diabetes self-management through acceptance, mindfulness, and values: a randomized controlled trial. *J Consult Clin Psychol.* Apr 2007;75(2): 336-343.

214. Johnsen BH, Eid J, Lovstad T, Michelsen LT. Posttraumatic stress symptoms in nonexposed, victims, and spontaneous rescuers after an avalanche. *J Trauma Stress.* Jan 1997;10(1):133-140.

215. Valentiner DP, Foa E, Riggs DS, Gershuny BS. Coping strategies and post-traumatic stress disorder in female victims of sexual and nonsexual assault. *J Abnorm Psychol.* Aug 1996;105(3):455-458.

216. Forman EM, Herbert JD, Moitra E, Yeomans PD, Geller PA. A randomized controlled effectiveness trial of acceptance and commitment therapy and cognitive therapy for anxiety and depression. *Behav Modif.* Nov 2007;31(6):772-799.

217. Twohig MP, Shoenberger D, Hayes SC. A preliminary investigation of acceptance and commitment therapy as a treatment for marijuana dependence in adults. *J Appl Behav Anal.* Winter 2007;40(4): 619-632.

218. Lachapelle DL, Lavoie S, Boudreau A. The meaning and process of pain acceptance. Perceptions of women living with arthritis and fibromyalgia. *Pain Res Manag.* May-Jun 2008;13(3):201-210.

219. Thompson BL, Waltz J. Mindfulness and experiential avoidance as predictors of posttraumatic stress disorder avoidance symptom severity. *J Anxiety Disord.* May;24(4):409-415.

220. Wicksell RK, Ahlqvist J, Bring A, Melin L, Olsson GL. Can Exposure and Acceptance Strategies Improve Functioning and Life Satisfaction in People with Chronic Pain and Whiplash-Associated Disorders (WAD)? A Randomized Controlled Trial. *Cogn Behav Ther.* Jun 13 2008:1-14.

221. Low CA, Stanton AL, Bower JE. Effects of acceptance-oriented versus evaluative emotional processing on heart rate recovery and habituation. *Emotion.* Jun 2008;8(3):419-424.

222. Jacobson NS, Christensen A, Prince SE, Cordova J, Eldridge K. Integrative behavioral couple therapy: an acceptance-based, promising new treatment for couple discord. *J Consult Clin Psychol.* Apr 2000;68(2):351-355.

223. Kranz D, Bollinger A, Nilges P. Chronic pain acceptance and affective well-being: A coping perspective. *Eur J Pain.* Apr 26.

224. Roemer L, Orsillo SM, Salters-Pedneault K. Efficacy of an acceptance-based behavior therapy for generalized anxiety disorder: evaluation in a randomized controlled trial. *J Consult Clin Psychol.* Dec 2008;76(6): 1083-1089.

225. Johnston M, Foster M, Shennan J, Starkey NJ, Johnson A. The effectiveness of an Acceptance and Commitment Therapy self-help intervention for chronic pain. *Clin J Pain.* Jun;26(5):393-402.

226. Westin V, Ostergren R, Andersson G. The effects of acceptance versus thought suppression for dealing with the intrusiveness of tinnitus. *Int J Audiol.* Nov 2008;47 Suppl 2:S112-118.

227. Karademas EC, Hondronikola I. The impact of illness acceptance and helplessness to subjective health, and their stability over time: a prospective study in a sample of cardiac patients. *Psychol Health Med.* May;15(3):336-346.

228. McCracken LM, Vowles KE. Acceptance of chronic pain. *Curr Pain Headache Rep.* Apr 2006;10(2):90-94.

229. Lundgren T, Dahl J, Melin L, Kies B. Evaluation of acceptance and commitment therapy for drug refractory epilepsy: a randomized controlled trial in South Africa--a pilot study. *Epilepsia*. Dec 2006;47(12):2173-2179.

230. Twohig MP, Hayes SC, Masuda A. A preliminary investigation of acceptance and commitment therapy as a treatment for chronic skin picking. *Behav Res Ther*. Oct 2006;44(10):1513-1522.

231. Woods DW, Wetterneck CT, Flessner CA. A controlled evaluation of acceptance and commitment therapy plus habit reversal for trichotillomania. *Behav Res Ther*. May 2006;44(5):639-656.

232. Bach P, Hayes SC. The use of acceptance and commitment therapy to prevent the rehospitalization of psychotic patients: a randomized controlled trial. *J Consult Clin Psychol*. Oct 2002;70(5): 1129-1139.

233. Gaudiano BA, Herbert JD. Acute treatment of inpatients with psychotic symptoms using Acceptance and Commitment Therapy: pilot results. *Behav Res Ther*. Mar 2006;44(3):415-437.

234. Twohig MP, Hayes SC, Masuda A. Increasing willingness to experience obsessions: acceptance and commitment therapy as a treatment for obsessive-compulsive disorder. *Behav Ther*. Mar 2006;37(1):3-13.

235. Marcks BA, Woods DW. A comparison of thought suppression to an acceptance-based technique in the management of personal intrusive thoughts: a controlled evaluation. *Behav Res Ther*. Apr 2005;43(4):433-445.

236. Varra AA, Hayes SC, Roget N, Fisher G. A randomized control trial examining the effect of acceptance and commitment training on clinician willingness to use evidence-based pharmacotherapy. *J Consult Clin Psychol*. Jun 2008;76(3):449-458.

237. Vowles KE, McCracken LM. Acceptance and values-based action in chronic pain: a study of treatment effectiveness and process. *J Consult Clin Psychol*. Jun 2008;76(3):397-407.

238. Abramowitz JS, Tolin DF, Street GP. Paradoxical effects of thought suppression: a meta-analysis of controlled studies. *Clin Psychol Rev*. Jul 2001;21(5):683-703.

239. Clark DM, Ball S, Pape D. An experimental investigation of thought suppression. *Behav Res Ther*. 1991;29(3):253-257.

240. Clark DM, Winton E, Thynn L. A further experimental investigation of thought suppression. *Behav Res Ther*. Feb 1993;31(2):207-210.

241. Wegner DM, Schneider DJ, Carter SR, 3rd, White TL. Paradoxical effects of thought suppression. *J Pers Soc Psychol*. Jul 1987;53(1):5-13.

242. Salkovskis PM, Campbell P. Thought suppression induces intrusion in naturally occurring negative intrusive thoughts. *Behav Res Ther*. Jan 1994;32(1):1-8.

243. Trinder H, Salkovskis PM. Personally relevant intrusions outside the laboratory: long-term suppression increases intrusion. *Behav Res Ther*. Nov 1994;32(8):833-842.

244. Purdon C, Clark DA. Suppression of obsession-like thoughts in nonclinical individuals: impact on thought frequency, appraisal and mood state. *Behav Res Ther.* Oct 2001;39(10):1163-1181.

245. Taylor F, Bryant RA. The tendency to suppress, inhibiting thoughts, and dream rebound. *Behav Res Ther.* Jan 2007;45(1):163-168.

246. Hofmann SG, Heering S, Sawyer AT, Asnaani A. How to handle anxiety: The effects of reappraisal, acceptance, and suppression strategies on anxious arousal. *Behav Res Ther.* May 2009;47(5):389-394.

247. Edgar L, Remmer J, Rosberger Z, Fournier MA. Resource use in women completing treatment for breast cancer. *Psychooncology.* Sep-Oct 2000;9(5):428-438.

248. Shapiro DE, Boggs SR, Rodrigue JR, et al. Stage II breast cancer: differences between four coping patterns in side effects during adjuvant chemotherapy. *J Psychosom Res.* Aug 1997;43(2):143-157.

249. Graham JE, Lobel M, Glass P, Lokshina I. Effects of written anger expression in chronic pain patients: making meaning from pain. *J Behav Med.* Jun 2008;31(3):201-212.

250. Barling J, Bluen S, Moss V. Type A behavior and marital dissatisfaction: disentangling the effects of achievement striving and impatience-irritability. *J Psychol.* May 1990;124(3):311-319.

251. Yan LL, Liu K, Matthews KA, Daviglus ML, Ferguson TF, Kiefe CI. Psychosocial factors and risk of hypertension: the Coronary Artery Risk Development in Young Adults (CARDIA) study. *JAMA.* Oct 22 2003;290(16):2138-2148.

252. Thomas SA, Friedmann E, Wimbush F, Schron E. Psychological factors and survival in the cardiac arrhythmia suppression trial (CAST): a reexamination. *Am J Crit Care.* Mar 1997;6(2):116-126.

253. Julkunen J, Salonen R, Kaplan GA, Chesney MA, Salonen JT. Hostility and the progression of carotid atherosclerosis. *Psychosom Med.* Nov-Dec 1994;56(6):519-525.

254. Mendes de Leon CF, Powell LH, Kaplan BH. Change in coronary-prone behaviors in the recurrent coronary prevention project. *Psychosom Med.* Jul-Aug 1991;53(4):407-419.

255. Rowe BH, Channan P, Bullard M, et al. Characteristics of patients who leave emergency departments without being seen. *Acad Emerg Med.* Aug 2006;13(8):848-852.

256. Frankl V. *Man's Search for Meaning: An Introduction to Logo Therapy.* New York: Simon and Schuster; 1970.

257. Jim HS, Purnell JQ, Richardson SA, Golden-Kreutz D, Andersen BL. Measuring meaning in life following cancer. *Qual Life Res.* Oct 2006;15(8):1355-1371.

258. Skaggs BG, Barron CR. Searching for meaning in negative events: concept analysis. *J Adv Nurs.* Mar 2006;53(5):559-570.

259. Park CL, Folkman S. Meaning in the context of stress and coping. *Review of General Psychology.* 1997;1(2):115-144.

260. Taylor SE. Adjustment to threatening events: A theory of cognitive adaptation. *American Psychologist.* 1983;38:1161-1173.

261. Thompson SC, Janigian A. Life schemes: A framework for understanding the search for meaningq. *Journal of Social and Clinical Psychology.* 1988;7:260-280.

262. Clucas JG. *Mother Teresa.* New York. : Chelsea House Publications; 1988.

263. http://www.cbsnews.com/stories/2006/06/23/health/webmd/main1748477.shtml?source=RSS&attr=HOME_1748477. Accessed October 19th, 2008.

264. Reinventing aging: baby boomers and civic engagement. *Caring.* Mar 2005;24(3):32-35.

265. Bamia C, Trichopoulou A, Trichopoulos D. Age at retirement and mortality in a general population sample: the Greek EPIC study. *Am J Epidemiol.* Mar 1 2008;167(5):561-569.

266. Alavinia SM, Burdorf A. Unemployment and retirement and ill-health: a cross-sectional analysis across European countries. *Int Arch Occup Environ Health.* Oct 2008;82(1):39-45.

267. Tsai SP, Wendt JK, Donnelly RP, de Jong G, Ahmed FS. Age at retirement and long term survival of an industrial population: prospective cohort study. *BMJ.* Oct 29 2005;331(7523):995.

268. Slingerland AS, van Lenthe FJ, Jukema JW, et al. Aging, retirement, and changes in physical activity: prospective cohort findings from the GLOBE study. *Am J Epidemiol.* Jun 15 2007;165(12):1356-1363.

269. Forman-Hoffman VL, Richardson KK, Yankey JW, Hillis SL, Wallace RB, Wolinsky FD. Retirement and weight changes among men and women in the health and retirement study. *J Gerontol B Psychol Sci Soc Sci.* May 2008;63(3):S146-153.

270. Krause N. Church-Based Volunteering, Providing Informal Support at Church, and Self-Rated Health in Late Life. *J Aging Health.* 2009 21(1):63-84.

271. Krause N. Church-based social support and mortality. *J Gerontol B Psychol Sci Soc Sci.* 2006;61(3):S140-146.

272. http://religions.pewforum.org/reports. Accessed April 13th 2009.

273. Puchalski C, Romer AL. Taking a spiritual history allows clinicians to understand patients more fully. *J Palliat Med* 2000;3:129-137.

274. Sessanna L, Finnell D, Jezewski MA. Spirituality in nursing and health-related literature: a concept analysis. *J Holist Nurs.* 2007;25(4):252-262.

275. Highfield MEF. Providing spiritual care to patients with cancer. *Clin J Oncol Nurs* 2000;4(115-120).

276. Ferrell BR, Smith SL, Juarez G, Melancon C. Meaning of illness and spirituality in ovarian cancer survivors. *Oncol Nurs Forum.* Mar-Apr 2003;30(2):249-257.

277. Meraviglia M. Effects of spirituality in breast cancer survivors. *Oncol Nurs Forum.* Jan 2006;33(1):E1-7.

278. Thompson P. The relationship of fatigue and meaning in life in breast cancer survivors. *Oncol Nurs Forum.* May 2007;34(3):653-660.

279. Folkman S. Positive psychological states and coping with severe stress. *Soc Sci Med.* Oct 1997;45(8):1207-1221.

280. Anagnostopoulos F, Slater J, Fitzsimmons D. Intrusive Thoughts and Psychological Adjustment to Breast Cancer: Exploring the Moderating and Mediating Role of Global Meaning and Emotional Expressivity. *J Clin Psychol Med Settings.* Apr 8.

281. Tolle E. *The Power of Now: A Guide to Spiritual Enlightenment* New World Library; September 1997.

282. Salsman JM, Yost KJ, West DW, Cella D. Spiritual well-being and health-related quality of life in colorectal cancer: a multi-site examination of the role of personal meaning. *Support Care Cancer.* Apr 20.

283. Teresa M, . *Mother Teresa: Come Be My Light - The Private Writings of the Saint of Calcutta*: Doubleday 2007.

284. http://www.time.com/time/world/article/0,8599,1655415,00.html.   Accessed October 20th, 2008.

285. Diener E, Biswas-Diener R. *Happiness: Unlocking the Mysteries of Psychological Wealth.* Malden, MA: Wiley-Blackwell; 2008.

286. *http://www.forbes.com/2008/12/22/billionaires-mitttal-ross-biz- billies-cz_lk_1222billieblowups_slide_11.html?thisSpeed=15000* [Accessed December 31st, 2008.

287. Thiele DM, Whelan TA. The relationship between grandparent satisfaction, meaning, and generativity. *Int J Aging Hum Dev.* 2008;66(1):21-48.

288. Debats DL, Drost J, Hansen P. Experiences of meaning in life: a combined qualitative and quantitative approach. *Br J Psychol.* Aug 1995;86 (Pt 3): 359-375.

289. Basoglu M, Mineka S, Paker M, Aker T, Livanou M, Gok S. Psychological preparedness for trauma as a protective factor in survivors of torture. *Psychol Med.* Nov 1997;27(6):1421-1433.

290. Rodriguez-Laso A, Zunzunegui MV, Otero A. The effect of social relationships on survival in elderly residents of a Southern European community: a cohort study. *BMC Geriatr.* 2007;7:19.

291. Updegraff JA, Silver RC, Holman EA. Searching for and finding meaning in collective trauma: results from a national longitudinal study of the 9/11 terrorist attacks. *J Pers Soc Psychol.* Sep 2008;95(3):709-722.

292. Hinkle LE, Jr., Wolff HG. Ecologic investigations of the relationship between illness, life experiences and the social environment. *Ann Intern Med.* Dec 1958;49(6):1373-1388.

293. Degner LF, Hack T, O'Neil J, Kristjanson LJ. A new approach to eliciting meaning in the context of breast cancer. *Cancer Nurs.* Jun 2003;26(3): 169-178.

294. Simonelli LE, Fowler J, Maxwell GL, Andersen BL. Physical Sequelae and Depressive Symptoms in Gynecologic Cancer Survivors: Meaning in Life as a Mediator. *Ann Behav Med.* Apr 3 2008.

295. Bauer-Wu S, Farran CJ. Meaning in life and psycho-spiritual functioning: a comparison of breast cancer survivors and healthy women. *J Holist Nurs.* Jun 2005;23(2):172-190.

296. Lethborg C, Aranda S, Kissane D. Meaning in adjustment to cancer: a model of care. *Palliat Support Care*. Mar 2008;6(1):61-70.

297. Taylor EJ. Factors associated with meaning in life among people with recurrent cancer. *Oncol Nurs Forum*. Oct 1993;20(9):1399-1405; discussion 1406-1397.

298. Rasmussen DM, Elverdam B. The meaning of work and working life after cancer: an interview study. *Psychooncology*. Dec 2008;17(12):1232-1238.

299. Carpenter JS, Brockopp DY, Andrykowski MA. Self-transformation as a factor in the self-esteem and well-being of breast cancer survivors. *J Adv Nurs*. Jun 1999;29(6):1402-1411.

300. Taylor EJ. Transformation of tragedy among women surviving breast cancer. *Oncol Nurs Forum*. Jun 2000;27(5):781-788.

301. Linn MW, Linn BS, Harris R. Effects of counseling for late stage cancer patients. *Cancer*. Mar 1 1982;49(5):1048-1055.

302. Kim SH. The influence of finding meaning and worldview of accepting death on anger among bereaved older spouses. *Aging Ment Health*. Jan 2009;13(1):38-45.

303. Vehling S, Lehmann C, Oechsle K, et al. Global meaning and meaning-related life attitudes: exploring their role in predicting depression, anxiety, and demoralization in cancer patients. *Support Care Cancer*. Mar 21.

304. Smith BW, Zautra AJ. The role of purpose in life in recovery from knee surgery. *Int J Behav Med*. 2004;11(4):197-202.

305. Lee V, Cohen SR, Edgar L, Laizner AM, Gagnon AJ. Clarifying "meaning" in the context of cancer research: a systematic literature review. *Palliat Support Care*. Sep 2004;2(3):291-303.

306. Lee V, Robin Cohen S, Edgar L, Laizner AM, Gagnon AJ. Meaning-making intervention during breast or colorectal cancer treatment improves self-esteem, optimism, and self-efficacy. *Soc Sci Med*. Jun 2006;62(12): 3133-3145.

307. Bower JE, Kemeny ME, Taylor SE, Fahey JL. Finding positive meaning and its association with natural killer cell cytotoxicity among participants in a bereavement-related disclosure intervention. *Ann Behav Med*. Spring 2003;25(2):146-155.

308. Krause N. Meaning in life and mortality. *J Gerontol B Psychol Sci Soc Sci*. Jun 2009;64(4):517-527.

309. van den Belt H. Playing God in Frankenstein's Footsteps: Synthetic Biology and the Meaning of Life. *Nanoethics*. Dec 2009;3(3):257-268.

310. Stiefel F, Krenz S, Zdrojewski C, et al. Meaning in life assessed with the "Schedule for Meaning in Life Evaluation" (SMiLE): a comparison between a cancer patient and student sample. *Support Care Cancer*. Jan 16 2008.

311. Gottman JM, Levenson RW. What predicts change in marital interaction over time? A study of alternative models. *Fam Process*. Summer 1999;38(2):143-158.

312. Covey SR. *The 7 Habits of Highly Effective People*: Free Press; 1990.

313. de Waal FB, Leimgruber K, Greenberg AR. Giving is self-rewarding for monkeys. *Proc Natl Acad Sci U S A*. Sep 9 2008;105(36):13685-13689.

314.   de Waal FB. Putting the altruism back into altruism: the evolution of em-
        pathy. *Annu Rev Psychol.* 2008;59:279-300.

315.   Cialdini RB, Brown SL, Lewis BP, Luce C, Neuberg SL. Reinterpreting the
        empathy-altruism relationship: when one into one equals oneness. *J Pers
        Soc Psychol.* Sep 1997;73(3):481-494.

316.   Steger MF, Kashdan TB, Oishi S. Being good by doing good: Daily eudai-
        monic activity and well-being. *J Res Person* 2008;42:22-42.

317.   Harbaugh WT, Mayr U, Burghart DR. Neural responses to taxation and
        voluntary giving reveal motives for charitable donations. *Science.* Jun 15
        2007;316(5831):1622-1625.

318.   Perry B. Conveying compassion through attention to the essential ordi-
        nary. *Nurs Older People.* Jul 2009;21(6):14-21; quiz 22.

319.   Smith-Stoner M. End-of-life preferences for atheists. *J Palliat Med.* Aug
        2007;10(4):923-928.

320.   Park CL. Religiousness/spirituality and health: a meaning systems per-
        spective. *J Behav Med.* Aug 2007;30(4):319-328.

321.   Nelson CJ, Rosenfeld B, Breitbart W, Galietta M. Spirituality, religion, and
        depression in the terminally ill. *Psychosomatics.* May-Jun 2002;43(3):
        213-220.

322.   Richer MC, Ezer H. Living in it, living with it, and moving on: dimen-
        sions of meaning during chemotherapy. *Oncol Nurs Forum.* Jan-Feb
        2002;29(1):113-119.

323.   Jim HS, Richardson SA, Golden-Kreutz DM, Andersen BL. Strategies used
        in coping with a cancer diagnosis predict meaning in life for survivors.
        Health Psychol. Nov 2006;25(6):753-761.

324.   Hogan NS, Schmidt LA. Testing the grief to personal growth model using
        structural equation modeling. *Death Stud.* Oct 2002;26(8):615-634.

325.   Park CL, Cohen LH, Murch RL. Assessment and prediction of stress-related
        growth. *J Pers.* Mar 1996;64(1):71-105.

326.   Tedeschi RG, Calhoun LG. The Posttraumatic Growth Inventory: mea-
        suring the positive legacy of trauma. *J Trauma Stress.* Jul 1996;9(3):
        455-471.

327.   Fegg MJ, Kogler M, Brandstatter M, et al. Meaning in life in patients with
        amyotrophic lateral sclerosis. *Amyotroph Lateral Scler.* Mar 17.

328.   Enright RD. *Forgiveness is a choice: A step-by-step process for resolving an-
        ger and restoring hope* Washington, DC: American Psychological Associa-
        tion.; 2001.

329.   Holmgren MR. Forgiveness and the intrinsic value of persons. *American
        Philosophical Quarterly.* 1993;30:341-352.

330.   McCullough ME. Forgiveness as human strength: Theory, measure-
        ment, and links to well-being. *Journal of Social and Clinical Psychology.*
        2000;19:43-55.

331.   Enright RD, & The Human Development Study Group. Piaget on the moral
        development of forgiveness: Identity or reciprocity? . *Human Develop-
        ment.* 1994;37(63-80).

332. Bleil ME, McCaffery JM, Muldoon MF, Sutton-Tyrrell K, Manuck SB. Anger-related personality traits and carotid artery atherosclerosis in untreated hypertensive men. *Psychosom Med.* Sep-Oct 2004;66(5):633-639.

333. Deshields TL, Jenkins JO, Tait RC. The experience of anger in chronic illness: a preliminary investigation. *Int J Psychiatry Med.* 1989;19(3):299-309.

334. Everson SA, Goldberg DE, Kaplan GA, Julkunen J, Salonen JT. Anger expression and incident hypertension. *Psychosom Med.* Nov-Dec 1998; 60(6):730-735.

335. Shimbo D, Chaplin W, Akinola O, et al. Effect of anger provocation on endothelium-dependent and -independent vasodilation. *Am J Cardiol.* Mar 15 2007;99(6):860-863.

336. Verrier RL, Mittleman MA. Life-threatening cardiovascular consequences of anger in patients with coronary heart disease. *Cardiol Clin.* May 1996;14(2):289-307.

337. Williams JE, Paton CC, Siegler IC, Eigenbrodt ML, Nieto FJ, Tyroler HA. Anger proneness predicts coronary heart disease risk: prospective analysis from the atherosclerosis risk in communities (ARIC) study. *Circulation.* May 2 2000;101(17):2034-2039.

338. Poole JC, Snieder H, Davis HC, Treiber FA. Anger suppression and adiposity modulate association between ADRB2 haplotype and cardiovascular stress reactivity. *Psychosom Med.* Mar-Apr 2006;68(2):207-212.

339. Lawler KA, Younger JW, Piferi RL, Jobe RL, Edmondson KA, Jones WH. The unique effects of forgiveness on health: an exploration of pathways. *J Behav Med.* Apr 2005;28(2):157-167.

340. Wilson T, Milosevic A, Carroll M, Hart K, Hibbard S. Physical health status in relation to self-forgiveness and other-forgiveness in healthy college students. *J Health Psychol.* Sep 2008;13(6):798-803.

341. Friedberg JP, Suchday S, Shelov DV. The impact of forgiveness on cardiovascular reactivity and recovery. *Int J Psychophysiol.* Aug 2007;65(2):87-94.

342. Harris AHS, Thoresen CE. *Forgiveness, unforgiveness, health, and disease.* New York: Routledge; 2005.

343. Friedberg JP, Suchday S, Srinivas VS. Relationship Between Forgiveness and Psychological and Physiological Indices in Cardiac Patients. *Int J Behav Med.* Feb 20 2009.

344. Bono G, McCullough ME, Root LM. Forgiveness, feeling connected to others, and well-being: two longitudinal studies. *Pers Soc Psychol Bull.* Feb 2008;34(2):182-195.

345. Thompson LY, Snyder CR, Hoffman L, et al. Dispositional forgiveness of self, others, and situations. *J Pers.* Apr 2005;73(2):313-359.

346. Romero C, Friedman LC, Kalidas M, Elledge R, Chang J, Liscum KR. Self-forgiveness, spirituality, and psychological adjustment in women with breast cancer. *J Behav Med.* Feb 2006;29(1):29-36.

347. Carson JW, Keefe FJ, Goli V, et al. Forgiveness and chronic low back pain: a preliminary study examining the relationship of forgiveness to pain, anger, and psychological distress. *J Pain.* Feb 2005;6(2): 84-91.

348. Hansen MJ, Enright RD, Baskin TW, Klatt J. A palliative care intervention in forgiveness therapy for elderly terminally ill cancer patients. *J Palliat Care*. Spring 2009;25(1):51-60.

349. Maio GR, Thomas G, Fincham FD, Carnelley KB. Unraveling the role of forgiveness in family relationships. *J Pers Soc Psychol*. Feb 2008;94(2):307-319.

350. Paleari FG, Regalia C, Fincham F. Marital quality, forgiveness, empathy, and rumination: a longitudinal analysis. *Pers Soc Psychol Bull*. Mar 2005;31(3):368-378.

351. Gordon KC, Hughes FM, Tomcik ND, Dixon LJ, Litzinger SC. Widening spheres of impact: The role of forgiveness in marital and family functioning. *J Fam Psychol*. Feb 2009;23(1):1-13.

352. Worthington EL, Jr., Scherer M. Forgiveness is an emotion-focused coping strategy that can reduce health risks and promote health resilience: Theory, review, and hypotheses. *Psychology and Health*. 2004;19:385-405.

353. Tartaro J, Luecken LJ, Gunn HE. Exploring heart and soul: effects of religiosity/spirituality and gender on blood pressure and cortisol stress responses. *J Health Psychol*. Nov 2005;10(6):753-766.

354. Carr L, Iacoboni M, Dubeau MC, Mazziotta JC, Lenzi GL. Neural mechanisms of empathy in humans: a relay from neural systems for imitation to limbic areas. *Proc Natl Acad Sci U S A*. Apr 29 2003;100(9):5497-5502.

355. Decety J, Chaminade T. Neural correlates of feeling sympathy. *Neuropsychologia*. 2003;41(2):127-138.

356. Peck MS. *People of the lie*. New York: Simon & Schuster; 1997.

357. McCullough ME, Bono G, Root LM. Rumination, emotion, and forgiveness: three longitudinal studies. *J Pers Soc Psychol*. Mar 2007;92(3):490-505.

358. Siassi S. Forgiveness, acceptance and the matter of expectation. *Int J Psychoanal*. Dec 2007;88(Pt 6):1423-1440.

359. Enright RD, Santos MJ, Al-Mabuk R. The adolescent as forgiver. *J Adolesc*. Mar 1989;12(1):95-110.

360. McCullough ME, Root LM, Cohen AD. Writing about the benefits of an interpersonal transgression facilitates forgiveness. *J Consult Clin Psychol*. Oct 2006;74(5):887-897.

361. Lambert NM, Fincham FD, Stillman TF, Graham SM, Beach SR. Motivating change in relationships: can prayer increase forgiveness? *Psychol Sci*. Jan 1;21(1):126-132.

362. http://www.cbsnews.com/stories/2008/02/14/60minutes/main3833797.shtml. Accessed April 12th, 2009.

363. Whited MC, Wheat AL, Larkin KT. The influence of forgiveness and apology on cardiovascular reactivity and recovery in response to mental stress. *J Behav Med*. Apr 3.

364. Enright RD, Group HDS. The moral development of forgiveness. In: Kurtines W, Gewirtz J, eds. *Moral behavior and development*. Vol 1. Hillsdale, N.J.: Erlbaum; 1991:123-152.

365. McCullough ME, Worthington EL, Jr., Rachal KC. Interpersonal forgiving in close relationships. *J Pers Soc Psychol*. Aug 1997;73(2): 321-336.

366. McCullough ME, Worthington EL. Promoting forgiveness: The comparison of two brief psychoeducational interventions with a waiting-list control. *Counseling and Values.* 1995;40:55-68.

367. Wade NG, Meyer JE. Comparison of brief group interventions to promote forgiveness: a pilot outcome study. *Int J Group Psychother.* Apr 2009;59(2):199-220.

368. VanLoon P. The practice of interpersonal forgiveness in the personal and professional lives of clergy. *J Pastoral Care Counsel.* Fall-Winter 2009; 63(3-4):7-1-9.

369. Lawler-Row KA, Karremans JC, Scott C, Edlis-Matityahou M, Edwards L. Forgiveness, physiological reactivity and health: the role of anger. *Int J Psychophysiol.* Apr 2008;68(1):51-58.

370. Al-Mabuk RH, Downs WR. Forgiveness therapy with parents of adolescent suicide victims. *Journal of Family Psychotherapy.* 1996;7: 21-39.

371. Lin WF, Mack D, Enright RD, Krahn D, Baskin TW. Effects of forgiveness therapy on anger, mood, and vulnerability to substance use among inpatient substance-dependent clients. *J Consult Clin Psychol.* Dec 2004;72(6): 1114-1121.

372. Coyle CT, Enright RD. Forgiveness intervention with postabortion men. *J Consult Clin Psychol.* Dec 1997;65(6):1042-1046.

373. Worthington EL, Jr., Kurusu TA, Collins W, Berry JW, Ripley JS, Baier SN. Forgiveness usually takes time: A lesson learned by studying interventions to promote forgiveness. *Journal of Psychology & Theology.* 2000; 28:3-20.

374. Freedman SR, Enright RD. Forgiveness as an intervention goal with incest survivors. *J Consult Clin Psychol.* Oct 1996;64(5):983-992.

375. Ripley JS, Worthington EL, Jr. Hope-focused and forgiveness-based group interventions to promote marital enrichment. *Journal of Counseling & Development.* 2002;80:452-463.

376. Harris AH, Luskin F, Norman SB, et al. Effects of a group forgiveness intervention on forgiveness, perceived stress, and trait-anger. *J Clin Psychol.* Jun 2006;62(6):715-733.

377. Hebl JH, Enright RD. Forgiveness as a psychotherapeutic goal with elderly females. *Psychotherapy.* 1993;30:658-667.

378. Levenson MR, Aldwin CM, Yancura L. Positive emotional change: mediating effects of forgiveness and spirituality. *Explore (NY).* Nov-Dec 2006;2(6):498-508.

379. Tibbits D, Ellis G, Piramelli C, Luskin F, Lukman R. Hypertension reduction through forgiveness training. *J Pastoral Care Counsel.* Spring-Summer 2006;60(1-2):27-34.

380. Rye MS, Pargament KI, Pan W, Yingling DW, Shogren KA, Ito M. Can group interventions facilitate forgiveness of an ex-spouse? A randomized clinical trial. *J Consult Clin Psychol.* Oct 2005;73(5): 880-892.

381. Reed GL, Enright RD. The effects of forgiveness therapy on depression, anxiety, and posttraumatic stress for women after spousal emotional abuse. *J Consult Clin Psychol.* Oct 2006;74(5):920-929.

382. Ingersoll-Dayton B, Campbell R, Ha JH. Enhancing forgiveness: a group intervention for the elderly. *J Gerontol Soc Work*. Jan 2009;52(1):2-16.

383. http://www.usatoday.com/news/nation/2006-06-22-friendship_x.htm. Accessed November, 28, 2008.

384. Stillman TF, Baumeister RF, Lambert NM, Crescioni AW, Dewall CN, Fincham FD. Alone and Without Purpose: Life Loses Meaning Following Social Exclusion. *J Exp Soc Psychol*. Jul 2009;45(4):686-694.

385. Cohen SD, Sharma T, Acquaviva K, Peterson RA, Patel SS, Kimmel PL. Social support and chronic kidney disease: an update. *Adv Chronic Kidney Dis*. Oct 2007;14(4):335-344.

386. Schwartz RS. Psychotherapy and social support: unsettling questions. *Harv Rev Psychiatry*. Sep-Oct 2005;13(5):272-279.

387. Regehr C, Hill J, Glancy GD. Individual predictors of traumatic reactions in firefighters. *J Nerv Ment Dis*. Jun 2000;188(6):333-339.

388. Turner SW, Bowie C, Dunn G, Shapo L, Yule W. Mental health of Kosovan Albanian refugees in the UK. *Br J Psychiatry*. May 2003;182: 444-448.

389. Giles LC, Glonek GF, Luszcz MA, Andrews GR. Effect of social networks on 10 year survival in very old Australians: the Australian longitudinal study of aging. *J Epidemiol Community Health*. Jul 2005;59(7):574-579.

390. Reichstadt J, Depp CA, Palinkas LA, Folsom DP, Jeste DV. Building blocks of successful aging: a focus group study of older adults' perceived contributors to successful aging. *Am J Geriatr Psychiatry*. Mar 2007;15(3): 194-201.

391. Brown WM, Consedine NS, Magai C. Altruism relates to health in an ethnically diverse sample of older adults. *J Gerontol B Psychol Sci Soc Sci*. May 2005;60(3):P143-152.

392. Steptoe A, Owen N, Kunz-Ebrecht SR, Brydon L. Loneliness and neuroendocrine, cardiovascular, and inflammatory stress responses in middle-aged men and women. *Psychoneuroendocrinology*. Jun 2004;29(5): 593-611.

393. Twenge JM, Zhang L, Catanese KR, Dolan-Pascoe B, Lyche LF, Baumeister RF. Replenishing connectedness: reminders of social activity reduce aggression after social exclusion. *Br J Soc Psychol*. Mar 2007;46(Pt 1):205-224.

394. Twenge JM, Baumeister RF, DeWall CN, Ciarocco NJ, Bartels JM. Social exclusion decreases prosocial behavior. *J Pers Soc Psychol*. Jan 2007;92(1): 56-66.

395. Konrath S, Bushman BJ, Campbell WK. Attenuating the link between threatened egotism and aggression. *Psychol Sci*. Nov 2006;17(11): 995-1001.

396. Ciechanowski P, Wagner E, Schmaling K, et al. Community-integrated home-based depression treatment in older adults: a randomized controlled trial. *JAMA*. Apr 7 2004;291(13):1569-1577.

397. White H, McConnell E, Clipp E, et al. A randomized controlled trial of the psychosocial impact of providing internet training and access to older adults. *Aging Ment Health*. Aug 2002;6(3): 213-221.

398. Twenge JM, Baumeister RF, Tice DM, Stucke TS. If you can't join them, beat them: effects of social exclusion on aggressive behavior. *J Pers Soc Psychol.* Dec 2001;81(6):1058-1069.

399. Park CL, Malone MR, Suresh DP, Bliss D, Rosen RI. Coping, meaning in life, and quality of life in congestive heart failure patients. *Qual Life Res.* Feb 2008;17(1):21-26.

400. Neff KD, Vonk R. Self-Compassion Versus Global Self-Esteem: Two Different Ways of Relating to Oneself. *J Pers.* Nov 28 2008.

401. Initial sequence of the chimpanzee genome and comparison with the human genome. *Nature.* Sep 1 2005;437(7055):69-87.

402. Wallace RK, Benson H, Wilson AF. A wakeful hypometabolic physiologic state. *Am J Physiol.* 1971;221(3):795-799.

403. Cardoso R, de Souza E, Camano L, Leite JR. Meditation in health: an operational definition. *Brain Res Brain Res Protoc.* Nov 2004;14(1): 58-60.

404. Fitzgibbon ML, Stolley MR, Ganschow P, et al. Results of a faith-based weight loss intervention for black women. *J Natl Med Assoc.* Oct 2005;97(10):1393-1402.

405. Tloczynski J, Fritzsch S. Intercessory prayer in psychological well-being: using a multiple-baseline, across-subjects design. *Psychol Rep.* Dec 2002;91(3 Pt 1):731-741.

406. Wachholtz AB, Pargament KI. Is spirituality a critical ingredient of meditation? Comparing the effects of spiritual meditation, secular meditation, and relaxation on spiritual, psychological, cardiac, and pain outcomes. *J Behav Med.* Aug 2005;28(4):369-384.

407. Leibovici L. Effects of remote, retroactive intercessory prayer on outcomes in patients with bloodstream infection: randomised controlled trial. *BMJ.* Dec 22-29 2001;323(7327):1450-1451.

408. Cha KY, Wirth DP. Does prayer influence the success of in vitro fertilization-embryo transfer? Report of a masked, randomized trial. *J Reprod Med.* Sep 2001;46(9):781-787.

409. Yanek LR, Becker DM, Moy TF, Gittelsohn J, Koffman DM. Project Joy: faith based cardiovascular health promotion for African American women. *Public Health Rep.* 2001;116 Suppl 1:68-81.

410. Matthews DA, Marlowe SM, MacNutt FS. Effects of intercessory prayer on patients with rheumatoid arthritis. *South Med J.* Dec 2000;93(12): 1177-1186.

411. Byrd RC. Positive therapeutic effects of intercessory prayer in a coronary care unit population. *South Med J.* Jul 1988;81(7): 826-829.

412. Harris WS, Gowda M, Kolb JW, et al. A randomized, controlled trial of the effects of remote, intercessory prayer on outcomes in patients admitted to the coronary care unit. *Arch Intern Med.* Oct 25 1999;159(19): 2273-2278.

413. Sicher F, Targ E, Moore D, 2nd, Smith HS. A randomized double-blind study of the effect of distant healing in a population with advanced AIDS. Report of a small scale study. *West J Med.* Dec 1998;169(6):356-363.

414. Helm HM, Hays JC, Flint EP, Koenig HG, Blazer DG. Does private religious activity prolong survival? A six-year follow-up study of 3,851 older adults. *J Gerontol A Biol Sci Med Sci.* Jul 2000;55(7):M400-405.

415. Ikedo F, Gangahar DM, Quader MA, Smith LM. The effects of prayer, relaxation technique during general anesthesia on recovery outcomes following cardiac surgery. *Complement Ther Clin Pract.* May 2007;13(2):85-94.

416. Astin JA, Stone J, Abrams DI, et al. The efficacy of distant healing for human immunodeficiency virus--results of a randomized trial. *Altern Ther Health Med.* Nov-Dec 2006;12(6):36-41.

417. Benson H, Dusek JA, Sherwood JB, et al. Study of the Therapeutic Effects of Intercessory Prayer (STEP) in cardiac bypass patients: a multicenter randomized trial of uncertainty and certainty of receiving intercessory prayer. *Am Heart J.* Apr 2006;151(4):934-942.

418. Krucoff MW, Crater SW, Gallup D, et al. Music, imagery, touch, and prayer as adjuncts to interventional cardiac care: the Monitoring and Actualisation of Noetic Trainings (MANTRA) II randomised study. *Lancet.* Jul 16-22 2005;366(9481):211-217.

419. Mann JR, McKay S, Daniels D, et al. Physician offered prayer and patient satisfaction. *Int J Psychiatry Med.* 2005;35(2):161-170.

420. Mathai J, Bourne A. Pilot study investigating the effect of intercessory prayer in the treatment of child psychiatric disorders. *Australas Psychiatry.* Dec 2004;12(4):386-389.

421. Palmer RF, Katerndahl D, Morgan-Kidd J. A randomized trial of the effects of remote intercessory prayer: interactions with personal beliefs on problem-specific outcomes and functional status. *J Altern Complement Med.* Jun 2004;10(3):438-448.

422. Aviles JM, Whelan SE, Hernke DA, et al. Intercessory prayer and cardiovascular disease progression in a coronary care unit population: a randomized controlled trial. *Mayo Clin Proc.* Dec 2001;76(12):1192-1198.

423. Matthews WJ, Conti JM, Sireci SG. The effects of intercessory prayer, positive visualization, and expectancy on the well-being of kidney dialysis patients. *Altern Ther Health Med.* Sep-Oct 2001;7(5):42-52.

424. Walker SR, Tonigan JS, Miller WR, Corner S, Kahlich L. Intercessory prayer in the treatment of alcohol abuse and dependence: a pilot investigation. *Altern Ther Health Med.* Nov 1997;3(6):79-86.

425. Levine EG, Aviv C, Yoo G, Ewing C, Au A. The benefits of prayer on mood and well-being of breast cancer survivors. *Support Care Cancer.* Jul 17 2008.

426. Steinhauser KE, Voils CI, Clipp EC, Bosworth HB, Christakis NA, Tulsky JA. "Are you at peace?": one item to probe spiritual concerns at the end of life. *Arch Intern Med.* Jan 9 2006;166(1):101-105.

427. Ross LE, Hall IJ, Fairley TL, Taylor YJ, Howard DL. Prayer and self-reported health among cancer survivors in the United States, National Health Interview Survey, 2002. *J Altern Complement Med.* Oct 2008;14(8):931-938.

428. Lissoni P, Messina G, Parolini D, et al. A spiritual approach in the treatment of cancer: relation between faith score and response to chemotherapy in advanced non-small cell lung cancer patients. *In Vivo.* Sep-Oct 2008;22(5):577-581.

429. Mueller PS, Plevak DJ, Rummans TA. Religious involvement, spirituality, and medicine: implications for clinical practice. *Mayo Clin Proc.* Dec 2001;76(12):1225-1235.

430. Elavsky S, McAuley E. Physical activity and mental health outcomes during menopause: a randomized controlled trial. *Ann Behav Med.* Apr 2007;33(2):132-142.

431. Elavsky S, McAuley E, Motl RW, et al. Physical activity enhances long-term quality of life in older adults: efficacy, esteem, and affective influences. *Ann Behav Med.* Oct 2005;30(2):138-145.

432. McAuley E, Konopack JF, Motl RW, Morris KS, Doerksen SE, Rosengren KR. Physical activity and quality of life in older adults: influence of health status and self-efficacy. *Ann Behav Med.* Feb 2006;31(1):99-103.

433. Levine JA. Nonexercise activity thermogenesis--liberating the life-force. *J Intern Med.* Sep 2007;262(3):273-287.

434. Weuve J, Kang JH, Manson JE, Breteler MM, Ware JH, Grodstein F. Physical activity, including walking, and cognitive function in older women. *JAMA.* Sep 22 2004;292(12):1454-1461.

435. Abbott RD, White LR, Ross GW, Masaki KH, Curb JD, Petrovitch H. Walking and dementia in physically capable elderly men. *JAMA.* Sep 22 2004;292(12):1447-1453.

436. Larson EB, Wang L, Bowen JD, et al. Exercise is associated with reduced risk for incident dementia among persons 65 years of age and older. *Ann Intern Med.* Jan 17 2006;144(2):73-81.

437. Podewils LJ, Guallar E, Kuller LH, et al. Physical activity, APOE genotype, and dementia risk: findings from the Cardiovascular Health Cognition Study. *Am J Epidemiol.* Apr 1 2005;161(7):639-651.

438. Lautenschlager NT, Cox KL, Flicker L, et al. Effect of physical activity on cognitive function in older adults at risk for Alzheimer disease: a randomized trial. *JAMA.* Sep 3 2008;300(9):1027-1037.

439. Forbes D, Forbes S, Morgan DG, Markle-Reid M, Wood J, Culum I. Physical activity programs for persons with dementia. *Cochrane Database Syst Rev.* 2008(3):CD006489.

440. Angevaren M, Aufdemkampe G, Verhaar HJ, Aleman A, Vanhees L. Physical activity and enhanced fitness to improve cognitive function in older people without known cognitive impairment. *Cochrane Database Syst Rev.* 2008(3):CD005381.

441. Winter B, Breitenstein C, Mooren FC, et al. High impact running improves learning. *Neurobiol Learn Mem.* May 2007;87(4):597-609.

442. Colcombe SJ, Kramer AF, Erickson KI, et al. Cardiovascular fitness, cortical plasticity, and aging. *Proc Natl Acad Sci U S A.* Mar 2 2004;101(9):3316-3321.

443. Griesbach GS, Hovda DA, Molteni R, Wu A, Gomez-Pinilla F. Voluntary exercise following traumatic brain injury: brain-derived neurotrophic factor upregulation and recovery of function. *Neuroscience.* 2004;125(1): 129-139.

444. Rojas Vega S, Struder HK, Vera Wahrmann B, Schmidt A, Bloch W, Hollmann W. Acute BDNF and cortisol response to low intensity exercise and following ramp incremental exercise to exhaustion in humans. *Brain Res.* Nov 22 2006;1121(1):59-65.

445. Tang SW, Chu E, Hui T, Helmeste D, Law C. Influence of exercise on serum brain-derived neurotrophic factor concentrations in healthy human subjects. *Neurosci Lett.* Jan 24 2008;431(1):62-65.

446. Blumenthal JA, Babyak MA, Doraiswamy PM, et al. Exercise and pharmacotherapy in the treatment of major depressive disorder. *Psychosom Med.* Sep-Oct 2007;69(7):587-596.

447. Blumenthal JA, Babyak MA, Moore KA, et al. Effects of exercise training on older patients with major depression. *Arch Intern Med.* Oct 25 1999;159(19):2349-2356.

448. Ulmer CS, Stetson BA, Salmon PG. Mindfulness and acceptance are associated with exercise maintenance in YMCA exercisers. *Behav Res Ther.* May 18.

449. Wu A, Ying Z, Gomez-Pinilla F. The interplay between oxidative stress and brain-derived neurotrophic factor modulates the outcome of a saturated fat diet on synaptic plasticity and cognition. *Eur J Neurosci.* Apr 2004;19(7):1699-1707.

450. Duan W, Guo Z, Jiang H, Ware M, Li XJ, Mattson MP. Dietary restriction normalizes glucose metabolism and BDNF levels, slows disease progression, and increases survival in huntingtin mutant mice. *Proc Natl Acad Sci U S A.* Mar 4 2003;100(5):2911-2916.

451. Lee J, Seroogy KB, Mattson MP. Dietary restriction enhances neurotrophin expression and neurogenesis in the hippocampus of adult mice. *J Neurochem.* Feb 2002;80(3):539-547.

452. Stranahan AM, Norman ED, Lee K, et al. Diet-induced insulin resistance impairs hippocampal synaptic plasticity and cognition in middle-aged rats. *Hippocampus.* Jul 23 2008.

453. Pollitt E, Lewis NL, Garza C, Shulman RJ. Fasting and cognitive function. *J Psychiatr Res.* 1982;17(2):169-174.

454. Mahoney CR, Taylor HA, Kanarek RB, Samuel P. Effect of breakfast composition on cognitive processes in elementary school children. *Physiol Behav.* Aug 7 2005;85(5):635-645.

455. Murphy JM, Pagano ME, Nachmani J, Sperling P, Kane S, Kleinman RE. The relationship of school breakfast to psychosocial and academic functioning: cross-sectional and longitudinal observations in an inner-city school sample. *Arch Pediatr Adolesc Med.* Sep 1998;152(9):899-907.

456. Michaud C, Musse N, Nicolas JP, Mejean L. Effects of breakfast-size on short-term memory, concentration, mood and blood glucose. *J Adolesc Health.* Jan 1991;12(1):53-57.

457. Kanarek RB, Swinney D. Effects of food snacks on cognitive performance in male college students. *Appetite.* Feb 1990;14(1):15-27.

458. Muthayya S, Thomas T, Srinivasan K, et al. Consumption of a mid-morning snack improves memory but not attention in school children. *Physiol Behav.* Jan 30 2007;90(1):142-150.

459. Bateman B, Warner JO, Hutchinson E, et al. The effects of a double blind, placebo controlled, artificial food colourings and benzoate preservative challenge on hyperactivity in a general population sample of preschool children. *Arch Dis Child.* Jun 2004;89(6): 506-511.

460. McCann D, Barrett A, Cooper A, et al. Food additives and hyperactive behaviour in 3-year-old and 8/9-year-old children in the community: a randomised, double-blinded, placebo-controlled trial. *Lancet.* Nov 3 2007;370(9598):1560-1567.

461. Tollefson L, Barnard RJ. An analysis of FDA passive surveillance reports of seizures associated with consumption of aspartame. *J Am Diet Assoc.* May 1992;92(5):598-601.

462. Walton RG, Hudak R, Green-Waite RJ. Adverse reactions to aspartame: double-blind challenge in patients from a vulnerable population. *Biol Psychiatry.* Jul 1-15 1993;34(1-2):13-17.

463. http://www.aasd.k12.wi.us/ACA/phys%20health.htm.Accessed December 5th, 2008.

464. Lieberman HR. Nutrition, brain function and cognitive performance. *Appetite.* Jun 2003;40(3):245-254.

465. Nardi AE, Valenca AM, Nascimento I, et al. A caffeine challenge test in panic disorder patients, their healthy first-degree relatives, and healthy controls. *Depress Anxiety.* Sep 6 2007.

466. Hindmarch I, Quinlan PT, Moore KL, Parkin C. The effects of black tea and other beverages on aspects of cognition and psychomotor performance. *Psychopharmacology (Berl).* Oct 1998;139(3):230-238.

467. Lu K, Gray MA, Oliver C, et al. The acute effects of L-theanine in comparison with alprazolam on anticipatory anxiety in humans. *Hum Psychopharmacol.* Oct 2004;19(7):457-465.

468. Cho HS, Kim S, Lee SY, Park JA, Kim SJ, Chun HS. Protective effect of the green tea component, L-theanine on environmental toxins-induced neuronal cell death. *Neurotoxicology.* Jul 2008;29(4): 656-662.

469. Sayegh R, Schiff I, Wurtman J, Spiers P, McDermott J, Wurtman R. The effect of a carbohydrate-rich beverage on mood, appetite, and cognitive function in women with premenstrual syndrome. *Obstet Gynecol.* Oct 1995;86(4 Pt 1):520-528.

470. Spring B, Chiodo J, Harden M, Bourgeois MJ, Mason JD, Lutherer L. Psychobiological effects of carbohydrates. *J Clin Psychiatry.* May 1989;50 Suppl:27-33; discussion 34.

471. 2002 A. S-Adenosyl-L-Methionine for Treatment of Depression, Osteoarthritis, and Liver Disease. In AHRQ (ed).

472. Hudson C, Hudson SP, Hecht T, MacKenzie J. Protein source tryptophan versus pharmaceutical grade tryptophan as an efficacious treatment for chronic insomnia. *Nutr Neurosci.* Apr 2005;8(2): 121-127.

473. Shaw K, Turner J, Del Mar C. Tryptophan and 5-hydroxytryptophan for depression. *Cochrane Database Syst Rev.* 2002(1):CD003198.

474. Gomez-Pinilla F. Brain foods: the effects of nutrients on brain function. *Nat Rev Neurosci.* Jul 2008;9(7):568-578.

475. Sinn N. Physical fatty acid deficiency signs in children with ADHD symptoms. *Prostaglandins Leukot Essent Fatty Acids.* Aug 2007;77(2):109-115.

476. Wu A, Ying Z, Gomez-Pinilla F. Dietary omega-3 fatty acids normalize BDNF levels, reduce oxidative damage, and counteract learning disability after traumatic brain injury in rats. *J Neurotrauma.* Oct 2004;21(10): 1457-1467.

477. Richardson AJ, Montgomery P. The Oxford-Durham study: a randomized, controlled trial of dietary supplementation with fatty acids in children with developmental coordination disorder. *Pediatrics.* May 2005;115(5): 1360-1366.

478. Helland IB, Smith L, Saarem K, Saugstad OD, Drevon CA. Maternal supplementation with very-long-chain n-3 fatty acids during pregnancy and lactation augments children's IQ at 4 years of age. *Pediatrics.* Jan 2003;111(1):e39-44.

479. Osendarp SJ, Baghurst KI, Bryan J, et al. Effect of a 12-mo micronutrient intervention on learning and memory in well-nourished and marginally nourished school-aged children: 2 parallel, randomized, placebo-controlled studies in Australia and Indonesia. *Am J Clin Nutr.* Oct 2007;86(4):1082-1093.

480. van Gelder BM, Tijhuis M, Kalmijn S, Kromhout D. Fish consumption, n-3 fatty acids, and subsequent 5-y cognitive decline in elderly men: the Zutphen Elderly Study. *Am J Clin Nutr.* Apr 2007;85(4):1142-1147.

481. Freund-Levi Y, Eriksdotter-Jonhagen M, Cederholm T, et al. Omega-3 fatty acid treatment in 174 patients with mild to moderate Alzheimer disease: OmegAD study: a randomized double-blind trial. *Arch Neurol.* Oct 2006;63(10):1402-1408.

482. Lin PY, Su KP. A meta-analytic review of double-blind, placebo-controlled trials of antidepressant efficacy of omega-3 fatty acids. *J Clin Psychiatry.* Jul 2007;68(7):1056-1061.

483. Molteni R, Barnard RJ, Ying Z, Roberts CK, Gomez-Pinilla F. A high-fat, refined sugar diet reduces hippocampal brain-derived neurotrophic factor, neuronal plasticity, and learning. *Neuroscience.* 2002;112(4):803-814.

484. Pinilla FG. The impact of diet and exercise on brain plasticity and disease. *Nutr Health.* 2006;18(3):277-284.

485. Engle PL, Black MM, Behrman JR, et al. Strategies to avoid the loss of developmental potential in more than 200 million children in the developing world. *Lancet.* Jan 20 2007;369(9557):229-242.

486. Otero GA, Pliego-Rivero FB, Porcayo-Mercado R, Mendieta- Alcantara G. Working memory impairment and recovery in iron deficient children. *Clin Neurophysiol.* Aug 2008;119(8):1739-1746.

487.   Vahdat Shariatpanaahi M, Vahdat Shariatpanaahi Z, Moshtaaghi M, Shahbaazi SH, Abadi A. The relationship between depression and serum ferritin level. *Eur J Clin Nutr.* Apr 2007;61(4):532-535.

488.   Bruner AB, Joffe A, Duggan AK, Casella JF, Brandt J. Randomised study of cognitive effects of iron supplementation in non-anaemic iron-deficient adolescent girls. *Lancet.* Oct 12 1996;348(9033): 992-996.

489.   Murray-Kolb LE, Beard JL. Iron treatment normalizes cognitive functioning in young women. *Am J Clin Nutr.* Mar 2007;85(3):778-787.

490.   Seelig MS. Consequences of magnesium deficiency on the enhancement of stress reactions; preventive and therapeutic implications (a review). *J Am Coll Nutr.* Oct 1994;13(5):429-446.

491.   Wilkinson TJ, Hanger HC, Elmslie J, George PM, Sainsbury R. The response to treatment of subclinical thiamine deficiency in the elderly. *Am J Clin Nutr.* Oct 1997;66(4):925-928.

492.   Mischoulon D, Raab MF. The role of folate in depression and dementia. *J Clin Psychiatry.* 2007;68 Suppl 10:28-33.

493.   Fava M. Augmenting antidepressants with folate: a clinical perspective. *J Clin Psychiatry.* 2007;68 Suppl 10:4-7.

494.   Durga J, van Boxtel MP, Schouten EG, et al. Effect of 3-year folic acid supplementation on cognitive function in older adults in the FACIT trial: a randomised, double blind, controlled trial. *Lancet.* Jan 20 2007;369(9557): 208-216.

495.   Przybelski RJ, Binkley NC. Is vitamin D important for preserving cognition? A positive correlation of serum 25-hydroxyvitamin D concentration with cognitive function. *Arch Biochem Biophys.* Apr 15 2007;460(2): 202-205.

496.   Letenneur L, Proust-Lima C, Le Gouge A, Dartigues JF, Barberger-Gateau P. Flavonoid intake and cognitive decline over a 10-year period. *Am J Epidemiol.* Jun 15 2007;165(12):1364-1371.

497.   Maczurek A, Hager K, Kenklies M, et al. Lipoic acid as an anti- inflammatory and neuroprotective treatment for Alzheimer's disease. *Adv Drug Deliv Rev.* Jul 4 2008.

498.   Perkins AJ, Hendrie HC, Callahan CM, et al. Association of antioxidants with memory in a multiethnic elderly sample using the Third National Health and Nutrition Examination Survey. *Am J Epidemiol.* Jul 1 1999;150(1):37-44.

499.   Ganguli M, Chandra V, Kamboh MI, et al. Apolipoprotein E polymorphism and Alzheimer disease: The Indo-US Cross-National Dementia Study. *Arch Neurol.* Jun 2000;57(6):824-830.

500.   Luchsinger JA, Noble JM, Scarmeas N. Diet and Alzheimer's disease. *Curr Neurol Neurosci Rep.* Sep 2007;7(5):366-372.

501.   Mokdad AH, Ford ES, Bowman BA, et al. Prevalence of obesity, diabetes, and obesity-related health risk factors, 2001. *JAMA.* Jan 1 2003; 289(1):76-79.

502. Elmquist JK. Hypothalamic pathways underlying the endocrine, autonomic, and behavioral effects of leptin. *Physiol Behav.* Nov-Dec 2001; 74(4-5):703-708.

503. Swinburn BA. The thrifty genotype hypothesis: how does it look after 30 years? *Diabet Med.* Aug 1996;13(8):695-699.

504. Spiegel A, Nabel E, Volkow N, Landis S, Li TK. Obesity on the brain. *Nat Neurosci.* May 2005;8(5):552-553.

505. Lowe MR, Levine AS. Eating motives and the controversy over dieting: eating less than needed versus less than wanted. *Obes Res.* May 2005;13(5):797-806.

506. Rolls ET, Critchley HD, Browning AS, Hernadi I, Lenard L. Responses to the sensory properties of fat of neurons in the primate orbitofrontal cortex. *J Neurosci.* Feb 15 1999;19(4):1532-1540.

507. Arana FS, Parkinson JA, Hinton E, Holland AJ, Owen AM, Roberts AC. Dissociable contributions of the human amygdala and orbitofrontal cortex to incentive motivation and goal selection. *J Neurosci.* Oct 22 2003;23(29): 9632-9638.

508. Kelley AE, Bakshi VP, Haber SN, Steininger TL, Will MJ, Zhang M. Opioid modulation of taste hedonics within the ventral striatum. *Physiol Behav.* Jul 2002;76(3):365-377.

509. Kim EM, Quinn JG, Levine AS, O'Hare E. A bi-directional mu-opioid-opioid connection between the nucleus of the accumbens shell and the central nucleus of the amygdala in the rat. *Brain Res.* Dec 10 2004;1029(1): 135-139.

510. Zahm DS. An integrative neuroanatomical perspective on some subcortical substrates of adaptive responding with emphasis on the nucleus accumbens. *Neurosci Biobehav Rev.* Jan 2000;24(1): 85-105.

511. Kringelbach ML. Food for thought: hedonic experience beyond homeostasis in the human brain. *Neuroscience.* 2004;126(4): 807-819.

512. Cohen DA. Neurophysiological pathways to obesity: below awareness and beyond individual control. *Diabetes.* Jul 2008;57(7):1768-1773.

513. Moors A, De Houwer J. Automaticity: a theoretical and conceptual analysis. *Psychol Bull.* Mar 2006;132(2):297-326.

514. Rolls BJ, Roe LS, Meengs JS. Larger portion sizes lead to a sustained increase in energy intake over 2 days. *J Am Diet Assoc.* Apr 2006;106(4): 543-549.

515. Wansink B, van Ittersum K. Shape of glass and amount of alcohol poured: comparative study of effect of practice and concentration. *BMJ.* Dec 24 2005;331(7531):1512-1514.

516. Painter JE, Wansink B, Hieggelke JB. How visibility and convenience influence candy consumption. *Appetite.* Jun 2002;38(3):237-238.

517. Tuomisto T, Tuomisto MT, Hetherington M, Lappalainen R. Reasons for initiation and cessation of eating in obese men and women and the affective consequences of eating in everyday situations. *Appetite.* Apr 1998;30(2):211-222.

518. de Castro JM, Brewer EM. The amount eaten in meals by humans is a power function of the number of people present. *Physiol Behav.* Jan 1992;51(1):121-125.
519. Kemps E, Tiggemann M. Working memory performance and preoccupying thoughts in female dieters: evidence for a selective central executive impairment. *Br J Clin Psychol.* Sep 2005;44(Pt 3):357-366.
520. Shaw J, Tiggemann M. Dieting and working memory: preoccupying cognitions and the role of the articulatory control process. *Br J Health Psychol.* May 2004;9(Pt 2):175-185.
521. Nielsen SJ, Siega-Riz AM, Popkin BM. Trends in energy intake in U.S. between 1977 and 1996: similar shifts seen across age groups. *Obes Res.* May 2002;10(5):370-378.
522. Zhong CB, Devoe SE. You are how you eat: fast food and impatience. *Psychol Sci.* May 1;21(5):619-622.
523. Ford AL, Bergh C, Sodersten P, et al. Treatment of childhood obesity by retraining eating behaviour: randomised controlled trial. *BMJ.*340:b5388.

About the Author:

Dr. Amit Sood is the Director of Research and Practice in the Mayo Complementary and Integrative Medicine Program at Mayo Clinic Rochester. An Associate Professor of Medicine, he chairs the Mayo Mind Body Initiative. Born in India, he finished his early medical training at Gandhi Medical College, Bhopal and All India Institute of Medical Sciences, New Delhi, India. He completed his residency in Internal medicine at the Albert Einstein School of Medicine, NY and earned an Integrative Medicine Fellowship from the University of Arizona, and a Masters in Clinical Research from Mayo Clinic College of Medicine, Rochester, MN. He has received several NIH and foundation grants for conducting research to develop and incorporate integrative and mind-body approaches into conventional medical care and to promote well being. He teaches workshops and educational courses nationally and internationally. He conducts his research and provides integrative and mind-body medicine consults to patients at the Mayo Complementary and Integrative Medicine Program in Rochester, MN.